Tom Taylor

Historical Dramas

Tom Taylor

Historical Dramas

ISBN/EAN: 9783337304317

Printed in Europe, USA, Canada, Australia, Japan

Cover: Foto ©Thomas Meinert / pixelio.de

More available books at **www.hansebooks.com**

HISTORICAL DRAMAS

BY

TOM TAYLOR, M.A.

LATE FELLOW OF TRINITY COLLEGE, CAMBRIDGE

London
CHATTO & WINDUS, PICCADILLY
1877

TO

MY TRUEST FRIEND AND BEST ADVISER

MY WIFE

PREFACE.

ALL the Plays included in this volume have been acted; and all but one may fairly be said to form part of the 'stock' or acting plays of the time. 'Anne Boleyn' is the only play in the volume which has not, as yet, been performed in any other theatre than that in which it was produced.

I have no wish to screen myself from literary criticism behind the plea that my plays were meant to be acted. It seems to me that every drama submitted to the judgment of audiences should be prepared to encounter that of readers. I have in all cases acknowledged in *notes* attached to the plays the sources to which I have been indebted for the suggestion of my subjects; not that I think Molière's rule, '*Je prends mon bien où je le trouve*,' less pleadable by the dramatic author now than it was when he said it.

But, as I have sometimes been spoken of by critics more confident than well-informed as one whose work has always been that of adapter rather than inventor, it may be worth while to say here, in the first edition of any of my plays likely to reach other than professional readers, that of more than one hundred pieces which I have given to the Stage less than one-tenth have been adaptations from foreign plays or stories.

Should this volume find readers, I may follow it up by one of Romantic Dramas, and another of Comedies and Comediettas.

TOM TAYLOR.

LAVENDER SWEEP,
April, 1877.

CONTENTS.

THE FOOL'S REVENGE

JEANNE DARC

'TWIXT AXE AND CROWN

LADY CLANCARTY

ARKWRIGHT'S WIFE

ANNE BOLEYN

PLOT AND PASSION

THE
FOOL'S REVENGE

A Drama

IN THREE ACTS

PREFACE

TO THE
FIRST EDITION.

This Drama is in no sense a *translation*, and ought not, I think, in fairness to be called even an *adaptation*, of Victor Hugo's fine play ' *Le Roi s' Amuse.*'

It originated in a request made to me by one of our most popular actors, to turn the libretto of Rigoletto into a play, as he wished to act the part of the jester. On looking at Victor Hugo's drama, with this object, I found so much in it that seemed to me inadmissible on our stage—so much, besides, that was wanting in dramatic motive and cohesion, and—I say it in all humility—so much that was defective in that central secret of stage effect, climax—that I determined to take the situation of the jester and his daughter, and to recast in my own way the incidents in which their story was invested.

The death of Galeotto Manfredi at the hands of his wife Francesca Bentivoglio is historical. It seemed to me that the atmosphere of a petty Italian Court of the Fifteenth Century was well suited as a medium for presenting the jester's wrongs, his rooted purpose of revenge, and the miscarriage of that purpose.

I should not have thought it necessary to say thus much, had not some of the newspaper critics talked of my work as a simple translation of Victor Hugo's drama, while others described it, more contemptuously, as a mere *rifacciamento* of Verdi's libretto,

PREFACE.

Those who will take the trouble to compare my work with either of its alleged originals, will see that my play is neither translation nor *rifacciamento*.

The motives of Bertuccio, the machinery by which his revenge is diverted from its intended channel, and the action in the court subsequent to the carrying off of his daughter, are my own; and I conceive that these features give me the fullest right to call the 'Fool's Revenge' a *new* play, even if the use of Victor Hugo's *Triboulet and Blanche* disentitle it to the epithet '*original*'—which is matter of opinion.

For the admirable manner in which the drama is mounted and represented at Sadler's Wells, and for the peculiarly powerful impersonation of Bertuccio, I owe all gratitude to Mr. Phelps. I must extend that feeling also to Miss Heath, Miss Atkinson, and the rest of the Sadler's Wells Company engaged in the representation of the 'Fool's Revenge.'

THE FOOL'S REVENGE.

*First Performed at Sadler's Wells Theatre,
on Tuesday, October 18th, 1859.*

CHARACTERS.

GALEOTTO MANFREDI (*Lord of Faenza*) MR. H. MARSTON.
GUIDO MALATESTA (*an old Condottiere*) MR. MEAGRESON.
BERTUCCIO (*a Jester*) .... MR. PHELPS.
SERAFINO DELL'AQUILA (*Poet and Improvisatore*).................................... MR. F. ROBINSON.
BALDASSARE TORELLI } (*Nobles*)... { MR. BELFORD.
GIAN MARIA ORDELAFFI }   { MR. T. C. HARRIS.
BERNARDO ASCOLTI (*a Florentine Envoy*) MR. C. SEYTON.
ASCANIO (*a Page*) .... MISS C. HILL.
GINEVRA (*Wife of Malatesta*).................. MISS C. PARKES.
FRANCESCA BENTIVOGLIO (*Wife of Manfredi*) .... MISS ATKINSON.
FIORDELISA (*Daughter of Bertuccio*) ...... MISS HEATH.
BRIGITTA (*Bertuccio's Servant*) .... MRS. H. MARSTON.

TIME—1488.   PLACE—FAENZA.

COSTUMES.

At *Sadler's Wells* the costume and scenery of this play were appropriate to the period of Francis the First, which is some years later than the actual date of Manfredi's murder. This departure from strict chronology is unobjectionable, when, as at *Sadler's Wells*, strict consistency is maintained in the dresses, architecture, and decoration of the piece.

In strict propriety, the costume of the *Duke* and nobles should consist of short, brightly-coloured jerkins, reaching just below the waist, with rather full sleeves, slashed, and confined at the wrists, embroidered belts round the waist, coloured tight hose, often worn of a different colour in the two legs, and velvet shoes. Short mantles may be worn by the young nobles. *Ascolti*, *Malatesta*, and the elder guests, may, with propriety, wear long velvet or silk gowns, of purple, crimson, or other rich colours, with borders of fur. The hair should be worn full and long, in the style familiar to us from Raphael's earlier pictures. The head-dress of the younger men is a small coloured velvet cap, with a raised edge, often scalloped and ornamented with a chain, and medal.

The *Fool*, of course, wears a motley suit, with a hood like that worn by Shakespeare's fools. His second dress should be a long gown, of sober colour. *Fiordelisa's* dress should be white, or dove-coloured, with scalloped sleeves and tight body. The *Duchess's* costume, of the same cut, should be of velvet, slashed, and embroidered with gold. She may wear a gold net; a silk or chenille net would also be appropriate to *Fiordelisa*.

THE FOOL'S REVENGE.

ACT I.

Scene I.

The Stage represents a Loggia opening on the Gardens of Manfredi's Palace; a low terrace at the back, and beyond, a view of the city and country adjacent. Moonlight. The gardens and loggia illuminated for a festa.
Nobles *and* Ladies *discovered* R. *and* C., *and moving through the gardens and loggia. Music at a distance.* Torelli *and* Ordelaffi *discovered.—Enter* Ascolti, L.

Torelli. Messer Bernardo, you shall judge between us—
Is Ordelaffi's here, a feasting face?
I say, 'tis fitter for a funeral.
Ascolti. An Ordelaffi scarce can love the feast
That greets Octavian Riario
Lord of Forlì and Imola.
Ordel. Because our line were masters there of old,
Till they were fools enough to get pulled down?
I was born to no lordship but my sword.
Thanks to my stout black bands, I look to win
New titles, and so grieve not over lost ones.
My glove upon't! I'll prove a lighter dancer,
A lustier wooer, and a deeper drinker,
Than e'er a landed lordling of you all.
Is it a wager?
Ginevra *passes with* Manfredi *from* L. *to* R., Malatesta *appears* L. *watching them.*
Torelli. My hand to that! There's Malatesta's wife,
The fair Ginevra. Let's try lucks with her?
Ascolti. Ware hawk! Grey Guido's an old-fashioned husband;

Look how he glares upon the Lord Manfredi.
Each of his soft words to the fair Ginevra's
A dagger in the old fool's heart.
  Ordel. Sublime! ripe sixty wedded to sixteen,
And thinks to shut the foxes from his grapes!
  Torelli. The Duke, too, for his rival! Poor old man!
  Ascolti. Let the Duke look to it. Ginevra's smiles
May breed him worse foes than Count Malatesta.
(*Whispering*) The Duchess!
  Torelli. Faith—'tis ill rousing Bentivoglio blood.
  Ordel. And she's as jealous as her own pet greyhound.
  Torelli. And sharper in the teeth. I wonder much
She leaves Faenza, knowing her Manfredi
So general a lover.
  Ascolti. She leaves Faenza?
  Torelli.   So they say: to-morrow
Rides to Bologna to her grim old father,
Giovanni Bentivoglio.
  Ascolti.   To complain
Of her hot-blooded husband?
  Torelli.   Nay, I know not—
Enough, she goes, and—fair dame as she is—
A murrain go with her, say I. There never
Was good time in Faenza, since *she* came
To spoil sport with her jealousy. Manfredi
Will be himself again, when she is hence.
  Ascolti. Hush! here she comes——
  Ordel.   With that misshapen imp
Bertuccio. Gibing devil! I shall thrust
My dagger down his throat one of these days!
  Torelli. Call him a jester; he laughs vitriol!
  Ascolti. Spares nothing: cracks his random scurril quips
Upon my master—great Lorenzo's self.
  Ordel. Do the knave justice, he's a king of tongue-fence;
Not a weak joint in all our armours round,
But he knows, and can hit. Confound the rogue!
I'm blistered still from a word-basting he
Gave me but yesterday. Would we were quits!
  Torelli. Wait! I've a rod in pickle that shall flay
The tough hide off his hump. A rare revenge!
  Ascolti. They're here—avoid!
    Ascolti, Ordelaffi, *and* Torelli *retire up*, C.
    and mingle with the Guests.

Enter FRANCESCA *and* BERTUCCIO, R., *followed by her two* WOMEN.

Fran. (*looking off, as if watching, and to herself*) Still
    with her! changing hot palms and long looks!
Hers for the dance—hers at the feast—all hers!
Nothing for me but shallow courtesies,
And hollow coin of compliment that leaves
The craving heart as empty as a beggar
Bemocked with counters!
    Bert. (*counting on his fingers, and looking at the moon*)
              Moon—Manfredi—moon!
    Fran. Ha, knave!
    Bert.   By your leave, Monna Cecca, I am ciphering.
    Fran. Some fool's sum?
    Bert.   Yes; running your husband's changes
Against the moon's. Manfredi has it hollow.
It comes out ten new loves 'gainst five new moons!
    Fran. Where do I stand?
    Bert. First of the ten; your moon was a whole honey
    one;
Excluding that, it's nine loves to four moons.
    Fran. You pity me, Bertuccio?
    Bert.   Not a whit;
I pity sparrows, but not sparrow-hawks.
    Fran. I read your riddle. I am strong enough
To right my own wrongs! So I am, while here.
    Bert. Then stay!
    Fran.   My father at Bologna looks for me.
    Bert. Then go!
    Fran. And leave him here—with her—both free,
And not a friend that I can trust to watch
And give me due report how things go 'twixt them.
Had I one friend——
    Bert.   You have Bertuccio.
    Fran. Men call you faithless, bitter, loving wrong
For wrong's sake, Duke Manfredi's worst councillor,
Still prompting him to evil.
    Bert.   How folks flatter!
    Fran. How, then, am I to trust you?
    Bert.   Monna Cecca,
You know the wild beasts that your husband keeps
Down in the castle fosse? There's a she-leopard

I lie and gaze at by the hour together;
So sleek, so graceful, and so dangerous!
I long to see her let loose on a man.
Trust me to draw the bolt, and loose *my* leopard.
 Fran. I'll trust your love of mischief, not of me.
 Bert. That's safest!
 Fran.   I must know how fares this fancy
Of Duke Manfredi for yon pale Ginevra—
Mark him and her—their meetings—communings;
I know you're private with my lord.
 Bert. (with a dry chuckle) He trusts me!
 Fran. Here! take my ring: your letters sealed with this,
My page Ascanio will bring me straight;
'Tis but three hours' hard riding—and in six
I'm here again. Mark! write not on suspicion,
Let evil thought ripen to evil act,
That in the full flush of their guilty joys
I may strike sudden, and strike home.
No Bentivoglio pardons.
 Bert.   Have a care!
Faenza is Manfredi's! These court-flies,
        [*Pointing to the* GUESTS.
Who flutter in the sunshine of his favour,
Have stings: the pudding-headed citizens
Love his free ways: he leaves *their* wives alone—
You play your own head, touching *his*.
 Fran. Give me my vengeance. Then come what come may.
Enough—I am resolved. Now for the dance!
They shall not see a cloud upon my brow,
Though my heart ache and burn. I can smile too,
On him and her—Bertuccio, remember!
     [*Exit* FRANCESCA, *followed by her* WOMEN, R.
 Bert. (looking at the ring) A blood-stone—apt reminder!
  Does she think
That none but she have wrongs? That none but she
Mean to revenge them? What? 'No Bentivoglio
Pardons.' There is a certain vile Bertuccio,
A twisted, withered, hunch-backed, court buffoon—
A thing to make mirth, and to be made mirth of—
A something betwixt ape and man, that claims
To run in couples with your ladyship.
You hunt Manfredi—I hunt Malatesta—
Let's try which of the two has sharper fangs!

MANFREDI *and* GINEVRA *appear in the background*, R.
The Duke and Malatesta's wife! (*He retires up.*)
    MANFREDI *and* GINEVRA *come forward*, MALATESTA
                watching them, L.
    Man. Not yet!—but one more round! The feast is blank
For me when you are gone. The flowers lack perfume,
Missing your fragrant breath. The music sounds
Harsh and untunable, when your sweet voice
Makes no more under-melody. Oh stay!
    Ginev. I am summoned, sir—my husband waits for me.
    Man. What spoil-sports are these husbands (*aside*) and
        these wives!
Per Bacco! I could wish Count Malatesta
Would lend my duchess escort to Bologna,
So were we both well rid.
                [MALATESTA *beckons to* GINEVRA.
    Ginev.   Your pardon, sir.
My husband beckons. It is I, not you,
Must bear his moods to night—I dare not stay.
    Man. I would not bring a cloud to your fair brow
For all Faenza. Fare you well, sweet lady!
            [*He leads her to* MALATESTA.
I render up your jewel, Malatesta;
See that you guard it as befits its price.
    Mala. Trust me for that, my lord.
    Man. (*to* GINEVRA)   Sweet dreams wait on you.
    Mala. (*aside*) This night sees *her* safe past Faenza's walls;
She's too fair for this liquorish court of ours.
            [*Exeunt* MALATESTA *and* GINEVRA, L.
    Man. A peerless lady!
    Bert. (*coming forward*) And a churlish spouse!
    Man. Bertuccio!
    Bert.   'At your elbow, sir,' quoth Satanus.
    Man. Come, fool, let's rail at husbands.
    Bert.   Shall I call
Your wife to help us?
    Man.   Out on thee, screech-owl!
Just when I felt my chains about to fall,
Thou mind'st me of my gaoler. Thank the saints,
I shall be free to-morrow for a while—
I'm thirsty to employ my liberty.
Come, my familiar, help me to some mischief—
Some pleasant devilry, with just the spice
Of sin to make the enjoyment exquisite!

Bert. Let's see! — throat-cutting's pleasant — but that's
    stale;
Plotting has savour in it—but 'tis tedious;
Say, a campaign with Ordelaffi's band,
So you may feed all the seven sins at once!
    Man. Out, barren hound! thy wits are growing dull.
    Bert. A man can't always be finding out new sins;
Think, they're as hard to hit on as new pleasures.
My head on't, Alexander had not run
So wide a round of pleasures, as you of sins;
And yet he offered kingdoms for a new one.
You must invoke Asmodeus, not Beelzebub.
    Man. What's he?
    Bert.   The devil specially charged with love;
He has more work than all the infernal legion.
There's Malatesta's wife—she's young, and fair,
And good, they say;—rare matter for *sin* there,
Though 'tis the oldest of them all.
    Man.   But show me
How to win *her!* She's cold as she is fair;
I have spent enough sweet speech to have softened
    stone,
And all in vain.
    Bert.   The monks say Hannibal
Melted the rocks with vinegar—not sugar.
    Man. But she is adamant!
    Bert.   When all else fails
You've still force to fall back on.—Carry her off
From under Guido's grizzled beard.
    Man.   By Bacchus,
There's mettle in thy counsel, knave! I'll think on't.
    Bert. It needs no brains neither—only strong hands
And hard hearts. Here come both.
    Enter TORELLI, ASCOLTI, *and* ORDELAFFI, C.
    Man. What say you, gentlemen; may I trust your arms?
Torelli. They're yours in any quarrel.
Ascolti.   So are mine!
Ordel.   And mine!
    Bert. One at a time. You said '*arms!*'—Of Torelli
You should ask *legs*! His did such famous service
In carrying him out of danger at Sarzana,
I think they may be trusted.
        [*All laugh except* TORELLI.

Torelli.   Scurril knave!
But I'll be even with thee.
   Bert.   That were pity.
A hump would be a sore disfigurement
Upon a back that you're so fond of showing!
   Ascolti. This rogue needs gagging.
   Bert. (*to* ASCOLTI)   What! for speaking truth?
I cry you mercy—I forgot how ugly
It must sound to a Florentine Ambassador——
   Man. Well thrust, Bertuccio?
   Ordel. (*angrily*)   My lord,—my lord!
The slave is paid to find us wit——
   Bert.   (*interrupting*) Hold there!
No man is bound to impossibilities—
'Tis a known maxim of the Roman law;
How then can I find wit for Ordelaffi?
                               [*All laugh but* ORDELAFFI.
But look—there's Serafino—big with a sonnet:
I must help him to reason for his rhymes——
   Man. Stay!
   Bert.   Not I! You're for finding out new sins;
With three such councillors, I am superfluous.
(*Aside*) The evil seed is sown—'twill grow—'twill grow.
                                   [*Exit* BERTUCCIO.
   Torelli. Toad!
   Ascolti.   Foul-mouthed scoffer!
   Ordel.   Warped in wit and limb!
   Ascolti. My lord, you give your monkey too much rope;
He'll soon forget all tricks in the scurvy one
Of making his grinders meet in our soft parts.
   Man. Nay, give the devil his due; if he hits hard,
He hits impartially.—I take my share
Of buffets with the rest. Best cure the smart
By laughing at your neighbour that smarts worse;
But for this business, where *your* arms may help me.
   Ascolti. Is it an enemy to be silenced?
   Ordel.   A castle
To be surprised? A merchant to be squeezed?
   Ascolti. Or aught in which ducats, or brains, of Florence
Can help?
   Man.   No.—Who was queen of the feast to-night?
In your skilled judgment, Messer Gian Maria?
   Ordel. I ought to say, your duchess, fair Francesca;

But, if another tongue had asked the question——
    Man. Speak out thy honest judgment!
    Ordel.   Not a lady
In all Faenza's worthy to compare
With proud Ginevra Malatesta!
    Torelli. I think I know a fairer,—but no matter!
    Man. I hold with Ordelaffi.—I have mounted
Ginevra's colours in my cap, and heart;
But she's too proud, or fearful of old Guido,
To smile upon my suit—'Tis the first time
I've found so coy a dame.
    Ascolti.   Trust one who knows them—
The coyest are not always chastest.
    Man. How say you, if I spared her shame of yielding
By a night escalade?
    Ordel. (*shaking his head*) Carry her off?
A Malatesta? Were it an enemy's town——
    Man. Hear him!—how modestly he talks!—Why, man,
Since when shrank'st thou from climbing balconies,
And forcing doors without an invitation?
    Ordel. Oh, citizens', I grant you—but a noble's,—
One of ourselves——
    Ascolti.   Remember, Malatesta
Is cousin to the old Lord of Cesena:—
The affair might breed a feud, and so let in
The sly Venetian.
    Torelli.   Be advised, my lord;
If you must breathe your new-fledged liberty,
Try safer game! Old Malatesta's horns
Might prove too sharp for pastime!
    Man.   Out, you faint hearts!
Do you fall off? Then, by St. Francis' bones,
I and Bertuccio will adventure it.
    Torelli. Bertuccio! My jewel to his hump;
'Twas he put this mad frolic in your head.
    Man. And if it were? At least he'll stand by me:
Perchance his wits may be worth all your brawn.
    Ascolti. Here comes one who may claim to be consulted
Upon this business.
            Enter MALATESTA, L.
    Man. (*disconcerted*)   Guido Malatesta!
Why, how now, Count? You left our feast so soon,
I thought you warm i' the sheets this good half-hour.

Mala. I had forgot my duty to your lordship;
So now repair my lack of courtesy—
To-morrow I purpose riding to Ceséna,
And would not go without due leave-taking.
 Man. (*aside*) This jumps well with my project. What,
  to-morrow!
You ride alone?
 Mala.   No, with my wife.
 Man. (*aside*)   The devil!
Why, this is sudden—she spoke no word of this
To-night!
 Mala. Tush! women know not their own minds,
How should they know their husbands'?
 Man.   But your reason?
 Mala. Your air here in Faenza is too warm,
And scarce so pure as fits my wife's complexion;
She's better in my castle at Ceséna;
The walls are five feet thick, and from the platform
There's a rare view. She'll need no exercise.
 Man. (*aside*) The gaoler! (*Aloud*). But what says the
  lady's will?
 Mala. I never ask that; and so 'scape all risk
Of finding it run counter to my own.
 Man. Faenza will have great miss of you both.
 Mala. Oh, fear not—I'll return; your wine's too good
To be left lightly. I'll be back to-morrow,
Before the gates are shut. Meanwhile accept
This leave-taking by proxy from my wife.
 Man. Not so; I must exchange farewells with her
To-morrow.
 Mala. We shall start an hour ere dawn;—
You'll scarce be stirring.
 Man. (*aside*)   Plague upon the churl!
He meets me at all points. At least, I hope,
This absence of your wife will not be long;
My duchess cannot spare her. (*Aside*) Saints forgive me!
 Mala. When your fair *lady* wants her, she can send:
I'll answer for her coming on *that* summons.
Good night, sweet lords. (*Aside*) How crestfall'n he
  looks!
Mass!—'tis ill cozening an old condottiere!
Did he think I had forgot to guard my baggage?
         [*Exit* MALATESTA.

Man. A murrain go with him! May the horse stumble
That carries him, and break his old bull-neck!
Oh, this is cruel—with my hand stretched out
To have to draw't back empty!—I could curse!
    Torelli. What if I helped you to a substitute
For coy Ginevra? passing her in beauty,—
One, too, whose conquest puts no crown to risk,
And helps withal a notable requital
That we all owe Bertuccio, you included.
    Man. What mean you?
    Torelli.   Guess what's happened to Bertuccio!
    Ordel. He's grown good-natured?
    Ascolti.   Or has dropp'd his hump?
    Man. He has found a monkey uglier than himself?
    Torelli. No—something stranger than all these would be,
If they *had* happened;—he has found a mistress!
                      [*All burst out laughing.*
    Man. My lady's pet baboon? Bertuccio
Graced with a mistress! (*He laughs.*)
    Ascolti.   She is blind, of course?
    Ordel. And has a hump, I hope, to match his own.
What a rare breed 'twill be—of two-humped babes,
Like Bactrian camels!
    Man. Bertuccio with a mistress!—why the rogue
Ne'er yet made joke so monstrous, or so pleasant!
                      [*They laugh again.*
    Torelli. Laugh as you please, sirs—on my knightly faith,
He *has* a mistress—and a rare one too!
Nay, if you doubt my word——Here comes Dell'Aquila—
He knows as well as I.
    Man.   We'll question him.
              Enter SERAFINO DELL'AQUILA, C.
    Man. Good even to my poet—you walk late!
    Aquila (*pointing to the moon*). I tend my mistress: poets
    and lunatics,
You know, are her liege subjects.
    Man.   They are happy!
    Aquila. Why?
    Man.   They have a new mistress every month,
And each month's mistress no two nights alike.
But jesters can find mistresses, it seems,
As well as poets. There's Torelli swears
Bertuccio has one, and that you know it.

Aquila. I know he has a rare maid close mewed up,
But whether wife or daughter——
    Man.   Tell not me!
A mistress for a thousand! But what of her?
How did you find her out?
    Aquila.   'Twas some weeks since,
Attending vespers in your house's chapel!
At San Costanza, I beheld a maiden
Kneeling before that picture of our lady,
By Fra Filippo—oh, so fair!—so rapt!
In her pure passionate prayers!—I tell you, sirs,
I was nigh going on my knees beside her,
And asking for an interest in her orisons:
Such eyes of softest blue, crowned with such wreaths
Of glossy chesnut hair—a cheek of snow
Flushed tenderly, as when the sunlight strikes
Upon an evening Alp, and over all
A grace of maiden modesty that lay
More still and snowy round her than the folds
Of her white veil. And when she rose I rose,
And followed her like one drawn by a charm
To a mean house, where entering, she was lost.
    Man. She was alone?
    Aquila.   Only a shrewish servant
That saw her to the church, and saw her home.
    Man. A most weak wolf-dog for so choice a lamb!
    Aquila. Methought, my lord, she needed no more guard
Than the innocence that sat, dove-like, in her eyes,
That shaped the folding of her delicate hands,
And timed the movement of her gentle feet.
    Man. You spoke to her?
    Aquila.   I dared not; some strange shame
Put weights upon my tongue. I only watched her,
And sometimes heard her sing. That was enough.
    Man. You poets are soon satisfied. Well—you watched?
    Aquila. And then I found that I was not alone
Upon my nightly post: there were two more;
One stayed outside, like me, and one went in.
    Torelli. True to the letter! I was the outsider
The third, and luckiest, was Bertuccio!
    Man. The hump-backed hypocrite!
    Ordel.   The owl that screeched
Still loudest against women!

Ascolti. But, is't certain
That 'twas Bertuccio?
 Torelli. I can swear to that!
 Aquila. And I!
 Ascolti. How do you know him?
 Torelli. By his hump—
His gait—who could mistake that crab-like walk?
I could have knocked my head against the wall,
To think I had been fool enough to trust
A woman's looks for once:—Dell'Aquila,
I know, holds other faith about the sex.
 Aquila. I would stake life upon her purity;
Yet, 'tis past doubt Bertuccio is the man,
The ugly gaoler of this prisoned bird.
 Man. Why, that's enough to make it a mere duty
To break her prison-house, and shift her keeping
To fitter hands—say mine. I'm lord of the town;
None else has right of prison here but I.
 Aquila. What would you do?
 Man. First see if she bears out
Your picture, Serafino—if she do,
Be sure I will not wait outside to mark
Her shadow. Shadows may suit poets—I
Want substance.
 Torelli. She's meat for Bertuccio's master,
Not for Bertuccio. When shall it be?
 Man. To-morrow.
I'm a free man! Meet me at midnight, here.
 Aquila. You would not harm her? Only see her face,
You will not have the heart to do her wrong.
 Man. What call you 'wrong'? To save so choice a creature
From such a guardian as Bertuccio?
He would have prompted me to play the robber
Of Malatesta's pearl;—let him guard his own!
 Ordel. If he resist, we'll knock him o'er the sconce:
Let me have *that* part of the business.
 Man. Nay, I'll not have the rascal harmed;—he's bitter,
But shrewdly witty, and he makes me laugh—
No, spare me my buffoon: who does him harm
Shall answer it to me.
 Torelli. 'Twere a rare plot to make the knave believe
Our scheme still held against old Malatesta—

That his Ginevra was the game we followed.
   Ordel. So give him rendezvous a mile away,
And, while he waits our coming, to break open
The mew where he keeps close his tercel gentle.
   Ascolti (*aside* to MANFREDI). Ne'er trust a poet. What
      if he betrayed us?
   Man. He's truth itself; and where he gives his faith,
'Tis better than a bond of your Lorenzo's.
   Ascolti. Swear him to secrecy.
   Man. (*to* DELL' AQUILA)   Your hand upon it.
You'll not spoil sport, by breaking to Bertuccio
What we intend?
   Aquila.   But think, oh, think, my lord!
What if this were no mistress—as—if looks
Have privilege to reveal the soul—she *is* none?
   Man. Mistress or maid, man, I will not be baulked;
'Tis for her good; I know the sex—she pines
In her captivity;—I'll find a cage
More fitting such a bird as you've described—
Your hand on't—not a whisper to Bertuccio!
   Aquila. You force me! There's my hand! I will not speak
A word to him!
   Man. (*taking his hand*) That's like a trusty liegeman
Of blind Lord Cupid! Hark—a word with you!
            [MANFREDI *and* LORDS *talk apart*, C.
   Aquila. I'll save her from this wrong, or lose myself.
What tie there is betwixt these two I know not.
How one so fair and seeming gentle 's linked
With one so foul and bitter—a buffoon,
Who makes even *his* vile office viler still,
By prompting to the evil that he mocks!
But I will 'gage my life that she is pure,
And still shall be so, if my aid avail!
            [MANFREDI *and* LORDS *separate*.
Once more, my lord—you'll not be stayed from this
That you propose?
   Man.   Unconscionable bard!
What—when you've set my mouth a-watering
You'd have me put the dainty morsel from me?
Go, feed on sighs and shadows—such thin stuff
Is the best diet for you singing-birds;
We eagles must have flesh!
   Aquila (*to* ALL).   Good night, my lords

(*Aside*) Keep to your carrion, kites! She's not for *you*.
[*Exit* AQUILA.

Man. But how to get sight of Bertuccio's jewel?—
I'd see before I snatch!

Torelli. Trust me for that!
I am no poet: When I found the damsel
Admitted such a gallant as Bertuccio,
I thought it time to press my suit—and so
Accosted her on her way from San Costanza——

Man. She listened?

Torelli. Long enough—the little fool—
To learn my meaning—then she flushed, and fled;
I followed—when, as the foul fiend would have it,
Ginevra Malatesta coming by
From vespers with her train sheltered the pigeon,
And spoiled my chase.

Man. You did not give it up?

Torelli. I changed my plan: the mistress being coy,
I spread my net to catch the maid—oh, lord—
The veriest Gorgon! You might swear none e'er
Had given *her* chase before—no coyness there;
A small expense of oaths and coin sufficed
To make her think herself a misprized Venus,
And me the most discriminating wooer
In all Faenza. 'Twill not need much art
For me to win an entrance to the house;
And when I'm in, it shall go hard, my lord,
But I find means to get you access too.

Man. About it straight; at dusk to-morrow night
Be here, armed, masked, and cloaked.

Ordel. While poor Bertuccio
Awaits our coming near San Stefano,
A stone's throw from the casa Malatesta.

Ascolti. He's here!

Enter BERTUCCIO, L.

Bert. Not yet a-bed!
Since when were the fiend's eggs so hard to hatch?
I left a pleasant little germ of sin
Some half-an-hour since: it should be full-grown
By this time.—Is it?

Man. Winged, and hoofed, and tailed.
If proud Ginevra Malatesta sleep

To-morrow night beneath old Guido's roof,
Then call me a snow-water-blooded shaveling.
  Bert. Ha! 'Tis resolved then?
  Torelli.   We have pledged our faith
To carry off the fairest in Faenza——
  Ascolti. Before the stroke of midnight.
  Ordel.   'Twas my plan
To gather one by one to the place of action;
Lest, going in a troop, we might awake
Suspicion, and put Guido on his guard.
  Bert. A wise precaution, although it *was* yours.
I wronged you, gentlemen; I thought you shrunk
Even from sin, when there was danger in't.
It seems there *are* deeds black enough to make
Even Torelli brave, Ascolti prompt,
And Ordelaffi witty. But the place?
  Man. Beside San Stefano.
  Bert.   The hour of meeting?
  Man. Half an hour after vespers.—There await us.
And now, good rest, my lords; the night wanes fast.
My duchess will be weary.
  ALL (*going*).   Sir, good night!
  Bert. Sleep well, Torelli. Dream of charging home
In the van of some fierce fight.
  Torelli.   My common dream.
  Bert. 'Tis natural—dreams go by contraries!
And you, Ascolti, dream of telling truth;
And, Ordelaffi, that you have grown wise.
  Torelli. And you, that your back's straight, your legs a match.
  Ascolti. And your tongue tipped with honey.
  Ordel.   Come, my lords,
Leave him to spit his venom at the moon,
As they say toads do!   [*Exeunt*, R.
  Bert.   Take my curse among you—
Fair, false, big, brainless, outside shows of men;
For once your gibes and jeers fall pointless from me!
My great revenge is nigh, and drowns all sense.
I am straight, and fair, and well-shaped as yourselves;
Vengeance swells out my veins, and lifts my head,
And makes me terrible!—Come, sweet to-morrow,
And put my enemy's heart into my hand
That I may gnaw it!

ACT II.

Scene I.

A Room in the House of Bertuccio, hung with tapestry; a coloured statue of the Madonna in a recess, with a small lamp burning before it; carved and coloured furniture; a carved cabinet and large carved coffer; in the centre a window opening on the street, with a balcony; behind the tapestry, a secret door communicating with the street, L. 2 E.; a door, R. 2 E.; a lamp lighted; a lute and flowers; a missal on a stand before the statue; a recess concealed by the tapestry, L. 3 E.

TORELLI *and* BRIGITTA *discovered*, C.

Brig. Hark, there's the quarter!—you must hence, fair signor.

Torelli. But a few moments more of your sweet presence!

Brig. Saint Ursula, she knows, 'tis not my will
That drives you hence; but if my master found
That I received a man into the house,
'Twere pity of my place, if not my life.

Torelli. Your master is a churl, that would condemn
These maiden blooms to wither on the tree.

Brig. Churl you may call him! why, he'd have the house
A prison. If you heard the coil he keeps
Of bolts, and bars, and locks! Lord knows the twitter
I've been in all to-day about the key
I lost this morning—it unlocks the door
Of the turnpike stair that leads down to the street.

Torelli. 'Twas lucky I came by just when you dropt it.

Brig. Dropt!—nay, signor, 'twas whipped off by some cut-purse,
That thought to filch my coin.

Torelli. That's a shrewd guess!
He must have flung it from him where I found it,
Not knowing (*bowing to her*) of what jewel it unlocked
The casket!

Brig. How can I pay your pains that brought it back?

Torelli. By ever and anon giving me leave
To come and sun myself in your chaste presence.

Brig. Alas, sweet signor! (*coquettishly.*)

Torelli (*in the same tone*). Oh! divine Brigitta!

Brig. But I must say farewell. Vespers are over; My mistress will be waiting—she's so fearful.

Torelli. As if her unripe beauties were in danger, While your maturer loveliness can walk The streets unguarded.

Brig. Nay—I am a poor, fond thing; Lord knows the risk I run to let you in.

Torelli. I warrant now You've some snug nook where, if your master came, You could bestow me at a pinch.

Brig. I know none, Unless 'twere here (*lifting arras*, L. 3 E.), behind the arras. Look! Here's a hole, too, whence you could peep to see When the coast's clear!

Torelli (*aside*). There's room enough for two. (*Sternly*) Brigitta!

Brig. Signor!

Torelli (*with feigned suspicion*). How if this had served For hiding others before me?

Brig. I swear By the eleven thousand virgins——

Torelli. That's Too many by ten thousand and ten hundred And ninety-nine! Vouch but by your virgin self, And I am satisfied!

Brig. (*whimpering*) Alack a-day! To be suspected after all these years!

Torelli. Pardon a lover's jealousy—this kiss Shall wipe away the memory of my wrong. (*Aside*) What will not loyalty drive a man to? (*Kisses her*) There!

Brig. (*aside*) He has the sweetest lips!—And now begone, Sweet signor, if you love me.

Torelli. *If*, Brigitta! Banish me then to outer darkness straight! Farewell, my full-blown rose—let others prize The opening bud, the ripe, rich flower for me!

Brig. Oh, the saints, how he talks! This way, sweet signor (*taking a key from her girdle*). The secret door—the key you found and brought me Unlocks it. (*Unlocking secret door*, L. 2 E.)

Torelli (*taking another from his girdle, aside*). Else why
    did I filch it from you—
And have this, it's twin brother, forged to-day?
    Brig. (*getting the lamp*) I'll let you out, and lock the door
    behind you—
'Safe bind, safe bind.'
    Torelli.   Good night, sweet piece of woman.
I leave my heart in pledge. (*Aside.*) Now for the duke.
BRIGITTA *holds open the door and lights him down—then
    locks the door.*
    Brig. He's gone—bless his sweet face! To think what risks
Men will run that are lovers—and indeed
Weak women too! Lord! if my master knew.
                                [*Getting on her mantle.*
'Tis lucky San Costanza is hard by—
I should be fearful else. Faenza's full
Of gallants—and who knows what might befall
A poor young woman like myself, with nought
Except her innocence to be her safeguard!
                                   [*Exit* BRIGITTA, R. 2 E.
As soon as she has closed the door the secret door, C. *opens,
    and* TORELLI *reappears.*
    Torelli. This way, my lord—the dragon has departed.
    Enter MANFREDI *from the secret door,* L. 2 E.
    Man. 'Tis time—I was aweary of my watch!
    Torelli. You were alone, at least. Think of *my* lot,
That had to make love to a tough old spinster!
I would we had changed parts. Why, good my lord,
I had to kiss her! Faugh! When shall I get
The garlic from my beard?—But here's the cage
That holds our bird! We must ensconce ourselves,
For they'll be here anon—vespers were over
Before we entered!
    Man.   Thanks to your device
Of the forged key!—yet that was scarcely needed;
I've climbed more break-neck balconies than that
                                   [*Pointing to window.*
Without a silken ladder! (*Looking about.*) So—a lute—
A missal—flowers!—more tokens of a maid
Than of a mistress!—Well, so much the better;
I long to see the girl! Is she as fair
As Serafino painted?
    Torelli.   Faith, my lord,

She's fair enough to justify more sonnets
Than e'er fat Petrarch pumped out for his Laura.
She is a paragon of blushing girlhood,
Full of temptation to the finger-tips.
I marvel at myself, that e'er I yielded
This amorous enterprise even to you—
But that my loyalty outbears my love.
    Man. I will requite your loyalty—fear not;
But where shall we bestow ourselves?
    Torelli (*lifting the arras from the recess*). In here;
The old crone showed it me but now,—there's cover
And peeping-place sufficient. Hark! they come!
Stand close, my lord. [*They retire behind the arras.*
        Enter FIORDELISA *and* BRIGITTA, R. 2 E.
    Brig. And he was there to-night?
    Fiord. Oh, yes! He offered me the holy water
As I passed in. I trembled so, Brigitta,
When our hands met, I fear he must have marked it,
But that he seemed almost as trembling, too,
As I was.
    Brig. *He!* a brazen popinjay,
I'll warrant me, for all his modest looks!
I wonder how my master would endure
To hear of such audacious goings on!
    Fiord. That makes me sad. My father is so kind,
I cannot bear to have a secret from him.
Sometimes I feel as I would tell him all;
But then, I think, perhaps he would forbid me
From going out to church;—and 'tis so dull
To be shut up here all the long bright day:
From morn till dark, to mark the busy stir
Under the window, and the happy voices
Of holiday-makers, that go out and in
Just as they please. Look at the birds, Brigitta;
Their wings are free, yet no harm comes to them;
I'm sure *they're* innocent! And then to hear
Sometimes the trumpets, as the knights ride by,
And tramp of men at-arms—(*a lute sounds without*)—
    sometimes a lute.
Hark! 'tis his lute! I know the air—how sweet!
My good Brigitta, would there be much harm
If I touched mine—only a little touch,
To tell him I am listening?

Brig.   Holy saints,
Was e'er such boldness! I must have your lute
Locked up. These girls! these girls!—Bar them from
    court,
And they'll find matter in church; keep them from
    speech,
And they'll make catgut do the work of tongue!
Better be charged to keep a cat from cream,
Than a girl from gallants!
    Fiord.   Nay, but, good Brigitta,
This gentleman is none.
    Brig.   How do *you* know?
    Fiord. He never speaks to me—scarce looks—or if
He do, it is but to withdraw his gaze
As hastily as I do mine. I've seen him
Blush when our eyes met; not like yon rude man,
Who pressed upon me with such words and looks
As made me red and hot—you know the time—
When that kind lady, Countess Malatesta,
Scarce saved me from his boldness.
    Brig.   Tilly-vally!
There are more ways of bird-catching than one;
He's the best fowler who least scares his quarry.
But I must go and see the supper toward.
Your father will be here anon.
                                    [*Exit* BRIGITTA, R.
    Fiord.   Dear father!
Would he were here, that I might rest my head
Upon his breast, and have his arms about me;
For then I feel there's something I may love,
And not be chidden for it. (*Lute sounds.*) Hark! again!
If I durst answer!
How sad he must be out there in the dark,
Not knowing if I mark his music!
(*Takes her lute, then puts it away.*)   No!
My father would be angry—sad enough
To have one joy I may not share with him.
Yet there can be no harm in listening—
I thought to-night he would have spoken to me;
But then Brigitta came—and he fell back!
I'm glad he did not speak—and yet I'm sorry—
I should so like to hear his voice—just once—
He comes in my dreams, now—but he never speaks—

I'm sure 'tis soft and sweet! (*Listening.*) His lute is
   hushed.
What if I touched mine, now that he is gone?
I must not look out of the casement!—Yes—
I'm sure he's gone! [*Takes her lute and strikes a chord*, L.
   Man. (*aside, lifting the arras*) She is worth ten Ginevras!
   Torelli (*holding him back*). Not yet!—
   Man.   Unhand me—I *will* speak to her!
   BERTUCCIO *appears at the door*, R. 2 3.
   Torelli. My lord! It is Bertuccio! In—quick!
BERTUCCIO *stands for a moment fondly contemplating*
   FIORDELISA. *His dress is sober and his manner composed. He steps quietly forward.*
   Bert. My own!
   Fiord. (*turning suddenly and flinging herself into his
      arms with a cry of joy*) My father!
   Bert. (*embracing her tenderly*) Closer, closer yet!
Let me feel those soft arms about my neck,
This dear cheek on my heart! No—do not stir—
It does me so much good! I am so happy—
These minutes are worth years!
   Fiord.   My own dear father!
   Bert. Let me look at thee, darling,—why, thou growest
More and more beautiful! Thou'rt happy here?
Hast all that thou desirest—thy lute—thy flowers?
She loves her poor old father?—Blessings on thee—
I know thou dost—but tell me so.
   Fiord.   I love you—
I love you very much! I am so happy
When you are with me. Why do you come so late,
And go so soon? Why not stay always here?
   Bert. Why not! why not! Oh, if I could! To live
Where there's no mocking, and no being mocked;
No la ughter but what's innocent; no mirth
That leaves an after-bitterness like gall.
   Fiord. Now, you are sad! There's that black ugly cloud
Upon your brow—you promised, the last time,
It never *should* come when we were together.
You know when *you*'re sad, *I*'m sad too.
   Bert.   My bird!
I'm selfish even with thee—let dark thoughts come,
That thy sweet voice may chase them, as they say
The blessèd church-bells drive the demons off.

Fiord. If I but knew the reason of your sadness,
Then I might comfort you; but I know nothing—
Not even your name.
  Bert.   I'd have no name for thee
But 'Father.'
  Fiord.   In the convent, at Ceséna,
Where I was reared, they used to call me orphan.
I thought I had no father, till you came,
And they needed not to say I had one;
My own heart told me that.
  Bert.   I often think
I had done well to have left thee in the peace
Of that still cloister. But it was too hard—
My empty heart so hungered for my child!—
For those dear eyes that look no scorn for me—
That voice that speaks respect and tenderness,
Even for me!—My dove—my lily-flower—
My only stay in life! Oh, God! I thank thee
That thou hast left me this at least! (*He weeps.*)
  Fiord.   Dear father!
You're crying now—you must not cry—you must not—
I cannot bear to see you cry.
  Bert.   Let be!—
'Twere better than to see me laugh.
  Fiord.   But wherefore?
You say you are so happy here—and yet
You never come but to weep bitter tears.
And I can but weep too—not knowing why.
Why are you so sad? Oh, tell me—tell me all!
  Bert. I cannot. In this house I am thy father:
Out of it, what I am boots not to say;
Hated, perhaps—or envied—feared, I hope,
By many—scorned by more—and loved by none.
In this one innocent corner of the world
I would but be to thee a father—something
August and sacred!
  Fiord.   And you are so, father.
  Bert. I love thee with a love strong as the hate
I bear for all but thee. Come, sit beside me,
With thy pure hand in mine—and tell me still,
'I love you,' and 'I love you'—only that.
Smile on me—so!—thy smile is passing sweet!
Thy mother used to smile so once—oh, God!

I cannot bear it. Do not smile—it wakes
Memories that tear my heart-strings. Do not look
So like thy mother, or I shall go mad!
 Fiord. Oh, tell me of my mother!
 Bert. (*shuddering*)   No, no, no!
 Fiord. She's dead?
 Bert.   Yes.
 Fiord.   You were with her when she died?
 Bert. No!—leave the dead alone—talk of thyself—
Thy life here. Thou heedest well my caution, girl—
Not to go out by day, nor show thyself
There, at the casement?
 Fiord.   Yes: some day, I hope,
You will take me with you, but to see the town—
'Tis so hard to be shut up here, alone.
 Bert. Thou has *not* stirred abroad? (*Suspiciously and eagerly.*)
 Fiord.   Only to vespers—
You said I might do that with good Brigitta—
I never go forth or come in alone.
 Bert. That's well. I grieve that thou should'st live so close.
But if thou knew'st what poison's in the air—
What evil walks the streets—how innocence
Is a temptation—beauty but a bait
For desperate desires. No man, I hope,
Has spoken to thee?
 Fiord.   Only one.
 Bert. (*fiercely*)   Ha! who?
 Fiord. I know not—'twas against my will.
 Bert. (*eagerly*)   You gave
No answer?
 Fiord. No—I fled
 Bert. (*in the same tone*) He followed you?
 Fiord. A gracious lady gave me kind protection,
And bade her train guard me safe home. Oh, father,
If you had seen how good she was—how gently
She soothed my fears—for I was sore afraid—
I'm sure you'd love her.
 Bert.   Did you learn her name?
 Fiord. I asked, it, first, to set it in my prayers—
And then, that *you* might pray for her.
 Bert. Her name?—(*aside*)—*I* pray! (*bitterly.*)
 Fiord.   The Countess Malatesta.
 Bert. (*aside*) Count Malatesta's wife protect *my* child!

You have not seen her since?
    Fiord.   No; though she urged me
So hard to come to her; and asked my name;
And who my parents were: and where I lived.
    Bert. You did not tell her?
    Fiord.   Who my parents were?
How could I, when I must not know myself?
    Bert. Patience, my darling; trust thy father's love,
That there is reason for this mystery!
The time may come when we may live in peace,
And walk together free under free heaven;
But that cannot be here—nor now!
    Fiord.   Oh, when—
When shall that time arrive?
    Bert. (*bitterly*)   When what I live for
Has been achieved!
    Fiord. (*timidly*)   What *you* live for?
    Bert. (*with sudden ferocity*)   Revenge!
    Fiord. (*averting her eyes with horror*) Oh, do not look so,
    father!
    Bert.   Listen, girl.—
You asked me of your mother;—it is time
You should know why all questioning of her
Racks me to madness. Look upon me, child;
Misshapen, as I am, there once was one,
Who, seeing me despised, mocked, lonely, poor—
Loved me—I think—most for my misery:
Thy mother, like thee—just so pure—so sweet.
I was a public notary in Ceséna:
Our life was humble—but so happy: thou
Wert in thy cradle then, and many a night
Thy mother and I sate hand in hand together,
Watching thine innocent smiles, and building up
Long plans of joy to come!
                  [*His voice falters—he turns away.*
    Fiord.   Alas! she died!
    Bert. Died! There are deaths 'tis comfort to look back on:
Hers was not such a death. A devil came
Across our quiet life, and marked her beauty,
And lusted for her; and when she scorned his offers,
Because he was a noble—great and strong—
He bore her from my side—by force—and after
I never saw her more: they brought me news
That she was dead!

Fiord. Ah me!
Bert.   And I was mad
For years and years, and when my wits came back,—
If e'er they came,—they brought one haunting purpose
That since has shaped my life—to have revenge!
Revenge upon her wronger and his order;
Revenge in kind; to quit him—wife for wife!
    Fiord. Father, 'tis not for me to question with you:
But think!—revenge belongeth not to man;
It is God's attribute—usurp it not!
    Bert. Preach abstinence to him that dies of hunger;
Tell the poor wretch who perishes of thirst
There's danger in the cup his fingers clutch;
But bid me not forswear revenge. No word!
Thou know'st, now, why I mew thee up so close;
Keep thee out of the streets; shut thee from eyes
And tongues of lawless men—for in these days
All men are lawless.—'Tis because I fear
To lose thee, as I lost thy mother.
    Fiord.   Father,
I'll pray for her.
    Bert.   Do—and for me; good night!
    Fiord. Oh, not so soon—with all these sad dark thoughts,
These bitter memories! You need my love:
I'll touch my lute for you, and sing to it.
Music, you know, chases all evil angels.
    Bert. I must go: 'tis grave business calls me hence—
(*Aside*) 'Tis time that I was at my post.—My own,
Sleep in thine innocence. Good night! good night!
    Fiord. But let me see you to the outer door.
    Bert. Not a step further, then. God guard this place,
That here my flower may grow, safe from the blight
Of look, or word impure, a holy thing
Consecrate to thy service and my love!
            [*Exeunt* BERTUCCIO *and* FIORDELISA, R.
Enter from behind the arras MANFREDI *and* TORELLI.
    Man. His daughter! That so fair a branch should spring
From such a gnarlèd and misshapen stock!
    Torelli. But did you mark how he raved of revenge
Upon our order?
    Man.   By the mass! I think
That Guido Malatesta is the man
That played him the shrewd trick he told the girl of.
'Twas at Ceséna, marked you—the time fits—

That's why he hounds me on after the countess
What! Must I be the tool of his revenge?
I'll teach the scurril slave to strike at nobles!
 Torelli. Hark! what's that? (*Listening.*)
 Man.   'Tis outside the window!
 Torelli (*listening*).   Yes,
By Bacchus, some one climbs the balcony!
 Man. A gallant?
 Torelli.   In, sir; see the play played out.
 Man. But I'll not be forestalled!
 Torelli.   We've time enough.
       [*They retire to the recess.*
   Enter AQUILA *from the balcony.*
 Aquila. Pardon, sweet saint, if I profane thy shrine.
I watched Bertuccio forth—he passed me close—
I feared he would have seen me. I have sworn
Not to betray their foul design to him.
And to warn her, this means alone is left me.
Hark! 'tis her gracious step she comes this way.
Enter FIORDELISA. *She kneels before the statue of the Madonna.*
 Fiord. Comfort of the afflicted—comfort *him!*
Turn his revengeful purpose to submission,
And grant that I may grow to take the place
My mother has left empty in his heart!
He's gone! And I had not the heart to speak
Of the young gentleman who follows me.
He asked if any spoke to me. I told
The truth—he never spoke to me.
     [*Turning round and seeing* AQUILA.
 (*In great terror.*)   Who's there?
Brigitta! help!—
 Aquila.   Silence! but have no fear—
I am not here to harm you—do not tremble.
I would die, lady, rather than offend you.
 Fiord. Oh, sir! how came you here?
 Aquila.   I knew no way
But by the balcony. Desperate occasions
Dispense with ceremony. My respect
Is absolute. Fear not: I am not here
To say, 'I love you,' nor to tell you how
For months your face has been my beacon star.
My passion never would have found a tongue,

It is too reverent; but your safety, lady,
I can be bold for that.
 Fiord.   My safety!
 Aquila.   Threatened
With desperate danger. Think you one so fair
Could even pray in safety in Faenza?
You have been seen: your beauty has been buzzed
In the Court's amorous ear: there is a project
To scale your balcony to-night.
 Fiord.   Oh, father!
 Aquila. He cannot save you—what were his sole strength
Against the bravoes that the duke commands,
For any deed of ill? My arm and sword
Are stronger than your father's—and are yours
As absolutely. And yet what were these?
I could die for you—but I could not save you.
 Fiord. What shall I do?
 Aquila   Have you no friends—protectors
To whom you might betake yourself?
 Fiord.   Alas!
I am a stranger here.
 Aquila.   Think—have you none?
 Fiord. Ha!—if the Countess Malatesta——
 Aquila.   What!
You know her?
 Fiord. She once rescued me from insult
Of a rude man; and promised help whene'er
I chose to seek it.
 Aquila.   She is good, and pure,
And powerful moreover. That's the chief.
Go to her straight—you have no time to lose.
Midnight is fixed for their foul enterprise.
 Fiord. But how to find the house? And then the streets
Are dark and dangerous. I've but one servant,
Brigitta——
 Aquila. Not a word to her! She's false.
Can you trust me? I'll lead you to the countess.
 Fiord. (aside) Were this a stratagem!
 Aquila.   I see you doubt me.
I know you have good cause to doubt all men.
Oh, could I bare my heart, and show you there
Your image set amongst its holiest thoughts,
Beside my mother's well-remembered face—

Could truth speak with the tongue, look from the eyes,
You would not doubt me! What can oaths avail?
He who could cheat you would not fear to cheat
God and his saints! Lady, it is the truth
That I have spoken! May heaven give you faith
To trust in me! but if not, I will stay,
And die in your defence.

  Fiord.   Sir, I will trust you!
And heaven so deal with you as you with me!—
Go with me to the Countess Malatesta—
I'll seek the shelter of her roof to-night.
To-morrow must bring counsel for the future.

  Aquila. Oh! bless you for this trust! Come—quick—
    but softly—
Put on your veil—fear not—I am your guard,
Your slave, your sentinel. I crave no guerdon—
Not even a look! Enough for me to save you.
       [*Exeunt* FIORDELISA *and* DELL'AQUILA.

  Man. (*breaking out from behind the arras,* TORELLI *following him*) Why did you hold me back? Our project's marred.
This moonstruck poet bears away the prize,
And I am fooled.

  Torelli.   Nay; trust my cooler brain.
I'll follow them to Malatesta's. Sure
He'll give her shelter?

  Man.   In his lady's absence?

  Torelli. Even so. The old ruffian can be courteous,
When there's a pretty face in question!

  Man.   Let him!
I'll break his house, or any man's that dares
Set his locks in the way of my good pleasure!

  Torelli. Why not? 'Twill give a double pungency
To our revenge upon Bertuccio.
We only looked to keep the foul-mouthed knave
Out of the way, while we bore off his pearl;
But now we'll use him for the robbery.
He shall see *us* scale Malatesta's windows;
But she whom we bear thence, muffled, and gagged,
Shall be the hunch-backed scoffer's pretty daughter!

  Man. A rare revenge! and so this brain-sick poet
And my curst jester may console each other.

Watch them to Malatesta's! I'll to our friends,
And find Bertuccio by San Stefano!
                    [*Exit by secret door*, L. 2 E.

SCENE II.

A Street near the Church of San Stefano: stage dark.
        Enter BERTUCCIO, L., *cloaked and masked.*

   Bert. The hour has struck—they will be here anon—
Trust them to keep tryst for a villainous deed—
I had need to whet the memory of my wrong,
Or my girl's angel face and innocent tongue
Had shaken even *my* steadfastness of purpose!
And Malatesta's wife has done her kindness—
I would she had not! But what's such slight service
To my huge wrong? Let me but think of that!
I grow too human near my child. I lack
The sharp sting of court scorn to spur the sides
Of my intent! With her I'm free to weep—
With them, I still must laugh—still be their ape
To mop and mow, and wake their shallow mirth.
True—I can sometimes bite—as monkeys do.
They'll make mirth of that too! Oh, courtly sirs!
Sweet-spoken, stalwart gallants! if you knew
The hate that rankles underneath my motley!
The scorn that barbs my wit—the bitterness
That grins behind my laughter—you would start,
And shudder o'er your cups, and cross yourselves
As if the devil were in your company!
Once my revenge achieved, I'll spurn my chain—
Fool it no more—but give what's left of life
To thought of her I've lost, and love of her
That yet is left me.
Enter MANFREDI, ASCOLTI, *and* ORDELAFFI, *masked and cloaked.*

   Man.   Hist! Bertuccio!
   Bert. Here, gossip Galeotto—you are punctual—
Ascolti, too,—grave Signor Florentine,
We'll show you how the gallants of Faenza
Treat greybeards who aspire to handsome wives.
Remember, *your* beard's grizzled—and beware—
   Ascolti. I will stand warned. You have the ladders here?
   Bert. The lackeys wait in charge of them hard by.
But where's Torelli?—we shall want his help.

Ordel. Pshaw! our three swords are plenty.
Bert. Cry you mercy!
'Tis not Torelli's sword we want.
Ordel. What then?
Bert. His marvellous quick scent of danger, man.
Stick to *his* skirts—I'll answer for't, you're safe.
Perhaps he smelt some risk of buffets here,
And so has ta'en him home to bed.
Man. Away
Towards Malatesta's house—'twas there he promised
To meet us. Sirrah fool, be it thy post
To hold the ladder while we mount—and see
Thou play'st us no jade's trick, or 'ware the whip!
Bert. Fear not, magnanimous gossip—do *your* work
With as good will as I do mine. The countess
Sleeps in the chamber of the balcony,
Which rounds the angle of the southern front:
I came but now by the palace—all was quiet.
Man. Set on then, cautiously—use not your swords,
Unless on strong compulsion: blood tells tales—
And I want no more feuds upon my hands. [*Exeunt*, R.

SCENE III.

Exterior of the Palace of Malatesta, with Street. The flat exhibits the corner of two streets. The Palace of Malatesta is on a set piece, L. C. E.—*A window on the first floor, with a balcony, practicable.—Night.*

Enter FIORDELISA *and* DELL'AQUILA, *followed by* TORELLI *at a distance. Through the scene between* FIORDELISA, DELL'AQUILA, *and* MALATESTA, TORELLI *watches and listens behind a projecting piece of masonry.*

Aquila. Be of good cheer—this is the house—I'll knock
And summon forth the count. (*Knocks.*)
Fiord. Oh, sir! what thanks
Can e'er repay this kindness?
Aquila. But remember
Who 'twas that did it: I am thanked enough.
Fiord. I'll pray for you, after my father—hark!
Aquila. They come!

Enter a SERVANT *from house.*

Serv. Two strangers who crave instant speech
Of the Count Malatesta. [*Exit* SERVANT.
Aquila. And should I see your father?
Fiord. Then you know him!

Aquila. Yes.
Fiord. And his business—occupations? (*He bows.*)
(*Sadly*) 'Tis more than I do, sir, that am his child.
I do not even know his name.
    Aquila.   What he
Keeps secret from you 'tis not mine to tell;
'Twere well you should not question him too closely:
He shall learn you are safe.
    Fiord.   And tell him, too,
That 'twas *you* saved me, sir. Promise me that.
                Enter MALATESTA, L.
    Mala. Who is it would have speech of Malatesta?
    Aquila. You know me, count?
    Mala.   Dell'Aquila, well met!
But your companion? (*Aside.*)   Ha! a petticoat!
So ho, my poet!
    Aquila.   Pardon, if I pray
This lady's name may rest a secret, count;
She is in grievous danger—one from which
Your house can shelter her. She owes already
Your countess much, for good help given at need,
So craves to increase the debt.
    Mala.   My house is hers;
But she should know my countess is not here.
    Fiord. Not here!
    Mala.   But if she dare trust my grey hairs
She shall have shelter.
    Aquila.   Nay, she cannot choose.
    Mala. I'll give her my wife's chamber, if she will;
Her women to attend her.
    Aquila.   All she needs
Is your roof's shelter for the night; to-morrow
Must see her otherwise bestowed.
    Mala.   Go in,
Fair lady; my poor house, with all that's in it,
Is at your service;—had my wife been here,
You had had gentler 'tendance; as it is
I'll lead you to her chamber, and there leave you.
    Torelli (*aside*). Now to the hunters: I've marked down
        the deer.
                              [*Exit* TORELLI, L. U. E.
    Mala. (*to* AQUILA) You will not stay and crush a cup
        with me?

Aquila. No—not to-night. (*To* Fiordelisa.) Did you
  well to trust me?
Farewell; think of me in your prayers!
  Fiord.   I cannot
Choose but do that, sir. (*Aside*). Oh, the thought of
  him
Will come, henceforth, betwixt my prayers and heaven!
              [*Exit* Malatesta, L., *leading in* Fiordelisa.
  Aquila. His child!—Since when did grapes grow upon
  thistles?
And yet I'm glad to know the tie that binds
The two together such a holy one!
Sweet angel!—sister angels guard thy sleep!
Now, to seek out Bertuccio, and tell him
The danger she has 'scaped and thank the saints
That made *me* her preserver.
                            [*Exit* Dell'Aquila, E.
Enter cautiously, L. U. E., Bertuccio, Manfredi, Ascolti,
  Ordelaffi, *and* Torelli, *with* Servants *carrying ladders*.
  Man. Softly, you knaves! with velvet tread, like tigers—
  Bert. Say rather, 'cats.'
            [*A light appears from the window*, L. 2 E.
  Torelli.   Which is the balcony?
  Bert. (*pointing*) That! I have noted in this summer
  weather
The window's left unbarred.
  Ascolti.   Ha, there's a light!
If she were stirring?
  Bert.   What, an' if she were?
A sudden spring—a cloak flung o'er her head:
If she have time to spring, you are but bunglers.
  Man. My cloak will serve. (*Takes it off.*)
  Ascolti.   If she alarm the house
It might go hard with us.
  Bert.   Oh, cats that long
For fish, yet fear to wet your feet! I'll shame you.
Let me mount first. Give me your cloak, Galeotto!
  Man. By your leave, fool, I'll net my own bird. Back!
Hold thou the ladder—that is lacquey's work,
And fits thee best. Ascolti and Torelli,
Guard the approaches! I and Ordelaffi
Will be enough to mount, and snare the game.

[*The light is extinguished; the* SERVANTS *set a ladder to the balcony.*

Bert. (*holds it*) All's dark now—Up!

Man. Why, rogue, how thy hand shakes! Is't fear?

Bert. 'Tis inward laughter, Galeotto,
To think how blank Guido will look to-morrow
To find the nest cold, and his mate borne off.

[MANFREDI *mounts the ladder, followed by* ORDELAFFI—*they enter the balcony.*

Bert. (*eagerly listening*) Ha! they are in by this time!
Cautious fools!
I had done 't myself in half the space! So, Guido,
You love your young wife well, they say: that's brave.

[MANFREDI *and* ORDELAFFI *appear on the balcony, bearing* FIORDELISA *in their arms, muffled in* MANFREDI'S *cloak — she struggles but cannot scream—*ORDELAFFI *descends first —* MANFREDI *hands* FIORDELISA *to him — they come down the ladder.*

Bert. 'Tis done!

Man. Away all—to my garden house,
There to bestow our prize!

Exeunt MANFREDI *and* ORDELAFFI, L. U. E.
The SERVANTS *carry off the ladder.*

Bert. Now, Malatesta (*shaking his fist at the house*),
Learn what it is to wake, and find her gone,
That was the joy and pride of your dim eyes—
The comfort of your age! I welcome you
To the blank hearth, the hunger of the soul,
The long dark days, and miserable nights!
These you gave me—I give them back to you!
I, the despised, deformed, dishonoured jester,
Have reached up to your crown, and pulled it down,
And flung it in the mire, as you flung mine!
Now, murdered innocent, *thou* art avenged!
But I have private wrongs, too, to repay:
This proud Manfredi—he you spat upon,
He you spurned such a day, set in the stocks,
Whipped—*he* is even with your mightiness!
Here is Francesca's ring; and here the letter,
To tell her that *her* vengeance, too, is ripe.
The blow shall come from her; but mine's the hand

That guides the dagger's point straight to *his* heart !
I cannot sleep ! I'll walk the night away :
It is no night for me—my day has come !

[Exit, R.

ACT III.

Scene I.

A Room in the Garden-house of Galeotto Manfredi, decorated with arabesques in the style of the earlier Renaissance. Folding doors at the back, communicating with an inner chamber; side entrances, R. *and* L., *covered by curtains; table, and chairs of the curule form.*

Enter Fiordelisa *from* R.

Fiord. (*pressing her hands to her temples*) Where am I?
    What has happened? Let me think :
Those men !—That blinding veil !—The fresh night air,
That struck upon my face. Then a wild struggle,
In strong and mastering arms ! Then a long blank—
I must have fainted—when I woke, I lay
On a rich couch in that room. Has he brought me
Into the very danger that he said
He came to take me from? Oh, cruel ! No,
Falsehood could ne'er have found such words, such looks.
Father ! Oh, when he comes and finds me gone !—
I must go hence ! (*Looking round.*) That door !—
(*She runs to side entrance*, L.)   'Tis locked !
(*Shaking door.*)   Help ! help !
How dare they draw their bolts on me? My father
Shall punish them for this ! I will go forth !
        [*Shakes door again—the door opens from without.*
At last !—
    Whoe'er you are, sir, help me hence !
        Enter Manfredi, L.
Take me back to my father ! He will bless you !
Reward you !
    Man.   Nay, your own lips must do that.
    Fiord. Oh, they shall bless you too, sir—
    Man.   To be blessed
With that sweet mouth were well—yet, scarce enough.

Fiord. Oh, sir, we waste time. Set what price you will
On the great service, I am sure my father
Will pay you. [MANFREDI *re-locks the door.*
Man. If we're to discuss your ransom
'Twere fairest we should do it with closed doors—
The terms can scarce be settled till you know
Your prison, gaoler, in what risk you stand.
First, for your prison—Know you where you are?
Fiord. No—
Man. In the Duke Manfredi's palace. Next—
Know you your gaoler?
Fiord. Who?
Man. Manfredi's self.
Fiord. (*wringing her hands*) Woe's me!
Man. What? Is the news so terrible?
Fiord. I've heard Brigitta and my father too
Speak of the Duke Manfredi.
Man. (*aside*) Here's a chance
To hear a genuine judgment of myself!
(*To her*) They said——
Fiord. That he was cruel, bold, unsated
In thirst for evil pleasures:—it was odds
Whether more feared, or hated, in Faenza.
Man. (*aside*) Trust the crowd's garlic cheers and greasy
caps!
The knaves shall know me worse ere they have done.
I thank you, pretty one—I am the duke!
Fiord. Then heaven have mercy on me!
Man. If report
Speak truth, your prayer were idle!—but report
Is a sad liar. Do I look the ogre
They painted to you? Nay, my fluttered dove,
Smooth but those ruffled feathers—look about you!
Is this so grim a dungeon?—Was your couch
Last night so hard—your 'tendance so ungentle?
I am *your* prisoner, fairest—not you mine.
Fiord. Then let me go.
Man. Not till you know, at least,
What you will lose by going. All Faenza
Is mine—and she I favour may command
Whate'er Faenza holds of wealth or pleasure—
I'll pour them at her feet—and after fling
Myself there too, to woo a gracious word

What's life, ungraced by love?—a dismal sky
Without sun, moon, or starlight!—'Tis a cup
Drained of the wine that reddened in its gold!—
A lute shorn of its strings—a table stripped
Of all its festal meats!—mere life in death!
A jewel like thy beauty is not meet
To be shut in a chest;—it should be set
To shine in princely robes—to grace a crown.
I would set thee in mine! (*Approaching her.*)
  Fiord.   Stand back, my lord.
  Man. Why, little fool, I would not harm a hair
On thy fair head. Think what thy life has been!
How dull, and dark, and dreary!—It shall be
As bright, and glad, and sunny as the prime
Of summer flowers!—Only repel not joy
Because it comes borne in the hand of Love!
  Fiord. Oh, you profane that name! Is Love the friend
Of night, and violence, and robbery?
Let me go hence, I say.—I have a father
Who'll make you terribly abye this wrong,
Lord as you are!
  Man.   Your father! By the mass,
She makes me laugh! Your father, girl! Bertuccio!
  Fiord. That I should learn my father's name from him!
Yes, duke, my father!
  Man.   Why, he is my slave—
A thing that crouches to me like a hound,
To beg for food or deprecate the lash—
My butt—my whipping-block—my fool in motley.
  Fiord. It is *not* true. This is a lie, like all
That you have said. Let me go forth, I say.
  Man. You're in my palace. Here are none but those
To whom my will is law; your calls for help
Will only bring more force—if I could stoop
To use force with a lady——
  Fiord.   Then you *have*
Some manhood in you. Look, sir, at us two—
You are a duke, you say—your power but bounded
By your own will. I am a poor weak girl,
E'en weaker than I knew, if what you say
Touching my father be the truth. What honour
Is to be won on me? Yet won it may be,
By yielding to my prayers to be set free—
To be sent home. Oh, let me go but hence,

As I came hither; I will speak to none
Of this night's outrage—even to my father.
   Man. Ask anything but this.
   Fiord.   Nothing but this!
You have a wife, my lord,—what if she knew?
   Man. The more need to take care you tell her not!
Come, little one, give up these swelling looks,
Though they become you mightily. (*Approaching her.*)
   Fiord.   Stand off! (*He
    pursues her; she flies.*) Help! help!
   (*Running to the* C. *door.*) A door! ha! (*She forces it
    open, rushes in, and closes it violently*).
   Man. (*locking it outside*)   Deeper in the toils!
   (*Laughs*) The lamb seeks shelter in the wolf's own den!
   Torelli (*at* L. *door, outside*). My lord!
   Man. (*unlocks the door*) Torelli's voice! How now,
    Torelli?
                  Enter TORELLI, L.
   Torelli. My lord, the duchess is returned.
   Man.   Why, man,
Thy news is stale; the duchess hath been here
These five hours; she arrived, post-haste, ere sunrise.
She must have ridden in the dark. 'Twas that
Prevented me from making earlier matins
Before my little saint here.
   Torelli.   Do you know
What brought the duchess back so suddenly?
   Man. Some jealous fancy pricked her, as I judge
From her accost when we encountered first;
And, as I gathered, she suspects contrivance
Betwixt me and the Countess Malatesta.
'Twas a relief, for once, that I could twit her
With groundless fears. I told her Malatesta
Rode yesterday with his lady to Ceséna,
And, for more proof, repeated what he said,
That on my wife's least summons she'd return;
So she *has* summoned her, in hopes, no doubt,
To catch me in a lie. Her messenger
Rode to Ceséna, just at daybreak. Soon
We may look for him back, bringing, I hope,
Ginevra Malatesta.
   Torelli.   This is rare.
So falls she off the scent, and leaves you here
To follow up your game with Fiordelisa.

Man. Even so: I excused me from her presence
By work of state, for which to this pavilion
I had summoned you and the Envoy of Florence—
Said work of state being no less a one
Than to lend me your presence at the banquet
I mean to offer our fair prisoner.
Bid Ordelaffi and Ascolti hither,
And send my grooms with fruits, and wine, and sweetmeats,—
All that is likeliest to tempt the sense
Of this scared bird.

Torelli. How did you find her, sir?

Man. Beating her pretty wings against the bars;
Still calling for her father. Shrewdly minded
To peck, instead of kissing, silly fledgling!
But I will tame her yet, till she shall come
To perch upon my finger.

Torelli. Where is she?

Man. In the inner room, whither she fled but now.
Fear not—I turned the key on her; she's safe.

Torelli. I'll send what you command, and warn the rest
That you attend them. Good speed to your wooing!

[*Exit* TORELLI, *by entrance*, L.

Man. Now for my prisoner! By gentle means
To gain her ear. Asmodeus, tip my tongue
With love's persuasion!

[*Exit* MANFREDI *into inner room*, C.

Enter the DUCHESS FRANCESCA, *masked, and* BERTUCCIO, *who has resumed his fool's dress*, R.

Fran. (*unmasking*) Was't not Torelli went hence, even now?

Bert. By the great walk? I think it was. Be sure
He saw us not in the pleached laurel alley.

Fran. Then you still bear me out, my husband lies?
That Malatesta's wife has *not* gone hence?

Bert. Trust a fool's eyes before a husband's tongue!
I say again, I was at hand last night
When *your* lord bore from Malatesta's house
Said Malatesta's wife. I saw the deed.
I heard the order given to bring her hither.

Fran. Then 'twas by force, not by the lady's will,
She came?

Bert. Force,—Quotha?—force! How many ladies
Have had to bless the 'force' that saved their tongues

An awkward 'yes.' See you not what an answer
'Force' finds for all? It stops a husband's mouth;
Crams its fist down the town's throat; nay, at a pinch
Perks its sufficient self in a wife's face;—
Commend me still to 'force.' It saves more credits
Then e'er it ruined virtues. After folly,
I hold force the best mask that wit has found
To mock the world with!
    Fran.   There's weight in that.
This violence would stand her in good stead,
Were she e'er called in question! Then what matter,
      [BERTUCCIO, *who has been moving round the room,*
          stops opposite the centre door.]
So I be wronged, if 'tis by force, or will?
Would I had certain proof!
    Bert.   Ha! You want proof?
Come here—(*the* DUCHESS *approaches him*).
Stand where I stand. Now listen—close.
    Fran. (*listening at door*) My husband's voice in passionate entreaty!
    Bert. Only *his* voice?
    Fran. (*starting*) An answering voice!—a woman's!
These are your state affairs, my gracious duke!
    Bert. If you would have more proof, I'll bring you where
You shall hear his humble tools in last night's business
Discuss the deed—all noble gentlemen
Who'd pluck my hood about my ears if I
Durst hint a doubt of their veracity.
    Fran. Do so—and if they bear thy story out
I know my part.
    Bert.   What, tears?
    Fran.   Tears! Death to both.
    Bert. Take care. His guards are faithful. Can you trust
A hand to do the deed?
    Fran.   I trust my own.
    Bert. Women turn pale at blood. Your heart may fail you,
When the time comes to strike.
    Fran.   Daggers for men.
I know a surer weapon.
    Bert. (*creeping up to her and whispering*) Poison?
    Fran. (*putting her finger on her lip*) Hush!
The Borgia's physician gave it me!
It may be trusted!

Bert. (*withdrawing aside*) My she-leopard's loosed!
[*Exit* BERTUCCIO, L.
Fran. (*still at the door,* C., *listening.*)
Past doubt a woman's tongue! And now my husband's!
How well I know the soft, smooth, pleading voice—
The voice that drew my young heart to my lips
When, at my father's court, I plighted troth
To him—and he to me! Oh, bitterness!
Now spurned for each new leman of the hour!
Oh, he shall learn how terrible is hate
That grows of love abused! (*Taking a phial from her bosom.*)
Come, bosom friend,
That hast lain cold, of late, against my heart—
As if to whisper to it—'Be thou stone,
When the time comes for *me.*' (*Looking at the phial.*) Each drop's a death!
What matter who she be? Enough for me
That she usurps the place which should be mine
In Galeotto's love! Hark! some one comes.
[*She conceals the phial and resumes her mask.*
Enter two CHAMBERLAINS *with white wands,* L., *followed by* ATTENDANTS *bearing a banquet, and pass into the inner room.—After them a* PAGE *with wine in golden flagon—goblets, fruit, &c., on a salver.—She stops him as he is going through the folding doors.*
Hold, sir, set down your charge.
Page.   By your leave, madam:
'Tis for my lord.
Fran.   Since when was that an answer
To give thy lady? (*Removes her mask.*)
Page. (*aside*) 'Tis the duchess! (*Respectfully.*) Pardon,—
I knew you not.
Fran.   Enough, sir—set it down,
And wait without—till I bid thee bear in.
[*Exit* PAGE, L., *after placing the salver on a table.*
What need of further proof? Is't heaven or hell
That sends this apt occasion? Galeotto,
I warned thee in the spring-time of our loves,
This hand could kill as easy as caress;
You laughed, and took it in your ampler palm,
And said that death were pleasant from such white
And taper fingers. Try it now!

[*She pours some of the contents of the phial into the flagons of wine.*
Re-enter BERTUCCIO, L., *hastily*.

Bert. Hide here, Madonna: here their lordships come!
I met them on the way—so brave and merry—
My gossip Galeotto bids them here,
To feast with him and *her!*   [*Exit* BERTUCCIO, L.
FRANCESCA *starts as if stung—then goes to the door and beckons.*
Re-enter PAGE, L.—*she signs to him—he bears in the wine.*
Fran. (*aside*)   Their doom is sealed!
   [*She retires behind curtained entrance*, R.
Re-enter BERTUCCIO, *with* ASCOLTI *and* ORDELAFFI, L.

Bert. It is your due;—you that go out bat-fowling
Lack wine o' mornings to keep up your hearts.
   Ordel. Why, thou wert there, knave; yet try thou to enter
Into the presence, and they'll whip thee back;—
His highness wants no fool to-day!
   Bert.   That's true—
With you two for his company. But tell me,
How will the lady relish o'er her wine
The cut-throat faces that she saw last night?
Methinks, 'twill mar her appetite.
   Ascolti.   Be sure
She will not look so scared at *us*,
As *thou* would'st at the sight of *her*.
   Bert.   Who—I?
Nay, I but held the ladder;—we, poor knaves,
Must take the leavings of your rogueries,
As of your feasts. But, pr'ythee, Ordelaffi,
How looked she in her night-rail?
   Ordel.   Would'st believe it?
Methought she had a something of thy favour;
As, if so crook'd a thing could have a daughter,
Thy daughter might have had.
          [*All laugh*—BERTUCCIO *starts*.
   Ascolti.   How now?—he winces.
There cannot, sure, be issue of thy loins!
Nature's too merciful: she broke the mould
When she turned *thee* out!
   Bert.   Nature, sir, proportions
Her witty fools to her dull ones: while she makes
Ascoltis, she must needs produce Bertuccios

To sting their hard hides now and then. But tell me,
Think you Ginevra needed all that force?
  Ordel. She struggled stoutly; but a lady's struggles,
I take it, are much like her ' no '—which often
Must be read, ' yes.'
  Ascolti.   Let's in, at once, my lords.
  Bert. I'll marshal you;—who said that cap and bells
Should be shut out?
  Ascolti.   Stand back, Sir Fool; 'twere best;
You may repent your pressing on too far.
  Bert. I fain would see the lady—'tis not often
That one can carry off a beauty at night,
And make her laugh i' the morning.
  Ordel.   Neither she,
Nor you, I think, are like to breed much mirth
Out of each other.
  Bert. Say you so? Here goes!
    [*He runs up to the door, a* PAGE *opens it and motions
    him back, two* CHAMBERLAINS *appearing at the
    open door.*
Why, how now, sirrah?—I'm the fool!
  Page.   Stand back!
  Bert. I!—why, I'm free o' the place—every place
Except the council-chamber, and in that
I sit by proxy!
  Page. 'Tis the duke's strict order
You enter not this room. [BERTUCCIO *is pressing forward.*)
  Back! or the grooms
Shall score thy hunch to motley. [*He closes the door.*
  Ascolti.   How now, sirrah!
Call you this marshalling?
  Bert.   I am right served!
I forgot fools in silk should take precedence
Of fools in motley!—Lead the way, my lords!
  Ordel. Look, here comes Malatesta.
  Bert.   Ha!—but stay
To hear me gird at him! You call me bitter;
Now you shall see how merciful I've been.
  Ascolti. Waste not your ears on him—the duke awaits us
Beside his beauty—metal more attractive
Than this curst word-catcher.
  Ordel.   Aye, aye—let's in.
    [*Exeunt* ORDELAFFI *and* ASCOLTI.

BERTUCCIO *goes hastily to* R. *entrance.*—*Enter* FRANCESCA.
   Bert. Now, now, Madonna—have you proof enough?
   Fran. Mountains of proof on proof—if proof were
     needed—
But had disproof come with them, and not proof,
'Tis all too late.
   Bert.   How?
   Fran.   I have drugged their wine—
They will sleep sound to night! (*She retires up.*)
   Bert. (*aside*)   Choose woman's hands,
You that would have grim work nimbly despatched!
Here's Malatesta! Looking black as night.
So, lord, I hope you liked your waking news!
Now—now—to gloat over his agony!
               Enter MALATESTA, L.
   Mala. (*not seeing the* DUCHESS) Ha!—knave—I'd see
     the duchess!
   Bert. (*looking at him curiously*) Marvellous!
   Mala. How now?
   Bert. To think—that they can make such caps
To hide all trace of them—
   Mala.   Of what, knave?
   Bert.   Horns.
   Mala. Rascal!
   Bert.   I hope your lordship had good rest?
And that my lady, too, slept undisturbed?
   Mala. What mean you, sirrah?
   Bert.   Nay—strain not so hard
To keep it down—You are among friends here—
A grievous loss, no doubt.—But at your age
You could scarce look to keep her to yourself—
Others have lost wives too—poor knaves who thought
To stick in their thrum caps jewels that caught
The eyes of nobles—needs were they must yield
Daughters—or wives—
   Mala.   Art mad, or drunk, or both!
My errand's to thy mistress—not to thee.
Where is she?
   Fran. (*coming down*) Here, my lord! (*They talk apart.*)
   Bert.   He bears it bravely.
But wounds will bleed under an iron corslet:
And how this must be bleeding! For he loved her—
The whole Court vouches it—as old men love:—

E

Husbanding their spent fires into a heat,
The fiercer, that it has short time to burn.
      [FRANCESCA *and* MALATESTA *come forward.*
 Fran. You say your lady slept not here last night,
But at Ceséna?
 Mala. Or the devil's in't.
I saw her safe bestowed there: I can trust
My own eyes—or, still better, my old bolts.
 Bert. (*amazed and aside*) Is this old man, too, of Manfredi's council,
To cheat his wife?
 Mala. I little thought to bring her back so soon;
But, on your summons, I have straight recalled her.
 Bert. (*breaking in eagerly*) And she is here: hold him to that. Madonna.
 Mala. Malapert dog!
 Fran. Pardon his licensed tongue.
I fain would see the lady.
 Mala. (*bowing*) You shall see her;
I have not far to fetch her. [*Exit*, L.
 Bert (*furiously*) 'Tis a lie!
A cursed lie!—to hide his own foul shame!
Believe him not!
 Fran. But if he bring the lady?
 Bert. (*laughing*) Aye, if he bring the lady, then believe him!
(*Aside.*) He robs me of my right—taking his wrong
With outward show of calm. *Mine* turned my brain:
I looked to see him mad—or drive him so!
 Man. (*within*) More wine, knave!
    Enter a PAGE *from* C. *door. passes out*, L.
 Fran. Ginevra, or another, what of that?
The wrong's the same—why not the same revenge?
 Bert. The same to you, but not the same to me!
I tell you Malatesta's wife sits yonder—
Sits at your husband's side: I saw her—I—
Borne off last night! I *saw*. There is no faith
In eyes, or ears, or truth, if 'twere not she!
Re-enter MALATESTA, L., *with* GINEVRA.—BERTUCCIO'S *back is towards the door.*
 Mala. Madam, my wife!
 Bert. (*turning, in amazement*) Ginevra here! Then who
Was that they carried from her bed last night?
Who is't sits yonder?

Fran.   Tell me, gracious, lady,
Where did you sleep last night?
     Ginev.   Where I scarce thought
To leave so soon, your highness; in Ceséna,
Within my husband's castle.
     Fran.   Pardon, madam,
That I have set you on a hurried journey;
Still more that I have wronged you in my thoughts!
     (*Passing her hand over her brow—laughter heard within.*)
     (*Aside*) They laugh! laugh on, my lord, while it is time.
     Ginev. Wilt please you grant me audience: you shall hear
To the minute how my hours went yesterday,
Down to this moment.
     Fran.   Come out in the air;
I stifle within hearing of their mirth.
(*To* BERTUCCIO) Stay here! see that the other 'scape me not!
                   [*Exeunt* FRANCESCO *and* GINEVRA, L.
     Bert. The other! Not Ginevra? (*To* MALATESTA) Good, my lord,
Your wife slept at Ceséna, yet her chamber
Was not untenanted last night, I'll swear!
     Mala. And so thou might'st, yet break no oath.
     Bert. Who slept in't?
     Mala. I know not; ask Dell'Aquila; 'twas he
Brought me the lady; craving shelter for her
From some great danger.
     Bert.   But you saw her face?
     Mala. And if I did—think'st thou I'd trust her name
To *thy* ass-ears?   [*Exit* MALATESTA, L.
     Bert.   Fooled—mocked of my revenge!
The sweetest morsel on't whip't from my teeth!
Oh, I could brain myself with my own bauble!
                Enter DELL'AQUILA, L.
(*Aside*) Dell'Aquila! *He* knows.
     Aquila.   Well met, Bertuccio;
I've sought thee since this morning; nay, since midnight.
     Bert. Ha!
     Aquila. For a matter much concerns thy peace.
Thou hast a daughter. (BERTUCCIO *starts*.) How I know thou hast
Matters not to my story.
     Bert. (*hastily*)   Hush—hush! hush!

If you know this, as you are Christian man,
And poet—poets should have softer hearts
Than courts and camps breed now-a-days—oh, keep
The knowledge to yourself!
  Aquila.   It is too late.
Torelli knew it—had set wolfish eyes
On her——
  Bert. Well?—well?
  Aquila.   Had rung her beauty's praise
Here in the court. Thou hast no friends here.
  Bert. (eagerly)   Well?
  Aquila. They plotted how to lure thee from the house;
And, in thy absence, to surprise her window,
And bear her off! They bound me by an oath
To keep it secret from *thee*—not from *her*.
I swore to save her, or to lose myself;
So found a desperate means of speech with her,—
And warned her of her danger.
  Bert.   Thanks—thanks—thanks!
But only warned her!
  Aquila.   Placed her, too, in safety.
  Bert. Oh, heaven! where?
  Aquila.   In the house of Malatesta.
  Bert. (hoarsely) My child in Malatesta's house last night!
  Aquila. Secure—even in the countess's own chamber!
  Bert. (with a wild cry) My child! my child! wronged!
   murdered!
  Aquila. Ha! by whom?
  Bert. (wildly) By me! by me! Her father—her own
   father!
That would have grasped heaven's vengeance, and have
   drawn
The bolt on my own head, and hers—and hers!
  Aquila. What do you mean?
  Bert.   I counselled the undoing
Of Malatesta's wife—I stood and watched,
And laughed for joy, and held the ladder for them,
And all the while 'twas my own innocent child!
Look not so scared—'tis true—I am not mad!
She's here—now—in their clutches! (*Laughter within.*)
         Hark—they laugh!
'Tis the hyænas o'er their prey—my child!—
And I stand here and cannot lift a hand!

Aquila.   Here's mine, and my sword too!
Bert.   Oh! what were that
Against their felon blades?
Aquila.   True—true! what aid?
Ha! there's the duchess!
Bert. (shrieks)   I had forgotten her!
    (*Drawing* AQUILA *to him and whispering hoarsely.*)
Man—she has drugged their wine—the bony Death
Plays cupbearer to them; if she drinks, she dies!
            Enter a PAGE *with wine,* L.
Look—look! Perchance, that is the very wine!
    (*He runs between the* PAGE *and the door, and assumes
        the fool's manner.*)
Halt there! for the fool's toll. No wine goes in
But pays the fool's toll.
Page.   Out, knave—stand aside!
        [BERTUCCIO *snatches the flagons from the salver.*
Bert. 'Tis forfeit by the law!
        [*The* PAGE *tries to recover the wine—in the struggle*
        BERTUCCIO *pretends to upset the flagons by accident,
        and the wine is poured out upon the stage.*
Page.   Thy back shall bleed
To make it up. Now I must go fetch more—
And brook the cellarer's chiding for thy folly.
            Enter TORELLI, L.
Bert. (to AQUILA) If he goes in—could we but enter
    with him,
A word of mine might save her from the poison.
            (BERTUCCIO *gets between him and the door.*)
Torelli. Good day, Sir Poet—stand aside, Sir Fool.
Bert. You are going in?
Torelli.   Aye!
Bert.   There's a shrewd hiatus
Needs filling at the table. You have War
And Love, but, lacking Poetry and Folly,
War is but butchery, and Love goes lame.
Tuck us beneath your wings, sweet Baldassare,
And you'll be trebly welcome!
    (*Seizing him by one arm, and motioning* DELL'AQUILA
        to take the other.)
Torelli. The duke for once has shut his doors against
Both Poetry and Folly. He is closeted
For grave affairs.

Bert. Tush—tell me not, sweet gossip.
Why, man—*I* know that there's a petticoat—
And more, I know the wearer.
Torelli. Thou!
Bert. You've lost
The rarest sport. Ascolti and Ordelaffi
Had their will of me. For once I'll own
You've turned the tables fairly on the fool!
That our Ginevra should be Fiordelisa,
And poor Bertuccio not know! Ha, ha!
Oh, excellent! It was a sleight of hand
I shall remember to my dying day?
Torelli. Nay, an' thou tak'st it so—
Bert. How should I take it?
Besides the pleasantness of it, there's the honour.
Think, my poor daughter in the duke's high favour.
Why, there are counts by scores had pawned their scutcheons
To come into such grace. I warrant, now,
You thought I'd swear, and storm, and rend you all,
So shut me out. But, lo you, I am merry,
And so shall *she* be, if you'll let me in?—
But let me in—I'll school the silly wench—
Teach her what honour she has come to—thank
The gracious duke, and play the merriest antics.
You'll swear you never saw me in such fooling—
But take me in.
Torelli. Why, now the fool's grown wise!
I'll tell the duke—perchance he'll let thee in.
[*Exit* TORELLI, C.
BERTUCCIO, *exhausted by his emotions, falls into a chair and writhes convulsively.*
Aquila. Lives hang on minutes here. Said you the duchess
Had mixed the poison—or but meant to mix it?
Bert. There it is, man—I know not which. Ev'n now
Death may be busy at her lips. Once in,
In my mad antics, I might spurn the board,
And spill the flagons, as I did e'en now;—
But here I'm helpless. Oh, Beëlzebub!
Inspire them with desire to see a father
Make laughter of the undoing of his child!
Ha! some one comes. They'll let me in!
[C. *door opens.*

SCENE I.]   *THE FOOL'S REVENGE.*   55

Torelli (at the door).   The duke
Will none of thy ape's tricks.
  (*He retires, closing the door.*—BERTUCCIO *wrings his
   hands and screams.*)
 Aquila (rushing forward).   What ho! Torelli!
And you within, you, my lord duke, 'fore all!
I do proclaim you cowards, ruffians, beasts!
Come out, if you be men, and drive my challenge
Back in my throat, if you've one heart among you!
 Bert. You speak to men—they're fiends!
 Aquila.   No hope, no hope!
Yes! here's the duchess; she's a woman still——
   Enter FRANCESCA *and* GINEVRA, L..
 Bert. Madam, and you, too—(*to* GINEVRA)—plotting your
  undoing,
I've compassed the destruction of my child,
The daughter that I loved more than my life.
'Twas she they seized last night, and she's in there.
       (*Pointing to* C. *door.*)
 Fran. Your child?
 Bert.   From death, if not worse wrong than death,
You still may save her. Have the doors burst open.
You can command here—next the duke. If not,
At least (*aside to her*) forbear the poison!
 Fran. (aside to him)   'Tis too late
The wine was here!
 Bert.   Then this alone remains.
   (*He rushes up to the door and shouts.*)
Come forth, my lords! The duke's life—all your lives
Hang by a thread! Come forth—all! For your lives!
 (TORELLI, ASCOLTI *and* ORDELAFFI *appear at the door.*)
Your wine is poisoned!
 Torelli.   Ha! Who did the deed?
 Bert. I!—drink not—for your lives!
   (*They are rushing upon him, drawing their swords.*)
 Fran. He lies! 'Twas I! (*A shriek is heard within.*)
 Bert. My child! my child!
 *Torelli (who has turned back at the sound, flinging the
  door wide open).* Look to the duke, my lords!
(*As the doors are flung open the interior of the inner room is
 seen, with the* DUKE *senseless on his seat, and* FIOR-
 DELISA *lying at his feet.*—TORELLI, ASCOLTI, *and*
 ORDELAFFI *support the* DUKE; BERTUCCIO *and*
 DELL'AQUILA *rush up to* FIORDELISA.)

Bert. Too late! too late!
Torelli. He's dead!
Fran. Before all men,
I'll answer this!
Bert. Before heaven's judgment seat.
How shall I answer *this?* (*Pointing to* FIORDELISA.)
 (DELL'AQUILA *has brought* FIORDELISA *forward.*
 BERTUCCIO *takes her in his arms.*)
 Dead!—dead!—My bird!
My lily flower!—Gone to thy last account,
All sinless as thou wert. My fool's revenge
Ends but in this! Cold! cold! (*Putting his hand on
 her heart.*) Ha! Yes!—a beat!
(*Putting his lips to her mouth.*) A breath! a full deep
 breath! She lives! she lives!
Say some of you—*she* drank not! and I'll bless
The man that says so—yea, so pray for him
As saints ne'er prayed! She breathes—still—Hark! hark!
 Fiord. (*faintly*) Father!
 Torelli. She never drank! Thou hast her pure as when
She kissed thy lips last night!
 Bert. Oh, bless you, bless you!
She lives—lives—lives! Leave us to pray together.
 Torelli (*to* FRANCESCA). Madam, you are our prisoner—
The duke lies foully murdered.
 Fran. Ha! what call you 'foully?'
Who but myself can estimate my wrongs?
For those who stand, like him, past reach of justice,
Vengeance takes Justice's sharp sword.
 Bert. No, no!
Vengeance is hellish!—Justice is from Heaven!
Look, Guido Malatesta, I am he.
Whose wife, long years ago, *you* stole from him—
I am Antonio Bordiga!
 Mala. You?
 Bert. I thirsted for revenge—for that I wrought
Upon the duke to carry off *your* wife—
Your innocent Ginevra;—seeking that,
See to what verge of terrible disaster
I brought my own dear daughter!—seeking that,
I've compassed the duke's death, whose blood must lie
Still on my head!
 Fran. (*proudly*) I take it upon mine!

My father, Giovanni Bentivoglio,
Stands at your gate, in arms !—Let who will question
Francesca Bentivoglio of this deed,
    Fiord. Father ! let's pray for her !
    Bert.   For her!—for me!
We need it both ! Ah, thou said'st well, my child !
Vengeance is not man's attribute—but Heaven's !
I have usurped it. (*Hiding his face in her bosom.*)
Pray—oh, pray for me !

    Ascolti,   Ordelaffi,   Torelli, *round the* Duke.
Mala. Ginevra. Bert. Fiord. Dell'Aquila. Fran.
R.   L.
                        CURTAIN.

JEANNE DARC

A Drama

IN FIVE ACTS

PREFACE.

So far as I know, mine is the only treatment, in play or poem, of the strange and stirring story of the Maid of Orleans in which the facts of her history have been, in all important particulars, adhered to. These facts are so immeasurably more startling and pathetic than the inventions of the many poets and dramatists, obscure or famous, who have taken her for their heroine, that it is difficult to understand how the truth should have been so widely, needlessly, in some cases even grotesquely, departed from.

So far from feeling any apology due for the retention in my play of Jeanne's agony and martyrdom, I feel that the apology should come from those who appear to have overlooked that such a death was the only fitting crown of such a life; and that, without it, the parallel in this saddest and grandest of all histories of human devotion to a noble cause, to that one divine history which goes beyond it in purity and self-sacrifice, would be incomplete.

There is no life and death of which we possess better and more trustworthy records than of Jeanne Darc's. The *Société de l'Histoire de France* have published, in five octavo volumes, edited by M. Quicherat, all the historical materials that concern her, including the testimony given in the *Procès de Réhabilitation*, directed by Pope Calixtus III., twenty-five years after her execution.

These five volumes have been most carefully and sympathetically condensed into two volumes by Miss Harriet Parr under the title 'The Life and Death of Jeanne D'Arc, called the Maid,' in 1866 (published by Messrs Smith & Elder).

JEANNE DARC (CALLED THE MAID).

A CHRONICLE PLAY, IN FIVE ACTS.

First Performed at the Queen's Theatre, on Friday, April 10, 1871.

DRAMATIS PERSONÆ.

JACQUES DARC (*Father of Jeanne*).
PIERRE (*her Brother*).
FATHER ISAMBARD (*a Franciscan Monk of Neufchateau*).
LA HIRE (*a Gascon Captain of Free Lances*).
DE BAUDRICOURT (*Captain of Vaucouleurs*).
JEAN DE METZ } *Knights.*
BERTRAND DE POUDANGY }
CHARLES VII. (*King of France*).
GEORGES DE LA TREMOUILLE (*Favourite of the King*).
THE ARCHBISHOP OF RHEIMS.
RAOUL DE GONCOURT (*Commandant of Orleans*).
THE EARL OF WARWICK.
THE CARDINAL OF WINCHESTER.
GUILLAUME BÉLIER (*Master of the Household*).
PIERRE CAUCHON (*Bishop of Beauvais*).
NICHOLAS L'OISELLEUR (*A Canon*).
A Cordwainer of Chinon, English and French Captains, Ecclesiastical Judges, Peasants, and Soldiers.
MARIE D'ANJOU (*Queen of Charles VII.*).
ISABELLE DARC (*Jeanne's Mother*).
HAUMETTE } (*Peasant Girls of Domremy, companions of Jeanne*).
MANGETTE }

JEANNE DARC.

ACT I.

The Maid Mystic.

Scene I.

An open place in the village of Domremy, on the Marches of Lorraine, surrounded by hovels. Entrance of the Village Church on the right. On the left Darc's *cottage. In the centre of the stage an old and spreading beech overhangs a spring, about which the peasant girls are dancing and singing.*

Song and Chorus.

Maidens. Spring is here, fair and clear,
   Winter is away;
 Hang the wreaths, to fairies dear,
   On the fairy May.
The flowers of the spring are the sweetest that breathe,
The flowers of the spring are the meetest to wreathe,
   Where the fairies play.

[*The last notes are sung by men and maidens together, while those who do not sing dance round the tree and spring to the air of the music. After the dance, which is led by* Haumette *and* Mangette, Jeanne's *companions, enter* Isabelle Darc, Jeanne's *mother, from her cottage.*

Isabelle. Saw you our Joan, Haumette—Mangette?
Mangette.   Nay, mother,
What should *we* know of Joan? Since that last summer
She passed at Burey——
 Haumette (*ironically*).   And at Vaucouleurs!
Don't forget Vaucouleurs!

  Isabelle.   Well, what of that?
Why should not my Joan visit her good uncle,
My sister's husband?—he's as honest a man,
And well-conditioned—though I say it that shouldn't,
That am Renne Laxart's sister—is Durand Laxart,
As e're a man in France, or Lorraine either,
Of his condition.
  Man.   Durand Laxart quotha!
Our Joan flies higher than Laxarts, or than Rommés;
She must consort with knights.
  Haum.   Who but our Joan!
Why, did not Durand tell you himself, good mother,
Nought would serve Joan but visiting Vaucouleurs,
Its castle and its captain, and speaking with him?
  Man. Nothing but knights for Joan!
  Haum.   Unless 'tis soldiers.
  Isabelle (*aside*). 'Tis e'en too true. She is growing the
    town's talk!
She that was wont to be as meek as a mouse,
Would shun knight, man-at-arms, or free companion,
As a bird shuns the cat, she's a changed thing.
No troop of soldiers passes but there's Joan,
Drawn by the glint of steel, as lark by glass.
  Haum. Art sure, good mother, *'tis* thy very Joan?
That the good people have not whipped her hence,
And put a changeling on thee?
  Isabelle.   Out on you
For a brace of magpies! Show me a better wench,
A gentler, in or out doors, or more helpful;
A nimbler at her needle or her wheel;
One that says *ave, pater,* and *credo* prettier;
Is earlier at mass and at confession.
Our Joan a fairy babe! If fairy babes
Be blessings—but not else.
  Man.   Fairy? Not she
Or she'd be fonder of the fairy May (*points to the tree*),
And fairy spring. Now, while we dance, and wreathe,
And hang our spring flowers out for the good people,
She's praying at the altar of our Lady,
In the chapel of Bermont yonder (*points up to the chapel
    on the hill*).
  Haum.   Give her saints
Or soldiers—masses or men-at-arms—all's well;

But maiden sport or maiden company
She turns up her proud nose at.
   Isabelle.   My Joan proud!
The humblest, gentlest, dutifullest child
That ever mother had—save in this haunting
Of men-at-arms.
  Enter JACQUES DARC, JEANNE'S *father, and* PIERRE, *her brother, from the field, with their implements of labour over their shoulders.*
   Jacques.   'Men-at-arms' quotha, wife;
We are like soon to have enow o' *them.*
The English and Burgundian companies—
A murrain rot them both!—are drawing hither—
So says a holy friar of Châteauneuf
I met on his way to their house at Vaucouleurs.
   Pierre. The father told me that the Gascon captain,
La Hire, is on his march from Vaudremont,
With some two hundred lances. Stout Sir Robert
Has ridden to seek his aid.
   Haum.   And shall we see him?
   Man. That will be brave!
   Isabelle (*ironically*). 'Brave,' will it? Look to yourselves,
Poor folks of either party. All is one
For the *sheep* when the *wolf* comes. Two hundred lances,
And La Hire for their captain; to say nothing
Of archers, grooms, and varlets; the wolf's brood
That snatch what the wolves spare—and they spare little.
   Jacques. Hark, Isabelle, I dreamed again last night
Our Joan had gone off with the men-at-arms.
   [HAUMETTE *and* MANGETTE *exchange signs.*
   Isabelle. Nay, Jacques (*remonstratingly*).
   Jacques.   It makes me mad! I'd sooner see her
Dead in her grave-clothes than a soldier's troll.
Sooner than she should go that road I'd drown her
With my own hand! I would!
   Pierre.   Nay—I know—father—— (*he pauses*).
   Jacques (*contemptuously*). Well, what dost *thou* know, springald?
   Pierre (*to himself, repressing what he was about to say*).
'Tis Jeanne's secret.
   Jacques. Thou knowest—*I* know! Be off to pen our beasts
In the island, quick—and tell thou through the village

The English and Burgundian companies
Are on the prowl, and may be here anon.
And if the foe come not, that friends are coming.

   Isabelle. Heaven help! 'Tis ill choice now 'twixt friends and foes.

   Jacques. I'll look up my old crossbow. Harkye, wife:
If soldiers are astir see Joan kept close,
Or *she* and *you* 'ware bowstrings.

   [*Exit* JACQUES *to his cottage*, L., PIERRE *going*, R., HAUMETTE *and* MANGETTE *go up talking.*

   Pierre. I'll to the river, mother, and pen the cattle (*he sees her wipe her eyes and returns*).
Nay, dry thine eyes. If his tongue's rough sometimes,
Thou knowest, and Joan knows too, his heart is kind.
In these unkind times kind hearts are most fretted.
Dry thine eyes, mother, and look cheerily. (*He kisses her and goes off,* R.)

   Isabelle. Oh, weary, weary days—where will they end?
Making men wolves, they should turn wolves to men.
But we must guard our homesteads against *both*,
And famine, too, and plague. Saints grant the spring
May bring some comfort, after such a winter!

   Haum. See, here comes Joan!
   Man. What said I? From the chapel!

   Enter JEANNE *from the chapel.*

   Jeanne. Did you call, mother?
   Isabelle. I was looking for thee,
But called thee not.

   Jeanne. I heard a tender voice
Call my name twice. I thought no voice but thine
Could sound so lovingly. (*To* HAUM. *and* MAN.) It was not yours?

   Haum. No—none of mine.
   Man. Nor mine, I'll swear.
   Haum. (*archly*) I know!
It was Jean Epinal's. Eh, Jeanne? Look, mother,
She's blushing red.

   Isabelle. Thy father bade me tell thee
The free companions may be here anon!

   Jeanne (*eagerly*). The free companions? Whose troop and *whose* colours?
France's or England's? But they must be *French*.
We are all true French here.

Under what captain, heard you—
La Hire, or Poton de Xaintrailles, or D'Illiers?
Oh, tell me, tell me——
  Isabelle.   Nay, I know not, girl.
But this I know—that thou must not go near them,
It is thy father's will.
  Jeanne.   I will obey him.
  Haum. And thou'lt dance with us round the Fairy May?
           [*They go up to tree.*
  Jeanne. No; I'll go with my mother; there is spinning
To do indoors.
  Isabelle. No more than I can see to.
So I know thou art at hand, it is enough.
Go with them. Take thy pastime while thou canst;
It needs young hearts to be merry now-a-days.
I was light-hearted when I was thy age.
     [*Exit* ISABELLE *into cottage.* HAUMETTE *and*
      MANGETTE *come down, with the wreaths*
      they have woven for JEANNE.
  Haum. For the good people—to hang on the tree!
  Jeanne. (*taking them*). Crocus and snow-drop, primrose, violet!
The earliest and the sweetest flowers I love
Better than summer ones, because they come
In winter times, defying snow and storm. (*Going to chapel.*)
  Haum. Not that way.
  Jeanne. 'Tis *my* way,—to our Lady's altar.
I'll hang my garlands there. [*Chapel bell sounds*
  Haum.   The Angelus! [JEANNE *kneels.*
[*Villagers appear at their doors and do the same. The men coming in from the fields take off their bonnets and kneel in prayer, hiding their faces in their hats.*
ISAMBARD *appears from the chapel.*
     [PIERRE DARC *rushes in with loud alarm.*
  Pierre. Look to yourselves! here's other work than praying.
The English companies have fallen on Greux
With fire and sword, sack'd house and barn and byre!
The poor souls who have 'scaped flock hitherward
With what they've saved.
  Father Isambard. Where's Joan? Where's my right
    hand?   [JEANNE *runs to him.*
See Father Francis warned—there will be wounded.

And tell Colette, at the presbytery, to have wine drawn
And soup set on. Thou, Nicole, warn Jacques Darc,
  [*To one of the boys, who goes off to* DARC'S *cottage.*
Thou, Jean Morel (*to another*), thou, Epinal, to make
 ready
Their barns to house the flyers—they're the biggest.
 Pierre Darc. I've seen the cattle safe penned in the isle
All I could find.
  Enter JACQUES DARC *with his crossbow.*

 Jacques.   Off, lads! muster the men
        [*Some men go off.*
You women! to the barns, and hide the corn;
We've little enough left for our own needs !
        [*Women go off.*
Get thy bow, Pierre ; and, Jean, bring me my sword.
      [*Exit* JEANNE *to cottage.*
I've my old arblast here. 'Tis good for more
Than birding still. The White Cross of Burgundy
Is a brave mark! We'll line the hollow way,
And give the wolves a welcome they're unused to.
 Jeanne (*looking off*).   Poor souls! poor souls!
 Jacques Darc. All who've the will or the weapons, follow
 me!
  [*Exeunt the men who have remained, led
  off by* JACQUES DARC.

  Enter JEANNE *from cottage with her father's sword.
  She looks at it in rapt ecstasy.*

 Jeanne. Oh, would I were a man, to strike with this
For all these hunted, harried, hapless souls !
How long, O Lord, how long? When will it come,
The time that thou hast promised, and the faith
That can move mountains—mountains such as lie
Between me and the work I have to do?
The need is sore; then wherefore stay thy help?
A woman's hand, or hand as weak as woman's,
Ere now hath wrought deliverance in *thy* strength—
Jaël and Judith, and the shepherd-lad
That went forth with his sling and stone of the brook !
I've seen him painted in the Abbey Church
At Vaucouleurs—no lustier than I.
I wonder if *he* heard the voices too?

Enter ISAMBARD. *Sees her absorbed, the sword in her hand.*
Isamb. What, idle, Joan? And so much work to do!
Joan. 'Twas of my work that I was thinking, father.
Great work, I think—strange work, for one like me.
Isamb. The nearest work is greatest.
Jeanne. Oh, 'tis near—
Near to my heart—near to the needs of France—
Near to such miseries as these about us.
Isamb. Joan?
Jeanne. Tell me, father, is there a God in heaven?
Isamb. Dost *thou* ask?
Jeanne. Yes, as one that believes there is,
And so believing, waits till He puts forth
A hand to stay and strike. Is it not time?
Look how my beautiful France is given a prey
To wolfish wills, to fire and sword and famine!
How brothers' hands are armed for brothers' throats;
How mothers curse the day that made them mothers,
Seeing their babes starve on their withered breasts,
Or grow up for such lives as men live now;
When no French soul lies down but fears to wake
With blood about his head, fire in his thatch,
And ravage in his homestead; when none sows
In faith to reap, or if, for English garners';
When our true king must hide his hunted head
Before usurping Bedford's ravening dogs,
That batten on our fields and foul our towns,
And trample down our Lilies—holy flowers,
By Angel Gabriel laid in Mary's lap!
Oh, is it wonder, father, such things make
My head burn, and my heart, as with a fire,
To lift up this (*takes sword*) and strike therewith for France,
Her uncrowned Dauphin, and deliverance
From the Fiend's thraldom and the foreign foes?
Isamb. Why, Joan, what's this?

Enter PIERRE DARC, *armed, followed by* JACQUES DARC, *with his crossbow.*

Pierre (*to* ISAMBARD). The English dogs turn tail!
They have heard La Hire and the Captain of Vaucouleurs,
With a brave company of men-at-arms,
Are hard at hand. The kestrels take to flight
From the ger-falcon. I'll see our best cask

Broached for the captains. They'll need wet their
  whistles.

[*Exeunt* JACQUES *and* PIERRE *to cottage.*
Jeanne. Father, is God's voice only heard in the church?
Isamb. Not only there, my child, but clearest there.
  Jeanne. I have heard it there, but heard it just as clear
In the oak wood, where I drive the sheep from the heat;
Or in the isle of the river, where I sit
At mid-day, while the cattle chew the cud,
And all is still but the crickets in the grass,
And the blue dragon-flies among the sedges;
And then my voices come, so sweet, so clear,
Like the gold trumpets that the angels carry
At Judgment, in the chapel at Bermont yonder.
  Isamb. What voices, child? Is thy brain turned of a
    sudden?
  Jeanne. I thought to tell you this long while—but I
    feared:
I did not know but it might be all a dream—
Sin, pride, the tempting of the Fiend perhaps—
But since last May I know, for I have seen them!
  Isamb. Seen whom?
  Jeanne. My sweet Saint Katherine and Saint Margaret,
And him, the mightiest angel of them all—
The Archangel Michael! It was in our orchard,
Upon Ascension Day, and I was fasting.
When nigh on compline, as I turned my spindle,
And thought of my sweet France and gentle Dauphin—
And my heart burned—it *still* burns with that thought—
Lo! a strange stillness fell upon the place,
And a great light shone through the apple trees.
It seemed a glory first too bright to look on,
As of the sun; but I looked and was not blind.
And then it softened, and out of the midst
Two sweet and saintly faces smiled on me—
I knew them for Saint Katherine and Saint Margaret—
I have seen them in Madame de Bourlemont's missal-book.
And with them was another—awfuller!
That held a sword. I knew then 'twas Saint Michael,
As he stands, cut in stone, o'er the church porch.
And they looked long and lovingly upon me;
And the voice came—I think 'twas Michael spoke—
'Why dost thou tarry? God hath a great pity

For France, its king, and people. It is time
That thou wast gone for their deliverance!'
I wept, and told them I was but a girl,
That knew to sew and spin, but nought of war.
And the voice answered: 'What God bids thee, do,
And have no fear. Saint Katherine and Saint Margaret
Will teach and help thee. Go to Vaucouleurs—
Sir Robert Baudricourt will give thee convoy
To Chinon, to the Dauphin—tell thy errand,
And he'll believe thee.' Then the glory passed,
And I fell with my face upon the ground,
And wept for joy and fear and thankfulness.
And ever since I knew the time had come,
  Isamb. (*aside*). She's mad! And yet could madness
   speak so calm,
And look so holy? Signs and miracles
Have never failed the Church. When was more need
Of miracles than now?—And did'st thou do
As the voices bade thee?—go to Vaucouleurs?
  Jeanne. I prayed my father's leave to help my uncle
At Burey, to keep house in his wife's sickness.
He had faith in me, and took me to the Captain.
  Isamb. And he?
  Jeanne. He had no faith. When I prayed still
For a horse and arms and men to ride to the Dauphin
He cracked a ribald jest, and laughed me off,
And bade my uncle whip me and send me home.
And then I thought I would set forth alone,
And took Pierre Laxart's clothes and started thence:
But still I thought of home—of them in there (*points to cottage*),
And their grief when they heard that I was gone,
Without their leave and blessing, and turned back.
  Isamb. Ah! *those* were voices it was safe to follow!
Have a care, daughter. Devils can take shape
And voice of angels; can breathe Satan's counsel
Into our hearts, so sweet, it seems the saints'.
'Tis pride o' the Fiend!
  Jeanne.   You have known me, father,
Since I could speak and spin. Have I been proud?
  Isamb. Ever most gentle, humble, and obedient.
(*To himself.*) If Heaven sought instruments, 'tis in such lives
They should be found.

Jeanne. And there's the prophecy
Of Merlin—how a maiden of these Marches,
From the oak woods, should rise to ransom France (*points to distance*).
There are the woods! Oh, should *I* be the maid!
Hark! Tramp of steeds and ring of armed men! (*She looks eagerly to the sound.* LA HIRE *without*, L.)
La Hire. Call a halt, Aymery! (*Command without, farther and farther off.*)
Voices. Halt! Halt! Halt! Halt!
Noise of armed men dismounting is heard. Enter LA HIRE, *a Gascon Captain of Free Lances*; DE BAUDRICOURT, *Captain of Vaucouleurs*; JEAN DE METZ, *an old Knight*; BERTRAND DE POUDANGY, *a Squire*; *a* PAGE, *and two Men-at-Arms.*
La Hire (*speaking off*). See pickets set! Thou, Gasquet, on yon hillock
That sweeps the ford; thou, Védille, in the field,
Above the hollow way. (*To* DE BAUDRICOURT.) By your leave, Captain,
We're in *your* country, but I know these Marches.
I rode them with Batifol, in old Armagnac's times,
And English hawks may be afield. I've learnt
The need of eyes, in tail as well as head,
When *they* are stirring.
De Bau. 'Tis a soldier's caution.
Those men you have posted now command the approaches.
La Hire. Trust me for that.
Mordioux! Our nags are cooling!
(*To* BERTRAND) Order the rogues of the place to look to them:
And feed the men. See my red roan rubbed down,
And let him drink when he's dry, like his poor master—
Who's usually dry. (*Exit* DE POUDANGY.) Now, Cadedis!
There should be a hostel handy.
Jeanne (*coming forward*). There's none, Captain,
Nearer than Greux; and at Greux, English thirsts
Have been before yours—it was sacked and fired
To-day.
La Hire. Tarare!
De Bau. What! In *my* bailiwick?
This is that rascal Bisset! He has surprised
The Castle of Joinville, some four leagues to the west.

La Hire. By Marne—a strong place. I held it to ransom
With jolly old Barbizan ; it brought us each,
I think, twelve thousand livres, besides the plunder
Of the merchants using the March-fairs. Nice picking
To be got out of Joinville. Thousand devils !
No hostel ! and I'm as thirsty as a monk
After a marriage.
  Jeanne (*coming forward*). Our wine is at your service.
My father's gone to draw some.
  La Hire.   Cap de Diou !
A lusty lass ! I'd rather *thou* drew for me,
My bonny belle, than thy father any day.
I like the spice of bright eyes with my liquor :
It improves good wine, and makes bad drink better.
Come, till I taste thy tap, let's taste thy lips.
  [*He approaches* JEANNE *to kiss her. She gives him a a look that checks him.*
  Jeanne (*appealing to* DE BAUDRICOURT). Captain, as you are gentlemen and soldiers !
  De Bau. Sure I have heard that voice and seen that face !
Why ! 'tis the mad wench that made such a coil
At Vaucouleurs ! How now ! did thy uncle whip thee
And send thee home, as I bade?
  La Hire.   The foul fiend do
Such bidding ! Whip a lass like this ! she's liker
To whip her whippers ! What must she be whipped for?
  De Bau. Ha ! ha ! I laugh still, when I think of her asking,
Thrice, faith—last year twice, and again last week—
A horse, and arms, and men, to ride to Chinon,
To the King.
  La Hire.   Mordioux ! a *cat* may look at a king,
They say—but a country wench !
  De Bau.   Oh, cry your mercy !
This *is* a cat, as well as country wench :
With claws to scratch the English out of France,
And draw the King to his crowning.—So she swears,
And vouches St. Katherine, St. Margaret, and St. Michael,
And the Lord knows what saints besides.
  La Hire. Peste de ma vie ! (*to* JEANNE) but we're of the same trade, wench :
I hate the Rosbifs too ; would do my best

To drive them out of their free quarters here,
Where they rob us poor native gentlemen
Out of all livelihood! Gascons are good
At pillage; but, Lord! *we're* bunglers to your *English!*
I *have* known a Scotchman steal after a Gascon;
But John Bull leaves the dish bare to the pewter!
  Jeanne. I would not plunder—I would fight.
  La Hire.   Sang Diou!
Fighting's all very well—I'm fond of fighting;
But fighting without plunder is like fishing
Without the fish! And so, thou'rt bent to drive
The English out of France? Suppose thou tried
To clear Champagne of them and the Burgundians?—
The work the Captain here seeks *me* to help in,
When I had other fish to fry—to gather
Money and men for Orleans?
  De Bau.   Nay, fair Captain,
Only aid me to drive these English hence,
Pay Harry Bisset back in his own coin,
And I'll help thee and Orleans.
  La Hire.   Done! a bargain!
Thou'rt witness, bonny belle. (*To* JEANNE) The witness puts
Her seal. (*Approaches her to kiss her. She shrinks back.*)
      Nay, then, if thou would'st rather not,
In good faith, I'll not force thee—kisses are
The one thing not worth stealing. You've a trick,
You women, of saying '*no*' when you mean '*yes*.'
A plain man ne'er knows when he has the wenches—
'Twixt looks that cry ' Come on,' and lips, ' Stand off.'
And so thou'dst see the King?
  Jeanne.   Indeed I would!
And must, and will—aye, before middle Lent:
Even though I wore my feet unto my knees!
I am not mad, nor merry—Oh, believe it!—
     [*Enter* ISAMBARD *from the chapel.*
When I say this. The Captain of Vaucouleurs
Knows if my voices told me truth last week.
(*To* DE BAU.) Did I not tell you there was sore disaster
Befalling the King's soldiers as I spoke?
  De Bau. You did; and, by my halidom, so it was!
  (*To* LA HIRE) 'Twas the day Falstaff beat the Count de
   Clermont.
  La Hire. The day of Herrings! Cadedis! I was there!

A villainous business.   Never were men thrashed
More roundly or more rascally.   Had but Clermont
Followed *my* counsel, we had cut off the convoy,
And drubbed stout Falstaff soundly as he drubbed us.
But hang your feather-bed soldiers !
  De Bau.   Well, she told me
How that day went—as it went——
  Isamb. (*comes forward.*)   And yet *you* mocked !
You did wrong then to mock this maiden's prayer;
You do wrong now to go back to your mocking.
Good Captains both—I speak for her pure life,
Good faith, and even blood, in all but this,
Touching her mission :—He that guides the world
May will to end the miseries of France,
And shame us all—priests, soldiers, counsellors—
By ending them with this weak woman's hand;
      [*Taking* JEANNE'S *hand in his.*
But, if weak, without stain.   Of what hand here
Could *that* be said?
  La Hire. Mordioux ! Sir Priest, well preached !
I like a bit of truth : best, because rarest,
Out of priest's lips !   And for this lusty lass——
  [*Enter* ISABELLE, *from the cottage, followed by* HAUM.
   and MAN., *with earthenware jugs of wine.*
Look, wench : if thou find'st means to get to Chinon,
And I'm there, ask for Etienne de Vignolles—
Known better as La Hire.   It shall go hard
But I will find thee convoy to the King.
Now, where's this wine?
    [HAUM. *and* MAN. *bring forward the jugs.* LA HIRE
   takes one, DE BAUDRICOURT *the other.*
Thanks, my brown beauty. (*Kisses* HAUM.)   *She* makes no
  objection.
   [*Gravely, to* DE BAUDRICOURT *stopping him as he is*
   about to drink.
By your leave, Captain—grace before good liquor!
    [*Takes off his cap, and says his grace reverently.*
Benedictus, benedicat! (*Drinks.*)   That's neat tipple!
(*To* PIERRE) Hark ye, my lad ! can'st show the road these
  English
Took from their morning's work?
  Pierre.   That can I, Captain.
  La Hire.   But lay us on their heels, and if we don't

Plunder the plunderers, never trust La Hire!
    [ISAMB. *and* DE BAU. *have been talking apart.*
 Isamb. Jeanne! He will give thee arms, and horse, and
  convoy to the King!
 Jeanne. He will!
      [HAUM. *and* MAN. *exchange looks of surprise.*
 De Bau.   'Tis more than eighty leagues
'Twixt there and here, and all Burgundian country,
Or English—three great rivers to ride, spring-swollen—
Enemies' towns to pass—their bands to avoid.
 La Hire. Rogues who rob the wrong side!
 Jeanne.   Fear not for these:
My Lord will guide my guides. Are there not angels
To guard us?
 La Hire. 'Tis no road for a woman's riding.
 Jeanne. I'll dress me like a boy. Here's Pierre, my
  brother:
I'll take his clothes!
 Pierre. Take Pierre's self, not Pierre's doublet!
If thou ridest, I will ride. I hate the foreigners
As I love thee, and put my faith in thee.
 Jeanne. My own true brother! [HAUM. *and* MAN. *go off.*
 Pierre. But our father, Jeanne,
How will *he* brook this?
 Jeanne.   Needs must that *you* tell him.
   [*Villagers assemble in the background.* PIERRE *exits
    into the cottage.*
 La Hire. Sound 'boot and saddle,' Aymery! (*Exit a
  Squire.*) My hands itch
To be about English ears—in English pouches. (*Trumpet.*)
See my red roan girthed tight. (*To* DE BAU.) By your
  leave, Captain,
We'll but give Bisset and his rogues a drubbing,
And join you straight. (*Calls.*) My helmet! (PAGE *brings it;
 he puts it on.*)   'Tis three days
Since I've seen lances levelled; a day more,
And my joints had grown stiff. (*Ordering off.*) Advance my
  pennon!
Two men-at-arms a hundred yards a-head!
Then our main battle. Archers in the rear!
These English hornets, with their cloth-yard stings,
Are ugly customers, until you close with them.
(*To* JEANNE.) Farewell, my lass! See thou look out for me

At Chinon. There's my hand! It keeps its promise
To friend or foe—for kindness or for cuffing.
St. Denis for La Hire! To horse! to horse!
            [*Exeunt* LA HIRE *and Men-at-Arms.*
  De Bau. (*who has been conversing apart with* JEAN DE
    METZ *and* POUDANGY, *to* JEANNE.) When would'st
    thou go?
  Jeanne.   The sooner, sir, the better:
Rather now than to-morrow—and to-morrow
Than the day after; only let me go!
  De Bau. Sir Jean de Metz, this grave and grey-haired
    knight,
And Bertrand de Poudangy, my stout squire,
Shall ride with thee; we'll find thee a strong roadster,
And Bertrand's mails shall furnish thee a suit.
I'll give thee letters to the King's treasurer,
Guillaume de Bélier, telling him thy errand.
  Isamb. And I will go with thee for priestly witness
To thy truth, piety, and blameless life.
  Jeanne. At last the time has come! I shall see the King!
My saints, I thank you! (*She kneels.*)
    Enter JACQUES DARC *and* ISABELLE. *The Villagers come
                    forward.*
  Jacques.   How now! what means this?
Joan ride with men, and furnished as a man!
Not if a father's curses or commands——
  Isamb. A Heavenly Father's high command is on her!
Cross it not! Father, mother, bless your child!
For this her errand, I proclaim it holy.
  Pierre. Let her go, father; and let me go with her—
To guard her, fight for her, fight *with* her—die for her,
If need be. Weep not, mother! Let her go!
  Isabelle. She still walked by our will, nor now would
    cross it,
But by compulsion of a higher will,
And holier, than a father's or a mother's.
She needs must go the road that bids her go,
Nor look if the cross ends it, or the crown.
  Jeanne. The cross for *me*, so but the crown for France!
I see it there, before me—shining fair!
Stay me not, father! mother!—let me go!
Follow me, friends, with prayers—not prayers for me,
But for France and her King!

Jacques. France and the King!
Look, all! To this cause Jacques Darc gives his child!
　Jeanne (*to Villagers*). All here that love me, dear friends
　　of my youth,
Weep not for me!—To this end I was born.
But keep me in your prayers and loving thoughts,
As I shall keep you still, when far away
About my work for France and her true King!
　Isamb. (*extending his hands over* JEANNE.) Go forth in
　　our love and the strength of Faith!

TABLEAU.

ACT II.

The Maid Missionary.—*Chinon, March* 9, 1429.

SCENE I.

Inner Court of the Castle of Chinon. Enter CORDWAINER *and*
　　SERVANT *of the Treasurer.*

　Servant. The hunting-boots for his Majesty! It is well!
I'll take them to the Intendant.
　　　　　　　[*About to take them from the* CORDWAINER.
　Cordwainer.　　　　　　　Not so fast!
Leather for livres—cash for Cordovan!
Pay me the money—you shall have the boots.
　　　　　　Enter GUILLAUME BÉLIER.
　Bélier. Thou knave! They're for the King!
　Cordwainer.　　　　　　　God bless his Majesty!
'Tis all my loyalty. I fain would have
A few of his Majesty's pictures—upon metal—
They're scarce with me!
　Bélier (*aside*).　　　Not so scarce as with *me.*
Leave them. I'll send the coin by a safe hand.
　Cordwainer. Where so safe as my own? Look, Master
　　Bélier—
Chinon's a loyal town! 'Twill give King Charles
His rights—her taxes—tolls—in cash or kind—
But it won't give its goods without money.
　Bélier. Why, rogue! do I not hold the privy purse?
　Cordwainer. That's it—so firmly doth your worship
　　hold it,
We none of us know the colour of its money.

Pay me and let me go—but *till* you pay me
I let not my boots go.
  Bélier.   Hence with thy boots!
If thoud'st not have them loose the dogs on thee!
I'll strike thee off the list of the King's furnishers!
  Cordwainer. I humbly thank you. Till the King's cofferer
Can pay down for goods furnished, I'd as lief
Be off the list. Meantime, when you want the boots,
You have but to send the coin by a safe hand.
            [*Exit* CORDWAINER.
  Bélier. Was ever royal cofferer aground
At such ebb tide! His Majesty's privy purse—
This blessed St. François's day—stands at four crowns!
And where to find the next—unless we pawn
The King's own crown—I know not. Nay, the Jews
Have all the jewels of that in pawn already,
And we make shift with shams. Men may make shift
With sham crown jewels better than with sham boots,
Sham doublets, or sham drinkables, or sham dinners.
And I've all these to find, and not a livre
I' the privy purse to pay for them withal!
And the King's credit as low as the King's coin!
      Enter COOK, R.
(*To* COOK.) Jean Andouillet, you are come in good time.
His Majesty entertains the Envoys from Orleans
At his own board to-day. You had your orders.
  Cook. And but wait till his Majesty's purveyors
Send in the fish, and fowl, and meat.
  Bélier.   'Tis well;
I'll see to 't. (*Exit* COOK.) Here's a pass! If luting, lilting,
Dancing, and dicing could but stay men's stomachs,
We've these enough and to spare. But as for victuals,
Or coin to buy them——
      Enter LA HIRE.
  La Hire.   How now, Master Bélier?
Four struck, and no horn sounded for supper!
Sang Diou! You forget that we've been on short commons,
And long to change our Orleans siege rations
For a brave tuck-out with the King—God bless him!
  Bélier. All in good time. His Majesty sups late.
  La Hire. Could'st shove the dial's nose a half-hour
  forward,

G

For special satisfaction of my stomach?
Meanwhile I'll let my belt out some three holes
In preparation. (*Turns up.*)

  Bélier (*aside*).   Faith! I've a good mind—
He should have money—and as free-companion
He should be free of it. Hark ye, fair Captain,
The supper lags—as doth the relief of Orleans,
And for the self-same reason—lack of money!

  La Hire. Tarare!

  Bélier.   The privy purse is at low water—
And but for what the King has caught this week
With his own hawks and hounds, his Majesty
Had often gone to bed without a supper!

  La Hire. Cadedis! I've known many a Gascon gentleman
In the same case.

  Bélier.   And how did *they* provide?

  La Hire. Mon Diou! They helped themselves! Eked
   out their needs
From other's superfluities. All France
Is the King's by good right. And here he starves
In fat Touraine, with a pack of silken courtiers,
And sleek priests, and smooth minstrels fattening on him;
While Bedford and his foragers squeeze the land,
Till north of Loire holds out no door or castle
For France and Charles but stout Mont St. Michel!
And now they close their hands on the throat of Orleans.
And when the Orleans burghers have given freely
Their blood and substance—burned down their fair suburbs;
Melted their pots and platters into bullets;
Spun their wives' hair for bowstrings; eaten up
Their household cats and dogs; stewed down their nettles;
And eked their wine out with their ditch-water;
And when the Bastard of Orleans sends us hither
To ask for men and money, arms and victuals,
The King can't find us so much as a supper
To stay our siege-pinched stomachs! With meat about
And drink for the taking! Oh, 'tis pitiful!

  Bélier. The King will have no taking!

  La Hire.   And so leaves
The more for the English takers—when they come—
As come they will—unless some miracle
Arouse him and breathe spirit in his friends.

  Bélier. The miracle is wrought!

La Hire (surprised). How?
Bélier. A mad maiden,
Out of Lorraine, says she comes to save Orleans!
La Hire. My wench of Domremy!
So she *has come*! I little thought to find her.
And our tryst! Well, she comes in a good cause.
Bélier. 'Tis thought she shall have speech of the King
to-day.
But, for this supper, to which the King invites you,
Might I make bold to borrow ten poor crowns,
You were soon served.
La Hire. Cor' Diou! This beats our Gascony!
Make a man pay for the supper you ask him to!
(*Unfastening purse at his girdle.*)
Here, Master Bélier, dip thy hand in it!
What little there is in it is honestly come by.
No coin there but was earned by good hard knocks——
Other folks' mostly—now and then my own.
Bélier (taking the purse joyously). Ho, knaves!

Enter Servants.

See that his Majesty's purveyors
Stir them to furnish out the royal table

Enter DE LA TREMOUILLE, *the royal favourite*; RAOUL DE GONCOURT, *an old warrior*; REGNAULD DE CHARTRES, *Archbishop of Rheims.*

Right royally! His Majesty gives a supper——
La Hire (aside). Gives!
Bélier. To his Envoys from his good town of Orleans.
De la Trem. (coming forward).
So, Master Belier! we're in funds again!
Bélier (hiding the purse.) Fair Count! I cry you mercy!
De la Trem. (pointing to purse.) By your leave——
La Hire (about to take the purse). By *my* leave! By your
leave—that purse is mine.
(*Takes it and buckles it on again.*)
De la Trem. Methought it was the King's.
La Hire. And so it is,
But not my Lord De la Tremouille's! I know
He usually dips i' the dish with the King—
Often before him; but not in *my* purse.
De la Trem. You are merry.
La Hire. Not I! Spare food and hard fighting

Are poor wit-breeders. To be merry, methinks.
One should be here in the gay court of King Charles,
To learn how cheerily a king and kingdom
May be diced, danced, and fiddled to the dogs!
    R. de Chartres. Your words, Sir Etienne, smack more of
        the camp
Than of the court.
    La Hire.   The steed will smell o' the stable—
I should have reek of blood and powder on me,
As you of civet. 'Tis the smell of Orleans,
And should stink in some nostrils here.
    R. de Chartres. If you mean ours that left the town——
    La Hire.   When victuals
Grew scarce, and nothing plentiful but hard blows.
    De Goncourt. We come to move the King.
    La Hire.   And faith moves mountains.
Nay, we're here, like your reverence, to move
Your reverence to move Sir Raoul de Goncourt
To move Count de la Tremouille to move
His mighty little finger to move the King.
'Tis a great moving—but the need is great,
And all hangs on the Count De la Tremouille's finger!
Pity so much should hang upon so little!
    De la Trem. Little as my hand is, 'tis big enough
To hold a sword! (*grasps his hilt*).
    De Goncourt.   A truce to gibes. The King!

Enter CHARLES VII., *with his* QUEEN, MARIE OF
ANJOU, *and Ladies, in the high horned head-dresses
of the period; with them Courtiers,* DE BOISSY, *the*
DUKE D'ALENÇON, *the* COUNT DE VENDÔME, *Courtiers. Huntsmen, and Attendants, carrying frames with
hawks, and leading greyhounds in leashes.*

    Charles (*to* DE LA TREMOUILLE).
Not booted yet, Tremouille! And such a wind
To fly a hawk! I've backed my Iceland falcon
'Gainst Vendôme's tercel gentle. Ha, La Hire,
We'll show you sport—the Touraine herons fly fast.
    La Hire. May all the King makes war on do the same!
But men or herons fly not unless they're hunted.
    Charles. You still go booted?
    La Hire.   For your Majesty's service—
But I've no stomach for hounds or hawks.
    Charles.   Sang Dieu!

But you've a stomach for what they catch! We live
On game here.
 La Hire. So I see—a gamesome court.
But *my* game's war—and, please your Majesty,
It should be *your* game too!
 Charles.   You are bold, Sir Captain.
 La Hire. Your Majesty's captains need be, since your courtiers
Have lost the trick on't.
 De la Trem. and Vendôme (laying their hands on their swords). How! Put the flout on us!
 Marie of Anjou. Draw before ladies!
 La Hire. Some men wear their swords
Chiefly to draw so—and be chid for drawing—
And put them up unfleshed. But, please your Majesty,
Chidden or no, I must make bold to urge
Once more the need of Orleans.
 Marie.   Pray you, sir,
To stay and hear the Captain.
 Charles.   Not a word
Till after supper—and we've supper still
To catch and cook. My sweet Queen should be weary
Of hare and partridge, mallard, crane, and bittern.
 Marie. The meat's still sweet that's shared with my sweet lord.
 Charles. That's sauce for any dish!
 La Hire.   Please you, to-day
Supper's provided.
 Charles.   How?
 La Hire (touching the escarcelle at his girdle). Out of my pouch!
 Charles. That's like a loyal subject! Trust thy King!
Nay, bring him money, instead of taking it of him.
(*To Courtiers.*) Gentlemen—an example for your following!
But since our supper's safe, we'll fly our hawks
For an appetite to eat it with. Come, madam.
(*To* LA HIRE). And after supper we'll talk to thee of Orleans.
      [*Exeunt* KING, QUEEN, *and Train.*
 La Hire. Now, a plague on this hunting, hawking court!
Orleans shall be relieved! aye, though I pawn
Fiefs, castles, horses, armour, coin, and jewels
To aid her. The King's needs have drained my purse!
Give me thy bonnet, Master Bélier—
 (BÉLIER *gives him his mortier-cap as* JEANNE *appears at back.*)

I'll do what I ne'er did before—turn beggar
For my brave Orleans. But I'll set example
Of giving ere I ask. See here, my chain—
 (*Takes gold chain from his neck and throws it into* BÉLIER'S
 mortier-cap)
For Orleans! (*To* REGNAULD DE CHARTRES.) Your turn,
 my Lord Chancellor.
 R. de Chartres.   My purse is lean—
 La Hire. As a churchman's purse should be.
 R. de Chartres. But such as it is I give it you for Orleans!
          (*Puts purse into the cap.*)
 De la Hire. And I this jewel!
   (*Takes jewel from his cap and puts it in cap.*)
 De Goncourt.   And I my dagger sheath,
Garnished with stones of price. (*Gives it.*)
 Jeanne (*coming forward*).   And I my life!
Thanks, my stout Captain; I said we should meet
At Chinon. I am here!
 La Hire.   And there's my hand
On our old bargain, made at Domremy. (*Gives her his hand.*)
 De la Trem. What malapert stripling's this?
 R. de Chartres.   Some country page
That knows us not.
 Goncourt.   Where's he that whips the pages?
 Bélier. Nay—'tis the maid I told you of!
 De la Trem.   A maid!
In *this* dress!
 R. de Chartres. One of the Captain's light o' loves!
What, in *our* presence! A Bishop's! To change hands
With your camp-trull!
 Jeanne (*half-pained, half-puzzled*). My Lord!
 La Hire.   By your leave. Bishop,
Soldiers mayn't be so close with their peccadilloes
As churchmen are. But I know manners better
Than flaunt my petticoat-sins before shaved heads.
This is an honest wench, whose errand here's
The same as mine.
 R. de Chartres. What mean you?
 La Hire.   To help Orleans! [*They laugh.*
Aye, you may laugh; but she brings Church's warrant.
(*To* JEANNE.) Thou hast the old priest's letters?
 Isambard (*coming forward*). Better still—
She has the old priest's tongue. I've ridden with her.

  De la Trem. No fooling, girl! What brings thee here?
  Jeanne (simply).   My voices!
They bid me drive the English out of France,
And take the King for his crowning into Rheims!
  De la Trem. A maniac!
  De Goncourt.   Or a trickster!
  R. de Chartres.   Or a witch,
Sent by the Devil.
  Isamb. (coming boldly among them). Led by saints and
    angels!
That she's come is best warrant for her coming!
My Lords, *I* doubted when I heard her first,
As you doubt now—'twixt madness, cunning, trick—
Delusion of the fiend. I doubt no longer.
Eleven long days, for ninety weary leagues,
I've ridden with her, and seen a guiding hand
Laid in hers, leading—or held o'er her head.
If ever angels held a mortal creature
In charge, they have held *her*, and brought her hither,
By signs and marvels, for the kingdom's good
And the King's glory!
  La Hire.   Well preached, priest, again!
  De la Trem. (aside) Satan chose well when he chose
    such a body
To lodge in.
  [JEANNE *turns painfully to the priest, and then looks
    with indignation on* TREMOUILLE.
  Isamb.   Hold thy peace, irreverent scoffer!
Look in her eyes! If they rebuke thee not
For thy foul thought, it is the fiend in *thee*,
And not in *her*, that kills the fire in them.
  R. de Chartres (sharply to ISAMBARD). And who art thou
That vouchest her so roundly?
  De la Trem.   Take her back
To her village, there to spin and tend her sheep.
  De Goncourt. Not bring her brain-sick fancies here to
    those
That need help of men's brains and swords.
  La Hire.   Hear! Hear!
  Jeanne. Such help I bring you. Men will follow me.
  De Goncourt. Men follow thee! A peasant's petticoat
For pennon! Sang Diou! Give her the ducking-stool,
Or the cart's tail!

De la Trem. (*to* ISAMBARD.) Hence with thy shepherdess!
Whether she's saint or sinner, witch or wanton,
Boots not to question.   She packs—and thou with her!
    Jeanne. Go back! When once my saints have brought
      me hither!
Father—I cannot go—I will die rather.
    La Hire (*interposing sturdily*). Thou shalt *not* go. And
      thou *shalt* see the King!
    De la Trem. Ha! Who rules here?
                            (*Lays his hand on his sword.*)
    La Hire.   My Lord de la Tremouille—
All but six feet of flesh, christened La Hire,
And some two feet of ground that that flesh stands on.
(*To* JEANNE.) I say, thou shalt *not* go—*shalt* see the King.
    R. de Chartres (*to* DE GONCOURT, *as* DE LA TREMOUILLE
      draws). Bailiff of Orleans!
    De Goncourt (*calls*).   Ho! On guard without!
    Bélier. My lords and gentlemen! In the King's castle!
    La Hire. Nay, if it comes to knocks—— (*Drawing.*)
      Keep near me, Jeanne;
I'll give thee thy first lesson!
    Bélier. Sirs, the Queen!

          Enter MARIE OF ANJOU.

    Marie. What's this, my lords? Swords out—and thun-
      d'rous looks!
    La Hire. It is my Lord De la Tremouille's breathing time:
Hunting is too hard for him. He but asks me
To try a pass of weapons—to help appetite
For supper, as I think.
    De la Trem. Even so, madam. (*Bowing, and sheathing
      his sword.*)
    La Hire. As queens are women, please your Majesty
To help a woman. (*Puts* JEANNE *forward.*) She would see
      the King!
    Bélier. 'Tis the strange maid I spoke of to your
      highness!
    La Hire. This good priest here, and this good—no, not
      good Captain—
Your poor knight, Etienne de Vignolles, vouch for her.
'Tis for his Majesty's good she see the King!
    Marie. Methinks such voucher scarce were needed, sirs.
All women can read faces—queens should read them

Better than other women—if occasion
Should measure cunning. I read in this face
Nothing but holy, humble maidenhood;
Yet, with that holiness and humbleness,
There's a light in those eyes, and on that brow
An awfulness—— (*To* ISAMBARD) Father, keep close to me!
(*Awe-stricken.*) Is she a holy thing? A thing of power
I feel she is.

   Isamb. Fear not, sweet Queen: the power
That crowns her humbleness is from the Highest!

   Marie.   Come with me!
(JEANNE *is about to kneel.*) Nay, 'tis I should kneel to thee!
(*Horn sounded.*) Hark! the King's horn! He is soon back
    from hunting.
My Lord De la Tremouille, he will look for you
At his unbooting. Come! (*to* LORDS.) (*To* JEANNE.) Thou
    shalt see the King. (JEANNE *kisses* QUEEN'S *hand.*)
           [*Exit* MARIE OF ANJOU, *leading* JEANNE, *followed
            by Ladies,* DE LA TREMOUILLE, DE GON-
            COURT, REGNAULD DE CHARTRES, *and* BÉ-
            LIER.

   La Hire (*gaily, to* ISAMBARD). We've won the barriers;
    and never yet
When barriers were well won did drawbridge hold.
But, priest—that girl has stirred strange thoughts in me!

   Isamb. Give them way, Captain.

   La Hire.   Will they give me way,
If I give them? Ours is an ugly life:
Needs hard hands, and a heart not easy softened.
Who knows if hand and heart will stand the siege
Of thoughts like those she wakens in a man?
I think she is a witch—but, by Mahound,
She is a white one. (*Passes his hand over his brow.*) Shall
    we to the King? [*Exeunt* LA HIRE *and* ISAMBARD.

SCENE II.

The King's Closet.   *Enter* CHARLES VII. *and* DE LA
                TREMOUILLE.

   De la Trem. How went your sport, my liege?

   Charles.   Ill, like my fortunes.
How should my hawks and hounds pull down their game,
When I, their master, so miss mine? A king!
Am I a king?

De la Trem.   Let any question it
In hearing of De la Tremouille!
    Charles (*affectionately laying his hand on his shoulder*).
    My George!
I have one friend, I know. "Tis much for one
So buffeted as I—so poor in means
To reward friends. But I am ill at ease.
By your leave, good Tremouille. (*Motions him to retire.*)
(DE LA TREM. *bows, and exit.*) Am I a king?
Is the blood in my veins the blood of Valois,
That fed my father's? She I must call mother,
Whom all but I call She-Wolf—Isabel—
Was she e'en then false to the marriage-vows
She made so light of afterwards with Orleans?
They say Heaven's hand is still about true kings—
Why is it against me, if I'm true King?
Why must I see my fair France, town by town,
Wrenched from my hold, upon my people's backs
All scourges laid at once—plague, sword, fire, famine—
And Burgundy and England in my seat,
With sovereignty to take, and tax, and toll?
Kind saints! vouchsafe some sign to show to me
If I indeed am the true King of France,
Or but a bastard birth of shame and sin!
That, if I be true King, 'twill please thee lift
Thy hand off me and France; or, if the sins
Of the fathers must be visited on the children,
Thou wilt be merciful even in thine anger,
And grant me, when vexed France shall cast me forth,
In Spain or Scotland some poor resting-place
From thy wrath and the malice of my foes! (*A knock.*)
Who's there?
    Marie (*without*).   The Queen.
    Charles.   My Marie! (*Opening.*)   Sweet, come in.
So sunshine should chase storm.
    Marie.   My gracious lord,
You are stayed for in the hall! But I've a boon
To ask——
    Charles. 'Tis granted.
    Marie.   Nay, but hear it first.
Wise wives prize no boons granted without asking.
'Tis that I may have leave to bring to audience
A maid from Domremy: the same that Bélier
Brought word of.

Charles. What! The girl that hath heard voices?
(*Laughingly.*) Merlin's maid—from the Marches of Lorraine?
Marie. Even so.
Charles. Let her come! She'll make us mirth,
Perhaps; and we have need enough of it here!
Marie. Nay, she will make us something beyond mirth,
Methinks. Oh, sir! this is a holy maid,
If ever holiness looked out of eyes
Or hallowed brow.
Charles. How now? St. Denis to aid!
She that so moves our gentle little Marie
Must have rare mettle in her. Thou shalt have
Thy boon—we'll see this marvellous maid of thine.
[*Exeunt* CHARLES *and* MARIE.

SCENE III.

The Great Hall of Chinon, with dais and chair of state. DUKE D'ALENÇON, DE VENDÔME, DE BOISSY, REGNAULD DE CHARTRES, DE LA TREMOUILLE, DE GONCOURT, LA HIRE, DE XAINTRILLES, *Churchmen, Courtiers, Pages, and Attendants.*

De Bélier (*announcing*). Their Majesties!
Enter Ushers and Pages preceding the KING *and* QUEEN, *the* QUEEN *followed by her Ladies.*

De la Trem. Will't please you I bid sound the horn
 for supper?
Charles. Forbear awhile. Where is our Treasurer?
(BÉLIER *advances and bows*).
'Tis the Queen's will we give speech to the maid
Whose coming three days since you told us of.
R. de Chartres. Were it not well my liege were first advised
She comes not in the strength of spells or witchcraft?
I have here clerks and doctors of the Church
To put her to the proof.
Marie. But see her, sir—
Methinks you will not doubt, whate'er she is,
That she's no witch.
Charles. Be it as the Queen wills.
And then, Archbishop, for thy clerks and doctors——
De la Trem. Some jugglcress, my liege, feed by Dunois,
To back these Captains' mission.—

La Hire. That she's not—
I crossed her first, in her red peasant's kirtle,
At Domremy, a fortnight gone, nor since
Saw her, or spoke with her, until to-day.
  Marie. She brings a sign, she says—a voice that guides her
Straight to the King!
  De la Trem. My jewel to a doit
Her sign's your royal robe and cap of state.
  Charles. I'll change them with Vendôme; if she hunt false,
(*To* DE CHARTRES) Then let your clerks and doctors have their will of her.
Come, Count (*to* BÉLIER) and Treasurer—no word of the change.
  [*The* KING *and* VENDÔME *retire, followed by two Pages. Exit* BÉLIER *on the other side.*
  Marie (*to* DE LA TREMOUILLE). Methinks, my lord, it is scarce fair of you
To set a trap.
  La Hire (*aside*). I have known hunters caught
In traps of their own setting!
  Re-enter CHARLES *and* VENDÔME, *the latter wearing the* KING'S *robe and cap of state*; *the* KING *with* VENDÔME'S *short mantle and cap.*
  Charles (*pointing to* VENDÔME, *who sits on the chair of state on the dais*). Sirs—the King!
May he find robe and circlet easier wearing
Than I have!
  Re-enter BÉLIER, *showing in* JEANNE *and* ISAMBARD.
  De la Trem. (*pointing to* VENDÔME.) The King! Thy knee!
  [JEANNE *looks at* VENDÔME—*then turns, and goes straight to the* KING, *who has mingled with the group of Courtiers, and kneels to him.*
  Jeanne. Save you, my gentle Dauphin!
  Charles (*pointing to the chair of state and* VENDÔME).
Not so—thy knee to the King.
  Jeanne. And so—to *you*,
Fair Dauphin—whom I may not yet call King—
Because you have not yet been crowned at Rheims
With the holy oil.
  Charles. I tell thee—there's the King.

Jeanne. I know not who sits there—or why he sits—
So bravely robed and crowned—I only know
    You are my Dauphin.
    Charles.   And how know'st thou that?
    Jeanne. My voices tell me.
    Charles. Do they tell thee naught
But this?
    Jeanne. They tell me you would have a sign.
Pray you, fair lords, to stand apart awhile.
    De la Trem. (*aside to* DE CHARTRES.) Is this the sheep-
    wench?
    Charles.   There's a power about her
Past our gainsaying. Do her bidding, sirs.
    (*The Courtiers fall back out of earshot, leaving* JEANNE
    and the KING *alone.*)
Now for your sign!
    Jeanne (*looking at him earnestly*). Doubt not, my gentle
    Dauphin,
That you are King (*very earnestly*) by right of the blood royal,
As you have doubted. And next time you pray,
Pray not to 'scape your foes, but conquer them.
    Charles. Who told thee of my doubt and prayer?
    Jeanne.   My voices—
That tell, too, how St. Louis and Charles the Great,
About the white throne even now are urgent
To have thee crown'd—the English swept from France.
    [*The* KING *beckons to the* QUEEN *and Courtiers.*
    De la Trem. (*aside to* DE CHARTRES.) The King is moved!
    Charles (*to* MARIE OF ANJOU). I'm glad I spoke with her.
(*Aside.*) Strange! she should so have read my secret heart!
My lords, I hold it well we hear her further,
And in *your* hearing.
    Jeanne (*to* ISAMBARD). Father, must I speak?
How shall I, that know neither A nor B,
Speak before all these lords and learned clerks?
    Isamb. Be of good cheer! He that hath guided thee
So far will guide thee now. Speak fearlessly.
    Jeanne. I am a poor maid, from the Lorraine March,
Come, at my voices' urging, to the Dauphin,
To bid him arm in aid of Orleans,
And beat the English thence—and Orleans cleared,
And all the King's towns on the Loire won back,
To come with me to Rheims, there to be crowned,

And after drive the English out of France
By hard blows, if they will not go for the asking.
  De la Trem. A modest mission!
  R. de Chartres.   Think'st thou to win faith
Without a sign?
  Jeanne.   I am not come to Chinon
To show you signs. But send me armed to Orleans,
And I will show you *there* a sign. But give me
Soldiers, or few or many, and I promise
To raise the siege.
  R. de Chartres.   If it were God's good will
To help France, he could do it without soldiers.
  Jeanne. The men-at-arms must fight that God may give
The victory.
  La Hire. Well answered! Mort de Diou!
I will ride with thee, Jeanne, if I ride single.
  Jeanne. Would I had fifty captains of thy mind
And mettle. But I *shall* have, when they know
All that my voices tell me—oh, so clear!—
How, when my Dauphin's crowned—but not till then—
He shall win back his own good town of Paris;
How the fair Duke of Orleans shall come home
From English bonds: and in this land of France,
Seven years hence, shall be no invader left
But those that hold six feet of her for graves.
All this I shall but help—not see fulfilled—
But that 'twill be fulfilled I know—I know!
  R. de Chartres. My liege. 'tis dangerous to let her speak
Till I have made close question of her faith.
I have clerks here to ask and write her answers.
  Jeanne. Nay, I will give them work for their clerk's cunning
Without your question. Take your pens and write:
(*She dictates.*) 'You, King of England, and you, Duke of
     Bedford—
Regent, so-called, of France—you, English captains,
Do right to the King of Kings and to the Maid,
Sent by his bidding—render up the keys
Of the French towns held by you wrongfully.
The Maid, if you do this. will grant you peace.
Knights, archers, and companions of war,
Gentle and valiant, that hold Orleans' leaguer,
Begone to your own land, or look for news
Of the Maid, who will come soon, to your dismay,

To fall on you with such a hunting cry
As was not heard in France this thousand years;
And prove on you which has the better right,
The King of Kings, or you, the King of England.
Written at Chinon, on the part of the Maid.'

La Hire (*to the* KING). Take her for secretary, good my
  liege.
She hath but framed the letter you've forgotten
To write this six months past. Sign, seal, and send it.
I'll be the bearer, if need be.

De Goncourt.   Enough,
My liege, of these ape's tricks.

La Hire.   Ape's tricks! Sang Diou!
She has spoke more manhood since she came to Chinon
Than these old walls have heard while Court's been kept here.
So say I—and will vouch it on my body
Against all comers, at all arms—lance, sword, axe,
Or dagger—the more the merrier!

Jeanne.   Nay, fair Captain,
I must be mine own champion against him
Or any man.

De Goncourt. How, wench? With crook and distaff?

Jeanne. Not so—with sword and lance, under my standard.
(*To* BÉLIER.) I sent your page to-day some four leagues hence
To Fierbois, to the Church of my Saint Katherine,
For a sword with five crosses on the blade,
That I must use. 'Twas shown me where 'twas buried—
Behind the altar. See if he have brought it.
       [*Exeunt* BÉLIER *and* LA HIRE.
(*To* ISAMBARD.) And, Father, there's the standard I had
  painted.
'Twas left in the outer chamber. Bring it me. [*Exit* ISAMB.
Sweet Queen, and gentle Dauphin, wonder not.
'Tis not of my own will I do these things
Or speak these words, but as my voices bid me.

  Re-enter BÉLIER *and* LA HIRE *with the sword.*

La Hire. The sword, with the five crosses on the blade!
Found, as she said, behind Saint Katherine's altar,
At Fierbois.

  Enter ISAMBARD *with the standard, while* JEANNE *takes
    sword and kisses blade.*

Isamb.   And the standard, as in vision

She saw it—white, as fits her purity.
With lily-flowers for France, and maidenhood;
And Heaven's King, with the world beneath his feet,
And angels with joined hands that pray for France.
    Jeanne (taking her standard).
At that King's bidding—with those angels' aid—
Who follows me to rescue Orleans
And ransom France?
    La Hire.   Sang Diou! I do for one!
      (*The crowd draw their swords and press forward with
        a general shout*).   And I!
    La Hire.   Under the leading of the Maid!
    Jeanne. Under *His* leading that leads her to Orleans!

          Act Drop.

ACT III.

The Maid Martial.

Scene I.

Room in the house of Jacques Boucher, *the Treasurer of the city, where* Jeanne *is lodged. Window, practicable, on one side. Door, practicable, on the other.*

    Enter Isambard, *meeting* Pierre Darc.

    Isamb. Now, welcome back from Domremy! How
        found you
All there?
    Pierre.   Well, Father. Sure the news I brought
Of Joan at Chinon was enough to make
Sick folks or sorry hale and happy again.
How mother wept, and father swore and prayed,
And cursed and crossed himself! How all the village
Talked till it buzzed again! While all remembered
Wonderful things that pointed Joan to this!
    Isamb. So runs the world—in hamlet or in city,
Cabin or palace. While the climber climbs,
Out on him! scoff! sneer! pluck him by the legs!
But when he *has* climbed—off hats! 'We told you so!
We said he'd win the height—and helped him to it!'
    Pierre.   What news of Joan
Since they gave her commission
To gather head at Blois?

Isamb. I ask myself
Sometimes if what I've seen these two months past
Be dream or waking truth. Where'er she moves
Spirits of strength and sweetness move with her,
Like angels, visible in their effects!
From all the Bourbonnais, Languedoc, Auvergne,
Flowed to her at Blois knights, men-at-arms, and archers,
Till, with a force some eight thousand strong
Of the best lances in all France, she rode
Like an avenging angel, armed in white,
Her standard borne before; while in the van
We priests, Faith's soldiers, marched with holy chaunts.
Rough soldiers left their oaths, and dice, and lewdness.
And she, you would have said, to look at her,
From her youth up she had borne arms herself
And captained those that bore them. So she led us
Safe hither, men and convoy, past the beards
Of the 'mazed English—shrank in their bastilles,
As if mere sight of her had palsied hearts.
But to tell you of her entering Orleans,
The town, that poured its life out on her path,
Its blessings on her head, as thrice ten thousand
Had lived, held, uttered one same life, heart, voice,
Is more than I have time or tongue for now.
    Pierre. And when was this?
    Isamb.   Eight days ago.
    Pierre.   And since,
How goes it?
    Isamb. Bravely—scarce a day but brings
Its sunshine of success; and she the sun!
You'd say that strength passed visibly from besiegers
Unto besieged!

              Enter DAME BOUCHER.

            Our worthy hostess here—Dame Boucher.
Good dame—tis Pierre Darc, brother of the Maid.
    Dame Boucher. Has she a brother? Methought a thing like her
Should be alone in the world. Her mother had
Know in *her.*
    Pierre. Nay, there are five of us.
    D. Boucher. Fair youth, you are blessed in a sister!
When my husband tells me of her feats of war

I marvel—seeing her still so good and gentle;
As humble and as helpful in the house
As I'd have my own daughter.
  Pierre.   That's our Joan
All over—such she was at home. Where is she?
  D. Boucher. At mass—at St. Pierre o' the Bridge, with
   my Karlotte. (*To* ISAMBARD.)
How the child loves her! will walk, pray, sleep with her.
Hark! where they come!
  Jeanne (*without*).   Now, Karlotte, doff thy hood;
And then for the story of the four sons of Aymon.

 Enter JEANNE, *leading* KARLOTTE, *a child of eight or nine.*

  Karlotte. But I must have a kiss before I go.
  Jeanne (*kisses her*). There, little one!
           [KARLOTTE *runs off.*
Now, dame—— (*Sees* PIERRE.) Ah, my own Pierre!
Returned at last! And at home?
  Pierre.   All is well.
  Jeanne. We'll have Domremy news anon. Dear Father,
You'll be as glad as I to talk it over.
But first, good dame—have you no work for me?—
No spinning, sewing? Ha! those bandages,
For the poor wounded souls in the hospital
By the New Market, that were hurt yesterday,
When we took Paris.
  Pierre.   Paris!
  Jeanne (*laughing*).   How he stares!
One of the ten bastilles our English friends
Have built to keep us safe. There's London, Rouen,
Paris—no, there *was* Paris—and soon shall be
No more of London, Rouen, and the rest
Than Paris now. Look where its palisadoes
Smoke still! (*Points* PIERRE *out of the window.*)
(*To* DAME BOUCHER.) Go, get the linen for bandages—
I've shown you I can use needle and scissors
Deftly as lance and sword—(*exit* DAME BOUCHER)—and like
   them better,
For all my steel coat—I can't put *that* off
Until my work is done. But let it prosper
As it has these six days! Even now, brother,
I await summons to the Captains' council,
For the attack that I've planned for to-day,
The lustiest and the last—my voices tell me!

Enter LA HIRE.

Look, here's my Pierre come back!
   La Hire (about to swear).   Mort——
                  (JEANNE *gives him a look.*)
                                By my baton—
—I'm glad to see him! Cry you mercy, Joan—
'Twill slip out, now and then.
   Jeanne.   What?
   La Hire.   A round oath.
But when I catch one 'twixt my teeth, I nip it
Half off—an oath's no oath unless it's round.
Nay, I have promised Jeanne to give up swearing;
And none can call La Hire a promise-breaker—
Though once I little thought to have made such promise,
And still less to have kept it after making.
But I'm bewitched.
   Jeanne.   Nay, but I let thee swear,
So 'tis an innocent oath.
   La Hire.   Ah! there's no savour
In innocent oaths. But think not I complain;
Though there's great comfort in a mouth-filling oath
When a man's chafed or in a perilous pass.
Maybe it brings the Devil to help his own.
I was *his* once—in the days I used to swear.
How I *did* swear!—Mort—that is—by my baton!
Before I knew thee!
   Jeanne.   Now, a truce to the past—
What of the present? When do the Captains meet
In council?
   La Hire. They *have* met.
   Jeanne.   And I not there?
   La Hire. Thou know'st thy council is enough for me.
But all are not as full of faith as I.
(*To* ISAMBARD, *who laughs.*) What are you laughing at?
                             I *have* a faith
In *Her*—and all that she believes and bids.
But 'tis no wonder, grey heads like De Goncourt's,
Or godless rogues like Cernoy and Valperga,
Or raw-boned, positive Scots, like old Hugh Kennedy,
Should fret to follow a woman—though she be
Such a one as the Maid. They've held their council
Apart from thee.

Jeanne. Then, I say, twas ill held!
What have they planned?
    La Hire. To try a feigned attack
Upon the bastille west the town—and then,
While English hands are full, loose our main battle
Upon the bridge. How dost thou like the plan?
    Jeanne. They have been in their council—I in mine;
And I believe my council will prevail—
Theirs come to naught! (*To* ISAM.) Be ready to say mass
Before the host—and still keep close to me
Throughout the day—I know I shall be wounded
And have blood on my breast. (*Loud shout and noise.*)
                      What noise is that?
    La Hire. The sound of battle. (LA HIRE *goes to the window.*) West the city too!
They've made their sally by the Rénart gate
Against the rampart of the wooden cross
'Twixt London and St Laurent. Ha! the English
Swarm out like wasps, and beat them from the ditch!
Now, by St. Denis, 'tis hot work!
    Jeanne. And I
Not there! and no squire nigh—or page—or horse!
All will go ill! Jean D'Aulon, ho! my helmet—
My sword, and standard! Where's that Imerguet?
Ever at play!
    La Hire. Here he comes up the street,
Leading thy horse!

    Enter KARLOTTE. *She seizes* JEANNE'S *skirt.*

Karlotte. Going without my story!
Jeanne (*kissing her*). I'll tell it thee anon. (*Kneeling to* ISAMBARD.) Thy blessing, Father!
Isamb. The God of battles hold his arm about thee!
Jeanne. My horse—my horse! Come, Pierre—La Hire!
My horse!

    [*Exit* JEANNE *impetuously, followed by the others.*

SCENE II.

The Gate of Burgundy (practicable). A wide gate, with flanking towers and vaulted doorways and passages. Portcullis down, inside the heavy clamped oaken doors, which are closed. The chains of the drawbridge visible inside the tower. In the flanking towers small portals. A crowd of armed men pressing towards the gate, with women and children anxiously watching and waiting, as if for news of their relatives engaged in the action without. The tocsin is tolling. The Guards of the gate are forcing the people back and remonstrating.

1st Guard. Back !
2nd Guard. No way by this gate.
1st Guard. To the Porte Rénart.
1st Citizen. There's fighting at St. Loup.
Two Others. And St. Jean-le-Blanc !
1st Woman (with a basket). It's a shame ! There's my Morin on bridge-guard
Since last night, and no victuals !
2nd Woman. And my man,
Hurt at the Belle-croix barriers !
1st Guard. Back, I say !
It is the Bailiff's orders.

Enter from the vaulted way, L., DE GONCOURT, *all armed but his head.*

De Goncourt. What's this coil ?
Am I King's Bailiff here, or am I not ?
Are we besieged inside, as well as out ?
Yon bell sounds for the muster at Porte Rénart,
Not here—the attack's o' the west side.
1st Citizen. The Maid bade us
Follow her from *this* gate.
De Goncourt. The Maid, quotha!
'Tis no maid, but a *man*, and the King's Bailiff
Bids you begone to the Porte Rénart, and help
The attack, as settled in council of the Captains,
Upon St. Laurent.
(*Cries heard without.*) The Maid ! the Maid !
De Goncourt (aside). Poor fools !
She turns your heads, if *I* can't !

(*A wounded man is borne in by two others at the side portal through vault in tower,* R.)

Now—who's this ?
Jean le Tonneur ! What, hurt ? How goes the day ?
Wounded Man (speaking with difficulty). Badly for us.
They've won the palisadoes

O' the bridge and ta'en our culverin, and killed
The cannoneer—and given me my quietus.
  De Goncourt. Call a leech. See to his wound.
    (*Cries without, louder*). The Maid! the Maid!

Enter JEANNE, *armed, the people crowding round her, and
    kissing her robe, hands, &c.*

  Jeanne. Now, where's my page and horse? Pray you, good people,
Stay me not. Form quick, all you that have arms.
    [*She comes on the wounded man, and shrinks back.*
  De Gon. Dost shudder, Jeanne? So women will—at blood.
If thou'dst keep up their faith, best hide thy fear.
  Jeanne. Fear! Nay. 'Tis true I ne'er see French blood flow
That my hair rises not. But 'tis not fear—
'Tis wrath and pity!
  Wounded Man. Let her touch my wound,
And I'll not feel it.
  Jeanne.   Be of good heart, good friend.
Now time goes. Frenchmen bleed, and yet they come not!
  De Gon. Who?
  Jeanne. La Hire, with his lances, and Don Cernay;
And Kennedy, with his Scots. They have command
To meet me here while my brother and D'Aulon gather
The crossbows of the Butchers' Guild, and bring
Maitre Jean, with his culverin.
  De Gon.   For what?
  Jeanne. To storm the Tourelles front and rear at once,
From the quay and the bridge.
  De Gon.   Nay. But thou knowest
The Captains have devised another plan
Of battle for to-day.
  Jeanne.   Let them devise;
I have to do—and *that* is this day's deed!
  De Gon. They hold 'twere best you stayed at home to-day
To rest, after the headache of yesterday,
From that big stone off St. Pouair rampart.
  Jeanne. When I want rest, I'll tell them.
  De Gon.   This day's work
Needs men to guide it.
  Jeanne.   Needs *me* to guide men!

Keep breath for battle, man, and fret me not.
Look, where my horse comes, and the men-at-arms,
Crossbows, and cannoneers. Ho, there! my horse!
> [*Her horse is brought on.*

De Gon. What! shall she ride down captains and King's
bailiffs
Like cabbage-stalks! (*Shouts without.*) Again!
(*Shouts without*) (JEANNE *mounts*). France! and the Maid!
De Gon. Look to the gate, men. Let no soul pass forth.
What! she shall learn the King and the King's Bailiff
Have still some say in Orleans! Keep the gate!

Enter JEANNE *on her horse, surrounded by a crowd of Citizens, Soldiers, and Women, the first files of the armed men showing behind her, with* LA HIRE, BERTRAND DE POULANGY, JEAN DE METZ, JEAN D'AULON, *and* PIERRE *and* ISAMBARD *near him.*

Jeanne. Give me my standard, you within the house!
> [*They hand her the standard from the upper window.*

Now, up portcullis! Down with bar and bridge!
De Gon. I hold this gate, as the King's officer,
And, by his captains' orders, I say none
Goes forth.
Jeanne. As captain of a greater King
Than thine, old man, I say I *will* go forth—
And these that follow. (*To Guards.*) Heed him not—heed
me!
La Hire. Clear the way there for France and for the
Maid!
[*They raise the portcullis, fling open the great gates, lower the drawbridge, and* JEANNE *dashes out, followed by the Soldiers, with loud cries, while the Women, Citizens, &c., form groups.*

SCENE III.

Scene changes to Fortress of the Tourelles. In flat, seen in perspective, a view of the bridge and town of Orleans across the river. Before them (practicable) the Tourelles, two large towers, with an archway, gate, and drawbridge between them, below which the river is supposed to run. Across the stage a palisade, with its gate, L. C., *about which, as the scene opens, the fight is fiercest. Cannon on clumsy wheeled carriages are run on from the wings and fired. Others reply to them from the palisadoes and gate. Cross-*

bow-men wheel on their large pavesses, or wooden screens, loopholed, and shoot from behind them; SIR WILLIAM GLASDALE, *in full armour, keeping the gate and smiting down the French, of whom several lie wounded about. The English man the palisadoes, the wall between the towers themselves, and rampart.*

    Glasdale. St. George for England! Down with the French frogs!

The English, pouring through the archway and from the gate of the palisadoes, drive back the French, against whom the English commander, GLASDALE, *keeps the gate. The French rally and raise ladders against the palisadoes, up which they climb, while the English defenders thrust and strike them down. Several ladders, with the men on them, are hurled into the ditch. Single figures are seen to fall into the ditch as if they had reached the top, been killed, and flung back.*

    Enter LA HIRE *as the French recoil.*

    La Hire. Give back to the bulldogs! Ah—France and La Hire!   [*He rallies them.*

    Glasdale. St. George for England! A Glasdale!

    La Hire. That's my man!

    [*Fight between* GLASDALE *and* LA HIRE. LA HIRE *is struck down.* PIERRE *rescues him.*

    La Hire (*wiping his brows*). The bulldogs have the luck! The day's against us!

    Pierre. When was fight lost with time to win it back? The Maid has ta'en the seaward barbican! And shall we fail her here? On! For the King!

    La Hire (*seizing the standard*). France! and the Maid!

        [*They renew their attack on the palisadoes.*

    Glasdale. St. George for England! Hurrah!

    Pierre. I'll change that cry for you. France, and the Maid!

A fierce assault of the French. The English are borne back. The gate is burst open, and the French pour through it and over the palisadoes, which are set on fire, crossbow-men and cannoneers continuing to shoot all the time. LA HIRE *is seen fighting on the drawbridge. The fire spreads to the hoarding over the gate and round the top of the towers. Amid the smoke and confusion of the fight* JEANNE *is seen to ride through the gateway, waving her standard. Loud shouts from the French.*

Jeanne. Glasdale is slain. The Tourelles are our own.
You have fought well, friends.
  All. France! France! and the Maid!
  Isamb. Victory! victory! Nor only here.
Dunois has ta'en their bastilles to west o' the town.
All round they raise their leaguer.
  La Hire.   Thy own Duke,
D'Alençon, and Vendôme, with a brave company,
Have crossed the bridge to greet thee.

  Enter D'ALENÇON, VENDÔME, *Ladies, and Nobles.*

  Jeanne.   They are welcome!
What said I, lords? I *have* raised Orleans' leaguer.
Now to sweep clear the Orleanists; and then
To crown my Dauphin King of France! To Rheims!

ACT IV.

SCENE I.

Rheims, Sunday, July 17, 1429.—*The Maid Manifest.
Room in the Inn of L'Ane Rayé, at Rheims, where* JEANNE
is lodged.

Enter PIERRE DARC, *showing in* JACQUES DARC *and* ISA-
BELLE, JEANNE'S *father and mother, who enter tremblingly.*

  Pierre. Nay, fear not, mother; she's thine own child still,
For all her great deeds and her state.
  (JACQUES *crosses himself.*)   What, father?
Crossing thyself?
  Jacques Darc. Nay, boy—a cross ne'er harms;
Who knows but crosses may be wanted here?
  Isabelle. What, where Joan lodges?
  Jacques.   Aye, wife, where Joan lodges.
They say in our parts there is that about her
That likes not crossing.
  Pierre.   That needs none, you mean.
  Isabelle. Heaven's grace is more than crosses.
  Jacques.   *Heaven's* grace, quotha!
(*Timidly.*) Nay, good be about us!—What o' the other place?
  (PIERRE *looks amazed.*)
Folks say, at Domremy our Joan began
Her fortune at the fairy tree—and since,
Hath helped it with worse aid.

Pierre. Whose?
Jacques.   The foul fiend's,
If thou *will* have it. There's thy mother, too,
Hath heard the town's talk, and been grieved by it,
As I have.
　　Isabelle. Aye, but not for the same cause—
Grieved thou couldst do such wrong to thine own child
As list these false, foul scandals. Tell her mother,
That nursed and knew her, from her cradle up,
The prayerfullest and dutifullest thing
That ever brought a blessing on a house,
My Joan owes aught she is or does to witchcraft,
Or any help but Heaven's! Were't other tongue
But my good man's and master's that dared say so,
I'd call down stroke of plague and palsy on it
For a black liar.
　　Jacques.   Nay, I but repeat
What burned my ears to hear, my tongue to shape.
　　Isabelle. The more thy shame to give such wicked lies
Or ear or tongue. Were I a man I'd thrust
The words down *his* vile throat that dared to speak them.
　　Pierre. Trust *my* hand to do that. Our Joan a witch!
Oh, father, ask the tens of thousands here,
That follow her with wonder and with worship—
Here comes one who could tell——

　　　　　　　Enter La Hire.

　　La Hire.   Now, my good Pierre!
Where's Jeanne? Who's here?
　　Pierre.   My father and mother, Captain,
From Domremy.
　　La Hire. Now welcome both—right welcome!
You come in happy time—to see the crown
Put on your child's head.
　　Jacques.   On the King's, you mean.
　　La Hire. If those that give crowns be above those that get them,
Your daughter should stand higher than King Charles.
His is the golden round, the holy oil,
The consecrated staff, and jewelled orb;
But hers the aureole that crowns the brow
Of saints and virgins—hers the oil of gladness,
Distilled from a regenerate people's love—
Hers the gold rod of heavenly rule, that tames

Hard hearts and hands—aye, hands and hearts like mine—
La Hire's—that speak to you as La Hire never
Had thought to speak or feel.
  Pierre.   And Joan's a witch!
Aye, Captain, they have told my father so,
Until he half believes.
  Isabelle.   The more shame for him!
  La Hire. Joan—witch! Leave that lie to Burgundian dogs.
Heaven fights upon her side—if ever heaven
Took part with earth. Look you, what she has done:
In ten days Orleans' leaguer raised—the English
Beat out of their bastilles—in eight days more
A clear sweep of them through the Orleannais—
Their towns ta'en, themselves beat, their noblest captains
Prisoners held, at ransom. Last, not least.
The King here for his crowning! Here's rare witchcraft!
And, rarer still, she has beat the devil in me;
Nay, the seven devils—dicing, drabbing, drinking,
Swearing and stabbing, swaggering and stealing.
Seven devils? Why, I've counted seven already,
And but begun my tale of sins. Look there!
     [*He points down to street. Cries without.*

  Pierre. See, father, how they flock upon her passage
And clutch her dress—how mothers clasp her hand
To touch their children's heads—how aged folk
Put life and limb in peril to come near her.
  La Hire. Marvellous like a witch, is she not, Gaffer?
  Isabelle (*looking out*). Now, bless her gracious face, 'tis the old smile—
The old sweet, humble look and loving eyes!
  Jacques. How shall we meet, how greet her? Prithee, Pierre,
Tell her first we are here. Come, wife, we'll wait
Apart, till she have signified her pleasure.
  Isabelle. Our Joan a witch! Oh, Jacques, for shame! for shame!
  La Hire (*clapping* JACQUES *on the shoulder*). Thou art well lodged at the Ass—the Striped Ass, too—
For thou deserv'st the stripes. (To ISAB.) Lay on him well!
  [*Exeunt* JACQUES *and* ISAB. (*Shouts without, getting nearer.*)

  Enter JEANNE, *attended by crowds of all ages, classes and sexes, kissing her dress and hands, holding up their children for her to touch, &c., &c.*

1st Woman. But bless my child!
Old Man (holding up rosary). An ave for my beads!
2nd Woman (with sick girl). Lay hands on my Toinette!
Jeanne (good-humouredly). Pray you, good friends,
Give me but breathing space.
    La Hire. Back, knaves! back, gossips!
    Isamb. What, have we Babel here?
    Jeanne. Nay, chide them not.
        [LA HIRE, ISAMBARD, *and* PIERRE *force out the crowd with difficulty.*
    Isamb. Is it well, Joan, to feed their folly thus?
    Jeanne. Poor folks! they know no better—'tis their love—
They hurt me not, if I do them no good.
I can't find in my heart to say them nay.
    Isamb. Thine enemies will make a hold of this.
Nay, who knows but it may breed pride in thee?
    Pierre. Pride in our Joan! Nay, you should know her better.
    Jeanne. Alas! I know I cannot bless or heal—
'Tis I need blessing, healing. Here's the scar
The arrow left at Orleans, and the bruise
Made by the great stone, through my helm, at Jergeau.
(*To* ISAMB.) 'Tis *thou* wert healer then—and blesser always.
    Isamb. (laying his hand tenderly on her head). Heaven bless thee still, I say, and keep thee safe.
What wonder if these rude folks pay thee reverence?
I, priest, and grey beard as I am——
    La Hire. And I,
Sinner and soldier, make no bones of kneeling—
And with more faith than e'er I knelt in church.
    Jeanne. Nay. (*Tries to prevent his kneeling to her.*)
    La Hire. By—(*she gives him a look; he ends his adjuration ruefully*)—my baton! 'tis the truth.
    Jeanne. Dear friends!
There is much fear lest I be spoiled by pride;
But 'tis *you* spoil me. Ah, well let it be—
'Tis not for long now. I have done my work.
I'll back to Domremy.
    La Hire. No, by—(*checking himself*)—my baton!
Not while a foreign bulldog kennels in France——
    Jeanne. Ah, me! I would I were at home again
With staff and spindle, by the quiet Meûse,
Under the elders, with the silly sheep,

Or hot i' the harvest-field—or hearing vespers
In the cool chapel.   Father (*to* ISAMBARD), let's go back
Together, as we came.
 Pierre (*aside*). Now is the time,
Joan; there are home-friends here.
 Jeanne.   From Domremy?
Oh! let me see them—I am sick for news
Of mother, father, Jean, Toinette, and all.
   [PIERRE *goes up and beckons in* JACQUES DARC
    and ISABELLE.
 Isabelle. ⎫
 Jacques. ⎬ Joan!
 Jeanne (*rushing into their arms*).   Mother! father! Oh,
  this joy—at last!
(*To* ISAMBARD.) How brave they look! (*To them.*) 'Tis Father
  Isambard.
He has been with with me still.   Oh, mother, mother!
How I have hungered for the sight of thee
And father!   And how is't with all at home?
Have the kine thriven since I left?   How look
The fields for harvest?   And Joan—and Toinette?
She sees to the orchard and my bees for me?
And Haumette—Mangette—still as mad as ever?
And—(*interrupting herself*)—oh! but I've so much to ask
  and hear!
I ne'er shall get all asked or you all answered.
 Isabelle. My own child! good as if thou wert not great,
That I should have thee in my arms, and feel
Thy heart against mine, as I used to feel it
Ere thou cam'st to this honour!
 Jacques.   Lord, forgive me,
That spoke of witchcraft!   That was ere I saw
Thine innocent face again.
 Jeanne.   My own dear father!
 La Hire (*aside*). I had a father and mother once—
I never saw them since I left the nest,
Scarce fledged—and now—ah, well——
   [*He turns aside to brush away an involuntary tear.*
 Enter Pages, who speak apart with PIERRE.
 Pierre (*hurriedly*). Joan, 'tis the Queen!
 Isabelle. Saints, give us grace!
 Jacques (*in great alarm*). And save her Majesty!
What should we do?   Wife!   Pierre!

Isamb. Fear not; she's kind.

    Enter MARIE OF ANJOU, *with her Ladies.*

Marie (*to* JEANNE). Save you, fair maid! (*To* ISAMBARD.) Your blessing! (*Gives her hand to* LA HIRE.) My stout Captain! (*To* JEANNE, *recognising* PIERRE.) Your brother, as I think. And who are these? (*Seeing the old folks.*)

Jeanne. My father and mother, please your Majesty—
Come from our village.
  Marie.   They have done well to come—
To see their child's work crowned by a King's crowning.
To know in thee, daughter of their love,
An angel sent to save both realm and King
In their dark hour—and make herself and you
Famous unto all time by her achievements.
Know the King, from whom I come to do thee honour,
Hath made thee noble and thy blood for ever—
Gives thee for blazon, on an azure field,
Three lilies, flowers of France, by thee restored
To rear their fair heads in the face of day.
Ask any boon my lord can grant to thee,
Or any that thou lovest.
  Jeanne.   Only this—
That he will free my Domremy for ever
From tax and toll and service—folks and land.
  La Hire. Well asked!
  Marie.   And gladly granted—so I leave you
Happy, as all are happy here to-day—
And I most happy. (*They are about to kneel.*)
         Nay—no knees to me.
Think of me as a friend who visits friends,
On some occasion fraught with joy to both.
So farewell—till we meet again at Notre-Dâme.
       [*Exeunt* MARIE *and Ladies.*
  Isamb. Solomon said, a good wife is a crown
To her husband; so the king is crowned already.
  Jacques. And I've looked on a Queen!
  La Hire.   So may a cat!
  Jacques. But what though? We are noble now!—I, thou (*to* ISABELLE),
Joan and Toinette, and Jean and Pierre—all noble!
  Pierre. I had rather have won knighthood, under sword,
On foughten field.

La Hire. And so thou shalt, Pierre, yet !
Under *my* sword—I promise thee a thwack
To make thy shoulders ache—remind me of it.
But time flies ; we must don our bravery
For Notre-Dâme.
    Jacques.   Shall we find find places, think you,
Among the nobles?
    La Hire.   Aye, faith—the new nobles.
Stick to my skirts ; I'll find your place anon,
When once I've seen to new apparel for you.
Nobles of the last mint are always brightest.
    Jeanne. Let them be as they are—I like that better.
Isabelle (*to* JEANNE). And where wilt thou be?
    Jeanne.   By the high altar, mother,
In white and gold—my standard in my hand.
    Isabelle. And wilt thou bear thy standard in the church,
There where the King is crowned?
    Jeanne.   Will I not, mother?
It shared the travail—it should grace the triumph !
    L'Oiselleur. Hist, Captain !
    La Hire.   What ! my bird-catcher ! Soho !
    L'Oiselleur. You had my message——
    La Hire. That had I, Master Nicholas.
But take me with you—Burgundy, you say——
    L'Oiselleur. And Bedford.
    La Hire.   True—will give my lances double
The King's pay ; and, moreover, leave and licence
To strip as foes those we now shield as friends.
    L'Oiselleur. I bear the Regent's warrant under seal
To offer these fair terms. He knows the worth
Of Gascon lances, with La Hire to lead them—
Above all, on the winning side !
    La Hire.   That's it—
Were one but clear which is the winning side.
    L'Oiselleur. Not this you fight on.
    La Hire.   'Twas the losing one,
That's certain, till last May ; but since the Maid
Has breathed a new life into the King's cause——
    L'Oiselleur. The Maid ! a witch, who sets her sheep-
        girl's face
Above tried captain——
    La Hire.   True—she leads us all.
    L'Oiselleur. To land you, in the end, in some foul ditch.
If Heaven help not the King, how should Hell help him?

La Hire. 'It needs a long spoon to sup kail with Satan.'
That's a Scotch saw of old Hugh Kennedy's.
So you, too, think her witch?
  L'Oiselleur.   Spawn of the pit!
'Twere as good deed as pray to clip her claws,
And hand her to the Church to exorcise
Her seven devils.
  La Hire. It were kindness to her——
  L'Oiselleur. And to the King, who, trusting in her aid,
Seems rising now to fall more heavily.
  La Hire. You set me thinking, Master Nicholas.
  L'Oiselleur. Make thoughts deeds, Captain, and I'll pay
    them nobly.
Leave the King, with your lances—bring her prisoner—
And I've five thousand crowns here for the asking.
           (*Touches purse.*)
She trusts you, does she not?
  La Hire.   As her own brother.
  L'Oiselleur. How could you earn five thousand crowns so
    easy?
  La Hire (*seizing him by the throat and taking his purse*).
Thus!—and poor pay enough for ridding France
Of such a double-damned rogue as thou! (*Shakes him.*)
  L'Oiselleur. You jest. Grip not so hard.
  La Hire.   The noose grips harder,
Though thou shouldst swing the lighter by this purse.
Thought'st thou to tempt me, rascal?
  L'Oiselleur.   Nay, not I.
They that hired me said thou wert to be hired.
But if thou'lt not be bought, is that a reason
I should be hung?
  La Hire. I play false to the Maid?
To her that hath raised France out of the dust,
And taught me—aye, and thousands more like me—
What goodness is, and nobleness, and faith?
And thy foul tongue has dared to call her witch!
Why, thou deserv'st the gallows but for that,
Apart thy treason. So prepare. I'll give thee
Ten minutes to repent. Wilt have a priest
For thy confession?
  L'Oiselleur. I shall want a week
To make it.
  La Hire. Hold! What if thou purge thy treason

To the King by turning traitor to Burgundy
And Bedford? Give me full particulars
Of all their forces, convoys, garrisons,
Their strong and weak points—all that's like to serve
My master, and hurt thine, 'twixt Rheims and Paris—
I'll think if hanging's not too good for thee.
  L'Oiselleur. Anything for dear life.
  La Hire.   But tell me truth !
I'll keep thee prisoner till I test thy tale.
If a point's false—thou swing'st—faith of La Hire !
            [*Exit* LA HIRE, *guarding off* L'OISELLEUR.

SCENE II.

The interior of the Cathedral of Rheims, crowded with Ecclesiastics, Nobles, Soldiers, Populace; JACQUES DARC, ISABELLE *and* PIERRE, *&c., &c., assembled for the Coronation of* CHARLES VII. DUKE D'ALENÇON, COUNTS *of* CLERMONT *and* VENDÔME, *the* SIRES DE LAVAL, DE GONCOURT, DE LA TREMOUILLE. JEANNE, *in her place at the high altar, with* ISAMBARD *near her, in a surcoat of white, fringed with gold, and the lilies of France on the breast, and holding her standard in her hand, forms the central figure of the picture. As the scene opens the* KING *is kneeling before the altar, supposed to be in the act of taking the Coronation oath. The* QUEEN *kneels near.* ARCHBISHOP *of* RHEIMS, BISHOPS *of* CHALÔNS, ORLEANS, *and* SÉEZ, *Canons and Clergy. The attendant Bishops and Nobles then raise the* KING *in his chair, to show him to the people, amid shouts of* ' *Noel ! Noel !* ' *and the shrill peal of trumpets; while two Bishops hold the crown over his head, and then crown him. The trumpets peal again, and a louder acclaim of* ' *Noel !* ' *rises from the crowd. They then crown the* QUEEN. *The* MAID *then hands her standard to* ISAMBARD, *and comes down from the altar-steps and kneels before the* KING.

  Jeanne. Now, fair Sire, His high pleasure is fulfilled
Whose will it was I should conduct you hither,
For the anointing of the holy oil,
And coronation that approves you King,
To whom of right belongs the realm of France—
And so I kiss your feet—weeping for joy.
And now my task is done. I pray your leave

I

To go back to my village, with my father
And mother, who have come to take me home.

[*The crowd murmurs and shouts ' No! No!'*]

    De la Trem. "Twere well, your Majesty, to grant her prayer.
    De Goncourt. And good luck go with her! prays an old soldier.
    Archbishop. Methinks the Court as little fits this Maid
As she the Court. So we all back her prayer!
    Queen. I too, my liege, pray with these Lords, but not
For these Lords' reasons. Not for hate or fear,
Or envy that this Maid is good or great,
But for dear love of her, I ask your leave
That she may go hence.
    Charles VII.   Be it as she will.
We cannot pay the debt we owe to her,
But what we can will pay—with fiefs and honours,
Charter and blazon of nobility,
That what she has done may stand known to all time—
The great work of the Maid of Orleans!
Fare thee well, Jeanne, and still trust Charles's love.
    Queen. And mine.
    Jeanne (*kissing the* QUEEN's *hand*). So help me saints as I trust both!
Farewell, most gentle King and gracious Queen—
Whose love hath blessed not only me and mine
But all in Domremy, for all time to come.
(*To* D'ALENÇON.) My gentle Duke, commend me to your wife.
And you, my Lords and Captains, whom perchance
My rough speech or my untaught country ways
Have sometimes crossed, I pray you pardon me,
That recked but of the work entrusted to me,
And was not nice in the doing, so 'twas done.
If I may not look for much love among you—
As I have grieved to get less than I gave—
I pray you let me take hence no misliking,
As I leave none behind. Now, father, mother,
Let us ride homewards.
    Isamb.   I will go with thee.
Henceforth my place is where thou art, my child—
Thou may'st have need of prayer and comfort yet.

Pierre. And of a stout arm and a loving heart.
I'll go too.
　　Jacques. We ride braver than we came—
The citizens of Rheims have lined my purse (*shows purse*),
And given us horses, and paid all our charges
At the Striped Ass.
　　Isabelle.　　　　And all for thy sake, Jeanne—
So still thou bring'st us blessing.
　　Jeanne.　　　　　　My own mother,
Lose no time ; I long sore to be afoot.
　　Jacques. We'll load the beasts, pay our shot at the inn,
And join thee here. Come, wife—hold up thy head—
Let's bear ourselves like nobles—that *have* nobles !
　　　　　　[*Exeunt* JACQUES *and* ISABELLE DARC.

The people have gradually deserted the Cathedral while this has been going on, leaving only a few distant groups about the aisles and nooks of the building, who pass out by degrees. At last there remain only some children, including KARLOTTE, *who peeps timidly at* JEANNE *from behind the pillars.*

　　Jeanne. And is the time come that I must give back
To Heaven the arms Heaven sent me for the work
That is this day fulfilled ? Is the time come ?
I cannot hear my voices. Speak to me,
My sweet Saint Katherine and Saint Margaret !
They will not speak ! They have left me to myself.
Of myself I have no right to these arms
That I have loved so. Come, helm, sword, and standard.
I hang you up before our Lady's Altar;
I never more shall need you where I'm going,
In Domremy—but I shall often think
Upon you hanging here, and the brave work
I wrought with you. Farewell, dear sword (*kisses it*)—
　　　farewell,
My standard, dearer still ! with which I clave
The waves of war and saw the foes of France
And her King sink like ships in a great sea,
While still thou rodest high above the storm,
Banner at once and beacon—fare thee well ! (*She kisses her standard and hangs it up, with her helm and sword, on a pillar near the altar.*)

Can this be Joan, the Maid of Orleans,
To whom Heaven spoke—whom soldiers feared and fol-
    lowed—
This weak and weary thing that longs to creep
Into some loving breast—to lean her head
And sleep a still, sweet sleep, and wake no more
In this sore-troubled and hard-judging world?

Enter LA HIRE.

La Hire. What's this, Joan—all amort!—unhelmed—un-
    sworded!
To-day of all days! In Rheims of all places!
Where are thy helm, and sword, and standard?
    Jeanne.   There.
My work is done—I have offered up its tools
To our Lady, ere I ride to Domremy!—
They wait for me—farewell!
    La Hire.   Farewell! from thee
To me? Unarmed farewell? With so much fighting
Still to do! while there's Paris to win back!
When I've learnt each weak joint in Bedford's armour;
When with a rush and a blow, and thee to aid,
Paris were ours! Thou hangest up thy arms!
Nay, Joan. It shall not, must not, cannot be!
List to thy voices, echoing, trumpet-tongued,
The 'No' that's in thy soul and on thy lips—
It cannot be!

  [JEANNE *rushes to the pillar and seizes her sword
      and standard.*

Jeanne. Once more I hear my voices!
They cry 'To Paris!'

Enter ISAMBARD, PIERRE, JACQUES, *and* ISABELLE, *with
    crowd and Soldiers behind, murmuring.*

Isamb. Now, Joan, we are ready.
Crowd. She must not go!
Soldiers.   They shall not take the Maid!
Jeanne. I will *not* go! My work is not fulfilled!
To Paris! On! For France and for King Charles!

[*The soldiers echo her cry as they press round her with uplifted
    weapons, amidst excitement of the crowd, amazement of*
    JEANNE'S *parents, joy of* PIERRE *and* LA HIRE.

ACT DROP.

ACT V.

May 30, 1431.—The Maid Martyr.

Scene I.—*Rouen.*

The Court of the Castle, R. *The portal of the Chapel, with closed door. A view, as from a height, of the town and distant country.*
LA HIRE, *in the disguise of a Burgundian soldier (the White Cross ragulé of Burgundy conspicuous on his surcoat), on guard with his partisan.*
PIERRE DARC *appears cautiously at door,* L. *He gives a low whistle, and advances to* LA HIRE, *who recognises him. He too wears the White Cross of Burgundy.*

    La Hire. Ha, Pierre! how goes our plan?
    Pierre (*points down*). I've horses ready
Yonder, outside the moat; our friends are posted
On the gate-guards. I hope, so you get speech of her,
All will go well.
    La Hire. Amen! and yet it irks me
We should be plotting, under this vile badge
Of Burgundy, not striking a stout stroke
For her that struck so many for us and France.
    Pierre. Where are the towns she helped, the lords she succoured,
The King she crowned?
    La Hire Put not your trust in princes!
So said the Chinon shopkeepers—so say I.
Hang kings and courts and courtiers! Why did Joan
Trust them, since that day we turned back from Paris
And left the gate of St. Honoré half-won?
Because the King, forsooth, lost heart and hope.
The King! a popinjay! King me no kings.
Now Charles leaves her unhelped that set her life
As dicer sets his stake, and won a crown
For him, a prison, and death—perhaps—for herself!
    Pierre. Oh, why was she so bold! why would she ride,
A handful 'gainst a host, out of Compiègne!
    La Hire. They had not taken her, had she but turned rein.

Pierre. She would not fly. She knew not how to fly.
Let her foes say their worst, none lives can say
He ever saw Joan's back on battlefield.
  La Hire. Her heart misgave her—ever after Rheims.
  Pierre. She said her work was done with the King's crowning;
Told me she should not last till midsummer.
'Twas May, last year, they took her—a whole year
She has lain here in close hold—chained, questioned—tortured.
Oh, I could go distraught but for the hope
To help her still!
  La Hire.   And I—whose soul she cleansed
From blood and mire—think you not *I* would give
The life she saved to save her?
                    Hence! her judges!
(*Proclamation heard without.*)
Way for his Grace the Bishop of Beauvais,
And for his worshipful Court of Ordinary!

Enter PIERRE CAUCHON, BISHOP *of* BEAUVAIS, *accompanied by English Lords, Abbots, regular and secular Clergy and Doctors of the Law. Among those around are* ISAMBARD DE LA PIERRE *and* NICHOLAS L'OISELLEUR.

  Bishop of Beauvais (*threateningly to* ISAMBARD).
Have a care, friar! that art still so ready
To counsel the accused, and thrust thy hand
Betwixt her and the court, lest, shielding her
From the fire, thou singe thyself. I marvel much
My Lord of Avranches should have pressed thee on me
As one skilled in the dealings of Church courts
With sorcery and witchcraft.
  Isamb.   In one point
The Church courts and my books agree—that none
Must be held guilty until guilt is proved.
  Bishop. What proofs like facts? Since this foul witch was taken
At Compiègne, by Heaven's help——
  Isamb.   And John of Luxembourg's.
A strange ally for Heaven!
  Bishop (*angrily*).   Again, Sir Monk!
I love not sneers on nobles. This year past
What have we done but pile mountains of proof

On her vile head? By questionings, in her prison,
In court, by judgment of the University,
Of bishops, abbots, of my Court of Ordinary,
The Holy Office itself, on the twelve articles
Wherein her subtle answers are digested.
And have not all agreed that she is guilty
Of heresy, and sorcery, and witchcraft,
And many more foul crimes and misdemeanours?
  Isamb. All *have* agreed. But even *their* agreeing
By the Church law 'mounts not to condemnation.
Ere you can hand her to the secular arm,
The Church's mercy grants her three monitions.
  Bishop. Two have been giv'n. We are called to hear the
   last.
  Isamb. Why have we left the hall where the Court sate
Till now?
  Bishop. To sit here—in the Torture chamber!
            (*Pointing* L.)
  Isamb. The Torture-chamber?
  Bishop.   That sight of the rack
May warn her of the end of contumacy.
Will you on, lords? The trial waits for us.

The procession, headed by the English Lords and the BISHOP, *enters the Torture-chamber.* LA HIRE *in the background.* ISAMBARD *lingers behind.*

  Isamb. (*shrinking back in horror as he approaches the portal.*) From the dark archway breathes a reek of blood.
The air seems thick with groans; and on the walls
Dank drops hang, like the sweat on tortured brows.
To think the rack is stretched even now for thee,
My noble, innocent, and ill-starred Maid!
For thee, to save whose life I risk my own!
'Tis vain, I fear—oh, why is she so bold!
  (NICHOLAS L'OISELLEUR *appears in the portal, listening.*)
Outspoken, trustful in her innocence?
Why will she not appeal to the Pope in Council,
As I have urged her?
  Nicholas L'Oiselleur (*with a low chuckle*). Why, good
   brother Pierre?
Because she has *my* advice to balance *thine.*
As friend and fellow-prisoner—you may stare—
'Tis the best joke—my name is birdcatcher.

I've had myself shut up in the same cell,
As a King's soldier and her countryman;
And, having wormed me into her full trust,
Have bent her quietly to her undoing,
Wrought on her to defy the Court, distrust
The Church, the Pope—and most, one Father Pierre,
That *was* her friend—and—shame on him!—is her judge!
So I serve English, Church and Bishop, self.

  Isamb. Wretch! fear'st thou not that Heaven will 'quite
   thy treason?
  L'Oiselleur. Leave me to square scores 'twixt my soul
   and Heaven.
  [LA HIRE *is about to rush on him, but restrains himself.*
  Isamb. I'll hear no more, lest I forget my coat
And calling.   Villain!
  L'Oiselleur.   Keep your breath for Court!
  Isamb. (*solemnly*). May He that guards the right and
   confounds evil
Deal between thee, destroyer, and thy victim!
      [*Exit* ISAMBARD *into Torture-chamber.*
  L'Oiselleur (*shrugging his shoulders contemptuously*). Here
   comes the prisoner. I'll to the Court!
      [*Exit* L'OISELLEUR *into Torture chamber.*

Enter JEANNE, *guarded and chained, in a woman's dress—a
white hood, and plain grey robe reaching to her feet. She
looks pale and worn, and walks weakly and languid, as
from confinement and illness.* MASSIEU, *the Usher of the
Court, in attendance.*

  Jeanne. Oh, blessed sunshine! and balm-breathing air!
'Tis so sweet after prison damp and darkness!
How fair the town shows yonder—and beyond,
The fields, snow-white with may, and fresh spring-green—
And the broad river, dancing in the sun! (*Guards motion
  her on.*) Oh, let me look!
  Massieu.   Nay, the Court waits.
  Jeanne.   At least
Let me say one short prayer, at the closed door,
Wherewith they shut me from the sanctuary,
And its sore-needed comfort.
  Massieu.   Pray thy prayer.
But be quick, or I may be chid for thee.
      [*She kneels at the closed door of the Chapel.*

Enter L'OISELLEUR, *followed by* ISAMBARD.

L'Oiselleur. How now, Sir Usher? Did not the Court order
She should be barred all service of religion,
Which she has outraged by her sorceries?

Isamb. Cruel as thou art crafty, hold thy peace!

L'OISELLEUR *re-enters the Torture-chamber.* MASSIEU *touches* JEANNE *on the shoulder. She rises, with the aid of* ISAMBARD.

Jeanne. Oh, Father Pierre! they say I should not trust thee—
That thou'rt no more my friend.

Isamb. A wicked lie!
Never so much thy friend as now, when friends
Are needed most.

Jeanne. To know *that* makes me glad.
Give me thy blessing, and stand by me still
On this last trial. Oh! I am so weary
Of this year's questioning, these heavy chains,
Those ruffian guards, whose gibes and curses drown
The voices that should bring me strength and comfort.

Massieu. Now—we waste time. [*He motions her on.*

Jeanne. But whither do they lead me?
Not to the Great Hall?

Massieu. To the Torture-chamber.

Jeanne (*shudders and shrinks back*). The Torture-chamber!

Isamb. (*soothingly.*) Not to torture thee.
They would not tear thy limbs, but tame thy courage.

Jeanne. That they shall not! I will pray Heaven for strength,
And then my voices, sure, will comfort me.
Lead on, sirs (*to Guards*).
[*Exit* JEANNE *into Torture-chamber.*

SCENE II.

The Torture-chamber, a vaulted room, of Norman architecture, surrounded by low arcades hung with black curtains. JEANNE *led in by her Guards. They leave her in the middle of the stage.*

Jeanne. Alone! (*To Guards.*) But tell me, sirs, where are my judges? [*Guards withdraw.*
They're gone, and will not speak. Dumb as these walls!

And yet, methinks, there's mercy in *their* silence.
Still hold your peace, kind walls! Stones as you are,
You have seen that has gone to your hard hearts.
How shall my heart of flesh hold up against
The horror of this place, mere thought of which
So pierces to my marrow! Anything,
But these black vaults, like graves! Where are my judges?
[*The curtains in all the arcades but the centre one are drawn,
and discover the Judges, seated in their places, including
the Cardinal,* WINCHESTER, *English Lords, the* BISHOP
of BEAUVAIS, *and* ISAMBARD.

    Bishop. Hear, Joan of Arc.—These before whom thou
       standest
Are men skilled in divine and human law,
Who with all clemency would deal with thee.
As thou art little learned, thou may'st choose counsel
From this Consistory—so in things of fact
Thyself make answer, swearing to speak truth.
    Jeanne. I thank you, sirs; but I have for my guide
A Counsel above yours. And for the truth,
I have spoke that to all you had right to ask.
    Bishop. Dost thou persist still in thy contumacy?
    Jeanne. I must persist in truth.
    Bishop.   And still refusest
Submission to the Church?
    Isamb. (*warningly*).   Have a care, Jeanne.
Appeal to the Council of Bâle.
    Bishop.   Who's that that speaks?
Peace, in the devil's name!
    Jeanne.   What is that Council?
    Isamb. A congregation of the Christian Church,
Where sit as many clergy of thy party
As Burgundy's.
    Jeanne.   To that Council I appeal.
       [*The Notary of the Court is about to write.*
    Bishop. Record not that appeal! The prisoner
May not appeal from this Court of Ordinary.
    Jeanne. 'Tis hard! You write down all that makes
       against me.
What would make for me, that you will not write.
    Warwick (*to* ISAMBARD). How dar'st thou prompt her!
       I will have thee flung
Into the Seine!

Bishop (*to* JEANNE). Wilt thou yield to the Church?
Jeanne. In all that's possible to me I *will* yield—
What is not possible, is to deny
What I have said—my voices and my visions,
And work enjoined on me—for these are true.
Rather than unsay truth I will say nothing.
    Bishop. Think; the familiars of the Holy Office
Stand ready with the rack unless thou answer.
    Jeanne. If you should make them tear me limb from
        limb,
I can but speak what I have spoke—the *truth*.
    Bishop. Beware! Not torture only, but the fire,
Will be thy portion, unless thou abjure
Thy heresies.
    Jeanne.   Were I set at the stake,
And saw the hangman with his torch alight,
Saw the pile kindled and the faggots blaze,
I could abjure no word that I have said! [*The Judges rise.*
    Isamb. (*appealing.*) Sirs, ere you sentence, grant me
        speech of her
Apart.
    Bishop (*bows consent*). 'Tis granted thee. The Church is
        kind.   [ISAMBARD *and* JEANNE *come forward.*
    Isamb. (*very earnestly to* JEANNE.) An abjuration wrung
        from thee by duresse
Binds not, nor stains the conscience. Do their bidding—
Abjure—yield to the Church. They'll loose thy chains,
Remove thee from thy cell into Church keeping,
Release thee from thy English guards.
    Jeanne.   For *that*
What would I *not* do! But, deny the truth!
Give me a little time. It is so hard!
    Bishop. Joan of Arc, called the Maid, thou hast received
The solemn admonitions that the Church
In mercy puts 'twixt proof of heresy
And the stern justice of the secular arm!
To the twelve articles of accusation
Thou hast, in contumacy, answered nothing
But blank and bare denial—yet the Court,
Ere it condemn and cast thee from the Church,
Would warn thee tenderly of what awaits thee—
The rack, that we can use, to force confession,

And the fire after, that will burn thy body,
If thou abjure not, and implore our grace.
    Jeanne. I can but say, as I have said already—
There is no truth in all you charge against me.
    Bishop. And that is thy last word?
    Jeanne.   My first and last!
    Bishop. Behold! (*The curtain of the centre arcade is drawn and the rack shown, with its two Executioners, in red gowns and hoods which cover their faces, with holes for the eyes.*) The Rack!
    Jeanne.   But still the truth's the truth.
Why will you try to make me soil my soul?
    Bishop. And after it the Fire!
    Jeanne.   Torture me not!
    Bishop. The Rack, and then the Fire!
    Jeanne (*in great agony*).   I will submit—
Abjure—say what you will. Spare me but this!
    Bishop. Thou has done a good work, and saved thy soul!
Behold, I have thine abjuration ready!
Sign it!
    Jeanne. I cannot.
    Bishop.   Better sign than burn.
    Jeanne. Alas! I cannot write!
    Bishop (*to* ISAMBARD).   Guide thou her hand.
    Isamb. (*comes forward and takes her hand—aside to her*).
    The deed and hand are naught.
    Jeanne.   Alas! alas!
I know not! Help me! (*Clings to him.*) Do not leave
    me, Father!
                [*She signs,* ISAMBARD *guiding her hand.*
    Isamb. (*to* BISHOP.) Now mitigate the sentence.
    Bishop.   As thou'rt come,
With contrite heart, back from thy heresy,
The Court takes off thy excommunication,
And doth award thee, in its Christian mercy,
That thou in prison pass the rest of life,
On bread of sorrow and water of affliction—
There to lament past sins—and sin no more.
    Jeanne (*in passionate entreaty*). But you will take me
    hence to your Church prison—
Not to that cell again—among those men?
So foul and cruel—and rude—they frighten me.

Bishop. We will consider of thy prayer—meanwhile
The learned Counsel given thee by the Court
Will teach thee how to speak thy abjuration
Publicly to the people, where the stake
Was raised to burn thee hadst thou not abjured.
   [LA HIRE, *in a hooded gown, comes forward from
    among the Judges.*
 Jeanne. Oh, cruel mercy! Not one friend!
La Hire (*hastily putting back his hood, so that she only
 sees him*). Thou hast!
Hush! (*Checking her surprise.*) Start not—speak not—
 ask not how I'm here.
(*Rapidly.*) Here is a file to cut thy chains and bars—
Thou'lt find a cord hidden within thy bed
Of length to let thee safe down to the moat.
I have fleet horses set without the castle—
Friends at the castle-postern and town-gates.
Thou hearest me? No word? Why dost not speak?
 Jeanne. I hearken for my voices—they are silent—
Alas! they've left me at my utmost need—
Left me, spite of my prayers, and tears, and sorrows,
This abjuration! Have I not denied them!
Then well may they desert me, false of heart,
And weak of faith! Oh! I have played with Heaven!
Tampering with the truth for fear of torture,
And terror of the burning. I will bear
Unto the end—not barter bliss eternal
For a brief remnant of unhappy life!
(*To* LA HIRE.) Farewell! 'Tis joy to know one true to me,
That *still* am true to France and to King Charles.
No word! Escape hence! Think no more of me.
      (LA HIRE *falls back.*)
Hear me, you cruel judges. Hear the Maid,
Not now abjure her faith, but witness it
In face of rack and pile! I hear my voices!
I see my sweet St. Katherine and St. Margaret
Again—they smile on me, and say 'Well done!
Endure unto the end—we will be with thee!'
Lo you—I here recant my recantation
And doom first to the fire the hand that signed it!
What I said of my voices and my visions
Was true. Do I not hear and see them now?
All I have done was well done—and from Heaven!

Bishop (*to Cardinal*). What said I to your Grace? She
    has abjured,
And yet we hold her for the fire at last!
(*To* JEANNE.) Accursed one! We cut thee from the Church,
And hand thee over to the secular arm!
To close thy record—as I close this book! (*The Judge
    closes his book.*)
To ring thy death-knell—as I strike this bell! (*The Judge
    strikes a bell.*)
And quench thy life—as I put out this light! (*All extin-
    guish their lights. Darkness.*)
    Bishop and Judges. Be thou anathema and maranatha!
[*Two familiars of the Inquisition lead* JEANNE *back into the
central recess, and the black curtains are drawn.*

SCENE III.

*Rouen; the old Market-place under the Church of St. Saviour.
In flat the Church; clustered against it and round the stage
the high-gabled houses and arcades of the Market-place. A
high pile with the stake* (*centre*). *On either side, running
obliquely, platforms, with the Cardinal,* BISHOP, *English
Lords and Judges of the last scene. The stage is crowded
with Citizens and Soldiers.* PIERRE DARC *in disguise.*

    1*st Citizen.* They'll never burn her, now she has abjured?
    Pierre. Abjured—what?
    1*st Citizen.*   Why, her witchcrafts.
    Pierre.   Witchcrafts, fool?
Her witchcrafts were to love France and fight for it,
And beat the invader hence. That's why she burns.
    1*st Citizen.* Think you her friends will help?
    Pierre.   Her angels should—
And you should—and all Rouen—were you men!
    English Soldier. Hear the vile Armagnac! Hold thy
        knave's tongue!
    2*nd Soldier.* Take him across the pate, Will.
    1*st Woman.*   For his pity?
It *should* be sin in *your* eyes!
    1*st Soldier.* Peace—you gillflirt!
    2*nd Soldier.* Clear the place of these cuckoldy Armagnacs!
        (*Levels his partisan.*)
    Pierre. St. Denis for France! (*Crowd repeat the cry.*)
    1*st Soldier.* Hear you *that*, lads? St. George
For England! (*Stir among the English and French mobs.*)

Pierre. Save the Maid ! Down with the English !
A rescue ! a rescue !
> [*English soldiers overpower and force back the unarmed crowd.*

Enter LA HIRE, *with the Burgundian badge.*

La Hire (*to Pierre*). It is too late—they have neither arms nor hearts.

Pierre (*aside to him*). You have had speech of her ? (*He nods.*) What hope?

La Hire. Alas !
She is too near to Heaven to care for earth !
She will not lift a hand to save herself.

Pierre. We'll save her in her own despite !

La Hire. Oh, Pierre !
My sword is lead ; now the heart in me's crushed
By what I've heard and seen.

Pierre. Mine burns like fire
To save her.

La Hire. It is hopeless—all the streets
Are guarded with their soldiers, every gate
Is held in force—*you* know if I'd count odds
For her—we can die with her—that is all !

Pierre. Oh, my sweet sister ! Pure and holy Maid !
Thou lily-flower of France—thus in thy spring
To be cut down and flung into the fire !

La Hire. I know not if to weep—or pray—or curse,
Becomes me most or least. To draw and strike
And die were best ! No—I'll live to avenge her !

Pierre. Look, where she comes ! Upon her way to death !

Enter procession of soldiers, clearing the way to the pile; then black monks and nuns chanting the De Profundis.
Then JEANNE, *barefooted and bareheaded, in a long black robe, attended by* ISAMBARD *carrying a crucifix. A buzz and murmur among the crowd : of love, pity, and sympathy from the French; hatred and exultation from the English.*

English mob. Burn the witch !

French mob. Bless thee, Jeanne ! Pray for the Maid !

Jeanne (*looking round her*). Oh, Rouen, Rouen ! that
    with thy proud towers
Look'st over Seine and the fair fields of France—
Tak'st thou my life, that had given mine for thee ? (*Turning to the Judges.*)

Lord Bishop, and you, Judges—(*To the* BISHOP *of* BEAUVAIS)
    —*you*, in chief,
I cite you to a higher judgment seat—
Where hearts are searched by Him who knows the truth—
May you confront the fires which *He* awards,
As I face this to which you have doomed me!
    Isamb. Forgive thine enemies!
    Jeanne.   Would my forgiveness
Could cleanse their souls, and make them clear as mine!
    Warwick. On with the witch to death! We waste the
       time
    Jeanne. Farewell, May-sun, whose light I change for fire,
Wherein foul souls are purged, pure made more pure!
    (*Stretching her arms to the crowd.*)
Farewell, friends! whom I would have died to save,
And but for striving to save whom I die! (*Looking up to
    Heaven.*)
Forgive my foes, and bless France and her King!
    Warwick. Heretic King, that trusted in thy witchcrafts!
    Jeanne. Saving your reverence, that is not true—
Say what you will of *me*, but spare my King.
Hear, all, my words—the last that I shall speak.
In seven years hence my fair France shall be free—
The invader beat from her, or buried in her!
And then peace shall bless France—and France shall bless
The memory of the Maid that now must burn!
Give me a cross, I pray.
    [LA HIRE *breaks his sword and gives her the fragment
       with the cross-hilt.*
    La Hire. Here, Jeanne, take this—
'Tis the best use that I can put it to.
Bless him once more, that will live on thy blessing
As long as life is left!
    Jeanne.   Bless thee, brave Captain!
And true friend.
    Pierre (*repressing his grief*). And *me*, Jeanne!
    Jeanne.   My Pierre—Heaven bless thee!
And all at home! Let them not weep for me,
Who, dying, loved them all, yet did not weep,
Thinking less of our parting than the joy
When we shall meet again.
    Warwick.   To the pile with her!
Must we be all day here?

Bishop. She is delivered
Unto the secular arm. 'Tis that must punish. (*Guards urge her on.*)

Jeanne. (*to* ISAMBARD). Keep near me, Father, near me to the last,
And hold the crucifix above the fire,
That I may see it while I have eyes to see.

[*She mounts the pile,* ISAMBARD *attending her.*

Isambard. Was it for this I held thee at the font,
Nurtured thy youth, and followed thee in faith,
Through thy brief glory to this bitter end?
Would I could give, not prayers, but life for thee!

[*The fire is kindled.* JEANNE *sees it.*

Jeanne. Look, where the flame steals up among the wood.
Go down quick, lest it hurt thee. Pray for me!
Look! 'Tis my sweet Katherine! My voices
Have not deceived me!

[*As the flames rise she gazes up to Heaven with a look of fervent faith and exultation. A groan bursts from the crowd.*

THE CURTAIN FALLS.

'TWIXT AXE AND CROWN

OR

THE LADY ELIZABETH

An Historical Play

(*First performed at the Queen's Theatre, Long Acre, May* 1870)

PREFACE.

THE subject of this play has already been treated by Madame Birch-Pfeiffer, the well-known German dramatist. Her play, *Elizabeth Prinzessin von England*, is in six acts, and begins and ends like the English drama.

The present play originated in a request that the Author would translate or adapt Madame Birch-Pfeiffer's drama for our stage. On reading it, it seemed to him that, though the German play as it stood was unsuited for adaptation, the subject was full of dramatic capabilities; and that an interesting drama might be constructed on the main lines of the German play—where these were well-laid—by resort to the historical materials of the period. In this way a new play has been built up, in which the original matter far exceeds, in bulk and dramatic importance, what is retained from the German play or suggested by it.

The character of Mary, a mere sketch in the German, has received a new aspect and development. The parts of Renard, Sir John Harrington, Isabel Markham, Rutter, and Paget are altogether new. Most of the scenes in which the acts culminate, as that of the introduction of Courtenay at Ashbridge Manor, that between him and Elizabeth, and the arrest of the latter—in the second act; the confronting of Wyatt, on his way to execution, with Courtenay; the plot of Renard and Gardiner for the destruction of Elizabeth, and the subsequent scene between Elizabeth and Courtenay—in the third act; the scene in which Elizabeth baffles Gardiner's attempt to procure her execution on a warrant unsigned by the Queen—in the fourth act; the scene in Mary's sick room, and the interview of Renard and Elizabeth—in the fifth;—are entirely due to the English Author. The only situations of stirring effect which he has adapted from the German, besides those in the first act, are that of Elizabeth's terror-stricken vision of queens in the Tower, and the concluding passage where the tidings of Courtenay's death clash with those of Elizabeth's accession to the throne.

Throughout the play, the Author has resorted to the German drama rather for the marshalling of incidents than for purposes of dialogue.

It seemed well that this should be explained, by way of rendering unnecessary any discussion as to the respective shares in the play of the German and English dramatists.

On the Subject and Treatment of the Play.

In the main, the historical data of the time, which covers the interval from Mary's accession, in 1553, to her death, in 1558, have been followed as closely as was compatible with dramatic effect. There is no historical authority for the visit of Courtenay to Ashridge, or for his presence at Elizabeth's submission to the Lords of the Council.

Events which really occurred, but which were separated by a longer interval than that represented in the play, have been brought together in time; *e.g.*, Courtenay's release from the Tower, and the execution of Wyatt; the letter and gift of Philip to Elizabeth, and the death of Mary; the death of Courtenay, and the accession of Elizabeth.

But, except in this compression of time, it is believed that the dramatic treatment of the subject is in its main lines warranted by sufficient historical authority. The character, conduct, and motives of Courtenay are among the disputed questions of the time. Mr. Froude, its latest and keenest investigator, takes a low view of both. But, except his retreat during Wyatt's attack on London, there is nothing on record that indicates lack of courage in Courtenay; and his conduct on that occasion is capable of an explanation quite compatible with his manhood.

If there be any faith in physiognomy, Courtenay was of dignified and noble nature; and there is abundant warrant in contemporary history for the higher view of him taken in the play.

In attempting to present a view of Mary's character making more demand on popular sympathy than has usually been ventured on in the case of this harshly-judged queen, I have but worked out the conclusions of Mr. Froude, who, decidedly Liberal and Protestant as are his sentiments, has been unable to resist the evidence that Mary was, in many respects, of a loving and womanly nature—warped by evil counsels, but struggling towards the light, as her weak vision apprehended it.

In these days of historical rehabilitation there are few objects of popular execration on whose behalf a plea, 'in confession and avoidance,' may be more fairly urged, than on that of 'bloody Mary.'

In the versification of this and my other blank verse plays there is a studious avoidance of rigid rhythm. The metre is arranged for speaking rather than reading. As this play is printed to be acted as well as read, the stage-directions will be found full, and fitted for purposes of representation. At the end of the play the scene and property plots, &c., will be found printed in an appendix for the convenience of managers.

DRAMATIS PERSONÆ.

BISHOP GARDINER (*Lord Chancellor and Confessor of the Queen*)
THE EARL OF SUSSEX ⎫
LORD PAGET ⎬ *Lords of the Council.*
LORD WILLIAM HOWARD ⎭
EDWARD COURTENAY (*Earl of Devonshire*).
SIMON RENARD (*The Spanish Envoy*).
SIR JOHN BRYDGES (*Lieutenant of the Tower*).
SIR THOMAS WYATT.
HARRINGTON (*Gentleman of the Chamber to Lady Elizabeth*).
PARRY (*Cofferer to the Lady Elizabeth*).
RUTTER (*a Tower Warder*).
MARY TUDOR (*Queen of England*).
THE LADY ELIZABETH (*Daughter of Henry VIII. and Anne Boleyn, her half-sister*).
DUCHESS OF NORFOLK.
ISABEL MARKHAM (*her Niece*).
CICELY (*Daughter of a Tower Warder*).
  Ladies of the Court, Courtiers, Guards, Pages, Attendants, &c.

PERIOD OF THE ACTION, 1553—58.

SCENES.

Act 1. *St James's Palace.*
Act 2. *Ashford Manor House.*
Act 3. *The Lieutenant's Garden in the Tower.*
Act 4. *A Room in the Lieutenant's Lodgings in the Tower.*
Act 5. *The Great Hall at Hatfield.*

'TWIXT AXE AND CROWN.

ACT I.

SCENE.—*Gallery in St. James's Palace. Large arch,* C., *and smaller ones at each side.* C. *arch backed by smaller arch, with rich crimson curtains down. A state chair, with canopy,* L., *with seats each side. Large illuminated window in recess,* L. *Door* 2 E. R. *The architecture and decorations in the style of Hampton Court—the Renaissance of the time of Henry VII. and VIII. Tapestry. Courtiers discovered grouped. As the curtain rises* LORD SUSSEX, *who is moving forward with his white wand, towards door,* R., *is followed by* GARDINER, *who has entered from* L. U. E.

Gard. (*as if claiming his attention*). My Lord of Sussex!
Sussex (*turning*). At your lordship's orders.
Gard. (*humbly*). Orders! Between your grace and me, 'tis mine
To take them, not to give. But there's a matter
Touching your office wherein it were well
You knew the royal pleasure.
Sussex.   What is that
The Queen wills and *you* ask, I should not do?
Gard. (*as the* L. *corner group move to back*). Yet 'tis a delicate business—craves nice handling.
Wary and well-weighed speech—that says but little
To what it means.
Sussex.   You said it touched my office.
Methinks, my lord, it needs a cast of *yours*.
Speak out, my lord, and roundly.
Gard.   'Tis my wont.

The Lady Elizabeth—of all those that love her,
And they are legion, thank the saints—
 Sussex.   And somewhat
Her own good gifts.
 Gard.   No doubt; I've heard men say
You love the lady.
 Sussex.   So I do, as a father.
Men call me proud, but, methinks, were I father
Of such a child I should go prouder still.
Scarce twenty, still on the edge of girlhood, ripe
Of wit, and firm of will, as few old men,
Yet very woman in each gracious gift
And grace of maiden. She holds Grindal hard
In Greek: caps Latin with him and his doctors.
The Envoy of Venice tells me her Italian
Has the true ring—it sounds like silver bells;
And Monsieur de Noailles says when she's Queen
She'll deal with French ambassadors single-handed,
And be a match for the Monsieurs, in compliment
As in contrivance. Yet she bears this load
Of learning lightly, and finds room with it
For all arts of her sex: comfits, confections—
She hath wrought the beds and chairs at Ashridge yonder,
Till the old hall's a plot of summer flowers,
And there, like a bird, she sits in the midst of them,
Setting her sweet voice to the virginals,
That travellers stop to listen.
   [*Group opposite throne,* L., *cross to* R. *and converse with
    the group there.*
 Gard.   You speak warmly.
 Sussex. I speak but as I feel. Warmly, quotha!
Was't but to hear her praise your Grace craved speech of
  me?
 Gard. I need not tell you, how, since Henry's marriage
With Katherine was held good in Parliament,
It follows that the marriage with Anne Boleyn
Is null and void, and that the Lady Elizabeth——
"Tis pity, but the law is pitiless.
 Sussex. Be like the law, make no parade of pity,
To say the Lady Elizabeth is a *bastard.*
 Gard. So says the law.
 Sussex.   The law lies in its teeth.
White is still white, though the law call it black.
The Lady Elizabeth is King Henry's daughter,

Even as the Queen is, and her right to reign
After the Queen remains as Henry will'd it;
And that *you* know, my lord, as well as I.
 Gard. (*humbly*). 'Tis a grave point, whereon were much
  to say
On either side. Suffices that her Majesty
Having noted that the Lady Elizabeth
Is used to take the seat nearest the throne,
Lays her commands on you to make known to her
That for the future she resign that seat
To her cousin, the Lady Margaret, Countess Lennox,
As first in the blood-royal—the *full* blood.
 Sussex. I will obey her Majesty, whate'er
My pain to pain the Lady Elizabeth!
But why this order? Come, be round with me.
 [C. *group move to* R., *and* R. *group go up and cross to* L.
 Gard. Queens less brook rivalry than lesser women.
 Sussex. Rivalry!
 Gard. Have you not seen, and wondered as you saw,
The sudden favour heaped on Edward Courtenay?
 Sussex. Seen and rejoiced—not wonder'd. 'Twas well
  done
O' the Queen to make that noble lad this payment
Of his fifteen years' penance in the Tower.
I ne'er drew gladder breath than when I saw
The new-crowned Queen upon Tower Hill kiss round
Those poor pale scarecrows, Courtenay and the rest—
She kissed them all, called them her prisoners——
 Gard. And straight was *his*, and hath been from that hour.
She ne'er forgot that kiss of Edward Courtenay,
Nor will forget. See you not she has given him
More than his father forfeited, lands, honours,
The earldom of his house?
 Sussex. A Queen's amends
For his long suffering, and a woman's pity!
 Gard. Pity! Past doubt! Most soft and tender pity.
Maybe the Lady Elizabeth, too, feels pity
For Courtenay! Warn her, good my lord—there's danger
 (*Enter* ELIZABETH, *followed by four* LADIES, *from* R 4th E.)
In subject's pity that dares cross a Queen's!
  [*All the Courtiers bow and come down on each
   side. The two Yeomen of the Guard present their
   partizans as* ELIZABETH *passes them.* ELIZABETH

*is plainly but tastefully dressed in white satin
and pearls. All bow, including* SUSSEX *and*
GARDINER.

  Eliza. Kind lords, fair ladies, my good Lord of Sussex!
   (SUSSEX, R.)
You see, my lord, how true I keep the hour—
One of your lessons in the happy time
When I had you for schoolmaster at Chelsea.
Why do you look so grave? Is it this dress,
Too plain and poor for my kind sister's court?
(*To* GARD. L.) But in this, my Lord Bishop, I make bold
To disobey her. I would still go thus,
For love of our dead brother, good King Edward.
He used to call me Sister Temperance,
And I still wear the white and pearls he chose me
One day, when he and I and the Queen, my sister,
Dressed for a baby masque at Hampton Court.
Then let me go as I pleased him, and look not
So stern on your old pupil.
   [GARD. *passes to back and converses with* SUSSEX.
  Sussex.   Now beshrew him,
That could be stern, when thy bright eye said nay!

Enter ISABEL MARKHAM *and the* DUCHESS OF NORFOLK
   D. R.

  Eliza. (*perceiving them*). Her Grace of Norfolk and my
   Isabel!
How's this? A month at Court, and never yet
A day for me?
  Isabel (*crossing to* R. C.). I dared not!
  Eliza.   Dared not, quotha!
Here's much to dare! (*To* DUCHESS.) She was not wont to fear me
Or Master Grindal either, when at Hanworth
She hid his staff and pinned his gown to his chair,
For plaguing her with Greek. How fares it, Isabel,
With thy Greek now?
  Isabel.   Methinks, at a pinch, your Highness,
I could make shift to read the alphabet;
But I must sweat for it!
  Eliza.   I warrant me:
Nature had cut the scholar's root in thee,
So Grindal said (*to* DUCHESS), but in a saraband
We were all lame to her. Dost thou remember

When I and Mildred Cook and sweet Jane Grey——
  [*The* DUCHESS *frowns;* ELIZABETH *pauses, with a passing emotion, but checks herself.*
I prattle idly. We'll talk o'er old times (*to* DUCHESS)
When your Grace gives her leave to come to me.
  (L. *group go up to leave room for* ELIZABETH *to take her seat* L. *of the throne.*)
Meantime to con my virginal book. Sit, ladies!
  [LADIES *sit* R. SIR J. HARRINGTON *approaches* ELIZABETH *and gives her her virginal book.* SUSSEX *shows signs of disquiet.* GARDINER *whispers to him.*
  Isabel (R.C.). You hear (*to* DUCHESS) she bids you, madam; you must bring me.
  Duchess (R.). Peace, fool! You would be maid of honour here.
The road to the Queen's grace lies not by *her* door (*glancing at* ELIZABETH).
  Isabel. (R.C.). They are sisters, aunt.
  Duch.   Sisters? Ay, marry are they!
Sisters by one side, and not o' the heart!
  Harr. (C. *advancing to* ISABEL). Fair Mistress Isabel!
  Isabel (*affecting surprise*). Sir John Harrington!
Now cry you mercy, I marked you not. (SUSSEX *converses with* GARDINER, R.)
  Sir J.   I marked *you.*
You at St. James's!
  Isabel.   And you *not* at Ashridge?
  Sir J. You note my absence?
  Isabel.   Gratefully—some folk's room
Is so *much* better than their company!
  Sir J. Still so sweet and so bitter! Must we ever
Be trying wits?
  Isabel.   Methinks with one of us
That were lost labour! I but pass at you
As the pages do at the Turk's head in the tilt-yard.
Weapons and wits are best tried on a block.
  Sir J. And the block has the best of it. He feels nothing,
And often blunts a sword or foils a wit!
Farewell, sweet mistress Malapert.
  Isabel (*with mock courtesy*).   Fare you well,
Doughty Sir Saracen's Head.
  Sir J. (*aside*).   A murrain on her!

Must I still stick my finger in the beak
Of my lady's parakeet? It serves me right.
> [*Goes up* C. *and talks to* PARRY. SUSSEX *comes down uneasily*, C., *as* SIMON RENARD *enters from* L. U. E. *and joins* GARDINER *at back*, R.

Eliza. (*observing* SUSSEX). What is it frets my good Lord Chamberlain?

Sussex. That chair! I have her Majesty's commands
To keep it for her cousin, the Lady Margaret,
Countess of Lennox. (*Aside.*) There, the ill word's out!
Pardon my tongue, your Highness, for my heart.

Eliza (*still sitting*). One of the truest beats this day in England!
My lord, you have done your duty—I know mine. (*Rises.*)
The Queen's command is law to me—as you.
I am her subject; but sit where I *may*,
Next to the throne or with the humblest here,
I am what I was born—King Henry's daughter!
> [*She walks across to* R. *and sits. Movement of Courtiers.*

Gard. (*advancing in front of her*). Not so, your Highness.
You mistake my lord,
Or he mistakes her Majesty. Your place
Is with the blood-royal, but not next the throne.

Eliza. My kind Lord Bishop, if with the blood-royal
I am to sit, I must sit next the throne.
Thence banished, I am banished utterly,
And so it pleases me to take this place,
So tell my Queen and sister, kind Lord Bishop.

Gard. (R.) Here comes her Majesty.

Sussex.   The Queen!
> [*By this time the curtains are up. The Courtiers fall down each side. Enter two Ushers and four Pages from* C. *arch. The* LORD TREASURER, *the* QUEEN, LORDS ARUNDEL, HOWARD, PAGET, *and other Courtiers crowd on and down each side.* ANNE OF CLEVES *and* COUNTESS OF DORSET *immediately behind the* QUEEN, *being of the blood-royal.* MARY *is a dark, stern woman of thirty-six, in a close-fitting scarlet dress, trimmed with ermine and closed to the neck; on her head the cap seen in her portraits. From her girdle hangs a rosary of pearl, with a large cross. Her look is shy and distrustful*

As she advances to C. *all bow. She surveys the group as if seeking for some one whom she misses, and her face darkens.*

Mary (C.). Greeting and thanks to all. (*To* ELIZ.) Ha! our fair sister!
They said you would prove rebel to command;
You shame them by obeying. (RENARD *gets* L. *of* MARY.)

Eliza. Good my liege,
As first among your subjects, it becomes me
To be first in obedience, whatsoe'er
It cost me to obey.

Queen.   It should cost little,
I think, to do what all say you do well. (*The* QUEEN *observes the* SPANISH ENVOY.)
Ha! Master Renard! We are glad to see you.
You have good news from Spain?

Ren.   That's as it pleases
Your Majesty to give me news for Spain.

Queen. How?

Ren.   'Tis your royal smile or frown that makes
Sunshine or storm in the Escurial.

Queen. A truce to Spanish compliment.

Ren.   So please you
I'm a plain Fleming. Were kings common men,
I should say that King Philip's sad and sick.

Queen. I grieve to hear it.

Ren.   Yet a word of yours
Would make him well, and you forbear to speak it.

Queen. Queens are not free to give hands as they will.

Ren. I pray your majesty to remember that,
If e'er your Council ask you to bestow
Yours on my royal master.

[*Group* L. *move up at indication of* LORD CHAMBERLAIN *to make room for* QUEEN *to pass to throne.*]

Queen.   'Twill be time
When they shall ask, that we should con our answer.

[*Turns away from him and takes place on the throne.* ANNE OF CLEVES *and* COUNTESS OF DORSET *take seats* L. *of the throne, leaving the one immediately next to it empty.*]

Queen. Methinks our whole Court is not yet assembled.

Gard. (C.). My liege, her Grace of Lennox's seat is empty.

Queen. 'Tis well—she's sick.

Enter COURTENAY, D. R.

Sussex (*announcing*). The Earl of Devonshire!

Queen. Ha! Is he late? I noted not his absence
(COURTENAY *kneels at foot of throne.*)
Late, but yet welcome, Earl of Devonshire.
I pray you rise, my lord.

Court. Let me still kneel,
Most gracious Queen, till I discharge in speech
What of my heavy load of gratitude
Can be so lightened. (*Rises.*) Was it not enough
To give me Heaven's free breath to breathe again,
After my fifteen years of close Tower air,
But you must crown my liberty with honour;
Giving me back, not the broad lands alone,
That were my noble father's—that were little,
But for the gift that goes with them—the name
My father bore? I cannot *speak* my heart;
Let me have leave, my liege, to show it in *act*.

Queen. Sir Edward Courtenay, Earl of Devonshire,
Restoring you to freedom, lands, and title,
So long denied you, I am yet your debtor.
There is a long arrear still to be paid;
We shall think how to pay it as befits
A Queen, near you in blood, nor far removed
In love.

Court. Your Majesty's poor servant ever.
[*He looks around as if for* ELIZABETH, *and by his looks shows surprise to see the seat on the right of the throne empty.* MARY *watches him.*

Queen. You are come in merry time. Now, gentle sister,
The virginals! In our withdrawing-room
There's place for all. The music waits. Set on.
(*Courtiers begin to leave gradually,* C.)
Your arm, Lord Bishop.
[*She leaves the throne, laying her hand on* GARDINER'S *arm, who offers it submissively for her support.* RENARD *watches* COURTENAY.

Court. (R. C., *approaching* ELIZABETH). Lady Elizabeth,
May I crave cousin's leave to take your hand?

Eliz. (*gently declining; aside*) We're watched. (*Crossing him.*)
Nay, cousin, for *your* good, not *mine,*

I pray you seek a fairer or more favoured.
An older arm is safer stay for me.
    [*She offers* SUSSEX *her hand, who is by* C., *and moves gently up with him to go off,* C., *followed by* SIR J. HARRINGTON. ISABEL, ANNE OF CLEVES, *and* COUNTESS OF DORSET *rise when the* QUEEN *rises, get to* C., *and goes off after* ELIZABETH. QUEEN *has been whispering to* GARDINER L., *while the dialogue passes between* ELIZABETH *and* COURTENAY.

  Queen (C. L.). You know my heart, as my confessor
    should.
He dreams not of his fortune. See he know it,
Here, and within this hour, and from *your* lips.
    [*She moves off,* C., *followed by Lords, Pages Yeomen of the Guard,* &c.

  Gard. (C., *aside to* COURTENAY). A word with you anon,
    here, and alone.   [COURTENAY *bows,* R.
  Ren. (R., *at back, plucking* GARDINER *by sleeve*). Is't
    friends, my lord, or enemies?
  Gard.   I'll tell you,
When I have sounded this young popinjay.
An English King for me.
  Ren.   In hopes 'twill prove
An English puppet. Better back my master.
If stiff to a *bishop,* he'll bend to the *Church.*
And I've five thousand crowns in a curious casket
I would fain show your reverence. You are curious,
I think, in such toys.
  Gard.   Aye, sir, by and bye.
    [*Exit* GARDINER, C. *Exit* RENARD, R. *Harp is heard, piano,* E. L.

  Court. (*solus*) Put my hand from her? For *your* good,
    not *mine.*
Those were her words! She look'd not hate nor scorn.
Her calm clear eye must needs have read my heart.
Oh, would I could read hers! Fair, close-sealed book,
So writ with wisdom, has it room for love?
Pardon, my sweet, that I misdoubt thee so,
Deeming thee poor in what is best of woman.
Thrust from her rightful place, how proud she took
Her lower room, for all the double crown
Of nature, as of blood, on her white brow,

And youth and beauty's crown, that crowneth these. ·(*Walks up and down.*)
How's this? Doth Edward Courtenay know himself?
The Tower hath been my bitter schoolmaster,
Tempering my manhood, as Spain tempers blades
I' the ice-brook of affliction.   Fifteen years
I've learned to wait, and crush with iron will
The thirst for liberty, hunger for revenge,
Youth's dream of heights to climb and fame to win!
And now that Heaven's sun has chased prison darkness,
When my worst chains are these of gems and gold—
                    (*Touching his jewelled collar.   Music stops.*)
With a Queen's favour beckoning on and up,
My iron will turns lead—my tempered purpose
Softens like wax (GARDINER *enters*, C.) under a woman's smile,
And all my past in love's sufficing present
Is drunk and drowned!   [*Takes stage*, L.
    Gard. (R. C.)   My Lord of Devonshire,
I'm sent to bid your Grace where bright eyes miss you.
    Court. (L. C.) So bright, they dazzle one scarce used to them.
    Gard. The more need of such user, wherein you,
Of all lords here. should chiefly school yourself.
Ruling, like serving, may be easy taught.
You've mastered one—needs now to learn the other.
Methinks 'twere soon learnt, were a crown the payment.
    Court. Crowns have brought small joy to the House of York.
    Gard. Power is a mighty spell to conjure with.
    Court. True, my Lord Bishop, it can call up scaffolds
For men too bold, women too nigh in blood;
Build prisons—lifelong graves for innocence.
None better knows than I what power can do—
I learned the lesson off by heart i' the Tower.
    Gard. (*glancing uneasily around*). Would you be back in your Tower school again,
That you so let your thoughts out at your lips?
The Queen knows all your sufferings.
    Court.   And hath amply
Made me amends.
    Gard.   Yet feels she owes you still
So much, she can but pay you with herself.
    Court. My lord!

Gard. 'Tis not enough that she has given you freedom,
Your houses, lands, and titles; unto these
She offers you, through me, a crown.
    Court.   What crown?
    Gard. The crown of England—as her princely consort.
Are you struck dumb, my lord? Nay, be a man.
    Court. I hold myself a man. But where's the man
Whom such a weight of fortune, so flung on him,
Would not strike into stone? I, Edward Courtenay,
But now, of the forlornest most forlorn,
Attainted, beggared, a State prisoner,
And now bid take my place right hand the throne!
This head, set all these years 'twixt axe and block,
Offered the consort's all but royal crown!
This hand I looked should be severed by the headsman,
And stuck to rot over a London gate,
Called to lie in the Queen's! My good Lord Bishop,
Say this is not a dream of mine or yours.
The Queen choose me?
    Gard.   And what choice worthier?
Your blood, my lord, is royal, is right English.
The people's voice, the will of Parliament
Point to you even now, will hail you gladly:
And these are voices the Queen's glad to follow,
Above all, when her own heart echoes them.
I see no marvel here.
    Court.   You *will* not see it.
    Gard. What if the choice were *mine*, ere 'twas the Queen's?
    Court. Then be advised, my lord; I am not the man
You think me, if you think to find in me
A willing tool, to fit his hand who made it.
I was a free man even in the Tower,
And ill can brook to be Queen's slave, or Church's.
    Gard. Methinks the *mis*-choice is of bride, not bridegroom;
Had *Lady Elizabeth's* hand proffered the crown,
The stiff back might have bent.
    Court.   Beware, Lord Bishop!
    Gard. Be *you* 'ware, Earl of Devonshire, and weigh
Your walking—it is perilous. The Tower
Has mouths that swallow easier than disgorge:
From Traitor's Gate 'tis short road to Tower Green.

Court. Fancy, like thought, is free.   I know no law
Makes liking or misliking treasonable.
I'm the Queen's loyal liegeman, bound to her
Beyond mere fealty, by the mighty debt
Of liberty restored, broad lands and honours.
I'll pay that debt with service, pains, or blood ;
But I'll no crown that makes me twice a slave—
The Queen's first, then the Priest's that rules the Queen.
(*Crosses to* R.)   No.   If I must wear chains, give me plain
   iron—
Sooner a prisoner in the Tower than here !
So tell her Majesty, in what phrase best fits
My fealty and her favour.   I have chosen !
                                      [*Exit* COURTENAY, D. R.
   Gard. The choice is *yours* to make.   I like his pride.
   Renard (*entering cautiously*, D. R.).   You've made your
      offer ?
   Gard. (L. C.) And been answered roundly.
Refuse a crown !
   Ren.   Coupled with such a wearer,
I marvel not.   But this works well for *us*.
   Gard. For *us* ?
   Ren.   *Me*, Spain—your lordship, Holy Church.
A woman's favour scorned is hate—a Queen's,
Destruction.
   Gard.   Let him look to his head !
   Ren.   Amen.
This clears my master's way ; better a Spanish
Than English prince, where Church must pilot State.
   Gard. So falls the favourite of the day !
   Ren.   And with him
Brings down a higher head—Elizabeth's !
While *she* lives, loved as she is of your gross English,
My master's way to the succession's barred,
And you, and Holy Church, both held at bay.
                          (MARY *appears at curtains*, C.)
'Tis but two lives to brush aside.
   Gard.   The Queen !
   Queen. (C.) We would be private.   (RENARD *bows, and
      exit*, D. R.)
(*Impatiently*.)   Now, Lord Bishop.   Courtenay—
I looked to find him.
   Gard.   He went hence e'en now.

Queen. But not before you saw and spoke with him?
Gard. I saw and spoke with him.
Queen (*feverishly*). Well, well?
Gard. Told him the grace
Your Majesty deigned proffer.
Queen. To the point!
You told him; and he? Speak! what said he, man?
Gard. Would that my tongue were cut out by the roots,
Sooner than utter——
Queen. Oh! thou torturest me!
Strike, and strike home. The Earl of Devonshire?
Gard. Hath spurned your hand and crown.
Queen. It cannot be!
He could not, would not, dared not! Priest! thou liest!
Gard. (*drawing himself up*). I am the Church's, and the
Church is truth.
Saying *I* lie, you give the lie to Heaven;
A deadly sin, that calls for bitter penance. [*Takes stage*, L.
Queen. Forgive me, holy father! Culpa mea!
(*Striking her breast.*)
Maxima culpa mea! Set me penance!
I'll fast, say aves, scourge myself to blood.
Have pity on your Queen—your penitent!
Spurned me—the crown! No, no; it cannot be!
Gard. It is—so spurned your love and crown, as tho'
'Twere odds which were the heavier load to bear.
Queen. Oh, woe is me! The first I ever loved.
A curse is on our blood! My mother died
Heart-broken and alone! I passed a youth
Sad as old age, uncheer'd by hope or love,
Knowing a mother's tears, no father's smiles.
Even on the throne, I sate with empty heart
Hungering for love; and when I would enrich
My life from his, looked to find in his arms
All my lost youth, my long arrears of joy,
My summer, the more sweet the more delayed,
He scorns my proffered heart and flings it back!
He spurns me! (*Sinks on seat*, R.) All is blank! What's
left?
Gard. Revenge!
Queen. I thank thee, Gardiner; I *will* avenge me.
(*Fiercely*) Avenge me as becomes my father's daughter,
That never let his vengeance halt or hold,

Till it was fed to the full! I may not have
His *heart;* I'll have his *head.* He shall not live
To say he scorned me!
  Gard.   So turns your revenge
Back on yourself. To scorn you was no treason.
Strain but the law against him, and you rouse
The people's wrath, unchain their evil tongues.
  Queen. But how, how? Teach me, Gardiner; you were wont
To be quick at devising vengeances
That keep the right side of the law.
  Gard.   I'll tell you.
He loves the Lady Elizabeth. [*Harp is heard.*
  Queen.   Ah! my heart!
It told me—Yes, I noted how their eyes
Changed lights, their voices softened as they spoke
Unto each other. Fool, blind fool that I was
Not to take order sooner! Look you, now;
Her mother stole my father's love from mine;
The daughter steals my love away from me.
(*Bitterly.*) She shall abye the theft as her mother did
Upon the scaffold, and he die the death,
Like Henry Norris! By the saints, he shall!
  Gard. So be it; but restrain the heady temper
Your father left you for inheritance.
Grasp not too much. Who aims at two hits none.
Both are beloved of the coarse multitude,
That, childlike, holds to its playthings, and will scratch
Ere it will give them up. First chain *that* fear.
Close hands with Spain, that offers you a husband
With her alliance. Philip seeks your love;
Accept it. Let the new fire kill the old.
'Tis odds the traitors who oppose the match
Seek tools in Lady Elizabeth and Courtenay.
Once let them *wink* at *treason.* There's the *law*
Serves your revenge, and offers you their heads.
  Mary. So be it; you say well. Forgive my heat
And the sin it engendered. Look, I kneel (*kneeling*)
To pray for absolution, and a blessing
Upon my purpose.
  Gard. (*blessing her*). That perforce must be
To Heaven's more honour, and the Church's good.

Mary. That music maddens me! Lord Chamberlain,
(*Curtains are drawn as* SUSSEX *appears*).
Silence those lutes!

Sussex. 'Tis the last spring, your Majesty;
The music's o'er. (*Harp stops.*) Here comes the Lady
Elizabeth.

Gard. Compose your face and voice. I'll leave you
with her.

[QUEEN *ascends throne.* ELIZABETH, *followed by* ISABEL, DUCHESS OF NORFOLK, ANNE OF CLEVES, COUNTESS OF DORSET, SIR J. HARRINGTON, PAGET, PARRY, ARUNDEL, HOWARD, *Lord Treasurer, and four pages, enter,* C. *All of these go down,* R. *Pages stand across front* C. *arch to keep the remainder of Court from advancing too far, so as to leave space behind* PRINCESS.

Eliza. Most gracious Queen and sister,
Grant me an audience; I would crave a boon.

Mary. So graciously you did *our* 'hest to-day,
What is there *you* could ask *we* can refuse?

Eliza. You know what, until now, my life has been—
How private and retired; for this month past,
Since your accession, you have kept me with you,
Therein a sister's kindness working in you
That craves and has my gratitude. But now
My spirit and my body both are sick
For wonted food of sweet air, quiet study.
My books, my birds, my 'broidery, my lute,
All woo me to them; and I crave your leave
I may return to my poor house at Ashridge.

Queen. A boon I little looked you should have asked me
Gard. (*aside to* QUEEN). Let her go.
Mary. Have your will. Return to Ashridge.
But we'll send with you one of our tried servants,
Sir Thomas Pope, to help you to control
Your household.

Eliza. Please you, I have mine own people.
Mary. 'Twere well you had mine besides.

[*Courtiers at back begin to move down,* R., *others crowd in at back, and the twelve Yeomen of the Guard stand at each side of the curtains.*

Eliza. Your Majesty

Would put me under guard! The Queen suspects
Her faithful subject—sister mistrusts sister?
    Queen. I mistrust youth, ill counsel, and wild thoughts.
As Queen and sister both behoves me guard
Your fame and honour.
    Eliza. (*proudly*).   These I guard myself!
But be it so; a fair life dreads no spies:
Elizabeth's lies open to the day;
It braves Heaven's eye, and need not fear the Queen's!
So I commend me to your Majesty.
To all friends here—and methinks all are friends—
A kind and loving leave till next we meet!
    [*She bows graciously to the Court; they return it.*
    ISABEL *runs up to her, kneels, and kisses her hand.*

END OF ACT I.

ACT II.

SCENE I.

The Queen's Oratory, St. James's. A tryptych or movable altarpiece; prie dieu, with Bible on it and cushion at foot under it. Doors R. *and* L., *1st entrances, with devotional pictures. Small table, with writing materials and high-backed chair,* R. C.

    Queen (*rising*). I cannot pray! Such black and bitter
        thoughts
Rise betwixt me and Heaven! Even the saints
Methinks look dark and frowningly upon me.
Within, my people's hard opinion—treason
Even in my Council—my own sister wishing,
Aye, compassing my death. The Church that fain
I would build up again I dare not, save
With faint and faltering hand—so I miss Heaven,
And find no fruit of earth but bitterness. (*Sits,* R. C.)
This Spanish lord! Heaven put some love in him
To counterpoise the hate they say his coming
Will quicken in the people. Oh, my subjects,
If you but knew how sore all's with me here,
                (*Lays her hand on her heart.*)

You would be gentler with your Queen.   (*Knock*, D. L.)
                                    Who's there?

(*Enter* DUCHESS *of* NORFOLK, D. C.

Duch. Pardon, your Majesty—but my silly niece,
Whom you had named, by your most gracious favour,
To take Kate Ashley's service down at Ashridge,
Swears she'll not go—will crave release of you,
The puling fool! 'Twere well you lessoned her.
  Queen. Not go when we had chosen her? By St. Luke!
But she shall go—so tell her.
  Duch.   It were well
She heard so much from you. She waits without.
  Queen. Bid her come in. (*Exit* DUCHESS.) My smooth Elizabeth,
We must have eyes about you we can trust,
And ears too.

(*Enter* DUCHESS *and* ISABEL, L.)

                    So, fair Mistress Isabel,
What's this we hear? You'll none of Ashridge service?
You craved it once.
  ISABEL (*crossing to* C.). While I expected 'twould be
      loving service
To one I love like a sister—you are one,
And know how warm that is.
  Queen.   Methinks I do.
  Isabel. But now my aunt says I must play the spy
On my sweet friend—must dog her, note her words,
Mark whom she sees and speaks withal—i'faith,
Set in my note-book what she has for dinner,
And with what appetite she falls to it!
I pray your majesty to find another
For such unworthy service. Isabel Markham
Would scorn espial of the veriest jade
E'er sate i' the stocks—how should she spy on *her*,
The sweetest maid, the gentlest gentlewoman,
Your liegest subject, and my dearest friend?
  Duch. Peace, malapert!
  Mary (*sadly*).   Nay, chide her not, good Norfolk
My sister can have love like that at will,
Even in danger's and disfavour's spite!
I could not buy it—no, not for my crown.

Even there she crosses me! Go, wench; I'll find thee
Another service.
    Isabel.   Thank your Majesty.
I told my aunt, for all they said of you,
You had a gentle nature.
    Duch.   Peace; you'd best!
She is the veriest prate-apace.
    Queen.   Let be:
She shows her heart. She is but young at Court.
There! (*Kisses her.*) Get thy aunt, not me, to lesson thee.
    Duchess (*aside to* ISABEL). Fool! thou shalt smart for this.
                                            (*Ready for knock.*)
    Isabel.   And what care I?
(*Comes back.*) Beshrew me but I could find in my heart
To love your Majesty—almost as well
As my Elizabeth.
    Duch.   Out, out, you fool!
Pardon her, madam; she knows naught of state—
How Queens should be accosted.
    Queen.   No, poor child.
She brings her country gifts, plain truth and love.
Go teach her, madam, what *you* bring a Queen!
                        (*Exeunt* DUCHESS *and* ISABEL, L.)
Still all the love for her—the hate for me,
That could so pay the love! (*Sits. Knock* L.) Again?
        Come in.

            Enter GARDINER *and* RENARD, L.

    Gard. (C.) Pardon our urgency, your Majesty,
That breaks in on your private hour—but news
Of weighty import——
    Queen.   Good or bad, sirs, which?
    Gard. (C.) As you may use them. Good, if wisely
        handled;
Evil, if weakly. First, here's Monsieur Renard
Brings you the articles of Spain, in answer
To our conditions.
    Ren. (*crosses to* C.) Granting all you ask;
And adding—should male issue bless this wedlock,
As Heaven will surely favour it therein—
Burgundy and the fat and fair Low Countries,
As annexations to the English crown.
My master, madam, gives with a large hand.

Queen. 'Tis bravely offered! Here's good news indeed!
Gard. So is what follows—black as it may look.
The gainsayers of Spain, knowing how hot
His Majesty the Emp'ror and yourself
Are for this match, grow mad and shape their spleen
In plots and treasons 'gainst the Spanish Envoys!
Nay—if need be—to seize your Majesty
And give you to safe keeping in the Tower.
 Queen. Now, let them come! By God's grace, they shall
  find
That Henry's daughter hath a man's heart in her;
A man's hand, too, to guard her head and crown!
 Gard. That's not all.
 Ren.   Nor the worst.
 Queen.   Is there a worse
Than to lay hands upon the Lord's anointed?
 Gard. Even so; lay hands on the Lord's own ark,
His holy Church.
 Ren.   The traitors aim at that,
Striking at you; they would bring back the order
Your heretic brother Edward—Heaven forgive him!—
Made for the Church in England.
 Gard.   Would put down
The sacrifice of the mass!
 Ren.   Have priests take wives.
 Queen. Now Heaven forbid!
 Gard. }
 Ren. }   Amen!
 Queen.   Not while we live.
 Gard. While you live all is well.
 Ren.   But Tower air's mortal
To lives of Queens.
 Queen.   Are they so bold?
 Gard.   Aye, marry;
And strong as they are bold. 'Tis coward's folly
To underrate the foe: they count on England,
To rise behind them——
 Ren.   And they count with cause.
 Queen. And this you call good news?
 Gard. (C.)   What news so good,
As that the foe has drawn his battle out,
When you hold in your hand the match that blows
His hosts in air?

Queen. And that match? Do we hold it?
Gard. So Monsieur Renard, here, will show your
  Majesty.
Queen. What is't?
Ren. The lives of Courtenay and Elizabeth!
They are the poles whereon this treason turns.
Theirs are the names to conjure with—the heads
To wear the crown, when it is pluck'd from yours.
  Mary (*rising*). My sister and the man I raised from the
    dust!
Now, by God's patience, they shall rue the day
They first smiled on each other! But the proof?
You have the proof?
  Ren. That I leave to my Lord
Of Winchester. (*Crosses behind table to* R. *of* MARY.)
  Gard. (C.) 'Tis making even now.
I've laid my lyme dogs on the track of Courtenay.
  Ren. Trust my lord to find proof!
  Gard. I hold the Council's voice for the consigning
Of Courtenay and Elizabeth to safe keeping.
Here are the warrants. (*Produces them.*)
  Ren. They but wait your hand.
    [QUEEN *takes the pen, is about to sign, but pauses.*
  Mary. Think!—'tis a sister's life hangs on my pen!
  Ren. Two—*yours* first, and the Lady Elizabeth's after.
Which head would you prefer to grace the block?
  Mary. I pray you give me time!
  Ren. Each hour that goes,
And finds her free, strikes a prop from your throne.
  Mary. But let me ply her first with gentler summons.
Invite her hither. In our very palace
She cannot plot.
  Ren. (*chuckles*). Ha! ha! Your Majesty
Has yet to learn the alphabet of plotting.
Not plot in the Queen's palace! 'Tis the place
She would ask for such pastime—if I know
The lady, whose best plot is to win hearts,
As she won Courtenay's.
  Mary. Out! thou madden'st me!
  Gard. But be it as you will. Invite her hither.
  Ren. If she refuse, but not till then, the warrant.
    [*He places it before her; she signs it.*

Gard. Now this—the Council's warrant to arrest
The Earl of Devonshire.   (*Produces it: she takes it.*)
  Mary (*eagerly*).   Aye, give me that! (*Grasping at it.*)
(*Pauses.*) It is his death, perhaps.   (*Pushes it from her.*)
                    I cannot sign.
  Ren. The crown he spurned when your hand reached it
    him,
He risks his *head* to win for Boleyn's bastard!
  Mary. The ingrate! He shall learn in Little Ease,
If we can make, we can unmake again.   (*Signs.*)
Prove but his treason, he shall die the death.
Oh! I am sick at heart. Call in my women.
                (GARDINER *signals off*, L.)
      [*Enter two* LADIES. MARY *crosses to them.*
Be gentle with him, Gardiner. Now, good Clarence!
Attend me, Renard; I would talk with thee
About my Philip.
  Ren.   A most proper man!
And bears a heart, your Majesty, none knows
How kind and fond! He wears it not, 'tis true,
Upon his sleeve. 'But she that finds it finds
A miracle.
  Mary. Thy words are balm, good Renard.
    [*Exeunt* MARY, *leaning on her women, and* RENARD,
      after exchanging a look of significance with GARDINER.
  Gard. We hold their heads. For this high-stomached
    boy,
Too stiff, forsooth, to bend to a priest's purpose,
I'll show him priests break those who will not bend.
For Lady Elizabeth—Renard counsels well—
Her fair head must come down, for all its craft.
I'll compass it's conveyance to Tower Green;
Anne Boleyn's block will fit Anne Boleyn's daughter.
                           [*Exit* L.
*Furniture cleared by two Yeomen of the Guard. Lights
        lowered. Change.*

SCENE II.

A Hall in the LADY ELIZABETH'S *Manor House of Ashridge
  Style of the* 16*th Century. Large folding doors, backed by
  staircase,* L. F. *Large* C. *opening in* R. F., *backed by illu-*

minated window of stained glass. *Large Fireplace* R.,
with logs burning. *Large window from* 4th *to* 2nd E. L.,
with boughs of trees covered with snow pressing against it.
Door 2nd E. L. *Secret panel* 4th E. L. *above window.*
Several large portraits of the period about the walls. A
Venus by Titian over recess, R. *Table, with candelabra,
book, etc., on it. Small table by door,* L., *with lute, embroidering frame, etc.* Wind howling.

Enter SIR J. HARRINGTON, *with a lantern, showing in* COUR-
TENAY *from* D. L., *booted, cloaked, and splashed.*

Harr. (*lighting candles from lantern*). Get to the fire, my
    lord, and thaw your boots,
While I find lights. Burr! (*Shivering.*) I am an icicle.
It is a cruel night.
    Court. (*at fire*). The very weather
For those who'd not be followed—yet methinks
I heard horse-hoofs behind us, from Hemel Hempstead.
    Harr. So did I; but I trow we gave them slip
At Gadsden Moor. Lord help the unhappy horseman
Dares to ride that sweet spot on a winter night,
Unless he knows the country like his hand!
We're housed—and so's our follower, I warrant me,
A'bottom of Gadsden ditch. There *requiescat
In pace!* (*Takes off cloak.*)
    Court. (R., *looking about*). And 'tis here she takes her
    pastime.
There are her books (*crosses to* L. *table*), her lute, her 'broidery
    frame—
A fair cage for my bird—and *yet* a cage.
I come to set thee free! Now, Harrington,
Show me where she is wont to sit. How uses she
The time?
    Harr. (*by fire*). Why, marry, at meal times she eats—
A good rule, and to be followed by her servants:
I'm hungry as a hawk—your lordship *should* be.
Remember, we are here hedged round with spies.
I've risked my life to bring you to the house.
If you're o'erseen 'twere pity of us both.
    Court. Where am I to bestow myself?
    Harr. (*lifts arras,* L.)   In here—
A secret cabinet—entered through this panel—
Unknown to all the household, save the cofferer
And me.

Court. (c.) But will the Lady Elizabeth
Certain come hither?
    Harr.   Past a doubt. 'Tis here
She holds her lonely vigils with her books.
But in; and if she storms, as sure she will—
And she storms royally, for all her sweetness—
To find your lordship here, I trust your honour
To keep my name close.
    Court.   By my faith I will.
But let me linger o'er these traces of her. (*At table, L..*)
    Harr. Footsteps! This way! now in, i' the fiend's
        name!   [*Puts him through panel,* L. U.

Enter ISABEL MARKHAM *from* D. L., *in riding skirt, splashed,
and masked.*

Just saved it! Who's this? As I live a woman!
        (*She takes off hat and mask.*)
Isabel Markham, muddy to the waist!
On such a night!
    Isab. (*by table,* R. C.) Good Sir John, keep thy wonder,
And help me with my skirt. There; now to thaw me
My hands and feet and tongue! (*Gets to fire.*)
    Harr.(L. C.)   Let that stay frozen.
'Tis an unruly member, and needs bonds.
But say what madcap wind has blown you hither?
    Isabel (*with mock tenderness*). Think you that I could
        long endure St. James's,
With thee at Ashridge? (*Gives him her hand.*) I must
        have my block,
To keep my hand in. But, in sober sooth,
I came to attend my lady—as a friend,
Being freed from turn of service as a spy.
My aunt had stayed me, so I asked no leave;
But took a horse and a knave who does my bidding.
    Harr. I know—e'en like a dog—and for dog's thanks.
                            (*Wind.*)
    Isab.   Nay,—
I'm very kind to *him;* and so rode hither.
His beast gave in wrong side of Hemel Hempstead,
And I was left on the moor, bogged and belated,
When you rode by, and for once served some purpose
As a guide-post. I made bold to ride behind you,
And here I am! And now, where's my lady?

But where's my supper, first?
Harr. Mine is prepared.
Suppose *you* eat it, and let we wait on you?
Isab. Agreed!
Harr. And all the wages I will ask
Will be a smile, 'twixt two sips of canary,
A kind word, 'twixt two bites of venison pasty,
And I'll sup upon *them*.
Isab. Faith, I've a mind
To take thee at thy word—But not for kindness,
Only for joy of eating up thy supper.

Enter PARRY *from* R. F.

Parry (R). Harrington come back! And who have we here?
How! Mistress Isabel Markham!
Isab. (C.) Come for service
Of my lady, when I've shifted me and supp'd.
(*Parry goes up* R. *and claps his hands.*)
Parry. My lady's women shall show you to a chamber.
(*Enter a* WOMAN, R. F.)
My lady will be marvellously glad to see you.
Isab. Hush! not a word to her that I am here.
I love surprises.
Harr. Do you? I'll tell you one.
Smile upon *me*, and give me one good word.
Isab. There's the smile—and good bye. That's two good words— (*Exit.* ISABEL, R. F.)
Parry. A wild wench, but a faithful.
Harr. A curst tongue
In the sweetest pair of lips—well, let them scold,
Till they learn kissing—so she lets me teach her.
Parry. None knows of thy return?
Harr. (L. C.) No; I came in
By the sallyport, and up the turnpike stair.
I care not that the gossips in the lodge (*Wind.*)
And buttery hatch and hall should note my goings
And comings on my lady's errands. Burr! (*Shivers.*)
Beshrew my lady, that sends men to ride for her
In weather that would freeze a Muscovite
Inside his furs! (*Shivers.*)
Parry. There's ill report of thee.
Harr. Of me?

Parry. 'Tis told me
Thou dost receive strange messengers—hast been seen
At the Bell in Hemel Hampstead, with a gentleman
Booted and belted, splashed with signs of travel.
  Harr. (*laughs*). Squire King of Wormenhall, to whom I
    promised
A greyhound pup! Lord, Lord, how folks will talk!
They'd make a plotter of poor Jasper King.
  Parry. Needs must her Highness's household should be
    careful
To give no hold to ill tongues these ill times.
England's a hive of plots.
  Harr.   The Queen-bee here!
England will none of these saucy Jack Spaniards;
All hopes and loves are centred in our lady.——
Needs but a stout stroke, Master Cofferer.
  Parry. Hush, man! Who knows but we have listening
    ears
Ev'n here? (*Going to arras over secret door.*)
  Harr. (*to prevent him gives a loud exclamation*). Oh, Lord!
  Parry. What is't?
  Harr.   I could have sworn
I saw a face looking in at the window.
  Parry (*goes to window and looks out*). Now—as I live—
    I see the glint of steel
Out in the pleasance! Look—more to the right.
  Harr. Horsemen—four—five—a troop in jack and
    morion!
What should this mean?
  Parry. Go, learn their errand—quick!
    (*As* HARRINGTON *goes off* L. PARRY *looks off* R. F.)
The Lady Elizabeth—paler, wearier,
And weaklier—day by day! it grieves my heart.

Enter ELIZABETH, C. R. *She is dressed more plainly than in the 1st Act, and looks pale and suffering.* PARRY *sets her chair by table,* R. C., *and supports her to it.*

  Eliza. Good even to my worthy Cofferer!
'Tis a wild night without. Ah, happy we,
With warmth and books and peace indoors! (*Sits, and
    leans her head on her hand.*)
  Parry.   Peace, madam?
They leave us little here, with their controllers,

Their yeomen, women, varlets from the Court—
An idle pack of spies. They'd prove you traitress
Out of your innocence.
    Eliza.   Let them do their worst.
I have a witness here (*puts her hand on her heart*) that bears me up
'Gainst their false speaking.
    Parry.   Nay, your heart is bold,
I know; but bodies will not answer hearts.
Look how you pine, lose spirits, appetite,
How your fresh cheek turns white and thin.
    Eliza.   Peace prithee.
At Court 'twas ill will plagued me—here, 'tis kindness.
Methinks the ill will is the best to bear. (PARRY *retires a little.*)

    Enter HARRINGTON, L. F.

    Harr. A messenger from the Court, strangely attended.
He brings this letter from her Majesty.
    Eliza. Is't the first letter that the Queen hath writ me?
Give it me—hare-heart. (*Holds her hand for letter. He gives it.*)
    Harr.   For the letter, madam,
It may be harmless, but I like not him
That brought it.
    Eliza.   Who?
    Harr.   Sir John Brydges, the Lieutenant
Of the Tower, with an armed troop.
    Eliza.   'Tis too much grace.
Read, Parry.
    Parry. (*Reads* C.)

'*Faithful and well-beloved,*—*These are to bid you that on receipt hereof, and all delay intermitted, you do repair to us at our Palace at St. James's. The bearer hath order ta'en for your journey; and, for your more commodity, we send our royal litter, to bring you hither by easy stages. Praying that God and the Saints may have you in their holy keeping, we rest your loving sister to command.*—MARY.'

    Eliza. 'Loving' and 'to command'—a gracious letter?

    Re-enter HARRINGTON, L. F.

    Harr. Sir John Brydges, madam, presses for admittance.
    Eliza. Let him in. (HARRINGTON *exit,* L. F.)
    Parry.   Nay, your Highness, go not with him!
There's some foul treachery hidden in this summons.

Eliza. I will be counselled by the occasion, Parry.

Parry. We've forty stalwart yeomen, in the house
And round about, who'd overbear his guard,
If need be.

Eliza. Lift hands on the Queen's livery!
'Tis treason, man, and he is my worst foe
That counsels it.

Harr. (*opening* C. D.) Sir John Brydges, please your
Highness. (*Exit*, L. F.)

Enter SIR JOHN BRYDGES (*in half-armour*).

Eliza. (*sitting*). 'Tis you, Sir John, who have brought
through this ill weather
This gracious message from our loving sister?

Brydges (C., *roughly*). Even so, madam, and in answer
to it
My order is to bring your Highness straight.

Eliza. My sister's love is pressing, and I thank her;
But I am ill at ease. A wasting sickness
Has been on me for weeks. I may not travel.
When I am well I will make no delay.

Brydges. The Queen looks you should start this very
night.

Eliza. So late, and in such bitter winter! Nay,
She hardly had meant *that*. It may not be.

[COURTENAY *is seen to draw the arras apart and listen.*]

Brydges. Yet so it is, your Highness, and so must be.
You would do well to set to preparation.

Eliza. Have you commission, sir, to counsel me?

Brydges. No; and yet, faith, good counsel should have
welcome.
Make no excuse, but *come*. That is good counsel.

Eliza. (*looks fiercely at him, as if amazed at his audacity,
but restrains herself to reply calmly*). My love and duty to her
Majesty.
I will come to her so soon as kind nature
Gives me the strength to come. You are free to go.

Brydges. 'Tis ill advised.

Eliza. (*with a queenly air of command*).
I said you were free to go.

Brydges. And I said what you said was ill advised.
So stout! Then be what comes on your own head.
(*Exit* SIR J. BRYDGES, D. L. F.)

Parry. Must you bear this?
Eliza. I have borne worse, good Cofferer.
He said, 'What comes must be on my own head.'
What meant he 'was to come?'
Parry.   No good, I'll swear.
Yet he dare scarce use force. I'll see our yeomen
Bestowed where they can meet it, if he try.   (*Exit*, L. F.)
Eliza. Heaven shield my heart, that has no guard on
    earth
But mine own innocency!
(COURTENAY *during last line has come from his hiding-place,
            turning bolt on* D. L. F.)
Court. (*kneeling at her feet*). And my sword!
Eliza. (*starting up*). Help, ho!
Treason! Who's there?
Court.   Hush! 'Tis I.
Eliza.   Courtenay!
Here! unbid, unpermitted, unannounced!
In my house!—nay, in mine own private chamber,
Like a night robber! Now, as I live by bread,
They shall abye it gave you entrance here,
And you that dared it.
Court.   Hear me first—then kill me.
Eliza. Kill thee!
Court.   It needs no sword. Let but thine eyes
Look on me thus—thy voice speak thus to me—
And Edward Courtenay's dead—his heart's life slain
By thy displeasure.
Eliza. (*with surprise*). He gives me 'thee' and 'thou.'
Court. Pardon! but when could tongue of ceremony
Speak the full heart of love?
Eliza.   Of love? Bethink you!
                        (*With dignity and pain.*)
I am alone, defenceless, a weak woman,
Set round with close espial; with no friends
To counsel or uphold me—my good name
My only jewel; and you set that name
For shot of evil tongues when you steal thus
Upon my privacy—the place and hour
So well contrived to blast my maiden honour
As my worst foe had not devised them better.
And then you talk of love! For shame—for shame!
It is unknightly done, Sir Edward Courtenay.

Court. Nay, I'll grant all but that. 'Tis rash, ill-counselled,
Cruel—crazed, if you will—but not unknightly.
When I took stroke of sword, 'twas under vow
To draw sword for the weak and the oppressed,
Woman and orphan. Lo, I draw for them!
(*Draws his sword.*)

'Twas under vow to hold my lady's love
Above all heed of case, or wealth, or life—
'Tis for my lady's love I put to hazard
All these, and on that hazard I am here.

Eliza. None come for noble purposes that come
Thus stealthily.

Court. When foxes ape the lion,
Lions may borrow cunning of the fox.
They *must* plot who would 'counter priests and Spaniards.
Oh! think not I am here for toys of love—
Though being here, blessed in thy gracious presence,
Love would not be withheld, but he must speak,
As pilgrims pass no shrine, but they will kneel
And breathe a prayer;—but my prayer has been breathed.
Pardon! the pilgrim will not sin again
By such ill-timed devotion.

Eliza. It is well. (*Sits.*)
How and why are you here?

Court. 'How' matters little,
So I know your ill wishers are not part
Or privy to my coming. For the 'why,'
Grant me your wariest wit and wisest brain
While I unfold what, in this house withdrawn,
Surrounded by your sister's spies, may be
Strange tidings to you. England is on fire
With hate of Spain and fear of Rome, sworn foes
Of free thought, free speech, and free Parliaments.
The Queen, all say, hath set her heart on Philip.
His envoys wait at Calais. In this pass,
The best and bravest blood of England's sworn
To bar the rule of Spaniard and of priest,
And England's brain and sinew asks no better
Than to march at the heels of such a leading.
Wyatt in Kent, Carew in Devonshire;
Croft on the Severn side, his Grace of Suffolk,
Northampton, and the Greys in middle England,

Draw towards London, that but waits for them.
Here are the names and forces each can warrant.
                              (*Producing a paper.*)
These gentlemen, knowing the strength that lies
In Right and the Blood Royal—knowing, too,
That England's lives and liberties were safe
In your good keeping, look but to *your* name,
So sweet and gracious in the common mouth,
As Queen and Head; and have commissioned me
To lay their lives and homage at your feet,
And in your name to raise St. George's banner
For England, England's Queen, and England's Law.
Let them not sue in vain; let me be first
To hail as Queen of England her that needs
No crown to be *my* Queen.   (*Kneels.*)
     Eliza. (*gravely and calmly*). Enough, my lord.
Here's weighty matter, truly. It is well
None saw you enter here. Give me those papers.
                              (COURT. *gives them.*)
Now, Edward Courtenay, I hold in my hand
Written proof of *your* treason. What's to say,
Why I should not summon my household straight,
And give you, on this proof, into safe charge
To meet a traitor's doom? Said I not well?
'He comes not for good ends that comes by stealth.'
You speak of love, yet do the work of hate;
You speak of loyalty, yet make yourself
The very tongue and hand and sword of treason—
Treason, that, black in all, is tenfold black
In you, whose blood comes from a line of kings—
In *you*, on whom the Queen you would unseat
Has heaped all favours! and that Queen my sister.
Oh! Edward Courtenay, see what you have done!
I would have sworn my life upon your faith.
I should have been forsworn.
     Court. (*kneels*).   Nay, take my sword
And thrust it through my heart—it would wound less
Than do your words.
     Eliza. (*rises*).   I think you had forgot
Whose blood runs in my veins—that I stand next
For England's crown—bidding me sign a paper
That lets loose English hands at English throats.
What were the short, sharp plague of priest or Spaniard

To civil strife? With Englishmen at *one*,
What can Queen do, or Spaniard, or priest,
'Gainst England's deep-based life? 'Twill outlive *them*;
And all their short-breathed tyranny can compass.
It is the house divided 'gainst itself
That saps its own foundations. The escape
From slavery lay never yet through treason,
Nor is it a light matter broaching treason
To a King's daughter, sister of a Queen.
                    (*Takes stage*, R.; *then goes up to fire.*)
  Court. My life and liberty are yours. I prized them
But as they might be used for you. You spurn them.
Then call your household—give me up for traitor.
You have the proof.
  Eliza. (*putting the papers in the fire*). Not so! there is *no* proof,
And Edward Courtenay from a fever-fit
Has waked and is himself. (*Comes to him*, C.) Oh! pardon me
My harsh reproof e'en now! I know—none better—
How hard this life's to bear: the more the courage
In bearing. My heart bleeds for my poor England!—
Would do her right—will do, if e'er I reign.
But, press that right upon me with the sword,
And, by Heaven, I would answer it with the axe!
                    (*Crosses to* L.)
  Court. (R. C.) Oh, noble lady! gracious mistress!—love
More loved than ever, now thou art my saint,—
I will learn patience of thee. Only grant me
To guard thy life. If they dare strike at that,
Treason or none, my sword must be betwixt thee
And danger.
  Eliza. (R. C.) Hark! I hear a hurried step (*Crosses to* R.)
Without! If you are seen?
  Court. (L. C.)   The bolt is drawn.
  Eliza. You dared do this! Oh, Courtenay, enemies
Ne'er drove me to drawn bolts: 'twas left for thee.
  Court. Forgive me!   (*Goes to door and unbolts it.*)
And let my life atone for it.   (*Exit through panel.*)
            Enter PARRY, D. L. F.

  Eliza. Now, what's to do?
  Parry.   Your Highness, Sir John Brydges
Is back i' the court, and with him from the Council

Lords Sussex, Howard, with Sir Edward Hastings,
Sir Thomas Cornwallis, and others.   They demand,
Rather than ask for, audience.
    Eliza.   From the Council!
'Tis weighty then.   Say they have leave to enter.
    [SUSSEX, HOWARD, *and three Lords, booted, cloaked, and
       splashed, enter,* D. L. F.   *They pass to* R. *corner, saluting*
       PRINCESS.   SIR J. BRYDGES *stands at door.*
How now, my lords?   You have not stayed for leave?
                                        (*Crosses to table*, R. C.)
    Sussex.   Forgive our haste.
    Eliza.   'Tis a cold night without,
I'll think you pressed to the fire.   My good Lord Sussex,
Lord William Howard, kind lords all, you are welcome,
Though it is late, and my distemperature
Must make me a poor hostess.
    Sussex.   Trust me, madam,
I had ridden twice as far in as bitter weather
To undo what we, perforce, are here to do.
    Eliza.   What is your errand?
    Sussex.   We are unwilling bearers
Of this.   (*Gives warrant.*)
    Eliza.   The Council's warrant for my arrest
And safe conveyance to the Tower, subscribed
By the Queen—strange!—even dated with this letter
Of gracious invitation.   (*Gives it to* SUSSEX.)
    Brydges (C., *at back*).   There, I told you
You'd better come for the asking.
    Sussex.   Peace, Sir John.
It wrings my heart, but so it is, your Highness.
Our order is, failing a willing journey,
To bring you against your will.
    Howard.   Beshrew the duty,
And those that laid it upon us!
    Eliza.   My lords,
You see me now—you saw me a month ago.
Your eyes will tell you, better than my tongue,
I speak plain truth telling you I am sick,
Unfit to face the winter and the night
And country ways.   Her gracious Majesty
May think me worthy of the Tower, but scarce
Would have me done to death by travelling thither.
I cannot go, so needs not say I will not.

Brydges. You hear, my lords. Warrants are not to play with.

Sussex. Nor your tongue to be wagged before your betters.

[SIR J. HARRINGTON, *with three or four of* ELIZABETH'S *retainers, armed variously, appear in recess of* R. F. BRYDGES *goes to* D. L. F., *beckons on a man and sends him off.*

Howard. Your Highness knows our love tenders you dearly.

Sussex. I'd sooner cut both hands off than lay finger
In force upon you.

Brydges (L.). Tush, my lords, we trifle.
Look where the corridor is filling fast
With her armed yeomen! We shall have hard knocks
For all this dilly-dallying. I'll take on me,
What you lords are too courtly for.
[*Advances to lay hands on* ELIZABETH. *She moves a little towards* R., *leaving* C. *open.*

Eliza. Back, traitor!
[COURTENAY *rushes out from his hiding-place and throws himself between the* PRINCESS *and* SIR J. BRYDGES.

Court. (C.) Or meet thy death on my sword's point.

Sussex. (R.) Who's this?
My Lord of Devonshire!

Brydges (*exultingly recognising him*). Ha! the White Rose!
Two birds killed with one stone! Ho, my stout fellows!
[*Men of the Tower Guard enter hastily from* D. L. F. *in double file, and stand* L.

(*To Guards.*) On your allegiance, seize Sir Edward Courtenay.
Seize him, I say, dead or alive!
(*By this time the recess in* R. F. *is filled with* ELIZABETH'S *retainers, headed by* SIR J. HARRINGTON *and* PARRY. *The Tower Guard take one step forward to seize* COURTENAY, *who retreats,* C.)

Court. Let him
That holds his own life light lift hand on mine.
Look, madam, your retainers! Force for force.
(*Rushes down to* R. *corner.*)

Harr. (*loudly, drawing and waving his sword*). Strike for the Lady Elizabeth!

[ELIZABETH'S *retainers advance. The Guards face round to meet them, and at the word of command from* BRYDGES *level their musquetoons.*

Brydges (L. *corner*). Level your musquetoons!

Eliza. (*rushes between, with a gesture of command*). Hold!
(*Pause.*)
Let drop your weapons
On either part.   (BRYDGES *signals Guard to recover.*)
How now?   For shame, my masters.
Bare blades and levelled guns before a woman!
My lords, Sir Edward Courtenay's intervention
Amazes me, as it amazes you.
How he found entry here I know no more
Than do yourselves. (*To* COURT.) Render your weapon,
   sir—
I need it not!   (COURTENAY *gives his sword to* SUSSEX.)
As for the Council's warrant,
I charge my Lord of Devonshire to obey it,
As I do. Look, my lords, I put myself
Upon your manhood to use needful kindness
To a sick woman.   I will ride with you.
(*Murmurs and movement among retainers.*)
(*To* LORDS OF COUNCIL.) Do you remember, lords, how six
   months since,
To help my sister to her throne, I raised
Two thousand horse, and rode with them by her side
Through Aldgate to the Tower? I tell you, sirs,
My heart will be more steadfast now than then,
Ent'ring the Tower. I feared *then* for a sister.
For myself, witness Heaven, I fear not now!

END OF ACT II.

ACT III.

April, 1554.

SCENE I.

Council Chamber at Whitehall. Murmurs heard, 1 E. R.
Enter GARDINER, SUSSEX, PAGET, *and* HOWARD.

Gard. (L.) A stormy Council! thanks to my Lord of
   Sussex.

Sussex. (L. C.) I did but speak my mind. 'Tis unsafe touching
A head so loved and guarded—unsafe keeping
Her Highness in the Tower, with nought made known
Against her to the people.
    Gard.   You are hasty;
We wait for perfect proof.
    Paget.   Folks have small faith
In proof that's waited for so long.
    Howard.   Her Majesty
Should know the truth—that England's hopes and thoughts
Are drawn more to the Tower than to Whitehall.
    Gard. 'Tis boldly said, Lord Howard. If 'tis truth,
Who is to blame for it so much as you?
    How.   As I?
    Gard. Aye, *you* that so drew out your journey,
Bringing the Lady Elizabeth to the Tower,
That her four days from Ashridge rather seemed
The progress of a Queen than of a prisoner.
    Sussex. Hush! lords—the Spanish envoy.

        Enter RENARD, L. 1 E.

    Ren.   Save your Lordships!
I come for the Council's answer to my master.
Is justice to be done upon the traitors
Who plot 'gainst the Queen's life and his?
    Gard.   You have told him
The warrant's signed for Wyatt's execution—
How my Lord Suffolk, Cobham, Crofts, and Arnold,
The Lords Grey, William Thomas, and other leaders,
Ere this, have paid their treason with their heads.
    Ren. Yes, and have made the most of the five score
Strung up in London, twenty-two in Kent;
More in the West and Midlands; counted up
The gibbets in Paul's Yard, on London Bridge,
Fleet Street, and Charing Cross—down to the four
Each with its rebel at St. James's Gate.
My gracious master's curious in such matters.
    Gard. Say hundreds more shall hang on proof of guilt.
    Ren. (L.) His answer is, what boot these carrion lives,
While the rebellion's root and soul and spring
Lives in the Lady Elizabeth and Courtenay?
He waits till justice has been done on *them*.
    Sussex. The King of Spain forgets what he calls *justice*

Is hampered here with that which *we* call *law*.
England is not so blest, sir, as your Spain,
Where kings may doom unquestioned. We have here
'Twixt head and block a world of tedious toys—
Court, judges, witnesses, trial and sentence.
  Paget (R. C.). These lacking, as they lack, to prove her
   Highness
Or Courtenay act or part in Wyatt's treason,
Her Majesty cannot procure your King
The marriage gift he asks, of their two heads.
  Gard. The proof that my Lord Paget so insists on
I hope her Majesty shall have to-day.
I have buoyed Wyatt up with hopes of pardon
If he'll confess all that he *could* confess
Against the Lady Elizabeth and Courtenay:
And have devised that on his way to the block
He shall be brought with Courtenay face to face,
Trusting, if he impeach him, that his journey
To death ends even there. The hope of life
May do what reverence for truth would not—
Induce him to speak out.
  Paget.   As I'm plain layman,
I marvel at my Lord of Winchester's courage,
That he can say such things, yet never blench
Nor blush.
  Gard. Why should I? Proof is proof, my lord,
However come by. 'Tis well to turn treason
On traitors!
  Ren. 'Tis most even-handed justice.
  Gard. And if that means fail, I've another yet;—
        (*Lords advance.*)
But which I take leave to keep to myself.
Your lordships are so keen at finding reasons
Why Justice should be lamed, when she'd lift up
Her sword against *these* lives, I'll bring the proof,
And then instruct you how I came by it.
The Queen will grant you audience, Master Renard.
    (*Exeunt* GARDINER *and* RENARD, R. I E.)
  Sussex (*to* HOWARD *and* PAGET). Will Wyatt keep touch?
  How. (R.) He is true as steel.
He will not speak; or what he speaks is true.
  Paget. (C.) H'm! I scarce know. The shadow of the
   scaffold
Is a rare man-queller. I've known it break

Many a soldier's courage, who had looked
Death in the face on twenty fields, nor winked.

 Sussex. This further proof of Gardiner's—it implies
Some devilish malice. Were it not well, my lords,
Some of us that are friends to Lady Elizabeth
Should be about the Tower to cross, if need be,
This subtle priest's foul play?

 Paget (*crosses to* L.)   'Tis well advised.
Have with you. Ho, there!—my barge to Tower Stairs!
       (*Exeunt*, L. 1 E.)

Enter QUEEN, RENARD, GARDINER, *and two Ladies*, R. 1 E.

 Mary. You have our whole thought. Heaven knows,
  my good Renard,
We long sore for the coming of your lord,
Our loving husband Philip; but herein
We are an English, not a Spanish sovereign.
What we do we must answer to the law,
So must deal by the law. Let our Lord Chancellor
Bring us proof, and although all England stood
Betwixt them and the scaffold—though our heart
Bled to undo a sister (*her voice trembles*), and a man
Whom we have favoured—both their heads shall fall.
And now to mass! Our duty done to Heaven,
Bring me your proofs, my Lord of Winchester!
     (*Exeunt* QUEEN *and Ladies*, L. 1 E.)

 Gard. (L. C.) So be it, then! A good day's work, good
  Renard!
Her Majesty's in most blessed dispositions!

 Ren. (R. C.) And Lady Elizabeth and her White Rose,
I think, a good lift nearer to the block.

 Gard. 'Tis pity of *his* life. There is no danger
In him apart from her.

 Ren.   While either lives,
England is no safe harbour for my master.
A bargain, my Lord Bishop—give us up
The heads of Lady Elizabeth and Courtenay,
And Philip shall give *you*, what, until now,
By my advice, he has refused—his aid
To plant the Holy Office of the Inquisition
Here, in your England, for the purging out
Of heresy, and more rooting of the faith.

 Gard. Your hand on *that!* With the same zeal, good
  Renard,

You serve your sovereign, I serve mine.

Ren. The Queen?

Gard. (*contemptuously*). The Queen! The power rules kings and queens—the Church!

(*Exeunt,* L.)

SCENE II.

Lieutenant's Garden in the Tower. A strong wall about 7 ft. high runs across the stage at fifth grooves, with heavy gate; C. *view of the White Tower on back cloth. The Garden House occupies the* 3 E. L. *Below this in* 2 E. L. *is a door, with grating in it. Lieutenant's house,* 3 E. R. *A corresponding door, with grating.* R. 2 E. *Large tree, with stone seat beneath it,* L. C. 4 E. *Trees and shrubs formally planted, but the general aspect of the garden sombre. No bright flowers. Large lock and bolts to postern gate,* C. *Two Warders are discovered talking together at postern. A group of three female citizens, one male, and two children,* R. 3 E. *Another group,* C., *of two females and two males and one child. As the scene opens two or three male and female citizens enter from* L. 1 E. *One joins the* R. *group, the others go off at the postern and* R. *Three men enter from* L. 1 E. *and go off at the postern; then man and girl from* L. 1 E., *and joins* L. *group. Three of the* R. *group, with child, go off. As the first people enter,* SIR JOHN HARRINGTON *and* RUTTER, *a Warder, enter from house,* R.

Harr. (L. C.) Constable me no Constables! They may put me
In Little Ease, an' they will, with the rats and toads.
There is worse company than toads and rats
In the Tower, saving your presence, Master Rutter;
But the Lady Elizabeth's men shall do their office
About the lady.

Rutt. 'Tis the Constable's right,
To have *his* men about prisoners of worship.

Harr. Aye, he's allowed his twenty shillings a week
For her Highness's gentlemen like *me*, so gets him
Poor rogues like you at ten, and pockets me
The difference. I know your jade's tricks! I was here
With the old Duke of Norfolk.

(*First portion of* R. *group go off,* C. R.)

Rutt. Tell me not.
Sir John must have men about her he can trust.

Harr. And *she* must have men about her *she* can trust.
Why, there's her meat—who knows how shrewdly spiced

It might be, an' we let cooks' hands of his
Pepper her pottage?   (L. *group go off.*)
(*Significantly*) I have heard of folks
Who sickened of Tower cooking.   Tell your master
The Lady Elizabeth had leave to bring her men.
The Lady Elizabeth means to keep her men ;
And the Lady Elizabeth's men are like the bears
Over in Paris Garden—he who'd move them,
Must lug them by the ears, and 'ware their claws.
    Rutt. Here's pretty order !   A Tower warder rated
Inside the Tower by a prisoner's serving-man !
    Harr. Serving-man !   Scurvy knave !—an' 'twere not
        hacking
One's hand off to draw here, I'd beat the word
Down thy knave's throat !   (*Bell.*)
    Rutt.   Have you no decency
To brawl and bluster here—and Wyatt coming
On his way to the block ?   If you've no manners in you,
To enjoy the sight yourself, needs not you spoil it
For decent people.
    Harr.   Wyatt coming hither !
How comes that ?   The Lieutenant's garden lies not
On his way to the scaffold ?
(*By this time the stage is entirely clear of citizens.   One man,
a boy, and three men back on from* R. C., *and take position
in front of house,* L.)
    Rutt.   He's brought round
By the Byward Tower and Postern to Tower Hill,
That he may be confronted here with Courtenay.
He's lodged in the Garden House (*pointing to it,* L.).
(*Three men and two women enter from postern, and get to* L.)
                                   We've been so full
Since mad Sir Thomas raised the men of Kent,
We had to stow our company where we could.
Courtenay's lodged here, where none have been bestowed
Since Cranmer went to Oxford.
    [*A stir among the crowd—some looking off and indicating
        by murmurs and signs the approach of the procession.*
                      Look, they're coming.
I must bring Courtenay forth.   Stand by there, knaves.
    [*Thrusts his way rudely through a group which has gathered
        in front of the Garden House.   Exit into house.*
    Harr. Now !   Pray Heaven Wyatt hold—a word kills
        Courtenay !   (*Shrugs his shoulders.*)

May my life ne'er hang on my best friend's truth,
When he can save *his* head by dooming mine.
        [*Bolts heard,* L.
  Re-enter RUTTER, *with* COURTENAY, L.
 Court. (L. C.) Nay, tell me, good friend, whither you would
  lead me,
And to what end?
    (*Crowd of citizens appear at postern.*)
 Rutt. You will know soon enough.
(HARRINGTON *exchanges a sign of recognition with* COURTE-
 NAY. *In answer to a look and gesture of* COURTENAY *asking where the* PRINCESS ELIZABETH *is,* HARRINGTON
 *answers by pointing to the Lieutenant's house, as if to indicate
 she is there. As he passes across near where* COURTENAY
 stands, he speaks to RUTTER, *so that* COURTENAY *may
 overhear.*)
 Harr. (R.) Look how the knaves crowd—bid the Yeomen
  clear
A path, or Wyatt will ne'er reach the scaffold.
 Court. (L.) Wyatt! I see now! This is Gardiner's
  malice.
 1st *Warder* (*pushing crowd back*). Stand back!
 2nd *Warder.* Uncover!
 3rd *Warder.* Room for the Lieutenant! (*Muffled drums.*)

[*Enter* C. R. *Lords of the Council,* SUSSEX, PAGET, HOWARD,
 &c., and go down R. *corner,* LORD MAYOR, *two Sheriffs,
 two Aldermen,* SIR JOHN BRYDGES, *and two Tower Guard.
 All go down to* R. *corner. Ten Yeomen of the Guard walk
 in oblique line, as if going off* L. 1 E. *Executioner masked
 and bearing axe.* SIR THOMAS WYATT *and Priest, with
 crucifix, and guard at each side. Ten Yeomen of the
 Guard follow. When* SIR THOMAS WYATT *is fairly in
 the* C. *the drums stop and procession also. Enter* GAR-
 DINER *and* RENARD *at back,* R.

 Brydges. Sir Thomas Wyatt, her Majesty in Council,
As knowing dying lips speak truth, has ordered
That on your way to death you be confronted
With one who, you admitted to the Council,
Was privy to your plot—Here stand you, Wyatt;
There stands Sir Edward Courtenay; therefore speak,
As one past fear or favour, what you know
Touching his part in your conspiracy.
 Wyatt. Tell my good Lord of Winchester I had

His message and understand it; but that Wyatt
Would sooner die i' the truth, than live by a lie.
Touching this lord, here on the edge of life,
When words should weigh, I take all here to witness
I charge no guilt upon him. All that man
Could do to bar our rising that did he,
Nothing to favour it. And neither he
Nor the Lady Elizabeth—Heaven bless her grace!—
        (*Crowd cheer.*)
Deserve a lodging in the Tower for aught
That Wyatt had to do with them, or knows.
        (*Loud cheering from crowd.*)
  Court. (L.) Thanks, noble Wyatt! I had judged thee better
Than our base enemies. What should they know
Of hearts e'en fear of death cannot turn coward?
  Brydges. You spake not thus before the Council, Wyatt.
  Wyatt. What I said there, I said; what I say now
Is true.
  Harr. God bless thee for't.
  Wyatt.   Amen, good friend!
The more honest men's blessings I take with me,
The lighter I shall come to my inn to-night.
Now, Sir John, we but keep my friend here waiting.
        (*Pointing to Executioner. Bell and drums.*)
His axe is heavy. Set on.
  (SIR JOHN BRYDGES *crosses, with his Guard, to head the procession.*)
                Give my greeting
To the Lady Elizabeth, and say Wyatt bade
A blessing on her, and prayed her to forgive
Her enemies, as he forgave all his.
Now, sir! (*To Executioner.*) Now, masters! (*To Guard.*)
Forward to Tower Hill!
  [*Muffled drums. Procession moves off in same order,* 1 E. L., *Citizens following last. Some few Citizens go off at postern. While the procession moves off,* CICELY, RUTTER'S *daughter, is seen to hide behind tree. Warder goes into house,* R. *The other Warder goes off at postern—shutting and bolting it.* GARDINER *and* RENARD *exeunt,* U. E. R.
  Court. A noble heart! Has England all so many
She can thus lightly fling them under foot?
May I bear me as like a gallant soldier,

When I must go the road he travels now.
    Rutt. Now, my lord, to your lodging.
    Court.   Nay, good Rutter,
Leave me an hour to breathe so much spring air,
Glad eyes with so much green as April brooks
Poor prisoners in the Tower.
    Rutt.   My lord, 'twere more
Than I dare do.
    Court. (L. C.) But tell me—nay, I know
Thou'rt a kind heart—Why, man, we are old friends.
    Rutt. (R. C.) That we are. Marry, I have known your
        lordship
From a slip so high—let's see—fourteen years—
Nay, by the mass, fifteen—you played about
Here and the Belfry Tower, with my wench Cicely.
You'll have forgotten Cicely?
    Court.   I forgotten!
'Tis you forget that scarce nine months have gone
Since we called sweethearts. Faith 'twas well I left you,
Or you might have been saddled with a Courtenay
For son-in-law. White Roses bring no luck
In wedding posies.—I forgotten Cicely!
The bud I watched to blossom! my sweet playmate,
Who brought me flowers, coaxed pardon for my fits
Of frowardness, and made within my prison
Its one bright gleam of sunlight! She is well?
    Rutt. Aye, grown a stout lass; serves at the Lieu-
        tenant's,
When we have worshipful ladies, as we have now.
    Court. 'Tis as I thought, then—Lady Elizabeth?
    Rutt. Is lodged at the Lieutenant's, in the rooms
The poor sweet nine-day Queen left for the block.
Faith! (*wipes his eyes*) 'tis a rare chance for a plain Tower
    warder
To have had two angels under lock and key;
But 'tis Dick Rutter's chance—first came Queen Jane,
And now the Lady Elizabeth.
    Court.   My good Rutter,
Tell me how she is handled?
    Rutt. (*shrugs his shoulders*). Hard enough.
    Court. How bears she up?
    Rutt.   Like a man.
    Court.   How doth she look?

Rutt. Like a woman—sweet and sad and pale, but firm
And fearless. I've had many in my keeping,
And great ones ; but, save poor Queen Jane, none e'er
So mated majesty and maidenhead.

   Enter a Warder at postern—takes RUTTER *aside
            and speaks to him.*

  Court. (*aside*). Here within sight and speech of where I
    stand.
  Rutt. Here's a coil! my Lord Bishop and the Lords
Of the Council are met in the Presence Chamber.
I must attend them. My Lord Bishop sends order
Your lordship may have leave to breathe the air
Here for awhile. (*Ready for bolts*, R.)
  Court. Thanks for the grace, though from an enemy !
  Rutt. (*aside, going*). And I'm to bring the keys of the
    vaults that lead
To the west postern yonder (*points to the door with grated
    aperture*, R. *to* E.) to my lords.
Strange—leave my Lord of Devonshire here alone ;
And bring the keys to the Bishop ! Ha ! I see.
He'd play the eavesdropper. Well, each man to his trade.
Bishops can do things warders would be ashamed of.
               [*Exeunt* RUTTER *and Warder at postern.*
  Court. Alone, in free air—and my love at hand.[1]
  [*Cicely* (*coming from her hiding-place*). All gone at last !
Edward ! my own White Rose !
  Court. What? Cicely! Joy on joy. How camest thou hither?
Who let thee in ?
  Cicely (*puts her finger to her lips*). Nay, I'm not Cicely
    Rutter,
Born and bred in the Tower, to answer questions
Without the rack. I was upon the wharf.
I saw them bring thee in at Traitor's Gate.
Oh, I cried so ! I was so sorry for thee—
So glad to see thee again—I know not which
Made me cry ; but I cried—Lord, *how* I cried !
Since then there's not a day but I asked father
To take me with him to thy lodging—let me
Bring thee a posy out of the Queen's garden,

---

[1] The scene between brackets, from this point to near the bottom of page 182, may be omitted in representation. In that case Elizabeth should enter from the Lieutenant's Lodgings at this point.

As I used.   There's no flowers here in the Lieutenant's
Ghost of a garden.   But my father chid me;
Said 'twas not seemly, now I am a woman,
I should be taking flowers to prisoners' lodgings.
  Court.   If he knew how their blessing's doubly blest,
Brought by thy hand and given with thy bright smile!
Let me look at thee! (*Takes her head in his hands.*) I swear
  thou hast grown
A head since I left here.
  Cicely.   And you are changed.
You are not so pale, and you are fuller fleshed,
And hold your head up braver; but methinks
I liked you better as my own White Rose,
That looked as it had pined for the fresh air. (*Pausing.*)
Your pardon.   Father says you're a great lord now,
And I'm too forward.
  Court.   Nay, sweet Cicely,
I'm still thy Tower White Rose—and like, I fear,
To wither as I grew—within stone walls.
  Cicely.   Now Heaven forbid! I think all will be well.
Oh, if my prayers could help, all would be well.
  Court. (L.) And whose prayers should find heaven, if
  thine do not?
  Cicely (R. *gets nosegay from hiding-place*). Look, I had
  made thee a posy, as I used.
But this is braver. (*Shows him letters wrought in nosegay with
  flowers.*) See, here's E and C.
The E's for Edward, and the C—(*pause*)—nay, guess;
For Courtenay—is't not rare? The Lady Elizabeth
Taught me to weave the letters so.   Here's pansies,
Violets, and primroses.
  Court.   The Lady Elizabeth?
Thou servest her!
  Cicely.   Oh, yes, I wait on all
That lodge at the Lieutenant's—and, oh, Edward—
      (*Stamping her foot impatiently*)
My lord, I mean—it breaks my heart sometimes;
Just when I've learnt to love some gentle lady
She's taken hence—to Tower Green. (*Shudders and then
  bursts into tears.*)   Oh, my saint,
My sweet, sad Lady Jane! Look, what she gave me—
This little heart. (*Shows cornelian heart worn round her neck.*)
She wore it (*kisses it*) that last day.

And now the Lady Elizabeth—that's as easy
To love as Lady Jane. Who knows but soon
They'll come for her? She uses to walk here.
Maybe if you stand by you'll chance to see her.
 Court. I know her, Cicely—love her, too, like thee.
 Cicely. Oh, if you know her, needs *must* you should love
  her.
 Court. When she comes hither wilt thou give her these?
        (*Shows her his flowers.*)
 Cicely (*pointing*). The posy that I made for thee? Nay,
  Edward.
But as thou wilt—'twere cruelly done of me
To say thee nay, the first thing thou hast asked me.
 Court. (*who while this is spoken has written on a leaf of
  his tablets and placed it in the posy*) *I must speak with
  her, and alone.* This paper—
None must know that it comes from me. Thou mind'st me?
 Cicely. Not all the racks and barnacles and pincers
And thumbscrews in the Tower should draw it from me.
'Tis near her hour to walk. (*Bolts,* R.) I hear them opening.
 Court. She comes! my sun shines out! Oh, blessed chance!

  Enter ELIZABETH *from house,* R., *attended by* ISABEL.
    ELIZABETH *looks sad and pale.*
 Eliza. (*looks around*). How now? Alone, my Isabel, you
  and I?
No Argus eyes on us? No listening ears?
What's this? Where's our she-Cerberus, Lady Brydges?
 Isabel. I cry you mercy, Chandos.
 Eliza. I forgot.
But Sir John's lordship's somewhat fresh.
 Isab. (*who has been waiting as if for some one to follow.*
  She comes not!
A blessed riddance. Is it not enough
To shut you in the Tower, but they must give you
A she-dragon for guard? (*Looking apprehensively* R.)
     They have not bolted
The postern yet. I fear she's coming still.
I love your Highness well, but never love
Was put to such proof as my Lady Chandos.
 Eliza. Nor love so needed as to help me bear with her.
[ISABEL *goes up anxiously to* R. D. *and looks off, then walks
  up garden.* CICELY *comes timidly forward with flowers.*

Eliza. How now, my pretty Cicely? What would you?
Cicely. This posy, please your Highness deign to take it?
Eliza. I take and thank you heartily.   (*Taking nosegay.*)
   Sweet flowers!
Pansies for thought, and primroses for spring,
And violets for sweetness.   And what's here?
An E and C twined in a true-love knot?
                              (*Pausing and kissing flowers.*)
What mean these letters, Cicely?
   Cicely (*timidly, and blushing, under her breath*). Edward
      Courtenay.
He bade me give them to you.   He is here
                              (*Hastily and in a low voice.*)
Hard by.   There is a paper.   Have a care
None see you reading it.   (*Exit* CICELY, R., *into house.*)
                    [ELIZABETH *turns up and reads paper.*
   Eliza.   My Isabel,
I grieve to rob thee of thy scanted air
And exercise.   But I left in my closet
Papers I would have fair and clerkly copied
For the Council. (*Showing paper.*) I learn 'tis met here e'en
   now.
Wilt go, sweet coz, and copy me those papers
Without delay?
   Isabel (*clapping her hands*).   Oh! now you make me
      happy,
Giving me something to give up for you.
                    (HARRINGTON *appears at door*, R.)
I'll have the papers writ so clear and fair
You'll swear they're none of mad Isabel Markham's.
[ELIZABETH *turns up reading* COURTENAY'S *paper, which she
   kisses passionately.   As* ISABEL *approaches house,* R., HAR-
   RINGTON *comes forward, holding the door for her to enter.*
   Harr. Sweet Isabel! let me help you rule the lines.
   Isabel (*holding up her hands*). I'll rule thy face with my
      ten finger rule
If thou com'st near me.
                  (*Exit* ISABEL, *followed by* HARRINGTON.)]
   Court. My lady and my love!¹
   Eliza.   Thou, Courtenay, here,
And thus!

---

¹ Throughout the following scene the passages between brackets
may be omitted in acting.

Court. And where should Courtenay be but where his heart
Is ever—where thou art? Oh! turn not from me.
We are not here in the hollow seeming court,
Where the tongue's fettered, if the limbs go free.
Here, if souls be not chainless, pity of them
That sit in these dark dungeons; light of mine,
Sun of the bright brief summer I have known
'Twixt prison spring and prison winter, pardon
That like the Indian I fall at thy feet
To tell thee I am worthier by all
I have thought and done since thy brave words at Ashridge
Taught me how great thou wert, how fallen I
From nobleness and duty! (*Kneels.*)
   Eliza.   Nay, I have heard
How since then you have borne you like a man—
Done all a man might do to hinder treason
From lifting its foul head; [and when its madness
Raised Kent at Wyatt's heels, how, while they left you
Free to draw sword, you drew to guard the Queen.]
It was a comfort in my prison here
To know you worthy of the worthiest thought
I held of you.
   [*Court.*   Aye! Treason might have brought thee
To a throne, and loyalty has brought thee here.
And thou hast lifted me so near thy height
I can say, from my heart, better a prison
With loyalty, than a crown bought with treason.
   Eliza. There speaks my own true knight!
   Court.   Here lay thy hand,
Where Mary laid her sword, upon my shoulder,
And dedicate me so, by holier vows,
To higher duties, as becomes thy knight.
   Eliza. We both are consecrate by the martyr's chrism
Of suffering undeserved and bravely borne.]
   Court. (*rises*). To what unlooked-for chance or what strange kindness
We owe this meeting I know not; but I pray thee
Let me bear from it with me to my prison
One word, one sweet word, that will make that prison
A present heaven—nay, plant the way to the block
With flowers, that I may tread it, head erect,
And mount the scaffold as the bridal bed

That binds our souls in one.
    [Eliza.   Nay, talk not thus.
I think they dare not doom thy head to the block
Nor mine for treason. Where can be the proof
More than 'gainst babe unborn of deed undone?
Their malice may stab sharply, but I wear
The harness of a conscience void of guilt:
And, so thou wear it too, as now thou wear'st it,
We may defy them. Think what life still owes thee
Of debt deferred—the long arrear of joys,
Hopes, fruits of youth's earlier and later spring,
Blighted in this Tower air.
    Court.   But all made up
By the full fruitage of this golden hour,
That warms me in the clear sun of thine eyes,
Thrills me with the pure music of thy lips,
Makes this poor garden heaven, and thee its saint,
Whose adoration lifts the worshipper
Nearer to her he worships. I was wont
To have blessed the Tower for teaching me to bear
The hunger of the heart; henceforth I'll bless it
For teaching me the rapture of its fulness.]
    Eliza. Take thou this ring from me—'tis a pure opal
That changes with the faith of her that gives it.
If I thought I should change, I would not give thee
The tell-tale stone. [Look, the gold bears my posy,
' True love and loyalty '—who holds the last
Deserves the first.] But be true to thyself!
Fear not Elizabeth will be true to thee—
Aye, even to the scaffold. Woe is me!
That love should pay the penalties of treason.
I think 'tis nothing worse has brought us hither
Than that we dared to love.
    Court.   Ah, there's love's curse!
[I that would die to serve thee, must I live
But to undo thee? Now thou hast vouchsafed me
Assurance that makes absence light to bear,]
If e'er I quit these walls alive, 'twill be
To crave the Queen's good will to wean myself
From England and from thee, till happier times
And thy sweet summons call me back again.
    Eliza. [Leave me! Till happier times? Who knows if e'er

Those happier times will come? But you say well.]
'Tis absence puts to proof the strength of love :
Ours should be proved i' the fire. Who knows the trials
I may be doomed to? I will steel myself
Against my heart. Let it cry as it may,
I will not listen. 'Tis not for *my* life
I fear, but thine.] Here thy way's set with pitfalls—
Thy wariest walking cannot keep thee safe.
From this day I claim half thy life for mine;
I would not have it risked.
  Court.   Fear not. Henceforth
It shall be precious. I will tender it
As heedfully as e'er I rashly ventured,
Knowing I hold it to bring back to thee. (*Bolts heard.*)
 [*Eliza.* Hark! they come hither.

      Enter ISABEL.

 Isabel (*aside*).   So she wanted papers
Fair copied! Holy Mother! Who'd have thought
She could lie with such grace?
 Eliza. (*perceiving her*). My Isabel,
Our secret's safe with thee—we have plighted troths.
 Isabel. Now amen!
 Eliza. (*sadly*). Yes, woe's me! our hands have joined
But to be severed. Let's think, be it death
Or absence parts us, 'tis but a span more.]
My true love, my brave knight, who leaving me
Bear'st down worse opposites, in thy heart and *mine*,
Than ever knight in lists or battle field,
Farewell! I thought I had my father's heart—
My mother's part in it is in this kiss—
The first, the last.   (*Kissing.*)
 Court. Until we meet again
Where love is free, be it this side the grave
Or its dark further shore, farewell!
 Eliza.   Farewell!
 [*They part after a passionate embrace. Exit* ELIZABETH
   into house, R. *Bolts heard,* R.

Enter RUTTER *by back postern, which he locks behind him.*

 Rutt. Now to lock up your lordship. Mass! I'm sorry
To shut you from the trees and the fresh air.

Court. All's one for that. Henceforth my joy of life's
Summed in remembrance, whereof nought can rob me,
Nor gyves, nor prison bars, nor rack, nor axe.
(*Pausing at door,* L.)
The dungeon's bright as day wherein doth shine
The never-dying light of faith and love.
      [*Exit* COURTENAY *and* RUTTER *into garden house,* L.

Enter from R. *grated door* GARDINER *and* RENARD. *Enter
   at same moment from* L. *door* SUSSEX *and* PAGET.

    Gard. (*surprised*). How now, lords! you were listening?
    Paget (L. C.)   Like your lordship—
But on the other side—my Lord of Sussex
O'erheard you bid them let the young pair meet—
We guessed 'twas that you might o'erhear their greeting.
    Sussex (*ironically*). Your lordship must rejoice, and
        Monsieur Renard,
This so feared treason ends in a love passage
'Twixt a hot boy and girl.
    Paget.   We are glad our witness
Will serve to bear out yours before the Council.
    Sussex. To whom we haste to carry the good news.
[*Exeunt* PAGET *and* SUSSEX *by postern.*

HARRINGTON *appears from wicket,* R., *from which* GARDINER
   and RENARD *have come out. Seeing them, he draws back,
   but listens.*

    Gard. (*taking stage,* L.) Foiled!
    Ren. (R.) Doubly! Wyatt staunch to the last! Elizabeth
As guiltless, or as guileful now as ever,
And their long ears between you and the Council.
I told you it was hopeless to seek proof
That would condemn her.
    Gard.   Yet without such proof
The Queen will not condemn.
    Ren.   The Council *will*—
If you but press them hot and hard enough.
Look, you count here six voices against ten—
Six voices of six lords, each soul and body
Your *alter ego*—drive them to a sentence
Of instant execution on the Princess.
For Courtenay, who's so sick for her bright eyes,

Take him at his own word—pack him o'er sea.
Once there, 'tis your own fault if he return.
    Gard. But the Queen's hand? She will not sign the
      warrant.
    Ren. Do the deed first—ask her to sign it after.
    Gard. Elizabeth's friends in the Council will be instant
About the Queen.
    Ren.   Aye, if you let them reach her.
Have the Tower gates shut, and let none go forth
Till her life is past praying for.
    Gard.   ·   Bethink you!
We risk our heads.
    Ren.   As an ambassador
Mine's safe. You should have wit to guard your own.
As for hers—'tis the price my gracious master
Sets on *his* hand—you best know what that's worth
To you and holy Church.
    Gard.   I'll dare the deed!
'Tis no sin, when the adder's coiled to spring,
To crush its head—though we leave the highway
To reach it. I'll wring warrant from the Council.
She shall not see another sun![1]
What ho there! (*Enter* RUTTER. GARDINER *gives him a
    paper.*)
This to Lord Chandos. See the gates are closed,
That no one leaves the Tower till further orders.
And harkye—let Lord Courtenay have the freedom
Of the garden, and of speech with Lady Elizabeth.
(*After a pause.*) So I have full report what passes 'twixt them.
    Ren. Knaves should have ears to serve: look to thine own
If they should fail his worship. Dost thou hear?
    Rutt. That I'm to play the spy or find a knave
To play it. Yes, I hear!
Stone walls have ears, they say—but I had rather
Your *lordship* found those ears than *I*.
    Gard.   How, sirrah?
Crack'st thou thy quips on me?
    Rutt.   No quip, my lord:
I did but speak my mind. [*Exeunt* RENARD *and* GARDINER.
Enter CICELY, *showing in* COURTENAY *from house,* L. *She
    then draws her father off, and* ELIZABETH *enters.*

---

[1] Here if time requires compression in this play, the Act may end, and usually does end in representation.

Court. (*coming forward*). My own dear lady!
Eliza. Oh joy! free once more!
Court. To see thee, speak with thee, hold thy dear hand,
To look into thine eyes, drink thy sweet voice,
Who calls this prison? It is Paradise!
Eliza. Thou had'st my letter?
Court. Yes—wherein thy heart
Speaks out so bravely, but so bootlessly.
Eliza. Say not so. Hear it! Shall I banish thee?
I that have risked life rather than be traitor
To the Queen, shall I play traitor thus to love?
Not so. I charge thee stay. Better trust love
To guard us, being true to him, than policy
That bids us, for love's sake, be false to love.
Court. Think'st thou, if I dare listen to my heart,
It would not echo thine? Ha! Harrington!

Enter HARRINGTON.

Harr. No hope that way—so no hope any way.
(*Seeing* COURTENAY *and* ELIZABETH.)
My lord—your Highness! I have played the spy
Upon your spies—eavesdropped your eavesdroppers.
Gardiner is even now wresting a warrant
For your swift execution from the Council.
Eliza. Old news.
Harr. But he has *here* the weight of voices.
Your friends are few—the Tower gate's barred, that none
Goes in nor out.
Eliza. They need my sister's hand
As warrant for the warrant.
Harr. They've resolved
That she shall sign when you are dead.
Eliza. Hold there!
One blood runs in my sister's veins and mine.
There's not a drop of it but will rise in flood
To sweep away such treason. What! usurp
The highest attribute of kings—the right
Of life and death! Now, as I live, they dare not.
Court. Could he but forth the Tower your life were safe.
Harr. No mouse can pass!
Court. 'Tis true; then we are caged.
To wear no sword! To have but one poor life
To give in thy defence, and give in vain!

These dark deaf walls between thee and the thousands
That love thee—Gardiner's courage, Renard's craft,
Against thee!
 Eliza. And one poor woman's wit
To match. Heavy odds! But, heart, hold up!
Be busy, brain! Methinks the swelling spirit
That came to me with my stout father's blood
Is stirring here! Feel, Courtenay, feel—my pulse
       (*Giving him her hand.*)
Throbs fast, but flutters not, and my heart's beat,
That checked a moment at this news, has ta'en
Its even pace again. I am armed to meet
The worst that can befal me. Heaven is here,
Even in the Tower.
 Court. And in thine innocence
Thou hast a stronger fortress of defence
Than have thine enemies in these grim walls
That frown so darkly on us. Unto Heaven,
And to thine innocence, commend thy cause!
   (*He draws her to her knees, and the act-drop falls.*)

END OF ACT III.

ACT IV.

SCENE.—*The* LIEUTENANT'S *Lodgings in the Tower, a picturesque tapestried room, but low and dark, with arched roof and grated windows in deep recesses; two doors,* R. *and* L.

 [ISABEL MARKHAM *discovered at her embroidery frame.*
  She puts it from her.

 Isabel. Heigho! It grows too dark for 'broidery!
I've naught to do but yawn, until my lady's
Done weeping for her lover. Poor White Rose!
He is a gallant gentleman. If I had
An inch of heart not filled with my sweet lady
I *could* be a shrewd rival. But she has witched me.
She's man and woman both, I think, for me.
So manly brave, and yet so woman gentle!
  [SIR JOHN HARRINGTON *enters, and listens until she*
   finishes her speech.
So merry, yet so wise! and here they shut her

In this dull, darkling, dreary, weary Tower.
And I must shut myself with her! More fool I!
    Sir John Harr. Amen!
    Isabel.   How now, sir?
    Harr.   You said, 'More fool I!'
I said 'Amen' to the confession.
    Isabel.   Did you?
Becomes you catch the Tower trick of eavesdropping.
    Harr. At least I owe it knowledge of the danger
That frowns more and more darkly on our lady.
    Isabel. Danger?
    Harr.   From Gardiner's malice! List, and learn
What passes, if he comes; 'tis of grave moment.
Isabel, 'tis no time for flirts and floutings.
You love her, as I love her; in *her* cause
I know you can be brave and grave and wise.
    Isabel. I am right glad you hold that thought of me,
That I am good for more than fooling with.
I have been curt and saucy.
    Harr.   It became you,
And it beguiled the time from darker thoughts,
But now, as there is a true love betwixt us—
                            (*She looks at him.*)
Much for our lady—something for each other—
Let's keep the wits that we have spent on jangling
To work in her defence.
    Isabel.   My hand on that!
              (*She gives her hand; he keeps it.*)
    Harr. A small, white hand; how well it looks in mine!
What if you gave it me, and I put in it
A heart no lady has so much a right to?
Don't let it drop—you'll break it.
    Isabel.   Nay, I warrant
'Tis tougher than you think. But let us know
Our lady clear of harm ere we waste breath
Or thought on such toys as *our* hearts and hands.
Once out of these black, blood-engrainèd walls,
You may remind me how my hand lay so,
And how I left it.
    Harr.   Execute the conveyance!
Say, 'I deliver *this* as my act and deed.'
                         (*Caressing her hand.*)
And there I set *my* seal (*kisses her*), and say the same.
So we are plighted—first to a common duty,

Then to a common—no, *un*common—joy!
    Isabel. You've taken more than I e'er thought to give.
But the deed's signed and sealed, and so no help!
    Harr. Now must I to the outer ward to learn
What I can of what passes in the Council,
While thy sharp wit stands sentry here. Farewell!
And bless thee, my own Isabel!
    Isabel.   Farewell!
                                      [*Exit* HARRINGTON.
How I shall miss my block! But a heart's better
Than a block, after all; and I have his,
And he has mine; and I think both are better
By the exchange. (*A knock.*) Who's there? Come in!

                    Enter GARDINER.
    Gard.   Fair mistress,
Say to the Lady Elizabeth the Lord Chancellor
Would speak with her.
    Isabel (saucily aside and going). I would fain speak with
        him,
An' I might speak my mind.   [*Exit.*
    Gard. Renard says she must die. And yet I'm sorry
To give so fair a head, so rich a brain,
So great a heart, to the worms! Ah! if but she,
And not her sister, had fall'n to my hand,
What might not our two heads have shaped together?
We had re-made the world! One way remains
To save her: if she'll wed the Duke of Savoy
She would be harmless being hence. I'll open
This last road of escape; that closed—no help—
She dies.
                    Enter ELIZABETH.
    Eliza. (with assumed humility). Good even to my kind
        Lord Bishop.
'Tis too much honour when the gaoler deigns
A visit to his prisoner.
    Gard.   Nay, your Highness,
Call not your best friend by so ill a name.
Be well assured I have given all my pains——
    Eliza. To keep me safe here. I *am* well assured,
And prize your friendship at its worth.
    Gard. You mock me.
    Eliza. Not I, or think you I would give you this?
                                          [*Gives letter.*

Gard. What's here?

Eliza. A letter that has reached me strangely—
So strangely, Isabel Markham swears it must be
A trap; but she's a fool. Who would set traps
Here in the Tower? Caged birds cannot need catching.

Gard. (*who has read the paper*). An offer from the French
    King to your Highness——

Eliza. Of his protection, and due maintenance
Fitting my rank, in Paris, at his court.

Gard. You have answered it?

Eliza.   Even so. I told the King,
Elizabeth would sooner be ill-handled
In England than dealt royally with in France.

Gard. 'Twas bravely said, and wisely.

Eliza.   For the wisdom
I leave *that* to your lordship. I but spoke
As Henry's daughter felt. Besides, my lord,
Had I sent other answer—say, accepted
The offer—who knows how it had been warped
Against me?

Gard. Not by *me*. Truth is my witness!
Be open with me. We are adversaries;
But let us play our game like gallant gamesters,
With fair cards and unloaded dice.

Eliza. (*proudly*).   *I* know
No other way of playing, my Lord Bishop.

Gard. While you are here in England, near the throne,
The restless flock will not sit quietly
Under a crown shared with a foreign prince.
Needs must, for the realm's peace and the Queen's life,
That you go hence. In this extremity
Heaven favours you, urging to seek your hand
The noblest, bravest, youthful sovereign Duke
Of Europe, Philibert of Savoy. He hath seen
Your portrait. If the *painted* image so
Have fixed him, what will not the *living* picture?
He has sent envoys asking you in marriage.

Eliza. 'Tis honour past my poor deserts.

Gard.   Think, madam:
A gallant husband, and a swift escape
From loss of liberty—nay, risk of life!
'Tis the Queen's wish you entertain his suit.

Eliza. Say to the Queen: Imprisonment or freedom,

My life or death, I will take from her hand.
Only *one* thing she shall not put on me—
That is, a husband whom I have not chosen;
And a home out of England, that I'll none of.
Tell her I'd sooner hold six feet of England,
Though 'twere my grave, than a realm over sea.
   Gard. Think, madam; 'tis not well to shut the door
That opens upon liberty and life.
   Eliza. 'Twere base to barter liberty and life
Against free love and native land; so tell
My sister.
      Gard.   'Tis your last word?
   Eliza. Aye, my lord,
Even if the scaffold were set up for me
Upon yon Green—as who knows but it may be?
   Gard. That I can rate you at your worth is cause
Why I would gladly serve you. Of my service
You'll none?   (*She makes a gesture of refusal.*)
Then be your doom on your own head! [*Exit* GARDINER.
   Eliza. That thou canst rate me at my worth! Proud
      priest!
Not so. So rates me none, but who can put
Honour and duty before life, and that
Thou canst not!
He counted without thee, my own White Rose,
That by a prior bond art sovereign lord
Of hand and heart, of love and life, and all
That is Elizabeth!
           Enter CICELY, *joyously*.
   Cicely. News! brave news, sweet lady!
Edward is free!
   Eliza. Free! Ha! another snare!
   Cicely. 'Tis true. He is set free on the Council's order.
My father told me—he was charged with it.
And hark! (*whispering*) I've coaxed father to send him hither.
   Eliza. But will they give him way?
   Cicely.   We will not ask them.
A stair in the wall from the Garden House leads hither.
He'll come and go by that, as the mice do.
Look where the arras stirs! And so I'll leave you! [*Exit.*
      Enter from secret panel, R., COURTENAY.
   Eliza. My Courtenay! free! A little while ago

I scarcely deemed life held this joy for us.
But now I urged thee hence. Methought 'twas brave
In me to speed thy flight across the sea,
Thinking but of thy safety. I was mad.
I counted not with love! I cannot bear
To send thee from me. Say thou couldst not go,
Now thou art free.

  Court.   My empress and my saint!
My life is thy life. They know that who freed me
On Gardiner's motion.

  Eliza.   Gardiner? Can it be?
Can devilish malice in a breath turn love?

  Court. What if *my* freedom were the gift of hate?

  Eliza. Ha! there's a sad foreboding in their eye,
And love can read hate's visage in love's mask.

  Court. Yes; they have set me free, and keep thee bound;
Lay thee perhaps under yet heavier durance.
Deeming that, free, I needst must use my freedom
To compass thine by force, and in that act
Make myself traitor, and help prove thee so.

  Eliza. But thou'lt be wise, and calm, and long-enduring?

  Court. Who knows if patience could hold out? Who
    knows,
If patience held, what malice might suggest,
Suborn, invent? Within these walls I learnt
Fifteen years' wisdom; then for a brief while
The joy of loving thee rased from my mind
All save that present heav'n; but now once more,
With love grown worthier, my ancient teacher
Hath ta'en me to his stern sad heart again,
To learn the old lesson, ' Renounce and forbear.'

  Eliza. What would'st thou?

  Court.   Leave thee, as I purposed,
And England; thereto I have bound myself
By oath to Sussex, Paget—thy best friends
And mine.

  Eliza. (*passionately*). Not so. Better captivity
Together than such freedom! Oh, forgive me!
If 'twas ill said—the woman spoke in me.
Look! I am not the thing I deemed myself—
The half-unsexèd heart where policy
Holds passion in a leash. Save as love prompts,
I know no policy for thee or me!

I only know I love thee—cannot live
Without thee. If thou'rt vowed to banishment,
Let me be banished also. Let me go
Where *thou* go'st !
  Court.   Hush ! thy life is not thine own.
     (*Laying his hand solemnly on her head.*)
This head is dedicate to England's Crown ;
This heart is sacred to a people's love !
Look how it yearns and cries for thee through all
The travail of this sore distracted realm !
Thou art its hope, its trust, its morning star ;
And when that star shines in the front of day,
Some ray of its far beam will strike to me,
And stir my heart, though it sleeps in the dust.
  Eliza. If e'er I hold the throne, thou shalt be next it.
Thy hand in mine, thy heart to stay my heart.
Or if not—hear me, Courtenay—bind myself,
To go down to my grave a virgin Queen !
  Court. Why should we plight with tongues, who have
    exchanged
The higher, holier plight of heart to heart ?
Though I am free, think not I'll quit these walls
Until I know thee safe from Gardiner's malice
And Renard's craft ! If I have not the power
To save thee, die for thee, I can die with thee !
      (*A knock heard at the panel.*)
Hark ! I am summoned ! One long look—the last !
One kiss ! that seals my soul upon thy lips,
   (*Tears himself from her after a passionate embrace.*)
And crowns thee Courtenay's Queen for life, for death !
  Eliza. (*trying to detain him*). Stay, Courtenay ! Leave me
    not ! He's gone ! Come, all
That seek my life (*despairingly*)—I give it you—a gift !
Beggared of love, what boots to strive with hate,
And draw out dull breath in a sunless world ?
Oh, I am sick at heart ! Alone ! alone !
How dark it grows and chill ! Methinks the day
Dies sooner here by a good hour than elsewhere,
Like a life cut off ere the time ! Alone !
Alone for ever now ! But one last look !
       (*Goes to the window.*)
An idle hope ! How now ? What is yon light
So red ? It turns the White Tower walls to blood !

[*The red light of torches is seen to gleam on the walls of the White Tower.*

(*Listening from the window.*)
And through the night sounds as of toiling hammers
On the side of the Green! Round my lone life
The shadows that have gathered long fall closer!
Is't the night-air that chills me, or the thought
Of the dark deeds of blood these walls have witnessed?
Down, terrible fancies! Fright me not from myself,
When I have *most* need to be all myself.
'Twas here Jane Grey was lodged. Out of this window
She saw her Dudley guarded to the block;
Saw him brought back anon, a headless corpse.
'Twas hence she walked, with calm face and firm step
To the scaffold, where her saintly head received
A higher crown than England's. Nay, who knows?
Perhaps 'twas here my mother waited summons
To the same scaffold. (*Shudders.*) Almost through the dark
I could think bodiless eyes were looking on me!
Pale shapes of Queens, with dim, discrowned brows,
And each a ring of red about her neck;
And youngest, fairest of them all, my mother!
One hand held to her throat (*clutches her own neck*), and one that points
Toward Tower Green! (*Shrieks.*) Oh, mercy! Isabel, come,
Or I shall go distraught! Help! Isabel!
ISABEL MARKHAM *enters from inner room.* ELIZABETH *recovers herself by a great effort.*
Keep with me, Isabel. Hush! it was nothing,
Or but a silly dream.
Enter GARDINER, *followed by* SIR JOHN BRYDGES, *preceded by a Yeoman bearing lights.*
(*Sits.*) Now, my Lord Bishop?
    Gard. We bring to you the sentence of the Council
Delivered even now.
    Eliza.   'Tis strange and sudden!
But I am bent to hear, deferring question
Till what I deem occasion. Read, my lord.
What says the Council?
    Gard.   It awards you death,
            (ELIZABETH *rises.* ISABEL *shrieks.*)
For treason done, in aiding and abetting
Wyatt's rebellion.

(Isabel *throws her arm round* Elizabeth, *as if to protect her.*)
                                    And for the estopping
Of riot among the peevish citizens,
The Council holds it best that execution
Be done on you to-night, within the Tower.
                                        [Elizabeth *starts.*
    Eliza. Give me the warrant.   [*Takes it from him.*
(*Starts, but suppresses her emotion.*) It is void, my lord,
                                        (*Returns it.*)
Not bearing the sign manual.
    Gard.   That I'll answer
To the Queen and the law.
    Eliza. (*stepping forward*). The Queen, whose conscience
You turn and wind as men a managed colt,
The law, in whose seat you set up *your will*,
Whose sacred sword you take to murder with!
                                        [*Moves to right.*
    Gard. Sharp speech will not avail you. Best employ
What brief time's left in pious preparation.
The chaplain shall attend you.   [*Moving towards door.*
    Eliza.   Hold, my lord!
If you mock right and justice, mock not heaven!
I need no priest to smooth my way to death—
No priest, I think, will have power to smooth yours!
Sir John, that you are true man and stout soldier
All voices here bear witness. Have a care
How you lend *your* hand to this deed of blood!
This unsigned warrant is no warranty
For what it dooms to the law or your conscience.
Law will prevail, and conscience will awake,
Howe'er this lord's strong force or glozing tongue
Have overborne the one and drugged the other.
You are set here to guard the Royal Tower;
Then how much more to guard the Royal life
That runs, part, in my veins! Or if your fealty
To the Queen be not in question, think of that—
The higher fealty you owe to manhood,
That bids you guard the weak, and set your strength
Between an unjudged woman and her death!
You have a *daughter*, nigh upon my years;
Think that she speaks in me!
    Sir J. Brydges (*after an inner struggle*). Now, by the Rood,

It shall not be. My Lord of Winchester,
As the Queen's soldier and the Council's servant,
Orders of Queen and Council I obey.
But neither without other. Have this warrant
Signed, as of wont, by Her Gracious Majesty,
I'll execute its sentence. Till it's signed
I'll make bold to refuse.   [*Holds out warrant.*
    Gard.   And put to peril
Your own head to save hers?
    Eliza.   Not so, my lord.
'Tis *he* rules here. His honest velvet coats
Obey *his* orders, not my Lord of Winchester's!
Thanks, my stout soldier. You shall find hereafter
Elizabeth forgets not timely service!
The scaffold that my lord bade you set up
I bid you to take down! I promise you,
When the law dooms me to it, you will find
I will make no delay, as I make now.
    Gard. (*to* SIR JOHN). On your allegiance!——
    Eliza.   It says 'disobey.'
    Gard. You dare defy the Council?
    Eliza.   He defies
Its boldest spirit and its basest—*You!*
    Gard. (*gloomily and baffled*). Then I have nothing here—
    Eliza. (*with marked but mocking courtesy*). Nothing, my
    lord,
But to take my best wish for your good rest.
(*Calls.*) Lights for my Lord of Winchester!
        (BRYDGES *kneels. She gives him her hand to kiss.*)
                              [*Exit* GARDINER.
(*Exultingly.*) I have won!
'Twas bravely borne! Help! Isabel, good wench!
    [*Overcome by the tension of nerve kept up through the
      scene, she reels and faints in* ISABEL'S *arms.*

ACT-DROP.

ACT V.

SCENE I.—MARY'S *Chamber at St. James's. A handsome chamber. State bed painted on* L. F.; *doors,* R. L. *Second entrances. Toilet table, &c.,* L.; *sofa and cushions,* C.; *small table, with medicine bottles, &c.,* R.; DUCHESS OF NORFOLK *at head of sofa,* R.; *and three Ladies, with* ISABEL MARKHAM, *at foot of sofa,* L. *Picture,* R.

Duch. Your Majesty's ill at ease. I'll shift the cushions.
Mary. Canst find the pillow that will rest a head
That aches and burns with burden of a crown?
The cushion upon which a sad, sick heart
Can leave its weight of sorrow? If thou canst,
Give it me, and I'll bless thee! Till thou canst
There is no ease for me! Set me the picture
Of my dear lord—that he sent me—in his armour,
As he fought at St. Quentin. (*Women set picture.*)
                              My brave husband!
Looks he not knightly? (*Sighs.*) How the painted semblance
Spurs longingly for the life! (*Feverishly.*) Have our posts come
From Dover—and from Harwich?
    Duch.   There is one
Come even now.
    Mary (*eagerly*). Ha! What news of the coming
Of our kind lord?
    Duch.   His Majesty was still
With the Commissioners for peace with France
At Cercamp.
    Mary. Woe is me! He will not come.
I shall not hold a husband's hand in mine,
Nor lean my head upon a husband's heart,
Till heart and hand are cold. If he but knew
How ill all's with me here! How sore my need
            (*Pressing her hands on her heart and brow.*)
Of some kind presence—some small word of love!
I do not look for much.
    Isabel (L.).   I love you, madam.
    Mary (C.). Good wench, I feel thou dost. Methinks
        my sister
May well be jealous of the Queen for once.
It will not be for long.
    Isabel.   Trust me, the Queen
Had never lieger subject than my lady.
I am rank rebel born: let who will scratch me,
Queen or aunt, I scratch back. But Elizabeth
Holds her wrath as you hold a hawk—to fly
But at the quarry she would have it strike.
It ne'er stooped at your Majesty—not when
Your hand was heaviest on us.
    Mary.   I believe thee.
I have been hard with her—but 'twas the Council.
Pray Heaven I was well counselled.

Isabel.   Now, amen!
I'm but a fool, my aunt says, but I judge
Trees by their fruits. If good of counsel comes,
I hold the counsel good; if evil, evil.
Your Majesty best knows the fruit you've gathered
From the seed sown by Gardiner and the rest.
    Mary. Who can read Heaven's high purpose but by
        light
Of Holy Church, whose servants hold the keys
That bind and loose. I have done as they bade me—
Made war on heresy, prisoned, hung, and burnt;
But, Heaven's my witness, with a heavy heart.
Mayhap *that* was my sin. (*Low and tremblingly.*)
I *must* have sinned;
Or why these plagues of famine, fever, murrain,
On man and beast? These wars unnatural
Of our most Catholic lord with the Holy Father?
Why is that master-jewel of our crown,
Calais, torn out, in France's diadem
To be re-set, and thence shoot scorn on England?
    Duch. Your Majesty frets too much. Let Calais go!
    Mary (fiercely). Let Calais go! the Leopard lift his paw
From off the throat of France, and let her up
To make her saucy brag in England's face?
To flaunt her lilies in our narrow seas—
Nay, plant them in our fields! (*With profound emotion.*)
                                 Open my heart
When I am dead, and in its core you'll find
The name of Calais 'graven. (*Falls back on sofa.*)
    Duch. (*looking off*, R.) "Tis Monsieur Renard, madam.
                    Enter RENARD, L. 2 E.
    Mary (reviving suddenly, with passionate impatience).
Ha! Renard. Quick! What news of our dear lord?
He's well? He bears us in his heart? His business
Will be disposed of soon? When comes he? Speak!
    Ren. (L. C.) Were wishes wings, his Majesty had been
        here
A month since; but, alas! love speeds not statecraft.
Meanwhile, this letter (*producing it*) utters all the passion
That paper can give tongue to, and conveys
His wishes to your Majesty.
    Mary (*seizing the letter and kissing it passionately*).
                      What joy (*taking knife from* ISABEL)

To work his will, whose will is his wife's law!
Whom to content is to content myself,
                    (*Opens letter with knife from table*, R.)
As I may not behold him.   Ha! what's here?
                    (*Putting her hand to her heart.*)
   Isabel (*rushing to her help*). Look, aunt—the Queen is fainting!
   Mary. Nay, 'tis not much—but a short, sharp pain here.
                    (*Weeps convulsively.*)
   Isabel.   Oh! what mean these tears?
   [MARY *stabs picture with knife in an agony of fierce grief and rage.*
   Mary. Out, painted semblance of a heartless husband;
And yet whose art is *truth* to the false face
That mocks me from thy canvass!   Would 'twere *he*,
And not his picture I were stabbing thus! (*Another stab.*)
Listen, sir—listen, Isabel!   Hear, all
What here he bids me do—to send the jewels
He left a gift with us unto Elizabeth,
With words of brotherly greeting—brotherly!
Cain's words were brotherly.   (*To* RENARD.) Tell him I obeyed.
(*To* ISABEL.) Get me the casket yonder—near my bed.
                    (ISABEL *gets it.*)
Fool! I still slept with it under my pillow. (*Opens it.*)
Fair stones! bright as my hopes, hard as his heart,
'Tis fit you crown *her*, who to all her gains
Now adds my husband's love. (*Gives jewels to* RENARD.)
                    Go, trusty Renard;
Leave my sick sun that sets for hers that rises.
Pay *thy* court to Elizabeth, like thy master.
   Ren. You wrong my lord. This gift to Elizabeth
Is policy, not passion—meant to bear
Her Highness still in hand, till we have proofs
That she's less loyal than you please to think her.
As for a messenger, I could find one
More welcome to Elizabeth than Renard.
   Mary. We're in no mood for riddles.   Speak!—whom mean you?
   Ren. Courtenay!
   Mary.   He is o'er sea.
   Ren.   He is in England—
Landed but now at Ipswich—cried 'A Courtenay!'
And raised your sister's banner.   The base herd

Flock unto him in crowds—to Yaxley Wood.

Mary. How know you this?

Ren. As I know every step
Of his since he went hence. My eyes were on him.
I have eyes that travel far and wide. He comes,
Doubtless, impatient—spurred with hope deferred
Of the crown he believes at point to fall
From off your royal head.

Mary (*proudly*). The crown that ne'er
Shall deck her brow or his!

Ren. And failing theirs,
Must be my master's, whom you have so wronged
By your suspicions!

Mary. Nay, but tell me, Renard—
It is but policy? He loves her not?

Ren. Loves her! He loves but one—your Majesty,
(*Aside.*) Himself!

Mary. Could we but feel assured of that! Alas!
They that long for assurance find it easy.
I am sorry I have so misused his picture.
Forgive me, my dear lord! But I was mad.
The fever in my blood, not I, was cause.
Hate bred of too much love may be forgiven;
And such is Mary's hate. Speed, trusty Renard,
To Hatfield. Let me hear thou hold'st these traitors
Against our peace and our dear lord's and husband's.
Our trusty Chandos will supply you force.
(*With sudden energy of will and passion.*) Think you the
    throne is empty, Edward Courtenay,
For you and your Elizabeth? You shall find
Scaffold and block lie yet 'twixt *it* and *you!*
    (*Falls back in hysterical laugh.*)

CLOSED IN.

SCENE II.—*A Room at Hatfield. First Grooves.*

Enter HARRINGTON, L.; PARRY, R.

Harr. (*ordering off*). Saddle Lord Paget's horses! Here's
    a coil!
(*To* PARRY.) Times are changed, Cofferer, since the old Ashridge days.
Then 'twas sour looks with us, spies, State controllers;
A prison, with the bolts and bars scarce masked:

Now, 'tis a crowd of courtiers and councillors,
That keep the road alive 'twixt here and London,
To fill innkeepers' purses and drain ours.
    Parry. Aye, Master Harrington, as the Queen's star dims
Our lady's brightens on the verge.
    Harr.   And draws
Courtiers' looks to her, as the sun sucks mist.
Here's my Lord Paget—a long head, that knows
Still to hold with the hare and hunt with the hounds.
Mark, he'll but step from favour into favour.
Faith, a wise man. I'll study him to learn
The art to thrive at court.
    Parry.   You are too bold.
These matters may be noted, but not spoken.
    Harr. 'Silence,' quoth Solomon. (*Putting his fingers on his lips with mock reverence, looking off.*)
                       But who comes yonder?
As I live, Master Renard! To him, Cofferer!
                               (*Exit* PARRY, L.)
Why should the fox visit our poultry-yard?
He licked his lips long for our pretty pullet,
But now I think he'll own her meat for his master.
Here he comes! So, Don Slyboots, I'm for you!
(*Calls, with elaborate courtesy.*) Place for his Excellence the Spanish Envoy!
(*Aside.*) Renard the Fox needs room to spread his tail.
(*Changing his tone to mock respect.*) This way, your Excellence.

    Enter RENARD, L., *followed by three Gentlemen of his suite.*

    Ren. (*as if recalling him*). Sir John Harrington,
I think: her Highness' gentleman of the chamber?
    Harr. The same; and proud to be borne in memory
By Master Reynard.
    Ren. (*correcting him*). Renard!
    Harr.   Pray you pardon!
Our English fashion's 'Reynard'—it means Fox—
A name of worship, and a type of wisdom.
I'll tell my lady you are here, so please you.
(*Aside as he goes.*) Show tail and claws—our chickens are safe cooped.   [*Exit*, R.
    Ren. A swaggering blade! who feels his fortunes planted

Right side the hedge—and they *are*. How the moths
Buzz to the light! 'Twixt this and London 'tis
A stream of horses, coaches, litters, showing
A back to Whitehall and a face to Hatfield!
I but swim with the stream. But be this news
Of Courtenay's rising true, the stream may turn
And land you at Tower Stairs again, fair lady,
So it please me set your barge bows that way.

      Re-enter HARRINGTON, R.

 Harr. My lady is in talk with my Lord Paget.
My lord despatched, she will see Monsieur Renard:
Meantime, so please your honour, a slight refection——
(*Aside.*) Say, of sour grapes.

 [*Exeunt* HARRINGTON, *ushering off* RENARD *and suite*, R.

CHANGE.

 SCENE III.—*The Great Hall at Hatfield. Fireplace*, R. *Two large portraits of Henry VIII. and Anne Boleyn at each side of fireplace. Window*, L., *with sunlight showing through. Low wainscot covered with tapestry from* 4*th* E. L. *and* R., *leaving the* C. *open. Table and state chair*, R. C. *Ladies and Gentlemen grouped.* PARRY, *attending* ELIZABETH, *discovered* C., *taking leave of* PAGET.

 Eliza. Take leave so soon! Nay, then, thanks, my
  good lord,
For this most welcome visit.
 Paget.   "Tis for me
To thank your gracious Highness for the courtesy
Kindly vouchsafed to one whom state occasions
Have often forced to hide his love.
 Eliza.   I know
My friends, Lord Paget, under all their faces;
And I know, too, how you and my Lord Sussex
And Arundel have stood 'twixt me and them
That compassed my undoing.
 Paget.   Whose chief head
Is fallen in Gardiner—a perilous man,
Who held the foul creed that what he thought good
Might be advanced by what he knew was evil.
 Eliza. Leave Heaven to judge him, that will judge us all;
Would that the seeds of blood that he and Pole

Have sown had died with the sowers! But even now
This poor land bleeds; disloyal and dismayed,
England sees her might mocked, her wealth decayed;
France flings her gage to us—we dare not lift it;
France takes our towns—we cannot win them back;
France smites us on one cheek—we turn the other!
And to crown shameful war a shameful peace
Is even now a-knitting. Oh, my lord,
My English heart burns sore to know all this,
Yet know I cannot help!
  Paget.   Heaven speed the time
When in the might of Law's true liberty
Our English Samson's strength shall be renewed,
And these base bonds, with which brave hands have bound
  him,
Be burst like green withes!
  Eliza. Methinks I see my England, like the eagle,
Pruning her unchained wing for freer flight,
Fuller in focus of the glorious sun
Than she e'er flew till now. Great deeds, great words,
That make great deeds still greater! Poesy
Fired with new life; her soldiers conquering,
Her sailors braving unknown seas, to plant
The germ of a new England in the West—
Acorn it may be, of a daughter oak,
Broader and stronger than the parent tree!
But I speak wildly, yet speak what I think,
As friend may speak to friend, and not be chidden.
  Paget. Ashes of age are grey upon my head.
Methought they had smothered my heart's fires as well;
But something glows beneath them, hearing you.
May Heaven speed the good time, and guard you, madam,
To make our England great and glorious
In men's deeds, as your words. For what 'tis now
I lay most charge upon the Spanish match.
Pray heaven your Highness lend no ear to those
That work on you to wed a foreign prince.
  Eliza. Elizabeth mates not—or she mates in England.
I have a vow for *that*.
  Paget.   Heaven grant you keep it,
And me to bless your mating, when it comes.
And now, farewell, sweet lady. I will take
Much comfort to our friends from this good news

Of your fair health and firm fix'd resolution.
                      [*He bows, kisses her hand, and exit,* L. C.
    Eliza.   Fare you well!   (*Exit* PAGET.)
Ah Courtenay, he dreams not that 'tis love's vow
I hold, not policy's! Oh, my true lord,
How heavy drags the time, waiting for thee!
Three whole months, and no tidings! I am sick
Of longing for his letter—but this audience
Of Master Renard. (*Exit* PARRY, L.C.) I see in his coming
Ill omen to my peace; but I am armed,
I think, against him, and all enemies,
With love and loyalty for talisman.
            Enter RENARD *and three of his suite,* L. C.
    Ren. (*kneeling*). Most gracious lady!
    Eliza. Your knee becomes you not, nor honours me.
An envoy should kneel only to the power
He bears commission to.
    Ren.   And such the power
You are to me. I come not as ambassador
Of Spain to England, but as messenger,
Trusted with Philip's duty to his sister——
    Eliza. In law.
    Ren.   And love; in witness of which love
I bring this letter, and this precious casket
Of jewels (*opens casket*) as my royal master's gift,
To her he prizes far beyond all measure
Of words or jewels. Pray you read this letter.
    Eliza. (*looking at letter, reading; after reading she starts,
        but masters herself*). Now, before Heaven—here is a
        gracious letter!
A kingly letter, and a husbandly!
And brotherly to boot!
Wherein King Philip offers **me** his hand,
On absolution first obtained from Rome,
After my sister's dead and duly mourned for.
He lays much stress on that; it shows his heart.
    Ren. Your Highness knows that heart, how it has stood
Betwixt you and your enemies in the Council;
Nay, saved you oft from peril of your life.
    Eliza. (*rising proudly*). No, 'twas the people's love that
        saved my life.
When the crown's mine I'll be the people's Queen,
And reign for them, by whom I lived to reign.

Ren. (L. C.) A most magnanimous purpose! Now, thank Heaven,
There's nothing stands between the crown and you
But a few sad hours of a sick Queen's life——
Which, let's pray, may be mercifully shortened!
It is that crown Philip would help you bear
With strength of policy and stay of love.

Eliza. (*with bitter irony*). Even such love as he has showed my sister,
Turning from her untended bed of death
With this unnatural tender of his hand!
(*With withering contempt, rising to wrath.*)
Say, did you take me for a fool or beast?
A monster without brains or without heart?
To come to me—you, and your worthy master,
With offers so accursed, and gifts so vile!
Out of my sight, lest I forget my sex
And strike thee!

Ren. Have a care, my passionate madam.
The Queen still lives, and a Queen's dying arm
Can strike when others guide. Even now a warrant
Of treason hangs suspended o'er your head.

Eliza. Treason!

Ren. Aye, treason. Courtenay is in England—
Has raised all Suffolk, in your name and his.
His treason is your treason; the first stroke
That Courtenay strikes finds echo in the fall
Of your head on the scaffold!

Eliza. So be it!
When Courtenay strikes that blow, let my head fall.
My life upon his loyalty!

Ren. You have staked
And lost! Without there! (*One of his suite advances*, C.)
This to Lord Chandos! (*Gives warrant.*)
(ISABEL'S *voice heard outside*, L. C.)
Stay me not! I must speak with her.

Eliza. What's that?
Isabel's voice! Returned!

Enter ISABEL, L. C., *with* SIR J. HARRINGTON, *both disordered, as if from rapid riding.* ELIZABETH *opens her arms to receive her.*

Isabel (*avoiding her embrace and sinking on her knee*).
Not so—my knee! (*Producing ring.*)

This token from Sir Nicholas Throckmorton.

 Eliza.   The ring I bade him send me
With tidings——(*Pausing with emotion.*) Oh, my sister! art
  thou gone?

 Isabel. I was beside her to the last—my hand
Was the last that she pressed.

 Eliza.   I'm glad of that.
(*To* Renard.) Look, sir; this news changes our fortunes
  strangely.
Now, sir, 'tis you are traitor—that dared call
The Queen of England traitor. But the charge
We pardon—not the lie that based the charge—
The slander on a brave and loyal Earl,
Sir Edward Courtenay.

 Ren.   What I heard I spoke,
What I spoke I believed—(*aside*)—and still believe,
Though this news has made loyalty of treason.
Your Majesty's answer to my master's letter?

 Eliza. But this—when next he honours us by writing
That he bethink him of a different message,
And send it by a different ambassador. (*Turns up.*)

      [Renard *bows and exits*, C. L.

  Sir John Harrington *and* Isabel *advance and kneel.*

 Harr. God save your Majesty! (*Points to* Isabel.) As
  she has set
Queen's crown on your head, please you set on hers
The crown of wife—giving her leave to marry
Your foolish faithful gentleman of the chamber.

 Eliza. How! Cat wed dog?

 Harr.   Even so, please your Majesty;
But we've done all our scratching before wedlock—
Henceforth we'll only purr.

 Isabel (*half aside*).   Speak for yourself!

    Enter Sussex, L. C., *and advances.*

 Eliza. Now good speed to your wedding! Such true
  servants
To me must needs be true unto each other.

  (*They kiss her hand, turning as* Sussex *has advanced.*)
My Lord of Sussex. (Sussex *kneels.*)

 Eliza. Rise, my good lord! Your face of gloom but tells
What we have heard already—the Queen's dead.

Sussex. The Queen ne'er dies, and so long live the
    Queen !
Eliza. You come in time—an hour, and you had met us
Escorted to the Tower.
    Sussex.   The Tower?
    Eliza.   For treason
In aiding and abetting Edward Courtenay,
Who, Master Renard late declared, has landed
And risen in arms in Suffolk.
    Sussex.   So 'twas bruited.
    Eliza. But 'tis not true ?
    Sussex.   No. 'Twas one Thomas Cleobury,
Who took my Lord of Devonshire's arms and title.
His levies are dispersed, and himself ta'en.
    Eliza. Ha ! Said I not ? Courtenay was *not* in England !
See a post straight despatched to him at Padua.
We would he first had news of our accession.
    Sussex. My liege, no post can reach him now !
    Eliza. What mean you ?
    Sussex.   He is dead.
    Eliza.   Dead ! Nay, my lord.
Here's too much death : one death that crowns a queen,
And one that robs a woman's heart of more
Than crowns can give. Dead ! When ? where ? Tell me all.
    Sussex. He died at Padua. His servants brought
The tidings to the Court just as I left.
    Eliza. Dead ! Was there nought—no word for me—no
    token ?
    Sussex. Pardon, madam.
This ring and letter——(*Holds them out.*)
    Eliza. (*passionately grasping them*). And thou keep'st
    them from me,
And let'st me prate and pule when I might hold
Something that he has touched, and breathed upon,
And warmed with his last breath of dying love;
                                       (*Looking at letter.*)
True friend ! lost lord ! sole love ! 'tis thy dear hand ;
And these blurred spots are tears, methinks—or kisses,
Thus let me put my tears and kisses to them. (*Kisses letter.*)
Thus only are we fated to be joined.
(*Reads.*) '*Dear love and lady,—When thou read'st these lines*
The hand that scarce can trace them will be cold.
My last breath went to pray all blessings on thee :

For thee my heart beat, till it beat no more.
They that severed hands have wedded souls:
We are one now and for ever—aye, one now—
And ever—and no separation more!

  [PARRY *brings down chair to nearly* C., ELIZABETH
   sinks into it. Burst of trumpets L.

         What's that?

    Enter HARRINGTON, C.

Harr. The Lords of the Council and the great ones
Of the City come to hail their gracious Queen,
Elizabeth.

 Eliza. (*sadly*). What love is left me now
But their love? What to live for, but to make
Them happier than their Queen can ever be?

  Trumpets. Enter Procession L. C. *Tableau.*

Omnes (*kneeling*). Long live Elizabeth! Long live the
 Queen!

Eliza. (*rising, with great emotion—lays her hand upon
 the crown*). Great King of kings! 'tis thou hast willed
 it me.
Guide me, that I may wear it, by thy will.

       (*Trumpets and cheering.*)

   CURTAIN.

The following plots of scenery and properties will be useful to managers in whose theatres the play is acted.

APPENDIX.

SCENE PLOT.

ACT I.

Arch, backed by corridor, with velvet curtain. Large arch and two smaller arches. Illuminated window; 3rd and 4th entrances R.; door, 2 E. R.

ACT II.

1. Queen Mary's Chamber. Doors, 1 E. L. and R.
2. Handsome Elizabethan Chamber. Large windows from 3rd and 4th entrances, L., and branches of trees covered with snow pressing against it. Secret panel, 5 E. L. from 2 E. L. Arch in R. F. showing into Library. Fireplace, R., extending from 5th to 3rd E. Large folding door, L. F., backed by staircase. Bolt on door.

ACT III.

1. Council Chamber.
2. Tower Garden House, 3 E. L. House, 2 E. R. Door, with gratings, 2 E. R. and L. Large tree, C. L., with stone seat. Large postern door, R. C. Wall, about 7 ft. high, running across at back. The White Tower on back cloth.

ACT IV.

Chamber in the Tower. Domed roof. Window, C., with White Tower seen through. Entrances R. and L. 2 E., covered by pieces of old tapestry. Fireplace, L. C.

ACT V.

1. Mary's Bedchamber. Doors, R. and L. 2 E.
2. Room in Hatfield House.

3. Hatfield Hall. Low wainscot, running from C. L. to wing and from C. R. covered with tapestry, leaving C. entrance. Fireplace, R., with large portraits of Henry VIII. and Anne Boleyn.

CURTAIN.

PROPERTY PLOT.

ACT I.

Throne, L. Three seats R. of throne, three L. of ditto. Crimson velvet cloth in front of ditto. Canopy to ditto. Rich velvet curtains to C. archway. Small table with crimson cloth, and seat in recess R. Five seats, R. Chamberlain's wand for Sussex ; wands for ushers. Virginal book for Harrington. Seat for harpist, L. Man to work curtains, C. Twelve spears for Yeomen.

ACT II.

1. Table and chair, R. C. Writing materials on table ; quill pens. Table. 4 ft. from flat. Prie dieu and cushions, L. Illuminated Bible on prie dieu. Two warrants for Gardiner.

2. Fire on hearth, R. Table and chair, R. C. Small table, with embroidery frame, books, lute, &c., L. Candelabra on R. C. table. Large pictures on walls. Wind and man to work it, L. Dark lantern and whip for Harrington. Whip for Courtenay. Lady's riding whip. A mask for Isabel. Twelve musquetoons for Tower Guard. Spears, swords, knives, &c., for retainers.

ACT III.

Keys for Butler ; keys for two warders. Crucifix and book for priest. Axe for executioner and mask. Spears and guns. Bolts, and man to work them, R. and L.

ACT IV.

Rude table and chair nearly R. C. Embroidery frame and needle. Chairs near fire, L. Fire, burning, L. 2. E. Old tapestry covering entrances, R. L. Socket over fireplace to hold lights. Warrant for Gardiner. Blank letter for Elizabeth.

ACT V.

1. Sofa, C. Table, with medicine bottles, &c., and knife. Toilet table, L. Portrait of Philip, in armour, 3 ft. by 2 ft., with piece behind for it to stand. Casket of jewels on L. table. Letter from Renard.

2. Table and chairs, R. C. Keys of the City on cushion ; keys of the Tower, ditto. Sword of State. Crown on cushion. Crozier.

LADY CLANCARTY

OR

WEDDED AND WOOED

A Tale of the Assassination Plot, 1696

An Original Drama

IN FOUR ACTS

(*First produced at the Royal Olympic Theatre, March 9, 1874*)

CHARACTERS.

KING WILLIAM III.	CARDELL GOODMAN.
THE EARL OF PORTLAND.	KNIGHTLEY.
LORD WOODSTOCK.	ROKEWOOD.
LORD CHARLES SPENCER.	VAUGHAN.
LORD CLANCARTY.	JAMES HUNT.
SIR GEORGE BARCLAY.	CAPTAIN GILLE.
SIR JOHN FRIEND.	TREMLET.
ROBERT CHARNOCK.	CLINK.

Officer of the Guards, Smugglers, Soldiers, &c.

LADY CLANCARTY.	SUSANNAH.
LADY BETTY NOEL.	MOTHER HUNT.

TIME.

JANUARY AND FEBRUARY, 1696.

SCENES.

ACT 1.—*The Hurst.—House-of-call for Smugglers and Jacobites in Romney Marsh.*

ACT 2.—*The Earl of Portland's Cabinet, Kensington Palace.*

ACT 3.—*Lady Clancarty's Bedchamber, St. James's Square.*

ACT 4.—*The Gate House at Westminster, and the King's Closet, Whitehall.*

[Copy of Original Bill.]

LADY CLANCARTY;

OR, WEDDED AND WOOED.

The leading incidents and personages of this Play are historical. The history of the Assassination Plot of 1696 has been told in detail by Lord Macaulay from materials furnished mainly by the State Trials of that date. The story of the marriage of Lord and Lady Clancarty while still boy and girl—a practice not uncommon at the time when it occurred—of their long and entire separation, their encounter as strangers, the husband's subsequent discovery of himself to his wife, the rapid growth of their love, Clancarty's arrest in his wife's arms by Lord Spencer, her brother; his condemnation to death under the High Treason Act, for being found in England without Royal License after filling high posts in the Armies and Councils of James II. at St. Germains, and the pardon obtained with difficulty from the King by the loving courage of Lady Clancarty, is also historical. The author is answerable for implicating Lord Clancarty in the Assassination Plot of 1696 (for most of the features and actors of which, as here represented, including the scenes and characters at the Hurst, there is historical authority), and for assigning to him the manly and courageous part in first revealing the plot to the king and the Earl of Portland, which was really played by Thomas Prendergast, a Jacobite gentleman of Lancashire. The Assassination Plot immediately preceded the reunion of Lord and Lady Clancarty, and the combination of the two series of incidents involved no violence to historical consistency.

King William III.... .... MR. CHARLES SUGDEN.
The Earl of Portland...(Groom of the Stole
    and Confidant of the King) .... MR. VOLLAIRE.
Lord Woodstock......(His Son and Private
    Secretary) .... MR. W. H. FISHER.
Lord Spencer...(Son of the Earl of Sunder-
    land) .... MR. W. H. VERNON.
Donagh Macarthy, Earl Clancarty .... MR. HENRY NEVILLE.
Sir George Barclay .... ⎫   MR. L. F. LEWIS.
Sir John Friend .... ⎪   MR. CANNINGE.
Cardell, commonly called ⎪ Jacobites en-
  'Scum,' Goodman ..... ⎬ gaged in the   MR. G. W. ANSON.
Charnock .... ⎪ Assassination   MR. VINCENT.
Rokewood .... ⎪ Plot of 1696.   MR. HODGES.
Vaughan .... ⎪   MR. JAMES.
Knightly .... ⎭   MR. ESCOURT.
Robert Hunt ..(Landlord of the Hurst, in
    Romney Marsh).................. .... MR. GRAEME.
Gille......Captain of a French Smuggling
    Lugger....................................... MR. CRICHTON.
Tremlett...(Usher at Kensington Palace) ... MR. BAUER.
Clink (Turnkey at the Gate House Prison... MR. CULVER.
The Princess Anne .... MISS EMMERSON.

Lady Clancarty...(Daughter to the Earl of
    Sunderland) .... Miss Ada Cavendish.
Lady Betty Noel .... Miss Fowler.
Susannah......(Lady Clancarty's Maid) ...... Miss Annie Taylor.
Mother Hunt .... Mrs. Stephens.

Time—JANUARY to FEBRUARY, 1696.

Act 1.—THE HURST, IN ROMNEY MARSH.
The Jacobites' Rendezvous.

Act 2.—THE EARL OF PORTLAND'S CABINET IN
KENSINGTON PALACE.
A Noble Traitor.

Act 3.—LADY CLANCARTY'S BEDCHAMBER.
A Meeting and a Parting.

Act 4.—DAY YARD IN THE GATE HOUSE PRISON, AND
ROYAL CLOSET IN WHITEHALL.
Woman to the Rescue.

LADY CLANCARTY.

ACT I.

Scene I.

The Hurst. Romney Marsh. A large rudely furnished room, with rough massive beams overhead. A broad fireplace, crossed by a heavy beam, with hearth and great logs burning, L. 2 *and* 3 E. *The broad stone or plate at the back of the fireplace is practicable, and conceals a hiding-place for smuggled goods. Door,* R. C., *communicating with the outside, with heavy bar for closing it inside. Low window in a recess or bay,* C. *Door leading to inner room,* R. 1 E. *Practicable traps leading to places of concealment (according to stage convenience). A rough ladder staircase,* R. 3 E., *leading to upper room, or place of storage for smuggled goods. Through the window, the Marsh Flat, in winter, under snow, with the sea and a late winter afternoon sky. Rude stools, heavy tables, with drinking vessels. As the curtain rises all is brisk movement. Smugglers are passing on kegs and packages from the open door, which others are depositing down the traps and in the hiding-place behind the fire, to reach which the Smugglers pass over the hearth, and stride themselves over the burning logs in their sea boots. Some carry or pass heavier packages up the rude staircase.* CAPTAIN GILLE *is directing.* MOTHER HUNT *and* HUNT *superintending storage of packages and tubs in places of concealment up staircase and down traps.*

Gille. Bear a hand zere! Cheerily, mes enfants. Cheerily, oh! Clear decks and a clean hold; and zen for grog and ze girls of St. Malo!

Mother. Keep them laces and silks for the loft, you lubbers! Set you up handling gentlewoman's gear!

Hunt (*speaking down a trap*). Harkee, you Miss Marjoram, don't you be blocking the marshway with them kegs, or we'll never get the horses loaded to-night.

Mother (coming up to CAPTAIN GILLE). Phew! All aboard, Captain, at last!

Gille. Tousand tanks, la mère. Ma foi (*mopping his forehead, sits on table*), it is ze heaviest cargo ze Belle Rose run dis winter.

Hunt (having shut trap, goes off R. *for bottle and glass*). A flash of lightning, Captain, to take the dust out of your weasand.

Gille (C., *drinking*). Ha, here's fair trade!

Hunt (R., *drinking*). And a misty moon!

Mother (L., *chucking off her glass*). Amen!

Gille. Now he is all stow, toi, Le-Bel, take ze hands down to ze lugger and receive ces Messieurs—for land zem and zere equipages (*shrugs his shoulders*).

[*Exeunt Smugglers, door* L. *back.*

Hunt. I tell you, Captain, I'd rather run a hundred cargoes o' silk and brandy than one of them plaguey papers and politicians. The one may get a man into Ryde Gaol and a 'Chequer fine, but the other leads to Newgate and Tyburn tree.

Gille. Ah, bah! Every bullet have his billet, and every rope's end his rascal. It is one comfort, Père Hunt, ze man dat is born to be hung will nevère be drown!

Mother (stops working). Hush! Hark! Horses outside on the causeway!

Hunt. Hawks, p'r'aps. Look out, Mother! (*Exit* MOTHER HUNT.) What a woman that is, Captain. There's a stowage o' brains inside her head that 'ud puzzle you to think where they was put away; for all the world like run goods on these here premises.

Re-enter MOTHER HUNT.

Mother. Now, Robin Hunt, Robin Hunt, on with thy Sunday coat. 'Tis that big black-a-vice gentleman from London, and some four or five o' the same kidney with him. They're seeing to their beasts.

[MOTHER H. *getting lanthorn.*

Hunt. A gallon o' Nantz on't, they're come to meet thy passengers, Captain.

Sir G. (without). Now, Mother Damnable! show a light in this devil's den of a stable.

Mother (*lighting ianthorn at fire*). Bless him! He makes himself at home. I'll light your honours. [*Exit.*

Gille. Ha! dat my friend, Sir George Barclay, swear like dat!

Hunt. You know him?

Gille. Parbleu! It is now two, tree, six time, I carry him across ze channel. One of your King James's right 'and men, for left 'and work (*motioning over the left, and drawing his hand across his throat*). I tell my gentlemen, Sir George arrive!

Enter SIR GEORGE BARCLAY, SIR JOHN FRIEND, CHARNOCK, *and* GOODMAN.

Sir G. (L.) So, Captain Gille, still at the old work, eh?

Gille (R.) Ma foi! oui, Sir George, all ze two of us—honest trade and honest treason!

Sir J. (L. C.) Hush, friend, hush! for prudence' sake. Pray remember, Sir George, we're a party of honest gentlemen come down to the marshes for snipe shooting.

Gille. And I have brought my Lord Clancarty and his friends across ze Channel for ze same sport. Sall I tell zem you arrive? [*At door.*

Sir G. (*at fire*) Do; and say we shall be glad of their company over a bottle. (*Smugglers go off with* CAPTAIN GILLE.) As gallant a spirit (*moves to fire*), my Lord Clancarty, as any the King has about him. Light-hearted, after his country's breed, but nice, devilish nice, upon the point of honour: so you had best mind your manners, Master Goodman!

Good. (*gets to fire and warms himself*). Prithee, leave my manners to mind themselves, Sir George Barclay (*swaggers to* C.) Will any gentleman here deny they've stood me in indifferent good stead—till now?

[*Twists his moustache and looks round swaggeringly.*
  A noise outside.

Voices—
  No, you shan't!
  Yes, I will!
  Make way, you scoundrels!
  There's company inside! [*Scuffle, clash of sticks.*

Sir G. How now! What's that?

Mother (*entering*). A difference of opinion outside. (*A heavy fall.*) That's settled it.

Enter LORD CLANCARTY, *carrying a stout stick, with* ROKEWOOD, KNIGHTLEY, *and* VAUGHAN.

Clan. (*to the company*). Mille pardons, messieurs ! (*throwing the stick off.*) There's your club, friend ! A stupid rogue of a smuggler that was after barrin' the way to us, so I had to open a road through his thick head.—I'm Lord Clancarty. [*All rise.*

Sir G. (L.) Glad to welcome your lordship on English ground. Let me make known Sir John Friend, Mr. Charnock, Mr. Goodman, all spirits of the right sort.

Clan. Glad to meet so many loyal gentlemen so close on our landing. But remember, Donough Macarthy has changed names, for the nonce, with one Captain Heseltine, a rascal in the Dutchman's service, taken prisoner at Namur, who's just made his escape from France. For these boys here, they've no need of aliases in this good company. Rokewood, Vaughan, Knightley, all of his Majesty's first regiment of Guards (*introducing* SIR GEORGE *to them*). Sir George Barclay, his Majesty's confidential agent in London.

Sir G. (*fills four glasses*). You'll join us in his Majesty's health?

Clan. (*stops him*). Have at you, in a bumper, as soon as we've got our cases ashore and under cover.

Sir G. What do you bring us?

Clan. Corn in Egypt, Sir George. The full equipment of a regiment of dragoons and their ammunition. Then, besides arms, I bring heads and hearts—gentlemen who know how to use them and teach their use.

[*Bows to his companions.* SIR G. *goes to table and writes.*

Sir J. (*aside*). Worse and worse!

Clan. The officers of my own regiment have all volunteered to a man. I can trust them, as the King can, to the death!

Good. (*offensively*). For trusty hands, I hope the cause need not look to foreign importations.

Sir J. We can surely breed our British loyalty at home, as we brew our British beer.

Clan. And both, I hope, unadulterated. But when heads are risked, it's well to know what one has to count on—flank and rear. [*Looks at* GOODMAN.

Good. So 'tis, egad! and so, the fewer Frenchmen, I say, the better!

Clan. I'm Irish, sir; these gentlemen are English. We have to thank France for nothing but hospitality.

Sir G. And claret. Come, try it, gentlemen, and drown all misunderstandings in sound Bordeaux.

Good. (*filling glass and bowing stiffly*). I ask your lordship's pardon. I took your lordship for a Frenchman.

Clan. (*front of table*). I shall be happy to prove my nationality by the best credentials (*touching his sword*)—against the enemy, Mr. ——

Good. Goodman. Cardell Goodman.

Clan. Ah, then, Cardell Goodman, is it?

Good. Perhaps your lordship may have heard my name?

Clan. (*looking him steadily in the face*). Indeed, then, I have, sir; tho', if I remember aright, it was with a shorter handle than Cardell at the head ov it.

Sir J. (*to* CHARNOCK, *chuckling*). A capital thrust at Master Scum.

Good. Handle? The only handle I own to, my lord, is Esquire. Ha! [*Looks round swaggeringly.*

Clan. There are many kinds of Esquire, sir, including Squires of Alsatia (GOODMAN *comes up inquiringly*)—alias sharpers, bravos, and bullies.

Good. I don't like quarrelling in company.

Clan. I don't see how you can do it by yourself.

Good. (*aside, shrinking back cowed*). Curse him! If I don't pay him off for this. [*Walks away* L.

Clan. But our stores must be unshipped by this time; and the sooner they are in safe hiding the better. (*Moving up at door.*) Then there's the dirty money I've in charge, still on board. Methinks I had better see it safe in my cloak bag. (*Comes down with* SIR G.) There may be those, even here, for whose hands louis d'ors will have more attraction than sword hilts. [*With a look at* GOODMAN.

Sir J. The money, gentlemen. By all means let's see after the money. [*Exeunt* SIR J. *and* CHARNOCK.

Good. (*aside, going*). Ah, 'tis not in French coin I look to pay his lordship. [*Exit.*

Clan. Faugh! The place is sweeter now he's gone. Faith! it should be a strong cause to carry as big a villain as that. How come you by this filthy rogue, Sir George? His reputation is so unsavoury, it stinks as far as St. Germains.

Sir G. Rough work needs rough tools, my lord. I found the fellow in our business, and have been forced to leave him there.

Clan. The more's the pity. I never knew flawed blade or damaged character but it failed you at a pinch. And then, in our Irish Brigade, a man gets used to fighting shoulder to shoulder with gentlemen. [*Exeunt.*

Enter C. *and* L. *Smugglers, who go up* R. *by table.*
Enter HUNT.

Hunt (*hurriedly*). Look alive, lads; the hawks are out. Mother Hunt! Mother Hunt! (*Enter* MOTHER HUNT.) Yonder's a carriage and four bogged off the Blue Wall, and company coming to the Hurst.

Mother. Run, Robin, and warn the gentlemen. (*One Smuggler runs off* C. R., *and re-enters shortly.*) They'd rather not be seen. In now, lads, and on with your smocks and smug phizzes. (*Smugglers hurry on smocks, which are hanging up,* R. 3 E. *and seat themselves at table, with mugs and pipes.*) We've no smuggling rogues here—only honest hinds and simple shepherds, over their tuppeny. Hoist thy Saints' day manners, Robin. (*To her husband.*) Where's my Sunday pinners? (*Speaking as she puts them on at fireplace, before a small glass.*) A murrain on them that they must go upsetting at our door. (*Hurries to door, and with change of manner.*) This way, your honours—this way, your ladyships; 'tis a poor place, but I'll warrant as honest as any 'twixt Hythe and Hastings.

Enter LORD CHARLES SPENCER, LADY CLANCARTY, LADY BETTY NOEL, *together, and* SUSANNAH, *and* LORD SPENCER'S *servant. The ladies wear hoods and mantuas, and their skirts are muddy.* HUNT *bows them in, and exit by table* R.

Spen. Thank ye, dame. Beggars cannot be choosers. Anything is better than the Marsh in a January sea fret. Come, mesdames, put a good face on't. It might have been worse. [*Ladies go to fire.*

Lady C. 'Tis our best comfort. (*Ruefully.*) We need some under all this mud.

Betty. For what we have received let us be truly thankful.

Mother. Good heart, how bedrabbled your ladyships be, to be sure. If I might make bold to offer you each a suit of my petticoats.

Betty. I should like it of all things; and a set of thy pinners, too, thou comical old creature. (*To* LADY C.) I vow, my dear, they would be madly becoming.

Lady C. Do, prithee, my lord, see about getting the carriage out of that Slough of Despond!

Mother (R. C.). Ah, the Blue Wall bog, where the supervisor was smothered—last Martinmas was a twelvemonth. (*Re-enter* HUNT *with jug, which he places on* R. *table, and fills the horns for Smugglers.*) They've been for mending it these ten sessions, and nothing done yet, Od rot the justices!

Spen. Meanwhile, can we have help to right the coach, and four fresh horses to carry us as far as Merstham Hatch? [*Goes to ladies.*

Mother. Here are these poor honest shepherds will help all they can. (HUNT *turns and comes down* R.) As simple God-fearing men as you'll easy find in the Marsh are our Hurst shepherds; and for horses, how say'st thou, James? My husband, your honour—a poor simple man too; and twice churchwarden! Keep us humble!

Hunt (R.). We've but our farm cattle, your honour, and 'tis a long stretch to the Hatch, and the roads sore foundrous. I 'most doubt!

Spen. Our horses have come from Ashburnham to-day, and they are dead beat. (HUNT *moves table, stools, and chairs up to staircase, reserving one chair for* LADY BETTY'S *business.*) I told you, ladies, it was impossible to make the journey without relays.

Betty. That's why I insisted. I love the impossible.

Spen. What say you, honest fellows, have you a will to earn a guinea by setting our carriage on its wheels?

Lady C. And keeping it there till we're clear of these dreadful marshes.

[*Smugglers whisper.* MOTHER HUNT *pretends to collect their answers.*

Mother (*up* R.). They're ready, your honours, and thankful, poor souls! Glad to do aught for an honest penny.

Spen. (*to servants*). Go with them and see they do no damage to the coach. (*Men go off with servants.*) I hope, Lady Betty, you repent of your mad freak by this time.

Betty. What! this voyage of discovery from Ashburnham to Merstham by a road no town coach ever travelled before! Nay, not I! I honour myself for the attempt, and I submit, heroically, to the shipwreck, and especially among such a vastly civil set of savages.

Lady C. And while you superintend the extrication of the coach we will rest here—at least here's warmth and shelter and the means of getting our clothes dried.

Spen. You won't mind my leaving you?

Lady C. Why, sure, here should be nothing to fear.

Mother. Fear, dear heart?—nay, barrin' the ager and the rheumatics. [*Goes off*, R.

Betty. And if there were, methinks I should enjoy it. I love a fright, something that makes one's blood run cold.

Spen. Then I'll e'en leave you in this good dame's care till I can announce all ready for the road. I don't know how I shall answer this to my Lord Woodstock, Lady Betty?

Betty (R.). Oh, if my Lord Woodstock cares not enough about me to give me his escort, I don't see I owe *him* an account. (*Exit* LORD CHARLES.) Methinks, of the two of us, I'm not the one he's most civil to.
[*With a look at* LADY CLANCARTY.

Re-enter MOTHER HUNT *with bottle and glass.*

Mother. Now, if your ladyships are for a sip o' strong waters, hot and sweet, we've some as neat Nantz——

Lady C. What's that? [*Rises*, L.

Mother (C.). Bless your ladyship's innocence. 'Tis our name for brandy in these parts.

Lady C. Brandy, my good dame! Why, what dost thou take us for?
[LADY B. *goes to table to fill glass;* LADY C. *interposes.*

Betty (C.) Do, prithee, let's try it, if 'twere but to horrify this precise brother o' thine.

Mother. Or what would your ladyships say to what, mayhap, you'd scarce expect in such a poor place—a dish of right Bohea, honest Dutch shipped?

Betty (C.) Tea here! You wonderful old woman!

Lady C. (L.) You said, Lady Betty, it was an untravelled route. Depend upon it, we've come upon the North-West passage unawares, and reached Cathay, where the tea comes from.

Mother (R.) I've a snug room in yonder, your ladyships, with a corner cupboard of gambroon China—simple as I stand here—to say nought of the tea to serve in it. I warrant the Hurst can hold up its head with houses in Rye and Winchester that think no small beer of themselves! This way, your ladyships. [*Exit*, R. 2 E., *followed by ladies.*

Betty (following). What an old fairy godmother it is! My dear child, I call this perfectly delightful.

Lady C. I can't say I do! but it might be worse. We might be on the Marsh Wall instead of under the Hurst roof, and I, with my own winter thoughts for company, instead of thy mad rattle!

Sus. And they can laugh! I call it dreadful.

[SUSANNAH *is about to follow the ladies, when she meets* MOTHER H. *at* R. *lower door, who re-enters with a china teapot in her hand.*

Mother H. Here's the teapot, mistress, and the tea in it. I suppose you know how to brew a dish of tea?

Sus. Well, I should think so. We drink it reg'lar at my Lord Sunderland's.

Mother H. Oh, indeed! [*Exit.* MOTHER H., R. D.

Sus. Real chany and real tea, too (*smells it*), and smells as good as you could buy at the Smyrna toy-shop in Bond Street! Only to think! and the old witch has made it as strong as if we'd not such a thing as a nerve among the three of us! Ah, there's the kettle.

[*Goes to hearth. As she lifts kettle the chimney-back opens and a huge Smuggler steps out.* SUSANNAH *screams, drops kettle, and goes into hysterics. The Smuggler takes her in his arms.*

1 *Smug.* A wench, and, curse me a woundy pretty one! Don't take on, lass!

[*Tries to bring her to. At her screams* LADY C. *and* LADY B. *appear at inner door,* R., *and Smugglers up trap,* L.

Lady C. Susannah!

Betty. What has happened?

1 *Smug.* Petticoats!

2 *Smug.* And pretty faces atop! Heave-to, my little rovers and show your colours!

[*The Smugglers assail the ladies and the maid.* LADY C. *is seized by two, and struggles in vain to extricate herself from their rude embraces.* LADY B., *more nimble, dodges two who attempt to grasp her, and escapes to door screaming.*

LADY B. *seizes chair that has been placed* R. *by* HUNT, *and throws it in the way of the* SMUGGLERS *who are trying to catch her, and exits,* C. L. *Enter* GOODMAN.

Good. Wenches! A brace! and buona robas! Here's

luck! Way there, you rascals! This is meat for your masters!

Lady C. Let me go, fellows! (*To* GOODMAN.) Sir, as you are a gentleman!

Good. Away, ye tarpaulins! What do you know of offering delicate attentions to a lady? (*Cuffs Smugglers aside and seizes* LADY C. *round the waist.*) There, no struggling! One's escaped, and I've a right to the other.

[*The men* (*up* C.) *remonstrate with each other.*

Lady C. (*appealing to Smugglers*). You are Englishmen! Will none of you protect me? (GOODMAN *tries to kiss her.*) Help! help!

Enter LORD CLANCARTY.

Clan. Back, you rogues! (*Draws and forces back Smugglers with sword.*) Back, for your lives!

1 *Smug.* Sheer off, lads. It's the gentry coves' quarrel now! [*Exit Smugglers by door,* C.

Clan. And you, sirrah! Let that lady go!

[*Lays hands on* GOODMAN'S *shoulder.*

Good (*shaking off his hand*). That you may take my place! Pooh, sir, I'm no Jack, to jump at your bidding.

[*Draw—they exchange a few passes, when* GOODMAN *is disarmed.*

Clan. (C., *to* GOODMAN). Take your life and your sword, sirrah, and learn to make a better use of both, tho', faith, I'm afraid 'tis too late in the day! (*To* LADY C.) Fear nothing, madam, you are safe under my protection.

Good. (L., *aside*). Curse him! One more to your score, my fine gentleman. [*Exit sulkily,* C. L.

Sus. (R.) Oh, my lady! Are they gone? And we're not robbed, murdered, and undone? [*Clings to* LADY C.

Clan. (L.) Sorry you can't have satisfaction, my dear. Hold your noise, girl, can't you? (*To Lady C.*) Be not alarmed, madam, the rogues will give you no more trouble.

Lady C. (R. C.) Oh, sir, you have saved me from a great fear, if not a great danger.

Clan. I hope it was more startling than serious. To be sure, there's no answering for these smuggling knaves—and in their drink too!—the unmannerly ruffians! Lean on me, madam. I'm better than the chair. I'd forgive their bilking the King's duties; but to forget their duty to a woman! Tho', methinks, the *gentleman*—heaven save the mark!—was the more dangerous of the two. But, pardon me, this is a strange, wild place. I hope you are not alone—that's to say, I hope you *are;* for then I can have the pleasure to be useful to you.

Lady C. We are on our way from my Lord Ashburnham's to Sir Edward Dering's, under charge of my brother. Our carriage has foundered in these terrible roads. They are dragging it out. My brother will be better able to thank you than I. Here he comes.

Enter LORD SPENCER *and* LADY BETTY, C. & L.

Betty. Safe, thank heaven!
Spen. My dear Elizabeth!   [*Goes to* LADY C., R. C.
Betty. (L.). Now I can enjoy a comfortable swoon. Support me, somebody.   [*Sinks into a chair.*
Clan. This is too much entirely!   [*Goes to her.*
Spen. (*impatiently*). For heaven's sake, madam! (*To* LADY C.) My dear child, what's all this? Nothing worse than a fright, I hope?
Lady C. Thanks to this gentleman. Who knows from what he has saved me!
   [*Staggers and grasps a chair.* LORD C. *approaches, solicitously.*
Spen. How now! You are hurt?
Lady C. (*smiling reassuringly, though still faint*). Nay, my dear, 'tis nothing. I never even felt faint till now, when there is no reason. See, Lady Betty, 'tis your bad example. Nay, 'tis nothing, Charles, but—(*almost fainting, to* LORD C.)— you will think me a sad coward.
Clan. (C.). It's what a woman ought to be, or where would be the use of men?
Betty (*dolefully*). Will nobody attend to me? Nay, then (*gets up and offers her salts to* LADY C.), I may as well make myself useful. (*To* SUSANNAH. *Goes* R.) Water, child! (SUSANNAH *pretends to be faint.*) What, thou presuming to swoon like thy betters!
   [*Shakes her; she runs off* C. *Crosses to* LADY C. *and offers her scent-bottle.*
Lady C. (R. C.). Nay, nay, this will never do. (*Reviving with an effort.*) My lord, you have yet to thank this gentleman.

Spen. (C.). I thank you, sir, heartily; and should be glad to know by what name—— [*Crosses to* L. C.

Clan. (L., *about to give his own name, but checks himself*) Heseltine—Captain Heseltine.

Spen. Like ourselves, no doubt, brought to this foul hole by some accident?

Clan. No, sir, by a smuggling lugger—landed not an hour ago.

Spen. (*suspiciously*). Landed by a smuggling lugger! From France, then?

Clan. (*with some confusion*). Exactly—from France, where I have been detained——

Re-enter SUSANNAH *with a glass of water.*

Spen. A prisoner?
Clan. A prisoner!
Spen. Since the battle of Landen?
Clan. Before that.
Spen. And you have been exchanged?
Clan. No such luck, sir. Where would I find friends to exchange me? I have made my escape, by help of an honest free-trader, who set me ashore hard by.

Spen. Ha! so much for the appearance of the rogues that so frightened thee, Bess. Doubtless this is the smugglers' house of call.

Betty. Smugglers! That explains the tea. Prithee, let's buy some. And, who knows, there may be French silks and lace to be had cheap. Oh, what a chance! (*Calling.*) Come forth, you gallant smugglers! Here's a brace of customers!

Lady C. Nay, you have not had the pleasure of such close acquaintance with the gentry as I have.

Spen. (*noting on his tables*) This will be news for Mr. Secretary. See, ladies, how, without knowing it, you serve your country. Thanks to your mad freak of following the sea-road, Sir William Trumbull and the revenue officers will have one smugglers' haunt the less to watch on Romney Marsh.

Clan. (L. *aside*) Methinks we'd better be changing our agent.

Betty. Oh dear, oh dear! I'm so sorry!

Lady C. Was ever so hard-hearted a brother! But for the smugglers, what should poor women do in these weary war times for French modes and lappets fit for a lady's wearing?

Spen. Smugglers or none, the rogues have set our coach on its wheels, and Master Hunt has found us horses. I've settled the reckoning. I've not included thy fright, Bess, nor a few other little items of my own noting; but mine host shall repay all scores yet, or I'm mistaken. Captain Heseltine, do you make for London?

Clan. I do, sir, at the best speed the Sussex roads will allow.

Spen. I trust we may meet there. If it should be in my power to repay your seasonable service, command me.

Lady C. And me, Captain Heseltine.

Clan. Pardon me, you have my name—I rather think you forgot to give me yours.

[LADY C. *is about to give it.* LORD SPENCER *stops her.*

Spen. I crave your pardon, sir; but our names had better remain a secret here, just now. This address will find me (*writes on leaf of tablets, tears it out, and gives it to* CLAN-CARTY), where there will be no reason for such mystery. Come, the coach waits, and we shall be late on the road.

[*Exit, leading the way.* LADY C. *and* LADY B. *turn back on the threshold and whisper.*

Betty. What! *you* won't? Nay, then, one incognito's enough, in all conscience. I'm Lady Betty Noel, at your service (*curtseying*); and am to be heard of at my Lord Gainsborough's, in Soho Square. [*Exit.*

Clan. (*gets round to* R.) Sure, I'll be glad to hear of your ladyship, and gladder still to see your good-looking face.

Lady C. Farewell, sir. I am sorry for the reserve my brother lays upon me. We have met strangely, but not, I hope, for the last time. My brother has offered you his service. Think what a claim you have on mine!

[*Exit,* C. L.

Clan. Claim! A fig for claims! When did an Irish gentleman ever acknowledge claims, in love or in law either? 'Tis the demands that come without a claim—debts of honour and loves of inclination—that bind a gentleman. (*Crosses to* L.) But for that sour-faced protector, I'd have had her name without asking; and a sweet name it should be, if it's like the face that owns it. Faith! 'tis well 'Im married, or it's leaving the King's business I'd be to follow my own pleasure, and that's in those beautiful eyes. What's here? (*Looking at papers given him by* LORD SPENCER.) 'For C. S., in St. James' Square.' The Court quarter of the town anyway. 'Right hand corner of King's Street. Present this.' Trust me for that, Mr. C. S. And when I see your charming companion, trust Donough Macarthy to improve the acquaintance. If this is the first-fruits of my borrowed name, it's mighty obliged I should be to Captain Heseltine for the loan of it! She is as high-born as she's beautiful—no need of a name to tell me that—and as kissable as she's high-born. Ah! now (*sighing*), what a coxcomb am I, letting my wits go wandering after her like this! Haven't I my work and my wife to think of? Either of them should be bother enough for a man, let alone both. (*Enter* SIR GEORGE BARCLAY.) How now, Barclay? You seem merry.

Sir G. (L.) A prize, my lord, a prize! Worth any three of the King's best privy councillors in an exchange of prisoners! Here's a chance to seize and ship him off to St. Malo under Gille's hatches! Why, man, 'tis Lord Spencer!

Clan. Lord Sunderland's son! The devil it is!

Sir G. The same—that Whig of Whigs! One of the little Dutchman's staunchest friends, and a main pillar of the Privy Council. My private advices told me of a scheme for inspection of the South coast defences, in preparation for the French invasion which we are here to second by a rising. My hopes of the Garter to a rotten orange, 'tis his inspection of the South coast defences has brought him into these Sussex wilds, and in this weather.

Clan. But what would he be doin' with the ladies on such a business? He doesn't look like a man to ask their company for diversion.

Sir G. Their presence is but a blind, and their visits to noblemen's seats in these parts but a cover for his inspection.

Clan. And who are they—who are they?

Sir G. Lady Betty Noel, my Lord Gainsborough's mad daughter.

Clan. I know her—'tis the other, man, the other?

Sir G. Lord Spencer's sister!

Clan. His sister—my—— (*Ends in a whistle.*) Hooroo! Hooroo! (*Tosses up his hat.*) 'Tis the happiest fellow I am—or will be! His sister!

Sir G. How now, my lord! Are you gone crazy?

Clan. Sure, isn't it enough to drive a man crazy? That darlin'—that angel—is my wife!   [*Crosses to* L.

Sir G. A wife you do not know, and that does not know you!

Clan. Faith, I doubt if that's such a novelty. The stranger thing and the pleasanter, is a couple ten years wedded, with their honeymoon still before them. And I feel as if honeymoons, like good wine, improved by keeping. We were buckled by my Lord Sunderland's contrivance, when she was twelve, poor innocent, and I was under fifteen. But then it wasn't *me* my lord was marrying her to, but my estates, that covered the best of two Irish counties then. It's my hat can cover them now. Man and wife parted at the church door, to go back to their school-rooms. In a few years I was swinging a sword, as long as myself, for the King—God bless him!—and my lord and father-in-law was praying as loud for the little Dutchman out of his Protestant prayer-book, as ever he'd prayed for the King from his breviary. Since I gave her my first and last kiss at parting, some ten years since, I've not clapt eyes on her till to-day. Even letters have been forbidden between the poor Irish Jacobite exile and the proud and politic minister's daughter. And now you ask me to introduce myself to my lady by clapping a pistol to her brother's head!

Sir G. Faith! I admit 'tis awkward.

Clan. Not but what I'd be glad to get rid of him in a more gentlemanly way. But as to kidnapping a brother-in-law, to say nothing of frightening the lady, upon my honour, Sir George, it goes against my feelings as a husband; I'm new to the business, and they are tender.

Sir G. I grant you, my lord, it does look objectionable. Well, we will spare my Lord Spencer to your relationship, all the readier that you may turn your connection with him to better account for us.

Clan. How's that?

Sir G. By making yourself known to your wife, winning her confidence, and through her mastering your brother's secrets—information, influence—to be used at need, on behalf of the cause. Zounds! This will be a better scheme than carrying him off prisoner.

Clan. Oh, you think it easier for me to play the spy than the kidnapper? Well, then, between ourselves, I don't.

Let us fight fair, if only because we have to fight our countrymen. There's no authority on fighting like an Irishman. You may trust me when I tell you this is not fair fighting!

Sir G. Odds blood, my lord, where did you pick up these scruples? Not at St. Germains, I'll be sworn! His Majesty is not so nice. *He* has no objection to catch his enemy napping—if it be from behind a wall!

Clan. Faith, they say that's Irish practice; but if so, we don't travel with it. I don't understand you.

Sir G. It is time you should; and here come our friends who *do!*

Enter SIR JOHN, CHARNOCK, GOODMAN, VAUGHAN, ROKEWOOD, *and* KNIGHTLEY, C.

Sir G. (C., *to* GOODMAN). Come, Mr. Goodman, you and my lord have had a tiff, I hear: you must shake hands upon it.

Sir J. (R.). Aye, aye; friends all, so say I. Friend by name and friend by nature.

Good. (R. C., *sulkily*). His lordship has given my right wrist a wrench that makes handshaking painful. If he likes the left——

Clan. (L.). 'Tis unlucky, they say, Mr. Goodman. Better wait till you have recovered the use of your right.

Sir G. In deference to his lordship's wish, our plan for clapping Lord Spencer under hatches is given up.

Sir J. 'Tis a grievous pity. 'Twas a good, safe, pleasant plan, with the least risk of broken heads.

Sir G. His lordship had scruples about kidnapping.

Good. Scruples! Pooh! You don't find us setting up scruples. 'Tis a gentleman's first duty to get rid of them.

Sir J. But if his lordship object to kidnapping a privy councillor, what will he say to our plan for kidnapping the great little Dutchman himself?

Clan. The devil! Kidnap the Prince of Orange! I'm thinkin' you'll find him a big mouthful to swallow.

Sir G. If 'tis not rendered unnecessary by a stray shot.

Clan. Come, we're among friends here. Suppose we call things by their right names, and say 'assassination' clean out?

Sir G. That's a word confined to *private* quarrel. In public 'tis called levying war. I hold here King James's commission to levy war on the Prince of Orange. We have

gained over some of the Blues who are on guard this month. Admitted to the gardens of Kensington Palace by their aid, we fire the place, and in the confusion carry off the King. We have a ship ready to receive him off Deal, unless——
                                               [*Pauses.*
  Clan. Unless——   [*All look at one another.*
  Good. (*slowly, and looking hard at* CLANCARTY). Unless, in the mêlée a bullet should let daylight thro' the Orange!
  Sir J. Quite by accident?
  Clan. Of course!
  Good. In which case we shall leave the Dutchman for his afflicted subjects and Westminster Abbey, or the foot of Tyburn gallows, as the case may be.
  Clan. Gentlemen, I beg you to believe me when I say that I never heard a whisper of this till now. I came here to aid and abet a Jacobite rising.
  Sir G. Of which this is the prologue.
  Good. And, like many prologues, better than anything in the play.
  Clan. Have you thought how England is likely to esteem the cause so ushered in? How posterity will judge it? How, even if the actors in it escape the gallows now, the terrible hand of History will gibbet them for all time to come?
  Good. Hang posterity!
  Sir J. And let posterity hang us, provided Jack Ketch be spared the office.
  Sir G. (*sarcastically*). If your scruples hold you back here, too, my lord, thank them for their care of your neck, and stand aloof till it is safe to strike in with us. Come, gentlemen, now the arms are safely bestowed we must be riding towards Rochester. While we saddle we will leave my lord to digest his squeamishness.
            [*Exit* SIR G., SIR J., GOODMAN, *and* CHARNOCK.
  Clan. (*alone*). Digestion follows appetite, and I've no appetite for this business; yet, for a healthy hatred of the little Dutchman, I'll yield to no gentleman at St. Germains. But between raising the country against him and shooting him in the back there's all the difference of soldier's work and stabber's. My sword and my service were engaged for war—not murder. If that's over-nicety, I *am* over-nice. (*Crosses* L.) And now, more than ever, that I know the jewel of a wife that's waiting for me; when I've the chance

to woo and win her, as win her I will, let them call it Irish fashion, ten years after wedding her. What! to bring a blush into that beautiful face—to lay in those pretty white fingers a hand red with blood, foully shed! Not at the call of all the Stuarts ever crowned, much less one of their Scotch agents. An Irishman wouldn't have done it. But 'tis not enough to hold aloof from the plot—I must set my wits to prevent it. How I may do this with honour I must think as we ride to London. (R.) Yes, if I put on the black mask 'tis not for the blood and booty of the road— 'tis to save my fellow *gentlemen* of the King's highway, as well as their victim! (*Enter* SIR G., SIR J., GOODMAN, CHARNOCK, ROKEWOOD, *and* KNIGHTLEY, *followed by* HUNT *and* MOTHER HUNT *with bottles and glasses.*) Come, the stirrup cup!

Sir G. (C.). A parting word, my lord, over our parting glass. Our horses are saddled; have you swallowed your scruples?

Clan. (R.). Anyway, I've circumvented them. Gentlemen, I will ride with you.

All. Well said, my lord!

Sir G. That's a brave heart! Come, friends, I'll give you our own toast. Fill all! (*They take glasses as* MOTHER HUNT *fills.*) Here's to the squeezing of the rotten Orange!

[*All repeat toast, with* Hip! Hip! Hurrah!

ACT-DROP.

ACT II.

SCENE.—*Duke of Portland's Cabinet at Kensington Palace, communicating by a door* C. *and outer corridor with the formal garden on which the windows look. The room is panelled in dark wood, and arranged in the style of the rooms in Queen Anne's suite at Hampton Court. In the panels are Dutch flower pictures. On the consoles and mantelpiece tall pieces of blue Dutch ware. Furniture, couch, clocks, &c., in the style of the time. A large writing-table or bureau. Console tables under the windows, settees, tables, chairs. In the angles,* R. *and* L., *corners, doors in panelling. Fireplace with high mantelpiece and picture over it. Folding doors,* C. *and* L., *opposite fireplace. Usher discovered at back of table arranging papers.* LORD

WOODSTOCK *enters, whispers* USHER, *who exits* L. D. *and re-enters almost immediately, announcing—*
Usher. My Lord Portland !

Enter LORD PORTLAND. LORD WOODSTOCK *rises and bows respectfully.*

Port. So, Harry, I am glad to find thee.

Wood. Sir John Friend attends your commands, sir, in the next room, and the Romney Marsh landlord and his wife are here, under guard.

Port. Ah ! ah ! my Lord Spencer's acquaintances ! 'Tis well. His lordship will be here anon. We will question them together, But, first, Harry, I have private business for thine ear. (*Sits* R. C.) Thou know'st the unlucky marriage contracted some ten years since between Lord Sunderland's daughter Elizabeth and the Jacobite, Lord Clancarty. My Lord Sunderland had a sharp eye to his own interest as usual ; but 'tis not the first time his shrewdness had led him astray. He has had bitterly to repent that marriage—to see his son-in-law an exiled traitor and his great estates sequestered.

Wood. Not altogether to my disadvantage, my lord.

Port. True. The King has been graciously pleased to invest thee with some of his baronies. (*Motions him to sit —he does so.*) It only needs a Bill of Divorce, easily to be procured on the score of his treason and desertion, to make her husband as dead to her in law as he is, in fact, already. Such a Bill has been prepared by agreement of my Lord Sunderland and myself. That passed, 'tis further agreed my Lord Clancarty shall give her hand to Henry, Lord Woodstock (WOODSTOCK *half rises*), whom the King is then to invest with the estates and titles of Donough Macarthy, Earl Clancarty. (WOODSTOCK *rises*). How say you, sirrah ? You know the lady. Is she not a prize worth winning ?

Wood. Worth winning indeed, my lord. But is this winning her ?

Port. Wed her first, man, and win her afterwards. 'Tis the safer way with a wife !

Wood. But what says the lady to this ?

Port. She has not been consulted, that I know of. No fear but she will prefer the substance of a husband to the shadow. Besides, not to flatter thee, Harry, thou lackest nothing that is most likely to please a woman ; and, not to flitter myself, my favour with the King makes our alliance well worthy of even my Lord Sunderland's ambition.

Wood. I see; my agreement, my lord, is taken as a matter of course.

Port. Lady and estate considered, I confess I had not thought needful to ask it; and, in truth, Harry, I had rather think thee unfettered than in the chains the town gives thee.

Wood. May I ask whose, my lord?

Port. That feather-headed daughter of my Lord Gainsborough's, Lady Betty Noel. (*Hand on* WOODSTOCK's *shoulder.*) Believe me, my dear lad, for all thy Dutch blood thou hast not ballast enough for two. She will be the better of a graver husband, and thou of a staider wife.

[*Usher announces* LORD SPENCER, L.

Enter LORD SPENCER, *bowing to* PORTLAND *and* WOODSTOCK.

Port. (R.). Exact to your hour as ever, my lord.

Spen. (*crosses to* C.). Methinks punctuality should be no credit to a gentleman; but in this case your praise is deserved, for I bring a lady, my sister, summoned with Lady Betty to attend her Royal Highness the Princess Anne, on this her first visit to Kensington since the Queen's death.

Port. May this reconciliation of the Princess and his Majesty help to foil the desperate designs of the Jacobite faction.

Spen. Amen! Besides, 'twill needs go far to dash the factious hopes founded on the Princess's accession. We want all the loyal strength of the kingdom to put down the pestilent traitors. Touching those designs—(*takes report from pocket*)—I bring, for his Majesty's eye, the report of my private inspection of the Southern coast defences.

Port. (*moves up* R. C.). 'Twere best you saw the King at once.

Spen. I am at your lordship's orders. (*Bowing to* WOODSTOCK.) My lord! [WOODSTOCK *bows.*

Port. Apropos (*comes down*), I have broken to my son the project your father has done me the honour to form for a union of our houses.

Spen. (*to* WOODSTOCK). Then I may hope soon to have in your lordship a brother, as well as a friend.

Port. This way, my lord, to the King's closet.

[*Exit* PORTLAND *and* SPENCER *by door in panelling*, R. *corner.*

Wood. (*crosses to* C.). Brother as well as friend! I fear the one relationship may spoil the other. This is intolerable! Grown man and woman's hands given away like christening-gloves! (*Sits.*) My Lady Clancarty is a charming woman. We have been excellent friends. Nay, my dear, mad Betty has been jealous of her more than once. But a man would revolt against Helen herself, were she flung at his head thus. (*Takes stage* R.) My Lady Betty Noel may be as feather-headed as my lord and father pleases; but I like feathers in a woman's head. They are as much in place there as in a peacock's tail. (*Crosses to* L. C.) I must see my Lady Clancarty, and put her on her guard. (*Goes to table.*) 'Tis lucky she's in the palace. Her woman shall slip my letter into her hand.

[*Goes to table and writes.* LADY BETTY *about to enter by secret door in panel* R. *corner, pauses on threshold.*

Betty (*aside*). Writing. To me, of course!

Wood. Now to find her waiting-maid. [*Exit* L. *door.*

Lady B. (*back of table*). There's the letter, unsealed, and undirected too—I wonder? For the Lady Betty Noel? No! (*Coming down* C., *while she reads direction,*) 'To the Lady Clancarty—privately, these.' Oh, the wretch! This accounts for his late barbarous neglect of me—his odious attentions to her. All the town talked of them! What does he dare to say to her? (*Takes up letter.*) I wish there *had* been a seal, that I might have broken it, as he does every vow that ought to bind a man (*reads letter*): '*Lord Woodstock begs most instantly a brief interview with my Lady C. in the Earl of Portland's closet. Lady C. will find the private stair from the presence room open.*' Oh, the villain! The passage he once gave me the secret of—'*The happiness of both may depend on what Lord W. has to break.*' (*Repeating*) 'What Lord W. has to break?' (*Flings letter on table.*) That's my heart! Oh, who would have thought Elizabeth such a serpent? (*Takes stage* L.) But I'll be a match for them! Never think, my lord, your inconstancy shall make me hang my head and fall into a silly, unbecoming green sickness. I'll revenge myself by being ten times more pervesre than ever. He called me a madcap. He little knows what I can be when I put my mad-cap on in sober earnest. (*Crosses to* R.) Here he comes!

Re-enter LORD WOODSTOCK.

Wood. Plague on't, I can't find her woman. (*Surprised.*) Ha, Lady Betty! you will be missed in the presence-room.

Betty (R.). Missed! scarcely by your lordship, at all events. There are others there to supply my place—far more agreeably. Can I carry any message—a letter—thither from your lordship?

Wood. So! this is fortunate You will much oblige me if you will give this to my Lady Clancarty, and unobserved, if possible. [*Goes to table for letter, which he seals.*

Betty (L. C., *aside, while he is sealing letter*). He seals it first. He little thinks I know its horrid contents. Vastly fine, my lord, vastly fine! (LORD W. *gives her letter.*) Sure, I am too happy to be of any service to your lordship and my Lady Clancarty (*bitterly and with an effort*)—as carrier of your correspondence, above all things.

[LORD W. *looks astonished.*

Usher (*announces*). Captain Heseltine!

Betty (*aside*). Here's a godsend! Captain Heseltine, my preserver!

Wood. (*after a puzzled glance at her, to* USHER). I do not know the gentleman!

Usher. He must see my Lord Portland, he says, on matter of moment.

Wood. Admit him. (*After a look at* LADY B., *takes back his letter; goes up* R.) I will not put you to the trouble. (*To Usher.*) Let one of the pages give this to my Lady Clancarty.

[*Exit Usher*, L. D., *with letter*, WOODSTOCK *opening the door ceremoniously and bowing to* LADY B.

Betty. No, my lord, no; I cannot leave the room without seeing Captain Heseltine.

Wood. Madam!

Betty. Oh, how I long once more to thank my gallant champion!

Usher shows in LORD CLANCARTY.

Clan. A lady! Egad, 'tis my luck! Madam, I have the honour. (*Aside.*) Who the plague is this, I wonder?

[LADY B., C., *affects confusion and interest.*

Wood. You know this gentleman?

Betty. Know him? Do I not know him?

Wood. (R.). My Lord Portland is engaged with his

Majesty; but I am his secretary—at your service. Madam, this gentleman is here for business.

Betty. What business can come before such thanks as I owe Captain Heseltine?

Clan. (L.). Madam, I vow—— [*Astonished.*

Betty (L. C.). Pray do not, sir, or, like the rest of your sex, 'twill be but to break it. I fear you do not recognise in me one of the ladies you so bravely rescued t'other day in Romney Marsh.

Clan. Recognise you, madam! I might have forgotten the service; but the ladies——(*Bowing courteously. Aside.*) Now, a plague on me if I knew her!

Betty. Gallantry, sir, can afford to forget, but not gratitude.

Clan. Your ladyship overrates my trifling service. 'Tis more than repaid by your recollection of it. But there's a rascally spoil-sport called business. (*Crosses to* LORD W.) My lord, I must press for an instant and private interview with my Lord Portland. (*Aside to* LORD W., *and very earnestly.*) Indeed, it is on matter of life and death.

Wood. I will tell my lord. (*Crosses to* LADY B.) Madam, may I offer you my hand to the presence-room?

Betty (L.). I am infinitely obliged by your lordship's attention, but I prefer to stay here. I hope I, too, my lord, may have my private interview—if not in your lordship's way and any other lady's.

Wood. (*angrily*). S'death, madam, have what you will. Thank my stars, I am not your guardian yet.

[*Exit by door in panel,* L.

Betty (L, *exultant*). He's angry! He's horribly angry! I've wounded him, the barbarous villain! Oh, sir (*to* LORD C., *very demonstratively, blushing and turning away*)—now I'm all of a tremble!

Clan. (R.). What the plague is she at? Am I going to be made love to at the point of the sword?

Betty (*in real confusion*). I am afraid you will think my behaviour very strange, Captain Heseltine.

Clan. Nay, madam. Why should I be thinking anything strange that procures me this pleasure?

Betty. But I hope you will not misunderstand. In truth, Sir, I am not the bold creature you must think me.

Clan. (*aside*). Faith! 'tis I am expected to be bold, 'twould seem. 'Pon my honour, madam, you owe me nothing (*goes to her*), not even an explanation. Compose yourself.

    [*As he takes her hand enter* LADY CLANCARTY *by door in panel,* R.; *mutual surprise and embarrassment.*

  Betty (*aside*). Oh, this is excellent! (*With an appearance of surprise.*) My Lady Clancarty!

  Clan. (*turns*). Confusion! That my darling should find me thus! Madam!   [*Bows to* LADY C.

  Lady C. (*down* R.). I beg your pardon! I expected to find——

  Betty (L. *bitterly*). My Lord Woodstock! I know—for a private interview. Nay, we will leave you to it. (*To* CLANCARTY.) Come, Captain Heseltine!

  Lady C. I am very glad, sir, to have the opportunity of thanking you in London.

  Betty. Nay, your lordship's thanks must wait, I fear. I have to ask Captain Heseltine's escort as far as the presence chamber. (*Aside.*) The demure minx! she shall not rob me of them both, I swear!

  Clan. (*to* LADY BETTY). I am more mortified than I can say, madam; but I dare not leave this room, where I await my Lord Portland. Besides, I would gladly have some friendly private speech of my Lady Clancarty, if she would vouchsafe me the favour.

  Lady C. I have no right to refuse Captain Heseltine even a greater request.   [*Bowing.*

  Betty (*very angrily*). The unconscionable coquette! She carries 'em all off, and I've nobody.   [*Exit* L.

    [*Pause.* LORD *and* LADY C. *remain for a moment silent and embarrassed.*

  Clan. Believe, me, madam, 'twas to an accident I owed my meeting with that lively lady.

  Lady C. Accident is very kind sometimes, sir!

  Clan. So 'tis, indeed, when it procures me the joy of meeting *you*.

  Lady C. A strange contrast with our last encounter.

  Clan. Would you think me very presumptuous if I ventured to prefer the occasion which enabled me to render you a service, however trifling?

  Lady C. And so left me heavily your debtor. Methinks debt is never pleasant.   [*Motions him to chair.*

  Clan. A man gets used to it, and so, I dare say, a lady might, if she'd try.

Lady C. I looked to our first meeting in London to pay off part, at least, if not all, of what I owe you.

Clan. I'm used to owing, madam, not to be owed to. (*Sits.*) Let me enjoy awhile the new pleasure of being creditor—your creditor, above all!

Lady C. I fear the burden might grow too heavy. No; I prefer paying! My brother has much influence, though I fear *I* cannot boast of any. I presume you are here to bespeak the favour of Lord Portland?

Clan. Nay, madam, strange as it may seem, I am here rather to render my lord service than to ask it of him.

Lady C. I am glad, for your sake, though I regret it for my own; for so I still must remain your debtor.

Clan. And yet I have a great favour to ask of you—a favour, not for myself, but for one who has been my best and closest friend during my long detention in France.

Lady C. And can I help him?

Clan. Indeed you can, madam; none so well!

Lady C. Who is he?

Clan. Donough Macarthy, Lord Clancarty!

Lady C. (*rises*) My husband! You have seen him, then —know him?

Clan. I have been his closest friend. (*Both rise.*) I know his inmost thoughts, as he knows mine; and I know there is no wish so dear to his heart as the desire to be re-united to you.

Lady C. Alas, sir, if that rested with me! But there is no one on whom it depends so little. I have had no more voice in our separation than in our marriage.

Clan. My friend knows that, madam! I never heard him breathe a word of blame on you, in all his unhappiness.

Lady C. Is he so unhappy, sir?

Clan. As far as nature will let him. He has a light heart, but a heart of air would be heavy, at times, in his predicament. Poor and proscribed—shut out from the honours and ambitions of his rank—an exile from country—his friends; and, strange as that may sound in a catalogue of privations now-a-days—his *wife!*

Lady C. Methinks *I* can be but little in his regrets. We were separated while still children.

Clan. Who knows, madam, but that may be the reason? (*Look from* LADY C.) Besides, levity apart, the heart has its own memories. I've heard him say he feels that, in separa-

R

tion from you, he loses all that would have made home heaven upon earth. And, upon my honour, madam, I think he is right.

Lady C. He is fortunate in a friend that can feel—that can plead for him so warmly.

Clan. For now, for the first time, his friend can understand what he has lost.

[*In a thoughtful manner crosses to* L., *then turning suddenly.*

Lady C. You are in correspondence with my lord?

Clan. I know 'tis little better than treason to own to it.

Lady C. Nay, sir, you may trust me even with treason, unless it be to my lord. Would I were as sure I could trust you.

Clan. Trust me *fully* and *freely.* Anything you may confide to me, madam, I will answer for reaching my Lord Clancarty as safely as if you had said it to him with your own beautiful lips.

Lady C. Then tell him, sir, that I feel deeply for him, and share his wish that our separation were at an end—that, tho' we have been so long and so entirely parted, I have had a woman's curiosity concerning him—that I have learned nothing of him to make me ashamed of his name—nothing that has not led me rather to honour and esteem him as a noble and true-hearted gentleman.

Clan. (*moves towards her*) Oh, madam, if you knew how —more than happy—how intolerably proud this news will make him!

Lady C. Methinks 'tis no little in my lord's favour that he should have made you so entirely his friend.

Clan. More than ever his friend, since I knew his wife, and what she feels for this luckiest—if most unlucky—of husbands.

Lady C. And yet, after all, my feelings can be but a fancy, like his own. Strangers as we are, how do we know but, if we met, we should soon be as indifferent to each other as I see so many couples about the Court?

Clan. (*movement*) I will answer for — my friend. Madam, you will have—nay—you *have* a husband who *adores* you!

[*Approaching her ardently.*

Lady C. (*slightly withdrawing*) Nay, sir; who adores some imaginary being his fancy has given my name to.

Clan. You forget, madam, I have had time to describe you to him since we met in Romney Marsh.

Lady C. I fear, from all I see of your style, that you have been a flattering painter.   [*Goes up.*

Clan. A bungling one. But what picture would not fall short of such an original?

[*Approaching to take her hand, she draws back with dignity, and re-seats herself.*

Lady C. We forget our main business. How can I forward my lord's wish for a reunion?

Clan. (*aside*) Now for a bold stroke! (*Aloud.*) The shortest way is the best.—By obtaining your father's leave to join your husband.

Lady C. Oh, if my wishes could prevail!

Clan. Then *you* desire it?

Lady C. I may speak freely to my husband's friend. (*Rises and comes* C. R.)   Think, sir, what it is for a woman, young, high-spirited, well-born, here, in a Court, with more flatterers than friends about her, yet with some true and tender friends—who would fain be more to her than friends— to have but a memory and a fancy to help duty in its watch over all she has given to her to guard, in her lord's name and her own honour. Methinks no man can understand this, yet only one who can know how I long to be with my lord—stranger to me as he is.

Clan. When he knows this, think you any danger will long keep you strangers? But promise me you will use all your influence with your family.

Lady C. I fear the attempt would be hopeless. Even if my father were less obdurate, my brother's prejudice against my lord, his party, his cause, his principles, is very, very bitter.

Clan. Methinks, madam, *your* pleading should be able to soften hearts of stone!

Lady C. And then my lord must not forget that, if I joined him, for me too this would be exile.   [*Pause.*

Clan. (R. C.) True! I fear your husband was but selfish; he but thought of his own happiness (*sighing*), not yours.

Lady C. (*approaching him*) Nay, sir, methinks 'tis I am selfish now. Strangers as we are, I am his wife, and bound to a wife's duty. My best happiness should be his.

Clan. (*passionately seizing and kissing her hand*) Madam, you are an angel.

Lady C. (*with dignity*, C.) Sir!

Clan. Pardon me, a man may call his best friend's wife an angel, and no treason!

Enter LORD SPENCER; *he catches sight of* LORD CLAN-CARTY'S *attitude of passion.*

Spen. (*aside*) Ha! he held her hand. How now, my lady? The Princess has asked for you. Who is this?

Lady C. (*crosses to* C.) Do you not know my preserver at the Hurst, Captain Heseltine?

Spen. I am glad to meet you, sir; and gladder still to meet you here. The Hurst was but a questionable place of encounter.

Clan. (*laughing*) I hope your lordship does not suspect me of any connection with the fair traders? (*Puts chair back*, L.) I wish my hands were as clean of all sins as of smuggled silks or laces.

Spen. (R.) Now we *have* met again, how can Lord Spencer serve Captain Heseltine?

Lady C. (C.) I have learned already, brother; Captain Heseltine is too generous to ask any favour for himself.

Spen. Faith, sir, in that you do not follow the London fashion.

Lady C. All his petitioning is for a friend.

[*Goes up to her brother.*

Spen. (C., *to* CLAN.) Your friend, sir, is fortunate.

Clan. (R.) Not so, my lord (L.), the most unfortunate of men; at once nobleman and beggar, husband and widower, a curse to those he loves best, an enemy to his brother-in-law—if not in love—and so amiable a brother-in-law!

Spen. You speak in riddles, sir.

Lady C. 'Tis but the truth, brother. (*Lays her hands pleadingly on her brother's arm.*) This gentleman's friend is my ill-starred lord!

Spen. The Lord Clancarty! (*Puts away his sister's hand;* CLAN. *bows.*) This is scarce the place to plead for a traitor. (*Crosses to* C.) I am sorry that you, sir, who wear his Majesty's uniform, and should be a loyal subject, are so ready to avow yourself the friend of one of the King's least pardonable enemies.

Clan. (*hotly*) Egad, sir, I'm not the only one that wears the King's uniform who has friends at St. Germains, though it is not the fashion to *own* them.

Lady C. He does not ask much for my lord—but that I may have the privilege of joining him in exile.

Spen. (*sternly*) I would sooner you joined him in his coffin! You may tell as much, sir, to my Lord Clancarty.

[*Crosses to* C.

Lady C. (R.) But not in such cruel words, sir, for my sake!

Clan. Your lordship is hard upon my poor friend.

Spen. If I am, do you think it is because he is an Irishman, a beggar, and an exile? It is for the cause that makes him two of the three at least; for his surrender of the liberties of his country, his adherence to that priest-ridden tyrant who calls himself King of England, yet plays into the hands of France at St. Germains!

Clan. (*angrily*) 'Tis but fair to remember, my lord, that this priest-ridden tyrant is the sovereign to whom Lord Clancarty has sworn allegiance; that this sovereign's faith is Lord Clancarty's faith; that if King James asks the aid of France, 'tis but to restore a true church and a lawful king to England.

Spen. These principles in this place!

Clan. They are Lord Clancarty's! I am speaking *his* thoughts, that there may be no mistake about him and them, in wife or brother-in-law. For myself, I will not presume to argue the public point with your lordship; 'tis for the private friend, the husband, I had dared to plead with my lady here.

[LADY CLANCARTY *is about to speak;* LORD S. *stops her.*

Spen. And it is by her brother that she answers you. Lady Clancarty (*keeps her hand*) knows too well what is due to her name, and her duty as a subject, to listen to any overtures from a traitor, most deservedly proscribed. Nay, more, if you are in commerce of letters with my Lord Clancarty, 'twere well you informed him that his wife's nearest friends are even now about freeing her from the tie that still binds her hand, though not her heart.

Clan.   } My lord!
Lady C. } What do you mean?

Spen. (*to* LADY CLANCARTY) Your father and my Lord Portland have already settled the heads of a Divorce Bill, which will leave you free for a happier and more fitting marriage.

Clan. (*aside*) So I am just in time, it seems.

Lady C. A Divorce Bill, and I learn this now for the first time!

Spen. Good news cannot come too suddenly. I give you joy of this prospect of freedom and happiness to come.

Lady C. And have my lords, besides thus kindly freeing me from *one* husband, been graciously pleased to find me another?

Spen. Their choice has agreed on my Lord Woodstock.

Clan. (*aside*) A highly creditable successor!

Lady C. (*ironically*) I am infinitely honoured. But methinks it would have been but mannerly in their lordships to take my will in such a matter. [SPENCER *goes up.*

Clan. Do you not see, madam, they *have* taken it in the shortest way they could—taken it for granted?

Usher. His Majesty!

Enter Pages and a Chamberlain preceding the KING, *who leads the* PRINCESS ANNE, *followed by* LADY BETTY NOEL, *and attended by* LORD PORTLAND, LORD WOODSTOCK, *and Lords-in-Waiting*, L.

King. Ah, my Lord Spencer, and my Lady Clancarty! We have promised her Royal Highness a sight of our last batch of beauties from the Hague (*bowing to ladies*)—I mean tulips, not ladies. I know Lord Spencer is an authority on these precious bulbs. I have told you, Portland, my Lord Sutherland's gardens at Althorpe shame ours at Kensington. (*Sees* LORD CLANCARTY.) Methinks I do not know this gentleman? (*To* PORTLAND.)

[CLANCARTY *bows.* WOODSTOCK *whispers to* PORTLAND.

Port. No, your Majesty; his business is with me.

King. I warrant 'twill keep till I have seen my tulips. Come, Anne, I fear I shall scarce be as ready in reviewing my flower-beds as my battalions.

[*Moves to door in flat, and exit.*

Port. (*to* CLANCARTY) Await me here, sir.

[LADY C., *following* PRINCESS, *turns and looks at* CLANCARTY.

Spen. (R., *aside*) Looks exchanged! There is an understanding between them.

Wood. (*aside to* LADY C.) I must see you alone.

Betty. (*aside*) Whispering! Nay, then, I will keep an eye on you both.

[*Exit* PORTLAND, WOODSTOCK, *and* LADY BETTY *at door into garden.*

Lady C. (*following, then turning back*) I must speak, and at once. Believe me, sir, this news of my brother is as startling to me as it must be to you—as it will be to your friend.

Clan. I do not like to think what a blow it will be to him. I said he had a light heart; this will make it a heavy one.

Lady C. Pray assure him that, strangers as we are, 'tis his misfortunes that make the strongest tie between us. There is nothing holds a woman like misfortunes bravely borne— as he bears his. Tell him that though his cause be not my family's, or mine, I rejoice to know him faithful to it, through disgrace, poverty, and exile. That I would not have him purchase my father's or my brother's favour by yielding one jot of his allegiance to the House of Stuart. That, so far as *my* determination can keep for him this poor hand, it shall be his still, in spite of all cajoleries, urgings, threats—his, in as simple faith as when, ten years since, it was given to him—child's hand to boy—at the altar.

Clan. Oh, madam, if you could but know how happy you have made—I mean, will make your husband by this assurance! Now that I know you, I can understand how your image, once stamped, even in a boy's heart, must needs be stamped for ever; how even the faintest memory of *you* might well be more to him than all present charms of other women. [*Seizes her hand.*

Lady C. I thought, sir, you said you were my lord's best friend!

Clan. I am, madam, and so fain would be yours—but only to plead *his* cause. You must not leave me till that cause is pleaded out—pleaded even to winning.

Lady C. To winning! Am I not wed? (*Wrenches hand away.*) The Princess awaits me, sir (*goes up*); and I think we have no more to say to each other. [*Up.*

Clan. (*moves up*) Oh, so much more, madam!

Lady C. No more, at least, that is becoming for your friend's wife to listen to.

Clan. (*seizing her hand in spite of her resistance*) I must see you alone.

Lady C. (*with dignity*) *Must!* Captain Heseltine!

Clan. Only to speak to you of the husband who languishes

for your love—for my friend—my brother—my second self. (*Has mastered her hand.*) You shall not go till you have promised me!

Lady C. Steps without! Rise, sir, rise; unhand me, sir! (*Hurriedly.*) There, then—I promise. [*Walks* L.

Enter LORD PORTLAND *and* LADY BETTY, C.

Port. There is your prisoner, Lady Betty.

Betty. So! (*Aside.*) Not with my Lord Woodstock, at least. (*Aloud.*) Come, my dear, the Princess is wondering at your absence. (*Comes down to* R. C.) Vastly sorry to interrupt any *tête-à-tête* of yours. (*Aside.*) Lovers! or I'm as blind as Cupid.

Lady C. Nay, our *tête-à-tête* admits a listener. (*To* CLANCARTY.) Tell my lord, sir, his cause has lost nothing in the mouth of his advocate.

[*During the above* LORD PORTLAND *is examining papers at the bureau. Exit* LADY CLANCARTY. LORD WOODSTOCK *meets her in the garden; they go off in eager conversation.*

Betty (R. C.) I am mightily concerned, captain, to have cut short my Lady Clancarty's confidences. (*Looks round and sees her with* WOODSTOCK.) There she goes now with my Lord Woodstock! Oh! I vow 'tis monstrous.

[*Exit hastily after her,* C.

Port. (*putting away papers. Sits.*) Now, sir, for your business. 'Tis urgent, you say. Make your story as brief as is consistent with clearness.

Clan. (R.) Short and sharp is my motto, my lord, for speech or sword. My business will go into two words, but they are weighty ones—Life and Death!

Port. To me, sir? [*Rises.*
Clan. To his Majesty. [*Crosses* L.
Port. (*comes down*) Not another Popish plot, sir? I warn you, neither I nor his Majesty are given to put faith in these murderous mare's nests.

The KING *appears at the garden door.*

Clan. 'Fore Gad, my lord, I should be glad if the eggs in my nest were less like hatching cockatrices instead of chickens. I come to tell you of real and *imminent* danger to the Prince of Orange!

Port. (*goes to table and is about to sit; checks himself*) So, let me hear it. But first, your price, sir?

Clan. Price, my lord!

Port. Aye, sir, price—what is it to be? Money, favour, employment? I am used to such bargains. Come, sir!

Clan. I do not understand your lordship.

Port. (R.) Pooh, man! you have your terms, of course. (CLANCARTY *is about to protest.*) Nay, I know the standing preface—your disclosures are prompted by loyalty—goodwill to the King—*après*——

Clan. No, my lord, I own no loyalty to your King—no goodwill to the Prince of Orange. (*The* KING *starts.*) He has not a more determined enemy than I in his dominions; and that's a bold word.

King (*aside*). More bold than pleasant.

Port. Then why this revelation of danger to him?

Clan. First and foremost, to save a brave man from a coward's death; then to keep a good cause clear of stain, and friends of a crime.

Port. Your friends, sir! You dare use the word when you avow their treasonable designs—your own privity to them—here under the royal roof!

King (*coming forward,* C.) Where better, my dear William? I will hear what this gentleman has to tell with my own ears. You may speak freely, sir. You have seen me before?

Clan. Faith, I believe no soldier ever saw your Highness behind. I was within short musket-shot of your Highness more than once at the Boyne, where I commanded a regiment of horse for his Majesty King James the Second.

King (C.) His *ex*-Majesty! Humph! A soldier (*half aside, scanning him rapidly*), and a likely fellow of his inches.

Clan. 'Tis a soldier's horror of foul play has brought me hither to disclose this danger to your Highness' life; but—but on conditions——

King. Ah! the price, after all! State them. [*Sits at table.*

Clan. That I shall be excused from disclosing names, and that nothing I say here shall be used against my friends, or for any other purpose than to secure your Highness' safety.

King (*takes up pen*). So much for your friends. Now for yourself.

Clan. That my name shall not be asked, and that on leaving the palace I shall not be followed.

King. Is that all?

Clan. All, sir.

King. I think we may safely grant these conditions, William?

Port. Pardon me, sir, without names, we have nothing we can lay hold of.

Clan. Sure, I don't want my friends laid hold of. The danger 'll neither be more nor less for the names. 'Tis a most determined and serious plot. First, to enter the palace gardens!

King (*making a note*). When?

Clan. At dark, to-night.

King (*looking at his watch*). So, a short hour hence.

Port. Hadn't I better at once take precautions, sir?

King. When we know the danger. Go on, sir. Enter the palace gardens, you say, and then?

Clan. Set fire to the palace!

King. Luckily one smells fire—and then?

Clan. In the smoke and confusion seize and kidnap your Highness, or, more likely——

King. Shoot me down! Ha!

Port. (*springing up*) Sakerment! What hellish scoundrels have we here?

King. Keep your temper, my dear William. Dutch blood should be cool. But the gardens are well watched. Sentinels at all the entrances.

Clan. Yes, sir, of your Oxford regiment. They have been bought over.

King (*rises, losing his coolness, moves* R. *and up*). So, plotting against my life! I'm used to that. But tampering with my troops—the dirty scoundrels! (*Walks up and down.*) Ah! William, had those precise Messieurs of the Parliament but left me my honest Dutchmen—but they were too faithful. [*Coughs; turns up* C.

Port. What are your Majesty's orders?

King (*who has recovered his coolness, refers to papers on table*). The King's Dragoons lie at Chelsea Barracks. Let them furnish a guard to relieve the Blues. Let the sentries have an eye on any strange or suspicious figures seen loitering near the palace. (*Movement of* PORTLAND.) But mind, no flurry. Let Keppel see to it. Give the orders yourself, privately and promptly.

Port. (R. *of table*) And leave your Majesty with this——
[*Pauses.*

Clan. 'Gentleman' will serve, my lord.

King. At the worst we are man to man. (*Looking at* CLANCARTY.) But I'll answer for this young fellow.

Clan. Your Highness does me but justice.

[*Exit* LORD PORTLAND, R. *panel.*

King. I'm inclined, sir, to believe your story, unpleasant as it is to know one's house destined food for fire, and one's self a mark for bullets. I like the feeling that makes full stipulation for your friends' safety, none for your own.

Clan. What else would I do as a soldier and a gentleman?

King (*sits* L. *of table*). I am glad my father-in-law has servants who are too brave to use the foul weapons his adversaries are not above putting into their hands. But let me recommend you to think over your conditions. Without names, your service is but half a service.

Clan. Anyway, 'twill be the half that includes your Highness's life!

King. True! And without names I should not be obliged to punish. Young man, why can I not call you my soldier?

Clan. Because, ever since I remember, I've called myself the King's—your father-in-law.

King (*sighing*). I should like to tempt you from him if I could. Think over the offer. Mine is the service for a soldier.

Clan. The King's, your father-in-law's, may be one o' these days.

King. Meantime, it is one rather for Jesuits than gentlemen.

Clan. Faith, your Highness will find Jesuits nearer than St. Germains.

King. You should be Irish?

Clan. I suppose I shouldn't, for it seems an offence this side the Channel; but, offence or not, I *am* Irish.

King. A warm-hearted, hot-headed people, the Irish.

Clan. Just the opposite of the Dutch.

King. Perhaps that's why we can't agree. I'm sorry for it. Kings need such servants as you, and my father-in-law is only playing at king; (*rises*) but, sir, friend or enemy, I am your debtor.

Clan. I hope your Highness will never have to pay the debt in the same coin.

Enter PORTLAND *by door in panel*, R.

Port. Your orders are given, sir. But here's a rogue, an old acquaintance of mine, seeking speech of me, if I mistake not, on the same matter, if not from the same motives, as this gentleman.

King (*to* CLANCARTY). One of the friends, sir, you are so careful to screen! Who is he?

Port. (R.) Cardell Goodman, sir, whom your Majesty may have heard of by his town title of 'Scum'—ruffler—gamester—poisoner—highwayman—who has stood more than once in the Old Bailey dock, and been burnt in the hand, if with a cold iron—and now a worthy agent of your precious father-in-law.

King (*to* CLANCARTY). I cannot congratulate you on your company, sir.

Clan. Any king, your Highness, may have a rogue among his servants—with all respect to the present company.

King. Come, we will overhear the rascal's information, though I will not do Master 'Scum' the honour I have done you, sir—of a personal examination. This way, sir.

Clan. They say listeners never hear any good of themselves, your Highness.

King. They sometimes hear the truth, even from rogues. 'Tis none the less useful.

  [*Leads* CLANCARTY *off by door in panel*, R., *which he
    leaves open behind him. Usher shows in* GOODMAN, L.

Port. (*sits, and with marked hauteur*) Well, Master Goodman, you are pressing.

Good. Your lordship must pardon my urgency, for my matter presses. It touches the King's life.

Port. You hinted as much in your letter.

Good. I am prepared to go beyond hints, my lord. I can put into your hands not only the designs but the names of the contrivers of his Majesty's assassination—their lodgings, places of meeting, watchwords, signs, and all that can help you to lay them by the heels at once.

Port. And your terms—waiving that virtue which is its own reward?

Good. Indemnity for myself as King's evidence. Then, as the town will be too hot for me after this, a thousand pounds down for outfit—a free passage abroad; and once there, some £200, or say £300 by the year, maintenance money as a gentleman.

Port. I am instructed not to chaffer about terms, if your revelations be as weighty as you promise. So now for your information?

Good. First, for the foiling the design on his Majesty's life. Not a moment is to be lost. The sentries have been secured, the palace gardens are to be entered, and the palace fired in less than an hour's time.

Port. (*rises*) Your warning comes somewhat late, Master Goodman.

Good. The desperate villains have forwarded the moment of execution, and I could not sooner get hither safely. I was watched. So much for evil consciences!

Port. And evil reputations!

Good. I do not understand your lordship's allusion.

Port. I said evil reputations, Master Goodman. I leave you to apply it.

Good. (*giving a paper*). This is not the moment for private quarrel. Here you will find the design, the plotters' names, and all other particulars. I have put crosses opposite the blackest of the flock; the biggest stands against the name of my Lord Clancarty. Secure him by all means—a most dangerous villain! To be punished, if all the rest be spared. (*Aside*) And so your halter's noosed, my bouncing bog-trotter. Faith, 'tis a comfort to have such a perilous load off one's conscience!

Port. And out of one's pocket. Found there, this paper had put your neck in peril. [PORTLAND *makes notes at table.*

Good. I hold it, like the rest of my poor person, at his Majesty's service.

Port. Or rather at that of his Majesty's representative, the hangman.

Good. Your lordship is pleased to jest—somewhat unsavourily.

Port. Jest with you, sir? Scarcely. Wait in that room till I recall you! [*Points to door*, L.

Good. Confound the stiff-necked Dutch upstart! In any case, my lord, it is a comfort to think one has done one's duty as a gentleman, a loyal subject, and a man of honour. [*Exit* L.

Re-enter KING *and* CLANCARTY *from panel.*

Port. (R.C.) You hear, sir, this villain's intelligence confirms this gentleman's every particular.

King. (C.) Here's a text, sir, if I wished to preach how Providence watches over the safety of lawful sovereigns, and treason ever breeds its traitors.

Clan. (L.) Your Highness might have learnt that sooner.

Port. 'Tis lucky your orders are already given, sir, or we might not have had time.

King. Give me that paper. (*Takes paper from* PORTLAND.) Strange! Persons of name and estate among them! Barclay—as I might have expected. Fenwick—a vacancy for Northumberland there. Friend—why can't the fool be content to improve his beer, instead of the succession? Charnock, Rokewood—old hands at this work. Ha! a new name—Lord Clancarty, the man this rogue warned you against, my Lord Sunderland's Irish son-in-law, of whom you spoke to me t'other day touching a Divorce Bill?

Port. The same, sir.

King. This will render the Bill unnecessary. (*To* CLANCARTY.) Your name may be amongst these, sir. If it is, I give you fair warning that within twenty-four hours every head here, dead or alive, will be worth a thousand pounds. Every road out of London will be patrolled, every outport watched. For those who do not succeed in escaping to-night there will be no escape to-morrow. You would be wise to leave the place unobserved. By the garden will be best. I have my master-key. Stay, I will see that the road is clear for you.   [*Going to garden entrance.*

Port. (R.) For prudence' sake, sir, do not expose yourself. Some of these villains may be lurking about, and the night is closing in.

King. My bullet is not cast yet, William. Or, if it is, think you I shall be sorry to receive my passport to the place where Mary is waiting for me? (*To* PORTLAND.) Go and finish with that rascal. (*Exit* PORTLAND. *To* CLANCARTY.) Await me here, sir.   [*Exit* KING.

Clan. (*alone*) I always said I'd a nose for a rogue! I scented this vermin from the first. Thanks to *his* treachery, I can see the shadow of a big gallows darkening over us all. Whatever comes, I have prevented this dirty villainy. I've saved the Prince; and faith, now you're all alone, Donough

Macarthy, you may as well own he's a born King, if he was ten times the Dutchman. Sorrow the vein in my body but runs the merrier that I've saved him. Thanks to him, I've still the night to escape in. But the others! Fly, and leave them to their fate? Hardly, Donough Macarthy. And my darling! Leave her—to lose her! Leave her to the tender mercies of this black and bitter Whig of a brother! Leave her, without once hearing my own name from her sweet lips, or drinking the light of her eyes when she knows me for her husband! No! I've called the main, I'll stand the hazard. If I live, 'twill be to know her—woo her—win her. If I die before she knows me, 'twill but set her free for a happier husband!

Re-enter the KING, C.

King. The garden is clear. Come, sir—I will be your guide! [*Motions* CLANCARTY *to door in flat.*

ACT-DROP.

ACT III.

Snow falling as Curtain rises.

SCENE.—LADY CLANCARTY'S *Bedchamber in* LORD SUNDERLAND'S *house, St. James's Square. Window,* C.F., *opening on to a balcony, with trees seen beyond, and near the balcony. Snow falling, and lying outside. Tall crimson-canopied bed, with high poles, like Queen Anne's bed at Hampton Court,* R. *Old-fashioned fireplace, with fire burning,* L. 2 E. *Toilet table,* R.C., *richly furnished in silver, between window and fire,* L. *Settees,* R. C., *and furniture of the period. Door,* L. 1 E., *to enter staircase. Door to dressing-room,* R. 2 E. *Candlesticks on toilet-table. Lights, in sconces, on the walls and on the mantelpiece.* NIGHT. *Lights half down.*

LADY CLANCARTY *discovered at toilet-table, with her Maid.*

Lady C. (L. C.) Do not fret me with dressing to-night. Light the candles, girl, and leave me. (*Exit* SUSANNAH, L. D., *after lighting candles on table.*) See him, and alone! I have promised. But when I think of his warmth and my weakness, I tremble! A proud woman am I, and thanks to my pride, if nothing nobler, a true wife, even to an unknown husband! Dare I look in this glass and tell myself it was his pleading for my lord that so moved me? When I go down into my heart, it whispers me that, had he so pleaded for himself, I had been content to listen. And this is my woman's pride, my wifely constancy! (*Rises.*) Oh, shame! shame! where is now the heart that was so boastful of its strength, while inclination was at one with duty? Weak bulwarks that we can raise, the best of us, against the fire of ardent eyes, the music of a winning tongue.

Enter SUSANNAH, L. D.

Sus. (L.) So please you, my lady—my lord, your brother, would see you in his closet.

Lady C. Say I will come. (*Exit* SUSANNAH, L. D.) Doubtless, 'tis on this project of divorce. It opens the way to freedom; for I should be free to follow my own will—not theirs. Oh, triple coward! To dream of being false to him who, if his friend may be believed, is so true to even the poor memory of me! Desert him in his low estate of loneliness and exile! No, not if Elizabeth Clancarty be what they have still called her—a true wife, and a strong-willed woman!

[*As she is going out*, L. D., SUSANNAH *reappears, holding door open for her; she then closes it.*

Sus. I wonder what has so moved my lady? (*Goes to window.*) Ugh! What a bitter night! (*Looks out.*) The snow falling fast. There goes a company of Guards across the square. Poor fellows! Cold work for them. (*Comes down to fire.*) Better snug and cosy here in St. James's Square, than bogged in Romney Marsh, between smugglers and Sussex roads.

[*Going to draw curtain at window*, C. *Enter* LADY BETTY, L. D., *in hood and mask.* SUSANNAH *turns, sees her, and is about to shriek.*

Betty. (*seizing her by arm*) None of thy airs, thou affected minx! leave hysterics to persons of quality. (*Takes off mask and mantua.*) 'Tis I—Lady Betty Noel! Dost thou hear? Where's thy mistress?

Sus. An't please your ladyship, with my Lord Spencer, in his closet.

Betty. Tell her I must see her instantly—here, in her chamber.

Sus. I will, your ladyship.   [*Exit* L. D.

Betty. (C.) Yes, 'tis time we came to an understanding. Either she takes Lord Woodstock, or I ; and I don't mean *she* shall without scratching for't. If *he* doesn't know his own mind, the more need she and I did. I know mine but too well—'tis to keep him all to myself. I wonder where she hides his letters ? (*Opens drawers in toilet-table,* R.) If the wretch writes to her those insipid compliments he used to write to me? How can she be so treacherous ? (*Rummaging. Enter* LADY C., *who stands watching.*) So false to her confiding friend ! One that would have trusted her with all her secrets. Nothing in *his* hand ?

Lady C. When you have done ransacking my drawers, my dear.

Betty (*confused*). I was only—only—looking for a knot of ribbon. No, I wasn't. (*Comes down* C.) I was looking for something to satisfy my sick, sore, suspicious heart. Oh, Elizabeth, say—am I still to love you as I have done, or to hate you worse than poison ?

Lady C. Hate me ! Are you mad, child ? Let this be my answer.   [*Takes her in her arms.*

Betty (*extricating herself*). No, no. That is no answer. Anybody can kiss and hug ; that counts nothing—not among women, you know. But tell me that you don't care for him —that you won't take him away from me—or, better still, that you hate him, as I do !

Lady C. (L. C.) Him ! Whom does the silly child mean ?

Betty (R. C.). Oh, thou hypocrite ! Who, but Lord Woodstock, to be sure ?

Lady C. Be comforted, my dear. If there were but one man in the world, and that man my Lord Woodstock——

Betty. And only two women, mind—thou and I——

Lady C. He should be thine for me.

Betty. Oh, I vow thou art the dearest girl, the best, the truest friend ! (*Checking the ardour of her embraces.*) But hold ! 'Tis very easy to say as much.

Lady C. Believe me, my dear Betty, my Lord Woodstock is less than nothing to me.

Enter SUSANNAH, L. D.

Sus. My Lord Woodstock asks leave to wait on your ladyship.

Betty. There, I knew it ! Oh, thou false creature !

Lady C. 'Tis true I sent for him, knowing he has been

S

closeted with my brother on a matter in which I am deeply concerned.

Betty. And what concern dost thou pretend to in him, or he in thee?

Lady C. That thou shalt hear. (*To* SUSANNAH.) Tell my lord I await his commands. (*Exit* SUSANNAH, L. D.) Into my closet, thou silly child, if thou wouldst learn how my heart stands affected to thy lover.

Betty. Ah, but how does his stand to thee? 'Tis that I care for.

Lady C. That let the man answer. In with thee, and lie close. [LADY BETTY *retires into dressing-room*, R. C.

Enter LORD WOODSTOCK.

Wood. (*eagerly approaching* LADY C.) How ever shall I thank you, madam, for this opportunity?

[LADY B. *appears at dressing-room door, in an attitude of consternation.*

Lady C. How now, my lord? You were all coldness this morning—and now——

Wood. Joy, madam, pure joy in the anticipation of liberty! You know, so your brother informs me, our fathers' projects for divorcing you from Lord Clancarty and uniting you to me. He tells me you have taken the proposal coldly—nay, more than coldly.

Lady C. Is that a grief to you, my lord?

Wood. Tout au contraire, madam. I have sought this interview that I might express to you my deep sense of the honour proposed for me, and, in the same breath, my regret at the insurmountable barrier that divides me from it.

Lady C. (R.) And I sent for your lordship hither to say just the same thing.

Wood. (L.) Then, madam, methinks here are two people easily made happy?

Betty (C., *coming forward and embracing* LADY C.). Three! Three! Oh, my dear friend! Oh, my dear Harry! (*Embraces* WOODSTOCK.) Nay, she knows—*she* knows! (*Takes a hand of each.*) Oh, you dear creatures! And so you *really* detest each other? Isn't it delightful! Now we are all in a mind, 'tis a league for life and death between us. Nobody shall marry any of us against the other's inclination. We swear!

Wood. Amen!

Lady C. Amen!
Betty. And if I can help you with the Captain——
Enter SUSANNAH, L. D.

Sus. My lady! My lady! Your brother has left his closet, and is on his way upstairs.

Lady C. He must think the rejection comes from me. Down on your knees, my lord—at my feet. So! Into my closet, child—quick!
  [*She throws herself into a chair,* R., LORD WOODSTOCK *at her feet,* R. C. *Exit* LADY BETTY *into dressing-room. Enter* LORD SPENCER, L. D.; *he pauses at door.*

Spen. (*aside*) As I could wish. He hath made his proposal.

Lady C. Rise, my lord. You have urged your suit eloquently. I am infinitely flattered by your offer. But you will pardon me reminding you, first, that it is premature; and next, even were I free, that my good brother, in disposing so kindly of my hand, has forgotten one trifling matter—his sister's inclinations.

Spen. (*coming forward*) What do I hear? Forgotten his sister's inclinations! Say, rather, has presumed upon them, because he believed his sister wise enough, in such a matter, to defer to the judgment of her father and brother.

Lady C. My lord, you once made me read law with you. Will you allow me to remember enough of our lessons to remind you that a woman's heart is not one of the personal chattels that can be taken into execution under a judgment —even so weighty a judgment as yours?

Spen. (*crosses to* R.) This is no subject for pleasantry— least of all, to-night. My lord, I hope you will not take this as a final answer.

Wood. (L.) Deeply as your sister's refusal wounds me, 'tis as much against my religion to put force upon a lady's inclination as on her person.

Lady C. (C.) At least, Lord Woodstock, more considerate than my brother, will have the gallantry to wait till I am a free woman. I am sorry my brother should need to be reminded I am still a wife.

Spen. (R.) You are no wife! though bound by the empty name of one to a traitor and an exile—nay, worse—I had hoped to spare you the knowledge of it to-night—to one who is likely to leave you a widow sooner than even the Bill of Divorce could have set you free.

Lady C. (*rising*) What do you mean, my lord?

Spen. I have but now received news by messenger from my Lord Portland, of a diabolical plot, just discovered, for the assassination of his gracious Majesty!

Lady C. (*rises*, C.) Of the King? Sure, Heaven watches over that precious life! I am glad the traitors have been discovered.

Spen. (R.) There is a proclamation, with their names, and a reward of £1,000 for the apprehension of any one of them—dead or alive! 'Twill be published to-morrow morning!

Lady C. May every one of them be a prisoner before to-night.

Spen. (R.) Have a care, madam! The list includes the name of your husband!

Lady C. Brother! But, no—I will not believe it.

Spen. (*shows paper*) Read there, madam.

Lady C. Yes, there stands his name. And yet methinks it should be impossible. Devoted to the House of Stuart he may be; all the more devoted, as a loyal subject should be, now that that house is fallen. But I have heard of him as a generous and honourable gentleman, not less capable of such a crime, Tory and Jacobite as he is, than any Whig and Spencer of you all. [*Returns paper.*

Spen. You forget, madam, killing the Prince of Orange is no murder in the eyes of James's confessor at St. Germains.

Lady C. Oh, if I had but known him, methinks this would never have been. But is he taken? [*Falteringly.*

Spen. The guards are even now about the arrest. They have intelligence, my Lord Portland informs me, of a rendezvous of the conspirators hard by, at the Nag's Head, in St. James's Street.

Lady C. And he may be taken, killed, in resisting, here, almost at my door! [*Sinks in chair.*

Wood. (L.) Take heart, madam; this paper may be untrustworthy; the whole plot may be a fiction, or your unfortunate husband may not be amongst those concerned in it.

Spen. My Lord Portland writes me that the truth of plot and paper may alike be depended on.

Wood. Then there is the chance of escape!

Lady C. Oh, thank you for that comfort. Pray heaven he may baffle his pursuers.

Spen. This concern for a traitor and an assassin, madam, is scarce becoming in one who bears our name.

Lady C. Pardon, my lord! you forget, I think, it is *his* name I bear. I still remember, as in a dream, the fair and gallant boy who kissed me, and called me his little wife, as we parted, and told me he would soon return. (SPENCER *expresses impatience.*) Is it a reproach if that dream will come back to me in this evil hour? Oh, 'twas cruel to join two young lives but to be thus miserably divided.
[*Throws herself in chair*, R. C.

Spen. (R.) It is too late for that regret. Let us rejoice that separation has come at length, though it might have come less painfully.

Lady C. (C.) My husband! My poor husband! So young, and yet so unfortunate! Who can say what possibilities of happiness will go with thee to thy untimely grave?

Spen. (*goes to* LADY C.) Remember, madam, if decency require mourning of most widows, neither feeling nor duty asks for even the show, much less the reality, of grief from the widow of Lord Clancarty. [*Crosses to* C.

Lady C. (*rising*) Oh, steeled by party hate against all kindly touch of nature! If you have no feeling for him, have some pity for me. At this sad moment I can think only what we might have been to each other!
[*Flings herself into a chair and sobs bitterly.*

Wood. Methinks, my lord, it were but humanity to leave her to herself awhile.

Spen. (*aside*) This grief is scarce natural. What if it were a blind? (*Aloud.*) My lord, when you have seen as much of the world as I have, you will be less tender to a woman's tears. (*Aside.*) I will watch her! (*Aloud.*) Come, my lord. (*Crosses to* L. D.) We will but leave you, madam, till reason has got the better of this distemperature.

Lady C. (*seated*, R. C.) Remember, my lord, I will admit no renewal of discourse on this project of separation. And for the present I would be alone with my sad thoughts.
[*Exit* WOODSTOCK.

Spen. Let me warn you, madam, they are not wholesome company.

Lady C. At least I may command the privacy of my own chamber.

Spen. (*aside*) Say you so, madam? Not while I keep the key. [*Takes key from door,* L., *and exit.*

Betty (*running out of dressing-room*). My poor, dear, unhappy friend! Now you leave me all his heart, my heart is all yours again. Oh, if I could but comfort you! (*A shot without.*) Hark! What's that?

Lady C. (*starting up*) A shot! (*Another.*) Another! Oh, mercy! Those arrests! He spoke of a Jacobite rendezvous in St. James's Street! Look out! Look out!

Betty (*opening window*). The snow blinds me. I can see nothing; but all seems quiet again. Ha! she is fainting!

[*Runs down, leaving window open, and busies herself with* LADY CLANCARTY.

Lady C. Nay, 'tis nothing; but a sudden and sickening fear. [LADY BETTY *goes back to shut the window.*

Betty. I'll close the window.

Lady C. Leave it; the fresh air revives me.

Betty. Trust to me, and forgive my foolish jealousy. I see now 'twas the other all the while. Thou hast helped me to my lover; I will do all I can to help thee to thine.

Lady C. My lover! Alas! I have no lover.

Betty. If you have no lover, I warrant you Captain Heseltine has a love. But never tell me. I can parse out of Cupid's Accidence — positive, 'love' — comparative, 'lover'—superlative, 'lovest'—'thou' understood.

Lady C. Captain Heseltine! A man I have only seen twice!

Betty. One has heard of love even at first sight.

Lady C. My poor lord's best friend!

Betty. And so half-way to being my poor lady's at starting.

Lady C. (*sits*) Hold thy wanton tongue, or I shall be angry. And leave me. I tell thee again I have no lovers; only memories, fancies, shadows, if thou wilt. But such as they are, I would be left alone with them to-night. Nay, prithee go. (*A noise at window.*) What's that?

Betty. But the tapping of a branch against the balcony. No! (*With cry of alarm.*) See—a man in the branches! He climbs the balustrade!

Enter LORD CLANCARTY *by window; he grasps for support at window-frame.*

Lady C. Captain Heseltine!

Betty. Captain Heseltine! Now I understand why thou wouldst be alone. (LADY CLANCARTY *about to speak.*) Hush! I said I would help thee to thy lover. Trust me to keep thy brother from the chamber. [*Going to* L. D.

Lady C. (L. C.) Stay—as thou art my friend: Captain Heseltine is no lover of mine.

Betty. No! no! no! But I will guard thy door, as if he were. [*Exit* L. D.

Lady C. This intrusion, sir; and by such a road, at such an hour! What does it mean? How dared you?

Clan. (*too exhausted to speak, and still grasping window for support*) Your pardon, madam—a moment's breathing-time. [*Comes down* R.

Lady C. You saw that lady; you heard her injurious thoughts. Go, call her back at once, that, in her sight, you may leave this room as you entered it.

Clan. If I leave this room 'twill be, not to recall that lady, but to choose betwixt arrest and a bullet in yonder square. My pursuers are at my heels. I hoped I might count on shelter here!

Lady C. No more, sir! 'Tis enough that you are in danger. You will be safe here. It is I who will leave the room.

Clan. (*coming down,* R. C.) Stay, madam (*seizing her hand*). At least, not till you have heard me!

Lady C. Captain Heseltine, must I again remind you that you call my husband your dearest friend?

Clan. Away with disguises! Do you see this ring? (*Shows ring.*) The counterpart should be on your finger, if you have kept your girlish promise.

Lady C. (*stretching out her fingers*) My betrothal ring! Look! 'Tis here! 'Tis here!

Clan. By that token—I am your husband!

Lady C. My husband! Methinks my heart had told me already! My husband, at last!

Clan. Your husband, who, a hunted and desperate man, makes this appeal to his wife's pity, if he dare make none to her love.

Lady C. My husband! thus hunted hither! But then,

'tis true, you are one of this wicked and desperate crew from St. Germains?

Clan. Desperate, it may be, but not wicked.

Lady C. Oh, Heaven! my husband in league with assassins!

Clan. Assassins! Then they have told you?

Lady C. Of this horrible plot to murder the King, just brought to light. They said your name was amongst the plotters. But it is not true! You are not of them? Oh, say you are not!

Clan. My name *is* on their roll!

Lady C. And 'tis as one of that murderous gang you seek shelter here? Oh, that it should be thus that husband and wife meet at last!

Clan. Hear me, madam. My name is among these men, 'tis true; but 'twas to prevent, not to forward, their design I joined them. When I saw you at Kensington to-day, I was there to put my Lord Portland and his master on their guard!

Lady C. What? Was it your warning revealed the plot?

Clan. Even so.

Lady C. Oh, my lord, which is worse—to join with such men, or to betray them?

Clan. I see, madam, you have yet to know your husband.

Lady C. (L. C.) Better, methinks, never to know him, than to know him thus. [*Turns away*.

Clan. (R. C.) My warning was one that gave Lord Portland neither name nor clue. It was enough to save the Prince; it could endanger no life—except my own. These arrests are a traitor's work, one of the base tools ever at hand for such ill designs. That I am guiltless of betraying my friends is best shown by my sharing their risk to the last.

Lady C. Oh, that I might trust his voice, his looks; and, stronger still, the feeling in my heart that tells me 'tis truth he speaks!

Clan. 'Tis like that death is close upon me, if not yonder, from those soldiers' bullets, a few weeks hence from the headsman's axe upon Tower Hill. Thus near the grave, I swear to you that my conscience is as free from the informer's shame as the assassin's.

Lady C. I believe you! I believe you! Heaven's

blessing on you for the faith I feel that it is the truth you speak—that we meet, at length, with danger—it may be, death—between us, but not dishonour. Take me, husband, in your arms, and kiss me as bridegroom kisses bride. (*Come together.*) 'Tis the first time our lips have met since boy and girl we kissed and parted, so long ago.

Clan. And there is no more, sweet wife, for thee or me to blush for in that kiss than in this. (*A long embrace.*) And now shall I call that lady back?

Lady C. No! no! no!

Clan. Remember, she but knows me as Captain Heseltine, thy lover!

Lady C. Methinks she saw with truer eyes than I. Ah, my dear, how dangerous it is for a husband to trust even his best friend at his wife's ear!

Clan. Nay; did I not plead lustily and loyally for my other self?

Lady C. But methinks thy praises of my lord drew most of their sweetness from the lips that spoke them. Oh, how I tried to be true to my shadow of a husband; but that perilous best friend would still thrust his substance across the shadow!

Clan. (R. C.) Nay; I swear I was true to my other self, save once or twice, when the odds stood heavy on Heseltine against Clancarty; and then, I own, I trembled for both of us.

Lady C. (L. C.) Nay; thou hast played thy part very, very badly, or Lady Betty would never have taken thee for my lover. But what matter what she thinks? Do I not know thee now, my husband, worthy of himself—of all I dreamed him—of all sacrifice his wife can make—if it be even of her good name? What matter, so 'tis given to save and shelter thee?

Clan. Then I am to be Clancarty's best friend once more, and his wife's into the bargain?

Lady C. For pity's sake, my dear lord, what trifling with the time is this! Let us be busy for thy concealment to-night, and to-morrow for thy escape from London, over sea. (*Takes his hand and puts it on her heart.*) Feel how my heart beats at the bare thought of all there is to do—to conceal to contrive. (*He takes her in his arms.*) How ever shall I find skill to mask my fear, prudence to plan for thee, or wit to work after thy planning?

Clan. Nay; I *may* lie concealed awhile. Faith, I'd like

it here with thee. But I must not fly the realm; I have other, sterner duty here than wooing thee, sweet wife. This vile plot was but the preface, writ in cypher, to a larger and a nobler work—the raising the King's friends throughout the realm, in concert with an invading force from France.

Lady C. Oh, hush, my lord, hush! Remember, if a Jacobite's wife, I am daughter and sister to two of the King's most devoted servants.

Clan. The Prince's, you mean. There is one King: he is at St. Germains.

Lady C. Oh, why need we differ about such words? What is Whig or Tory, James or William, to us? We are man and wife—long parted, and strangely met; bound by a holy tie which, but for these hideous factions, might be as happy as it is holy. Oh, Heaven! what curse has fallen upon our country, that even this strange joy that almost bewilders me must be darkened by the shadow of danger—nay, perhaps of death?

Clan. (*crosses to* R.) Trust me; I will be careful. I never rated my life at its right value till now.

Lady C. Then let us think without more delay how we may best preserve it for both. Oh, would this poor fluttering brain be but calm awhile! Ha! as thou saidst, what asylum so safe for thee as here? Who would look for thee in this house—in my own chamber—*our* chamber now?

[*Lays her head on his shoulder.*

Clan. (L. C.) My own true-hearted wife! Strange how, in spite of thy father's brother's bitterness against me—the gulf of faction between us—'twas ever thus I thought of thee —thy hand in mine, our hearts beating against each other, as if they must but draw the closer at last, for all the time they have been sundered. Ah, yes, believe me, I will be careful of a life henceforth thus linked with thine. But sit, dearest; thou art all trembling.

Lady C. (*sits* L. C.) But tell me of thy escape. Now thou art safe, I long to hear of the danger, and how bravely thou hast baffled it.

Clan. (C., *kneeling by her*, R.) Thanks to the Prince, I knew of Goodman's treachery—that our places of meeting were disclosed. No time was to be lost. I hurried to our rendezvous, hard by here, to warn my comrades they were betrayed. Some doubted; some defied the danger. While yet I urged instant dispersal, the Guards surrounded and summoned the house. Once in sight and sound of the redcoats, I felt my hand steady, and my head, all of a sudden, as cool as the weather outside. In a storm of shots and sword-cuts, I slashed a passage thro' the soldiers with our old Milesian ' Faugh a Ballagh '—that means ' clear the way,' darling—and, faith, they cleared it—showed my pursuers a clean pair of heels; and, after threading a labyrinth of alleys, emerged, haphazard, in St. James's Square, recognized this house and thy window, scaled the balcony, and here I am!

Lady C. But how knewest thou my window?

Clan. Sure, I saw thee at it twice yesterday, and spent last night under it, in the hope to see thee again.

Lady C. That cold, cruel night! And didst thou see me?

Clan. Thy shadow. 'Twas not all I wanted, but 'twas something to dream on; and then I heard thee singing to thy lute, and I set the shadow to the music, and was happy.

Lady C. And I sate warm and thoughtless here, and thou wert watching lonely in the bitter dark!

Clan. You forget the fire in my heart—that was more than a match for the snow.

Lady C. Ah! If the snow should betray thy footsteps? If they should track thee hither?

Clan. (*rises*) Nay; the fast-falling flakes must have hid all traces already.

Lady C. Thank Heaven for that! And now for thy concealment here. Methinks, with care, it will be easy. My maid is faithful; but she is foolish. I will dismiss her for the night. Lock my door!

Clan. That were best done at once.

[*As he approaches door, enter* LADY BETTY *in consternation.*

Betty. Hide, sir; my lord is coming! He suspects something! I could not detain him. Hide! Quick!

Lady C. Lock the door!

Betty. He has the key! By the balcony! By the balcony!

Clan. (*rushing to window*) There are men below!

Betty (*wringing her hands*). Oh, what *is* to be done?

Lady C. In my closet! Oh, mercy! he is here! Too late!

Enter LORD SPENCER, L.

Spen. (*seizing* LADY BETTY *by arm*) Hold, madam! (*Puts* LADY BETTY *to* L. *door.*) What may pass here is for me and my sister and this gentleman. Leave us!

[*Motions her to door,* L.

Betty (at L.D., *pleadingly*). My lord!

Spen. (L.) Leave us, I say. (*Exit* LADY BETTY.) Captain Heseltine, you rank as a gentleman. Your presence admits of no explanation but one. [*Touches sword.*

Lady C. (R. C.) Oh, my lord! I confess, I confess! This gentleman (*crosses to* C.) is here by my invitation—by my contrivance. (LORD S. *turns away. To* LORD C., *in undertone.*) Hush! hush! you don't know him as I do. (*To* LORD S.) He is blameless: the shame is mine—be mine the punishment.

Clan. (R.) Not so, my generous darling. [*Takes her hand.*

Spen. These endearments in my very hearing!

Clan. You shall not sacrifice your good name for me. My lord, your sister is innocent. I am here without her knowledge. I entered by that window—uninvited—unexpected.

Spen. (L.) No man climbs a lady's balcony unless he knows the reception that awaits him. (LADY C. *attempts to speak.*) Be silent. shameless hypocrite, who could put on a wife's sorrow as a mask for the welcome of a lover. And you, sir, once more, draw and defend yourself.

Lady C. Brother! brother! you do not know. It is my—— (*Checks herself in the act of giving the name of her husband.*) It is Captain Heseltine, my preserver!

Spen. We waste time—draw, I say!

Clan. (C.) My lord, I wear no sword for you.

Spen. Coward, as well as seducer! Will this rouse the man in you?

[*Strikes him with flat of sword.* CLANCARTY *catches the sword in his hand.*

Clan. I am this lady's husband! Your brother-in-law!

Spen. Clancarty!

Clan. Her husband and your prisoner! (*Crosses to* R.) The defenceless fugitive from your Prince's soldiers puts himself at your mercy.

Spen. Fugitive! Say, the proscribed traitor—the accomplice of assassins!

Lady C. (*crosses to* C.) 'Tis a lie! a foul and wicked lie! You know him not; I know him!

Spen. What should I call the man who shrinks not from conspiring with his country's enemies to let loose on his country the scourge of invasion, as well as the horrors of civil war?

Clan. (R.) 'Tis no time to bandy words. Enough, I own myself the enemy of your Prince and the present usurping Government of England; ready to do all I can by fair warfare to subvert it. But I am no assassin!

[*Movement of* SPENCER.

Lady C. (C.) But hear his story. Brother, hear his story, as I have done, and you will believe him as I do.

Spen. (L.) As *you* do! Poor credulous dupe of a ready tongue and a bold bearing. What do you know of traitors and their sophistry? They can cheat themselves; how should they not succeed in cheating thee? Hark you, my lord, 'tis well you should know escape is impossible. I have posted armed servants below that balcony. I command this door. (*Shows key.*) You must await my return with a warrant for your detention. Sir William Trumbull's house is next door—the Guards are at St. James's—a few minutes will suffice. Follow me, madam.

Lady C. My place is here, at my husband's side!

Spen. As you please. I thought to spare you a painful passage.

Lady C. But you will not, cannot give him up to justice. (*Flings herself at his feet, and seizes his arm to detain him.*) He is my husband. I was given to him at the altar, in the sight of Heaven. Oh, spare him, for my sake—he is no assassin! At my prayer he will cease even to be an enemy. 'Tis but to conceal his presence here—none know of it— none need know. He will go hence, unseen, as he came. I will go with him. I will answer for him. We will cross the sea—we will live together, harmless and happy. Oh, spare him, brother! spare him to thy sister's love!

Spen. Poor weak woman! Ask me to play false to my duty as statesman and subject, that my sister may be the companion of a traitor's flight! You little know me! (To LORD CLANCARTY.) I need not ask your undertaking to remain here (CLANCARTY *lifts her up*). I know the store men of your creed and cause set by promises. I have better security. [*Points to balcony, shows key, and exit.*

Lady C. Lost! Lost!

Clan. Do not weep. A true wife must not unman her husband!

Lady C. That a *brother's* hand should seal thy doom! And I can do naught but wring my hands and cry—these silly, cowardly woman's tears—for the husband I have found but to lose him; the husband whose blood must lie at my brother's door! [*Sinks in chair*, L. C.

Clan. Do not reproach him, my dearest. He but does his duty as he sees it. For myself, such a death has little terror, and no surprise. And I had rather steel than rope, though it be the axe. My grief is that I must grieve thee. Better we had never known each other, than know this brief blessedness but to lose it.

Lady C. Nay, husband, that is treason to love! Let us thank Heaven we have tasted the joy, though we must put the cup from us so soon. (*Footsteps outside.*) Hark! the tramp of soldiers!

Clan. (*slowly*). 'Tis the Guards! Keep a stout heart, dearest. The time is come!

Enter SPENCER, *with Officer of the Guards and Soldiers, who halt in doorway; followed by* LADY BETTY *in consternation.*

Spen. Donough Macarthy, Lord Clancarty, I hold here a Secretary of State's warrant for your arrest on a charge of high treason. Do your duty, sir. (*Officer takes* LORD CLANCARTY'S *sword.*) There is a coach below.

Lady C. (*crosses to Officer*) You will not separate us— you will let me go with him, sir? I am his wife. (*To* SPENCER.) Tell them, my lord, I am his wife!

Officer. I am sorry, madam, but no one can be allowed to accompany the prisoner.

Lady C. But his wife, sir! I tell you I am his wife that asks the favour. Donough, dearest—husband—husband— take me with you! [*Faints.*

Clan. God bless thee, my poor girl! (*Kisses her forehead. To* SPENCER.) Do not be more cruel to her than her fate. 'Tis no fault of hers that we are enemies.

Spen. (*motions to door*) For the last time, sir!

Clan. (*To* LADY BETTY) Take care of her. Tell her she shall have leave to come to me.

Betty. But will she?

Clan. I know not, but tell her so. One last look—one

last kiss. Heaven comfort her! (*to* SPENCER) and make this night's work sit easy upon you. [*Tableau.*

ACT-DROP.

ACT IV.

SCENE I.—*Day Room in the Gate House Prison, Westminster, with wide opening on to outer court and entrance-gate of the prison* (C. F.), *in which is a wicket with a grated aperture, both practicable. Cell doors* (R. *and* L.) *opening on Day Room. Rough furniture, as heavy tables and stools. As the curtain rises the Prisoners, including the Jacobite Conspirators of the First Act, except* BARCLAY, GOODMAN, *and* FRIEND, *are seen in dishabille, clustering about the Gate House at back.* MOTHER HUNT *is seen looking through the grating in the wicket. Noise without, as of angry mob. The Prisoners crowd and crush on* MOTHER HUNT, *so that she keeps her place with difficulty.*

Clink. Order, gentleman, order in the yard there, or Master Rivet will overhear and have you all clapped up in your chambers.

Mother (*backing the crowd off*). Stern all, my masters, or how's a body to see the sport? Trust me to report signals. (*Looks out.*) Now they've got the rogue. (*Yells outside.*) That's your game! Pelt and pump! Pelt and pump! Tally ho! Tally ho!

First mob (*without*). Hang the rascally informer!

Second mob (*without*). Cut his ears!

Mother. Clip his tongue first, that's like to be the hanging of so many of his betters. [*Yells and clamour without.*

Enter SIR JOHN FRIEND *from cell* L. *in nightcap and dressing-gown.*

Sir J. Here's a disturbance! Was ever such an ill-governed prison? How is an unfortunate prisoner to compose his mind to his situation? Will nobody tell me what's the matter?

Mother (*coming from her place by wicket, which is immediately occupied by other Prisoners*). 'Tis only the Sanctuary mob have caught that peaching scoundrel Scum Goodman, and are giving him a bit of their mind—Tothill Fields fashion.

Sir J. The Lord forgive him! If I am hanged—there's an *if* for a respectable alderman, the head of a large brewery and a large family!—I lay my death at his door.

Cry outside. The soldiers! The soldiers!

Mother. Soldiers! What a plague! I warrant they must be spoiling sport as usual.

[*Elbows her way up to wicket.*

Officer (outside the gate). Open in the King's name!

[*The gate is opened by Turnkey.* SCUM GOODMAN *is half-pushed, half-flung into the prison, pale, bleeding, his clothes torn, and in mortal terror.*

Good. Save me! Lock them out, or I'm a murdered man! [*Yells without.*

Officer. The rogue will be safe here. See to him, Master Gaoler. (*To his men at the gate.*) Drive the rascals back! Rear rank, right about! By your right! Forward! March!

[*Renewed yells. The gate is closed behind the Soldiers.* GOODMAN *crouches down, a miserable object, with the Prisoners gathered threateningly about him.*

Good. Save me, Mr. Gaoler. Don't leave me to them, or I'm a murdered man! For mercy's sake!

Clink. E'en settle it with your friends here. 'Tis none of my business. [*Walks away.*

Prisoners. Informer! Traitor! Villain!

Sir J. Oh, thou filthy knave!

Prisoners. Kill the rascal! [*Yells.*

Good. Spare me! Spare me, Sir John—I faint. Mercy! Mercy! [*Clings to* MOTHER HUNT'S *skirts.*

Mother. Let me go, thou cringing cur! Thinkest thou to shelter under my skirts?

Good. They'll murder me!

Mother. Tit for tat. Who murdered them? Away with the snivelling toad!

Good. (*in mortal terror—they seize him*) Help! help! for the love of Heaven!

Enter LORD CLANCARTY, *from his cell,* L. 3 E.

Clan. What poor devil have we here? Ten to one's foul odds. Come, gentlemen, hands off. Let the man breathe.

Prisoners. No! no!

Clan. Nay, then, we wear no swords here. But I carry a brace of Irish fists at my side; and by the powers I'll use them! Come, I must have my way in this. (*Forces* GOODMAN *out of the hands of the Prisoners, taking him by the collar.*) Thou most unredeemed villain!

Good. But spare my life!

Clan. Thy life! Better the death that lies before us than such a life as thine. But take it, wretch, to repent, if thou canst; if thou canst not, to suffer a foretaste here of the torments thou may'st count on hereafter.

Good. Oh, bless your lordship's goodness!

Clan. (*contemptuously*). A blessing from *thy* lips! Here, gaoler, take the knave hence; help him to a surgeon, and a suit less like the dirty soul inside of him. I'll stand the shot.

[*Turnkey supports* GOODMAN *off amidst the execrations of the Prisoners.*

Sir J. (L.C.) I hate violence; but if ever I could have enjoyed dousing a rogue within an inch of his life—if not nearer——

Clink (*up at back*). There's Master Rivet has heard the disturbance, and orders you all to your chambers. So in, gentlemen.

Sir J. I, too, friend?

Clink. You, too, Friend!

Sir J. Saucy rogue! (*Ruefuly.*) He might have said Sir John.

Clink. Come, my lord.

[*Exit Prisoners, grumbling, to their cells.*

Mother. Harkee, Tom Clink (*aside to Turnkey*), I've a bladder of right Nantz, crying 'come, tap me.' But thou'lt never lock up my lord here.

Clink. Nay, his lordship keeps order, instead of breaking it. He's free o' the yard. So I'll e'en lock him out of his chamber, instead of into it.

[*Locks* LORD C.'s *cell door outside.*

Mother. And here's the laundress has brought his lordship's linen. She's waiting for her pass outside. She asked me to forward the matter for her as I came in half an hour ago.

Clan. Nay, mother, my linen, what there is on't——

Mother (*aside*) Stow whids, my lord. (*Pushing* CLINK

T

to gate.) Now, man, 'tis a shame to keep a decent young woman waiting among that rakehelly Westminster crew, that's boiling like a cross tide round Dungeness. (CLINK *goes to gate. Aside to* LORD C.) I'll take Tom Clink in tow. Lay aboard of your laundress while I keep the coast clear for you!

Clan. (*aside*) What does she mean? I scarcely dare to hope——

[*The gate is opened. Enter* LADY C., *disguised as a laundress, with a linen-basket.*

Mother (*aside to* LADY C.). Keep your countenance. (*To* LORD C.) Here's your lordship's linen, and while you count it, come, Tom Clink. I've a word for thee—and a skin of the right sort, my lad o' wax. [*Exit with* CLINK.

Clan. My darling! My clever, cunning darling!

Lady C. Husband! Dearest! But are we alone?

[*They embrace.*

Clan. By the strangest chance the prisoners are locked up—all but thy happy husband! (*Another embrace.*) My brave sweetheart, I swear thou look'st prettier in thy mob than in thy laces!

Lady C. I am so glad! I hope the real laundress has as happy a heart under her grogram jacket.

Clan. To think of thee at this drudgery, among that howling mob outside! But, methinks, they could have none but kind words and looks for thee.

Lady C. I felt as bold as a lion. When they told me how bright my eyes were, and one of them asked a kiss, I was not a bit dashed, but tossed my head and told them I was keeping my lips for one in the prison; and there they are, sir, if you care to take them.

Clan. If I care to taste Heaven's cordial!

[*A passionate kiss.*

Lady C. They knew I was there to comfort some poor prisoner inside, and that made them all kind. Methinks if I had not known thee, and all this trouble, I should never have learnt how tender rough hearts can be. That's another debt I owe thee! There's Mother Hunt—'twas she found her way into our house with smuggled lace, and so got speech of me, for my brother has kept me well-nigh a prisoner; she counselled me this disguise, and found it for me; and lo! it has done what I tried in vain, by prayers to Mr. Secretary and his secretaries, to my father, my Lord

Woodstock, my Lord Portland, the King himself—it has let me in to thee!

Clan. It lightens my heart to see thy cheek so bright, and thine eye so blythe.

Lady C. And when should I be glad if not now—that I can hold thy hand once more, and lay my head on thy bosom; and think of the misery of the last month as of a horrible dream? Methinks I should be a wicked, ungrateful creature if I did not feel happy thus.

[*Breaks down in a passionate fit of sobbing on her husband's bosom.*

Clan. My poor love! Be comforted—compose thy dear fluttering heart.

Lady C. Forgive me. I could not keep it down; but these are tears of joy—they are indeed.

[*Another burst of grief.*

Clan. I feared this for thee, my brave darling; thy spirit is above thy strength.

Lady C. You have no right to think that, still less to say it. Would'st thou unman thy wife? Donough, 'tis I am the man now. 'Tis I must scheme and cajole, and make friends outside. 'Tis I must work to save thy dear life, that is my life now. And there is so much to be done, so many to be seen and pleaded with, and won to our cause!

Clan. And how does it go with my little warrior in her brave battle?

Lady C. If I could but have speech with the King! I have written and written, so often and so urgently; but no answer reaches me. I fear 'tis my brother—some one—intercepts my letters. I have tried all means to obtain an audience, but access to the closet is so guarded! The King will listen to no prayers, they tell me. Methinks mine would be such prayers that he *must* listen.

Clan. And thy brother?

Lady C. No, his face is set like flint against me and thee. 'Tis strange to think we once were children together, with one heart between us; and now so utterly divided. No, there is nothing to be hoped from my brother.

Clan. No hope in favourite or brother! Then we must e'en make our minds up to the worst.

Lady C. Husband, what coward words are these? I will not give up hoping, striving, praying—not till the day of doom has dawned—not till the hour of doom has struck—

not till the axe has fallen—not till I hold thy dear head to my heart. And then 'twill be a new hope that that heart will break, and bring us once more together!

Clan. Oh, to die, and lose such a woman!

Lady C. Lose me, cruel husband? Said I not that I would straight be with thee, in that happy place where there is no more parting? [*Sinks into his arms.*

Clan. They say that marriages are made in Heaven. Methinks ours will be spent there. 'Tis best so. 'Twill be a wedding with no waking out of the sweet dream of love to life's hard battle.

Lady C. Think not I am beaten in that battle yet. Keep up thy heart, and hope—thou needst them sorely here—while I make a last attempt upon the King, by aid of my truest friend, Lady Betty Noel. Ah, they call her featherhead, but I know her heart of gold. The King is good and just, for all he seems so cold and stern. But let me gain the closet, I have a secret weapon of my own by which I can reach his heart.

Clan. Why, how's this? Another assassination plot!

Lady C. My spirits are too heavy for jesting. But surely, if the King knew 'twas to thee he owed his first warning of the plot, he must step between thee and the axe.

Clan. Had my Lord Portland been of the Council when I was examined, or in court when I was tried, he might have said as much. 'Twas not for me to tell them. 'Twould have been said I had spoken but to secure my own life, not save the Prince's.

Re-enter CLINK, *flushed with drink, and* MOTHER HUNT.

Clink (*up* C.). How now, my lord? Have you not settled scores with your laundress yet? How now, mistress? Empty thy basket and begone!

Clan. Empty her basket! Out here, in the day yard! 'Tis thy fault, clumsy rogue. Thou hast locked me out of my chamber. Where was she to bestow the linen?

Clink (*going to cell door*). Plague on't, that's true! You see, my lord, I was bid to make you free o' the yard. Was I to give you choice 'twixt yard and chamber? But an' I locked you *out* then, I'll lock you *in* now. So, to crib with your lordship; and thou, wench, despatch!

[*Motioning her to cell.*

Clan. Come, my good girl.

Lady C. (aside) One last kiss.
　　　　　　　　　　[*Exit with* CLANCARTY *into cell.*
Mother H. (aside) It goes to my heart to see 'em parted, poor lambs! This way, Tom, for another sly caulker!

Clink (tipsily). Wouldst thou corrupt an officer of the Gate House prison? I've a mind to round on thee, thou drunken Jezebel, bringings—srp—surup—suruptitious liquor into the King's gaol to fuddle the King's officer! (*Calling into cell.*) Now, then, will the wench be all day about her business? (*Enter* LADY CLANCARTY *from cell, with empty basket.*) In good time. This way. (*Going towards gate and opening wicket.*) A buxom lass! Ere thou goest, there's thy prison fees to pay! Come, garnish! garnish!
　　[*Tries to kiss her. She gives him a smart box on the
　　　　ear, which sends him reeling.*

Lady C. Hands off, thou drunken rogue!

Mother Hunt (aside) Well hit, my lady. (*Hits* CLINK *on the other side.*) There's t'other broadside, to put thee on an even keel.

　　　　　　　　　(*Shut in.*)

SCENE II.

Antechamber in Whitehall.

Enter PORTLAND *and* SPENCER *in conversation.*

Port. Yes, the plot is a godsend. 'Twill give the King a new lease of public favour. What think you of this scheme of an association for the protection of his precious life, and the condign punishment of all who strike at it?

Spen. 'Tis of very likely action. Nothing your Englishman hates like assassination.

Port. You see, thus far, the juries have not acquitted one of those concerned in this vile plot.

Spen. 'Tis true, the citizens have done their duty like men.

Port. If but the King will do his. He is so loath to punish.

Spen. 'Tis his worst weakness.

Port. An amiable one, you must admit.

Spen. Kings and statesmen cannot afford amiable weaknesses. The rank of many of these conspirators, the atrocity of their design, the head their detestable faction is gaining in the country, all forbid clemency, and demand a terrible example.

Port. I have brought the King to admit it, though with mighty difficulty. He has promised that he will see no petitioner, read no petition, on behalf of any of the prisoners.

Spen. 'Tis a stern necessity. I needs must feel for him, who have to steel my heart against my unhappy sister.

Port. My Lady Clancarty has indeed been unwearied with all about the King. Never was petitioner so hard to resist—so brave as she is with all her womanliness—so unyielding in her perseverance—so tenacious under her tenderness. If your voice backed hers, I should despair of the King's firmness.

Spen. Have no fear, my lord, of any irresolution on my part. When you recommended suppression of my sister's frequent letters to the King, did I hesitate?

Port. Did you read ere you destroyed them?

Spen. I dared not trust myself.

Port. All know your lordship is of Spartan constancy—strong enough to resist even the fear of being thought unnatural.

Spen. Do you think the cloaked Spartan felt the fox's fangs the less because he uttered no cry. To your lordship I need not fear to own that I have the Spartan's feeling as well as his fortitude.

Port. Clancarty's death will relieve us of the pain and publicity of a divorce.

Spen. Your pardon, my lord, if I cannot think of that now. My poor sister's will be no formal widowhood. I doubt if we shall ever bend her to our wishes.

Port. Nous verrons. Woman is a weathercock, and Woodstock is accustomed to obey orders.

Spen. You know she has given him one rebuff.

Port. Let him wait for a second. Two negatives are equivalent to an affirmative. And now to the King, to confirm his resolution against clemency to the condemned, and to take his final orders as to their execution.

[*Exit with* SPENCER, R.

Enter on the other side LADY BETTY, *in hood and mantua, and* LORD WOODSTOCK, *she clinging to his arm, he encouraging her.*

Wood. Courage, my darling; thou wert not wont to be so fearful.

Betty. I know not. I used to be bold enough, single;

but since our marriage I've been as full of tremours and twitterings. I can only cling to my husband, instead of crowing over him. I hope 'twill not be *ever* thus.

Wood. I fear it will not.

Betty. Or I shall know nothing of the pleasure of command. I always looked to that as the best privilege of wedlock—to have one's own will and one's husband's as well. But lo! I feel as timid——

Wood. Believe me, the mood becomes thee infinitely. If thou wilt be ruled by me, thou wilt not change it.

Betty. I know, if I do not change it, I *will* be ruled by thee. But that's not what I married for—if, indeed, we are married, and 'tis not at all a dream.

Wood. No dream, dearest; a sober certainty of waking bliss.

Betty. Too sober by half—a stealthy, secret, sneaking wedding at the Savoy, by a parson with a rusty cassock and a red nose.

Wood. Better enter wedded life by the gate of horn to come to that of gold, than t'other and more beaten way.

Betty. But thou must own, Harry, 'tis very, very hard! (*Whimpering.*) No wedding clothes, no wedding coaches, no favours, and no flowers!

Wood. For wedding clothes, have we not the *couleur de rose* of the future to make them of? For coaches, a hackney chariot is the true car of Hymen. Going to church, its pace gives time for repentance; and coming home, it prolongs the bliss of the first *tête-à-tête*. For favours, what ribbons like the blush of thy cheeks, with the white of the bosom below them; and for flowers——

Betty. I must be fain to put up with thy flowers of speech. But, worst of all, there's the breaking of the awful news. Thy terrible father! how will he take it?

Wood. Whether as philosopher, politician, or Dutchman, he has long ago learned to put up with the inevitable.

Betty. Even in the shape of a daughter-in-law.

Wood. If his heart were marble——

Betty. I verily believe 'tis Dutch tile.

Wood. Thy smiles would melt it.

Betty. I always understood minerals were melted with vinegar. And then I thought I was to keep all my smiles for thee.

Wood. While they go to my father, at least they won't be spent out of the family.

Betty. The first favour I mean to buy with them is access to the King for my poor dear Elizabeth.

Wood. My father has refused a hundred petitioners on her behalf.

Betty. So he refused thee leave to marry; but as we took French leave in that, I mean to take it in this. You have my Lord Portland's master-key here. Give it me!

Wood. I hold it as his secretary.

Betty. You hold it as my husband.

Wood. To give it to thee were a grave breach of official duty.

Betty. In obedience to matrimonial. The lower duty must make way for the higher.

Wood. I tell thee 'tis impossible!

Betty. Impossible! And within an hour of marriage? (*Coaxingly, and clasping her hands on his arm.*) Harry, darling, thou wilt not say no to thy poor little, simple, submissive, affectionate Betty, who kneels thus humbly to her lord and master? [*Kneels at his feet.*

Wood. Prithee, my darling; this is childish.

Betty. And what am I but a child? A poor little helpless, harmless child, that must have its plaything, and will pay for it more than 'tis worth, in Cupid's coin—kisses. (*As she kisses him she gets the key from his pocket.*) There! Now I have the key, and my friend shall reach the King.

[*Going.*

Wood. (*following*) Plague on't! This is folly! Give it me back, I tell thee! Nay—I shall be angry!

Betty (*turning, smiling, shaking key, and putting up her mouth as to kiss*). I defy thee!

Enter Usher.

Usher. A lady to see your ladyship.

Betty. Who is it?

Usher. She is veiled, and will give no name.

Betty. Admit her. (*Exit Usher.*) I hold thee a thousand, Harry—kisses, I mean—'tis my sweet friend, come to me for help to the King. Away, my lord. You shall have the key—when we have used it. You shan't be compromised. I'll say I stole it. Away!

Wood. An ominous opening of married life. Trapped, tricked, and turned out of the room—and obliged to submit.

Betty (*kissing him*). There's for submitting with a good grace. [*Exit* WOODSTOCK.

Enter LADY C., L., *veiled. She unveils.*

Betty. Elizabeth! my poor suffering sweet one, how pale thou art!

Lady C. I have come to thee as a last hope. Lord Portland has again refused me. I must see the King myself, and to-day. To-morrow 'twill be too late. Thou art full of womanly arts. Thou art all-powerful with Lord Woodstock.

Betty. I *was* yesterday. To-day he is all powerful with me.

Lady C. What do you mean?

Betty. We were married in the Savoy Chapel scarce an hour ago, with nobody's leave but our own. 'Twas the tapster from the Precinct Coffee-house gave me away. Such a brandy-faced old rogue of a father! Bought for a broad piece! Faugh! I'm ashamed of him! So now I'm a married woman, like thyself.

Lady C. Not like me, I pray. For then would thy life be sorrow, thy double life a double agony. Yet, no—even the sorrow that is partaken between true hearts is better than the selfish joy that comes and goes unshared. But I waste time. Canst thou—will'st thou help me to speech of the King? Oh, do not say thou canst not.

Betty. Look, my first matrimonial trophy, won at the point of the lips—Lord Portland's master-key. [*Holds it up.*

Lady C. That opens the private stair to the King's closet, from the poor Queen's apartment! The passage she showed thee and me, when we were maids of honour—that the King has kept shut to all since her death——

Betty. The same! the same!

Lady C. I see! A light of hope dawns on me, even out of the tomb of that dear mistress. Come, come, quick!

[*Exeunt together.*

SCENE III.—*The Royal Closet in Whitehall. Oak fittings in the style of Charles the First's time. The pictures in the panels represent sieges and battles by Van der Meulen, and Dutch flower pieces, and furnish the sole decoration, with the exception of a full-length portrait and bust of the Queen. Door concealed in panel, R.C., windows looking on the garden in flat, C. Entrance doors R. and L. Furniture of the period.*

The KING *discovered at a table* (R.C.) *with papers.* PORTLAND *and* SPENCER *in attendance.*

King. Next Monday be it, then. The commoners at Tyburn, the noblemen on Tower Hill. There are the warrants. (*Handing papers to* PORTLAND. *To* SPENCER.) I am sorry for your sister. [*Rises.*

Spen. (*with a sigh*) So am I.

[*Walks up and down uneasily.*

Port. (*anxiously*) But you will not see her, sir?

King. Have I not promised I will not?

Port. And you will own, sir, that the promise commends itself to your better judgment.

King (*stopping opposite Queen's portrait*). My better judgment has left me. Had she been here, you would scarce have had your will of me so easily. My Mary, thou wert ever on the side of mercy; what wilt thou think of thy husband to-day? You have given me a sleepless night between you. Good afternoon, my lords, unless you will join me in the garden. But not another word of these miserable men and their fate.

Enter LADY BETTY, *peeping, from panel.*

Betty. The coast is clear. (LADY C. *follows.*) Courage, and good speed! [*Kisses her and retires through panel.*

Lady C. Here is the battle-field. Now for the last struggle. The fight for life or death! Father of all that suffer, give me strength to bear me bravely, and crown a wife's devotion with the conquest even of a conqueror and a king. (*Addresses portrait of Queen.*) And thou, good and gentle mistress, be my intercessor in that Heaven where thou art at peace, save for our sorrows, and in the heart of the husband who loved thee better than any e'er dreamed he could love, but thou——

King (outside). Farewell, my lords, you have even poisoned my pleasure in my flowers.

Lady C. The King coming this way and alone! Now is my time.

Enter KING *from garden with down-bent head, his hands clasped behind him, walking slowly, as if in deep and painful thought. He seats himself, not seeing* LADY C., *who kneels at his feet.*

Lady C. Mercy, your Majesty! Mercy for my husband, Lord Clancarty!

King. You here, madam? In spite of my strict commands! I had forbidden my closet to all petitioners—to you, above all. Who has dared to disobey my orders?

Lady C. No one has disobeyed. I have asked none—I came here without permission.

King. How?

Lady C. (in a low voice). By the private staircase from the Queen's apartment.   [*Points to it.*

King (struggling with profound emotion). That staircase, madam, the use of which I have forbidden to all! How dared you!—— [*Pause.*

Lady C. Because 'twas on an errand for which she would have opened it for me—for which she would have taken me by the hand, and kneeled at my side, had need been, at your gracious feet, to pray with me, in her sweet voice, all tremulous with pity, for the life of my husband, Donough Macarthy, now lying condemned to die!

King. Who gave you access to that staircase?

Lady C. My despair.

King. You knew 'twas sacred to my sorrow.

Lady C. Not so sacred to yours, sire, but there was room in it for mine. (*With increasing earnestness.*) Think of the gentle and gracious lady in whose service I learned the secret of that passage—of her love for her husband—of his for her; and then believe that as she loved her husband, I love mine —as she would have pleaded for her husband's life, I plead for mine—as she would have died to save her husband, I will die for mine. We were wedded as children; we have lived apart ever since. Oh, think of the long arrears of happiness that are due to us, now that we have learned to love each other with the strong, swift love that grows in affliction, and ripens in the shadow of the scaffold.

King. Your friends have urged all this already.

Lady C. But death is so much nearer now.

King (*rising*). Assassins deserve no mercy.

Lady C. (*passionately*) But my husband is no assassin! That is what I have striven so that you should know. He was in the plot, but not of it. He was too noble to take part with assassins. He warned my Lord Portland (KING *turns*); he warned your Majesty—'twas on the day fixed for the deed.

King (*quickly*, R.). What! That young soldier who saw my Lord Portland and myself at the Palace?

Lady C. The same! the same!

King. Who refused to give up his friends' names or to disclose his own; but made no stipulation for reward or indemnity?

Lady C. That was my Donough. My brave, self-forgetting, self-sacrificing husband.

[*The* KING *writes hastily and rings.*

Enter Usher.

King. This to the orderly officer of the day. Let him send a mounted man with it at once. Bid hither my Lord Portland and Lord Spencer. (*Exit Usher.*) How came it this was not given in evidence on your husband's trial?

Lady C. My Lord Portland, the only one who could have recognised my lord, was absent from Council and Court both, on a secret mission over sea. My husband's lips were sealed by his own nobleness.

King. But how came it I never knew?

Lady C. I wrote it to your Majesty, letter after letter.

King. I received none.

Lady C. Ah, I feared as much; but I would not listen to my fears.

King. Through whose hands did those letters pass?

Lady C. Alas! that I should say it!— through my brother's.

Enter PORTLAND *and* SPENCER. *They come down*, R.

Port. Lady Clancarty!

Spen. My sister here!

King (*significantly to* SPENCER). Though I have *not* received her letters.

Port. Is it thus your majesty keeps your promise?

King. I did not undertake, that I remember, to defy a woman's courage or a wife's devotion. My Lady Clancarty is an intruder without leave. She has been urgent in her pleading. [*Looking at her.*

Port. Urgency is not enough, sir; there is also justice.

Spen. And retribution. An eye for an eye—a tooth for a tooth.

King. And a life for a life, I presume you would say?

Spen. Even so, your Majesty.

King. Methinks the obligation should hold for life saved, as well as life taken.

Enter Captain of the Guard.

Officer. The prisoner is here, your Majesty.

King. Bring in the gentleman. Your veil, madam, for a moment. [LADY C. *veils herself.*

Officer shows in LORD CLANCARTY.

Clan. The Prince! my Lord Portland! Lord Spencer! Why am I brought hither?

[*The* KING *bows to* LADY C., *who throws off veil.*
Lady C. (*stretching her arms to her husband*) Donough!

Clan. My darling! (*Rushes to embrace her.*) Must I ask your Highness's pardon?

King. By no means. Consider us absent for the moment. My lords.

[*Beckons* PORTLAND *and* SPENCER *apart, and they group,* R.

Lady C. (*faintly*) Saved! saved!

[*In her husband's arms.*

Clan. She is swooning.

Lady C. No—no—'tis joy! only joy! true joy this time. [*Sobbing convulsively in his arms.*

Clan. Be composed, my own true-hearted girl! But how is this? Why art thou here, and these, and I? (*To the* KING.) I hope, your Highness, she has asked no grace for me—no grace, at least, on terms befitting not my duty as a loyal subject. 'Tis very hard to part from new-found happiness, and happiness like this. But I had rather die in the service of my King than purchase life by changing it for yours.

King. Why live for King's service at all, sir; why not rather for that of your liege lady here? The woman who has begged your life—to whom I have given it. Nay, no heroics, young sir, as a pure matter of barter, in exchange for my own; and with your life, sir, take your pardon.

Spen. Pardon, your Majesty, for an offence like *his?*

King. There are other offences, not so easily pardoned, my lord—offences against nature—like *yours.*

Spen. I do not understand your Majesty. For my Lord Clancarty's service to your Majesty, I learn it now for the first time.

King. Had you been more gentle with your sister she would have been more open to you.

Enter LADY BETTY *and* LORD WOODSTOCK.

Betty. God bless your Majesty, for the most merciful and magnanimous of Kings! (*Kneeling,* L. C.) On that mercy we throw ourselves.

King. We! and how comes Lady Betty Noel in the plural number?

Wood. Lady Woodstock now, an't please your Majesty, and you, my lord and father.   [*To* LORD PORTLAND.

Port. Lady Woodstock! zounds! But it doth *not* please me, puppy.

Betty. What cannot be cured must be endured; so, if I might ask a blessing for both of us! (*To* WOODSTOCK.) Kneel, my lord.

Wood. (*to* PORTLAND) You always said, my lord, I had no right to a will of my own. I was used to take yours instead. Now I take hers, and kneel as she bids me.

Port. Married to this madcap—without my leave or license!

Betty. We found a desperate Savoy parson, my lord, who dispensed with it.

King. Come, William, 'tis idle to look sour—you and I should know better than to cry over spilt milk. (*To* LADY B.) I warrant we shall steady this feather-head with a dowry. Grant to me, if not to them, your blessing on their union.

Port. (*shrugging his shoulders*) 'Tis hard, sir; but needs must——

King (*interrupting*). When the Dutchman drives. We'll find a sufficiency of manors for your Harry nearer home than Ireland. And now for you, my lord. (*To* CLANCARTY.) We must see your revenues re-rounded.

Clan. Your Highness is determined to leave me in my normal state of debt after all.

King. At least I will not press for payment; I will not even ask you to take service with me. Enough that you promise not to serve against me.

[CLANCARTY *is about to speak.* LADY C. *puts her hand on his lips.*

Lady C. He promises, sir—he promises!

King. There is Hamburg—safe neutral ground. Why not live happy there with your Elizabeth? Come, leave me one pleasant passage in my day's work to sleep upon, after all.

Clan. What say'st thou, sweetheart? Canst thou sacrifice court and country for thy husband?

Lady C. My court is where thou art—my country is in thine arms! [*Embrace.*

CURTAIN

ARKWRIGHT'S WIFE

An Original Domestic Drama

IN THREE ACTS

DRAMATIS PERSONÆ.

ORIGINAL CAST.

RICHARD ARKWRIGHT	MR. CHARLES KELLY.
PETER HAYES (*a reed-maker and mechanical inventor*)	MR. J. STEELE MACKAYE.
HILKIAH LAWSON	MR. HENRY FERRAND.
DICK O' JOHNS	MR. CHARLES ANSTRUTHER.
BOB O' CHOWBENT	MR. HARRY ST. MAUR.
CHADWICK	MR. JOHN INMAN.
ORMROD	MR. WM. MACFARLANE.
SIR RICHARD CLAYTON	MR. BAUER.
HAWORTH	MR. MELTON.
BAILIFF	MR. JOHNSON.
MARGARET HAYES	MISS HELEN BARRY.
NANCY HYDE	MISS A. M. KELLY.

Soldiers, Rioters, Charity Children, Village Lasses.

	TIME.	PLACE.
ACT 1	1767	*Leigh.*
ACT 2	1768	*Preston.*
ACT 3	1786	*Birkacre, near Chorley.*

To face p. 291.

RICHARD ARKWRIGHT'S ORIGINAL MODEL OF HIS SPINNING MACHINE,
PATENTED 1796.

(*Given as a guide to the construction of the model to be used
in the play of ' Arkwright's Wife.'*)

ARKWRIGHT'S WIFE.

ACT I.

SCENE.—*Poorly-furnished room in* PETER HAYES'S *house, Leigh. Low window* (C. *in flat*) *looking on village. Door in flat*, L. C. *Stair leading to upper room*, R. 2 E. *Fireplace, wide and open*, L. 2 E. *Door*, R. 3 E. *Everything betrays poverty— furniture old-fashioned. Table, two chairs, clock, and spinning-wheel.*

Nancy (*without*). Maggie, lass! (*Enters.*) Not at her wheel! Eh, but that's a sight, Saturday as it is, and all Leigh out at market. (*Apostrophising wheel.*) Thou should be glad of a rest, ou'd bumbler, for it's few thou gets wi' Maggie. It's well there's one pair o' hands in the house that addles since the ou'd man ceased to work at his reed-making. Though there's more spent than saved at back end, I reckon, for all thy huzzin' and buzzin', ou'd chap; and there's not a spinner in Leigh turns out as much weft i' the week as Margret Hayes. But the ou'd man taks every penny!

[PETER *appears at garret door with part of a model in his hand.*

Peter. Now, Maggie, lass, what's come o' t' breakfast? I'm fair clemmed. Drat that wheel, dost hear?

Nancy. Nay. It's none Marget It's nobbut me, Nan o' Jacks. I've come wi' a word for Maggie.

Peter. You can leave it wi' me, can't ye? (*Coming down.*) Happen I can still be trusted wi' a lass's message, though it's little else they'll trust me wi' in Leigh now-a-days—the blind buzzards.

Nancy. That's what comes o' knowing more than your neighbours, Mr. Hayes.

Peter. Ah, there's nought so like a fool among wise men as a wise man among fools.

Nancy. Why, down i' Bob o' Dick's bar the folks say you're little better than a warlock—that you spend neets on neets i' your garret yonder, castin' figures and reading fortuns i' the stars.

Peter. Ah—fortuns should be easy readin' if all folks had their dues.

Nancy. But schoolmaster says he'll be bound your seeking Lucifer's stone. Please, whatten a stone's that, Mr. Hayes?

Peter. Philosopher's stone—not Lucifer's! Thou'rt only confoundin' the doctors with the devil—like thy betters; a stone mony wise men and more fools broke their shins over for mony a hundred years—the stone that turns all metal into gold, lass.

Nancy. Lor' a massy! and be there such a stone, Mr. Hayes?

Peter. Aye, lass!

Nancy. But you've none found it?

Peter. Not yet. But I may be nearer to it than these Leigh wiseacres think, for all I'm not seekin' it o' the road they fancy. (*Rises.*) I tell thee, Nancy Hyde, there *is* a way to turn brass and iron into gold, and I'm on 't. You may tell t' schoolmaster that much next time you see him, but no more—no more. Old Peter Hayes mayn't be able to keep the pence in his pocket till he can jingle shillings against the sots and Solomons at the 'King's Yead,' but he can keep his own secret—he can keep his own secret.

Nancy. And mine, too, I hope—the secret I came to tell Maggie. Hilkiah will be fair savage if he knew I had letten it out. (*Whispers.*) They're goin' to seize t' sticks here to-day for t' rent.

Peter. Nay, niver! Will Learoyd's a hard chap, but he would niver do that—why, we were lads together.

Nancy. But Hilkiah knows. He's to help t' bailiffs. Nay, it's no use looking at me like that, Mr. Hayes. So I thought I would warn Marget. Happen there was something I could smuggle out o' t' place before they seize. There's Marget's wheel.

Peter. Rot her wheel! What's to come o' my machine-models—the fruit I've watered wi' my brain—sweat for days and nights, and weeks and years—my hard long life's work, lass—and just as it is comin' to bearin'! Lose them! lose all! all! I'll ha' them packed up, and out at garret window, and ower house-top into your place i' the turn o' a crank. Thy father will gi' them house-room. (*Rises and staggers.*) My models—my models!

Nancy (*supporting him*). Mind, Mr. Hayes. Tak haud o' me—you're weak i' t' legs.

Peter. It's nobbut want o' meat. But what matter o' meat now? My models, lass—my models!

[*Makes his way eagerly up stair.*

Nancy. Poor oud chap! There's my porridge waiting for me. I can want it better than the oud man. I'll slip it into their cupboard before Marget knows; she's ower proud to owe meat or money! Here she comes; 1 mun slip out at back door. [*Exit* R. 3 E. *door.*

Enter MARGARET *with basket; sets it down; goes to cupboard* (L.), *opens it, sighs, shakes her head sadly.*

Margt. Nay, where should the meat come from? Did I think father was the wizard Leigh folks call him to conjure bare boards into bread? [I've brought myself down to begging. If 'twas but asking credit for a stone o' meal it was still begging. There's a bill at the shop already. 'We'd trust thee, Marget, and welcome, but thou knows what comes o' thy earnings.' The old tale I've heard since 1 were a lassock. His flesh and blood must keep his bits o' brass and iron, and can't do it, though they work eyes blind and fingers sore. (*Turning to wheel.*) Well, I must fast till I've finished this hank. Bob o' Dicks will be round for weft this afternoon. I can clem a bit, easy enough, but there's poor father.]

Peter (*at garret door*). Ah, Marget, back at last. (*Comes down.*) Thou mun hurry porridge, lass; I'll eat it standing, and then thou can help me to take my bits o' things to pieces.

Margt. Take thy models to pieces, father? You're none tired o' them?

Peter. Nay, lass, nay—scarce likely. It's to save them out o' t' place—t' bailiffs are coming to seize for t' rent, Nancy Hyde tells me.

Margt. The bailiffs?

Peter. It's hard to think Will Learoyd could be such a fool. Why, I told him the road I was upon.

Margt. Easy enough to know that, I'm afraid.

Peter. Nay, niver. I keep it as close as the grave. Thou's not let on to anybody? What, lass, what?

Margt. Why, father, I thought you knew me better. I've none made a poor lip, not even when our want was sorest; but what need o' words to tell the gait we're goin'—wi' empty platters and cold hearthstone, and t' house place nigh as naked as the cupboard? Don't all Leigh see we're gettin' poorer and poorer?

Peter. Poorer and poorer, thou chicken heart, when every penny I lay out is bound to come back wi' a million behind it! When I've machines up yonder that only want a bit more time and brass to finish, and a world wi' fewer fools to work in, and Peter Hayes and his lass may be the richest lord and the grandest lady between Lune and Mersey.

Margt. Still fooling thyself with that dream, father?

Peter. Dream! Is that wheel a dream? That hank o' flax—that spindle—that treadle—these hands o' thine? As sure as they can turn out their day's tale of weft in a day, there's my bonny little iron spinner, hard on birth, up yonder, that will do a thousand times their work, in a tenth o' the time, at a hundredth o' t' cost. Ha, ha, ha! I like that —a dream! Ha, ha, ha!

Margt. Father, you forget how often I've heard that song. I heard it when you gave up reed-making—I was a bairn then, in answer to mother's prayer that you'd stick to the craft that had kept a good roof over t' Hayes's heads for more than a hundred years; and when she sickened o' hard times and sore sorrow, and clemmed sooner than ask help— it was wi' that song you tried to stop your bairns crying for their mother and for bread! And when brother and sister died of the weakness that followed the fever, and that craved better meat and drink than you had to give them, and I was left alone to help, that song was all we had to comfort us over those little coffins. And what has it come to? Money, and more money still, for wheelwright, and clockmaker, and turner, and caster, and carpenter—money and mockery and misery—delusion, disappointment, and despair!

Peter. Oh, that my own bairn should turn against me like this!

Margt. Nay, thou knows I'd give thee night's work and day's work; I'd clem for thee.—Have I not begged for thee?—if I believed what thou'art seeking could be found, and found for good. But thou sees what thy labour and thought comes to, and thou'rt not the only one by many. Why, there's Kay at Bury, and Hargreaves at Blackburn, and Paul at Birmingham, and a many more that Parson Trafford told us of only last week. It's been with them as with thee —not one but is a branded and a broken man.

Peter. Nay. They're on the wrong scent—gone astray after windin' and cardin', weavin' and dressin'. It's the spinnin' I'm after, lass—that's the root o' the matter— that's the problem—how to do wheel's work without wheels, and a thousand times better, and cheaper and faster.

Margt. And so starve all the spinners, and stop all the wheels in Lancashire!

Peter. Ah, the old fool's reason!

Margt. Much good that'll bring the country, and much love that will breed him that brings it, even if your invention did all you say. What is making one rich to keeping a hundred poor?

Peter. Oh, these women—(*crosses to* R.)—these women! As if it were not enough to fight wi' fools out o' doors, but I must fight my own bairn on my own hearthstone! But I'll punish thee. Thou shall not set finger to my models. Thou'rt not worthy to look at them, much less touch them.
[*Going towards stairs.*

Margt. Nay, let me help thee.

Peter. Stand off! Thou'rt no child o' mine to say what thou hast said e'en now.

Margt. Forgive me, father; I'm sore tried! We're alone in the world now. We mustn't be too hard on one another.

Peter. Stand off, I tell thee. I mun work my own work after this. [*Exit upstairs.*

Margt. Nay, then. Heaven help him and me! If we have not love left us, what have we?

Enter NANCY *with basin in hands.*

Nancy. Here, Maggie, lass; I've brought thee a basin of our porridge—we'd more than we could sup. There's enough for thy father, too, and it's hot as hot, and made wi' sweet milk. Now, Maggie, woman, I'll run up to thy father wi' it. Here, sup, lass, and put a little life in thee.

[*While speaking she has been fussing about, getting spoons, &c.*

Margt. Thou'rt a good lass, Nancy. May'st thou never want as bad; and if thou dost, may'st thou find as good a heart as thine own to help thee. [*Sups.*

Nancy. Hout! Here's a stir about a sup of porridge! (*Goes upstairs; knocks at* PETER'S *door.*) Here, Mr. Hayes —here's thy porridge.

Peter (*within*). Set it down.

Nancy. Margret says you mun sup it hot.

Peter. Margret be damned!

Nancy. Oh!

Peter. I'll take nought at her hand.

Nancy. Then you mun tak' it at mine. (*Puts in basin; comes down.*) Summut ha' set his back up. He's told thee what's coming?

Margt. Aye, has he. 'Twas scarce news. I've seen it getting nearer and nearer this long while. Oh, Nancy, whatever shall we do without a roof over our heads?

Nancy. There's room under ours till you can look about you. It's not the first time we've been bedfellows. But I've better news for thee than t' bailiffs. Dost want to earn three golden guineas in as many minutes, lass?

Margt. Do I? That's quicker than weft-spinning. How?

Nancy. Thou know'st me and Hilkiah's been asked these two Sundays. No lass o' the Hydes ever went to her man empty-handed Here's what I've got to help our housing—(*shows grey stocking, with money*)—a matter o' ten pound—seven pound ten saved at spinning, and the rest out of my own yead.

Margt. Out o' thy own head? Nay, that's like poor father's talk.

Nancy. Look here, lass. (*Unties handkerchief, worn round her head; shows close-cropped hair.*)

Margt. Why, Nancy, whatever's come o' thy hair? Thou's shaved close as a lad.

Nancy. Aye! t' crop's cut, and sold and paid for; and it brought me two pound ten. And thine should bring twice as much, for it's twice as long, and more than twice as bonny. T" man that buy's 'em is i' t' market-place e'en now; he's a Bolton chap; [Arkwright, they call him; and his tongue is as sharp as his scissors; and he has a box wi' scents and essences, that you would swoon to smell at, they're so sweet; and all sorts of dyes for the wig-makers, he says; and orris-powder, and Sheffield razors, and the Lord knows all what. Aye, and] wi' money in his pockets, they say, to buy all the good heads o' hair i' Leigh.

Margt. He buys none o' mine, I can tell him.

[*Nancy.* Nay, I told him o' that bonny wig o' thine. There's not another like it for twenty townships round. I gave him thy name, and showed him the house.

Margt. Then thou took'st too much upon thyself, Nancy Hyde.] While I've hands to spin I'll none part wi' my hair.

Nancy. Hush! Here's Hilkiah. (*Puts on handkerchief.*)

Enter HILKIAH.

Hilkiah. Good day, Marget. Nancy's told thee? Learoyd's bent on seizin'; I don't know what they couldn't do to me for tellin'.

[*Nancy.* I know what I'd a' done to thee if thoud'st not told.

Margt. I take it very kind o' thee, Hilkiah.

Hilkiah. Well, it *is* kind. I've searched books in our office, Newgate Calendar and all, and I can't find a case of t' sort; but I reckon I'm something like an accessory before the fact, and that's hanging sometimes.] But I thought you'd like to save the wheel, at least.

[*Margt.* And father's models.

Hilkiah. What! yon bits o' gim-cracks up in t' garret? Nay, they'll none be worth seizing. But the wheel 'll fetch a price.]

Nancy. Never fear, Maggie; I'll tak charge o' that.

Margt. When are they like to be here?

Hilkiah. As soon as old Crookmouth can get down his pint at the King's Yead; him and Learoyd's wetting t' writ.

[*Nancy.* I wish the pint might choke him.

Hilkiah. Amen. I don't see but Leigh might get over t' loss.]

Margt. I must prepare father for their coming—help him to take his models to pieces—the inventions he hopes such wonders from. [He must never know they're not even worth seizing.] [*Exit, upstairs.*

Nancy. Thou's been a good lad i' this, Hilkiah, and I'm proud o' thee for once.

Hilkiah. That's a comfort! [But lawyers' lads, that

hopes to be lawyers one day, ought to follow their masters' example.

Nancy. How dost mean?

Hilkiah. Never advise without a fee. I might ask thee six and eightpence, but I'll tak' it short, as they say at Ormerod's bank.

Nancy. Whatten way's that?

Hilkiah. Come here till I show thee.] (*Kisses her, and in the struggle her handkerchief comes off and shows her cut hair.*) Lord save us! Why, whatever hast thou been and gone and done? Had thy head shaved?

Nancy. I was forced to have it cut off. So many oud sweethearts wanted bits o't, now I'm going to swop the lot o' them for thee.

[*Washes up dishes with hot water from kettle.*

Hilkiah. I don't like it, I tell thee. Since we've been asked i' the church I've what the law calls a vested interest i' thee. Thou hast no right to give away so much as a single hair without my leave and license, let alone a whole head on't. That's law, lass. Dost hear?

Nancy. But possession's nine points of the law. My hair's mine while it's on ; and when it's off, it's his I choose to give it to

Hilkiah. Give it to?

Nancy (*putting back the kettle*). Aye, give it to. Thou'lt get quite as much as thy deserts if thou gets Nancy Hyde without her hair.

Hilkiah. [I don't like it, I tell thee.] I don't know that I'm bound to go on wi' banns after this. You contracted to deliver a certain article with its appurtenances ; one of t' appurtenances is gone. The corpus of the contract has been damaged before delivery.

Nancy. Who do you call Corpus?

[*Hilkiah.* But I say, Nancy—(*coaxingly*)—you're joking? You never let t' chap have it?

Nancy. Yes, I did. He wanted it so bad, I couldn't say him nay.

Hilkiah. I wish I had his head under my hands, that's all ; I'd take thy head o' hair out o' his, I would. But there's another Sunday's asking.] Suppose, when Parson Trafford inquires if anybody knows any just cause or impediment why Hilkiah Lawson and Nancy Hyde should not be joined together in holy matrimony, I was to get up and say ' I do ; Nancy Hyde has getten her head shaved?

Enter ARKWRIGHT, *briskly*.

Arkw. I beg pardon. (*Recognises* NANCY.) Ah, my pretty customer, I think this is the house you showed me; and now for the famous head o' hair I was to see.

Hilkiah. Oh! ho! So you're the chap that looks after lasses' heads o' hair. [*Going up to him.*

Arkw. And lads' too; only lasses' are longer, and bonnier, and easier working into wigs. Ecce signum! (*Points to* NANCY.) I couldn't offer much for yours, though I'll bid as high as any man i' the business.

Hilkiah. Business?

Arkw. Aye, sir. I'm not above it, I'm thankful to say. Dick Arkwright, of Bolton. 'Easy shaving; ladies' and gentlemen's hair cut and dressed; wigs dyed, dressed, and made to order after the newest London and Paris fashions.' That's a flam; but nothing else goes down. Can I do anything for you, sir? A touch o' comb and scissors could do no harm to your thatch. Excuse me, if I can't call it hair, wi' hers fresh in my box.

Hilkiah. Fresh i' thy box! I'll box thee.
[*Squaring out.*

Arkw. Excuse me—(*brandishes scissors*)—but these are my weapons. I keep my hands for more useful employment than bruising.

Hilkiah. But how do I know thou'rt a barber?

Arkw. The proof of the pudding—excuse me, but your beard is decidedly stubbly. If I might suggest a shave.

Hilkiah. I'll shave thee——

Arkw. Au contraire, as they say in Paris. Suppose I shave you? Here's towel, hot water, and everything at hand.

[*As* HILKIAH *approaches, angrily, A. pushes him into a chair, whips the jack-towel round his neck, knotting it behind, and so tying him to the chair with it by neck and shoulders; then nimbly out with shaving-box, dips his shaving-brush into the basin in which* NANCY *has poured hot water, after* MARGARET *had eaten her porridge, and lathers and shaves* HILKIAH, *while he talks; stopping every attempt of* HILKIAH's *to speak by thrusting the shaving-brush into his mouth.*

Nancy. That's right, man! he grudged thee my hair;

tak his beard to balance it, and prove thou'rt no sweetheart, nobbut a barber.

Arkw. Delighted to oblige any friend of yours in the way of my trade. Yes, 'barber' is the vulgar version of it, but you might add, wig-maker, inventor of hair-dyes, and hair-merchant to boot. The more know Dick Arkwright the better. No. 9, King Street, Bolton, one flight down the area stairs. 'The subterraneous barber,' as they call me, because, for want of a shop, I am content wi' a cellar. But what tho'? Business is business; small profits make quick returns. If any man shave for a penny, I'll under-shave for a halfpenny. There you are, sir, a cleaner and a cooler man, I'll be bound. Nobody ever felt the worse for a shave yet, especially when, as in this instance, the beard was three days old, the razor sharp, the soap sweet, the towel smooth, and no charge made. (*During this speech he has shaved, wiped, and untied* H. *Presents him with his hat, barber-fashion, with a bow.*) Your hat, sir. (*To* NANCY.) Allow me to offer you this bottle of the Queen of Sheba's essence; supposed to be compounded after a receipt given her by King Solomon, and of sovereign virtue for making short hair shoot again in all its native luxuriance.

Hilkiah (*looking in small hand-glass*). Ah, but he's a rare 'un to shave. Come, lad, I like thy impudence.

Arkw. The quality of our trade; like a ready tongue and a nimble pair o' fingers.

Hilkiah. But what right hast thou to this lass's head o' hair?

Arkw. The best of all rights—that of bargain and sale.

Hilkiah. Bargain and sale?

Nancy. Aye, thou gommock! He's bought and paid for't, and here's the brass—(*jingling her stocking*)—though I doubt it's going a bad road—to Hilkiah Lawson's pocket, when he takes Nancy Hyde 'for better for worse.'

(*On his trying to take the stocking out of her hand, she raps him over the fingers.*)

Nancy (*to* ARKWRIGHT). The lass I told thee of will be here by-and-bye. Now shoulder th' wheel, Hilkiah, and be off wi' 't to our place.

Hilkiah (*takes wheel*). Bilking t' bailiffs! I doubt it's felony i' the eyes of the law.

Nancy. Bother the law! It's kindness in the eyes of

honest folks. If thou couldst carry big table, best bed, and eight-day clock to boot, I'd like to mak' thee.

Hilkiah. And leave nought at all for bailiff? Nay, that would be hanging straight off, without benefit o' clergy.

[*Exit door* L. *flat.*

Arkw. Ho, ho! an execution in the wind. Bad off here, are they?

Nancy. Desperate bad. She's as hard-working a lass as ever turned a wheel; t'best spinner in Leigh or miles round. But the father takes it all; he hasn't done a stroke o' work these three years.

Arkw. A drunkard, eh?

Nancy. Worse! What he calls an inventor.

Arkw. And what may that be?

Nancy. Nought good, whatever 'tis—nobbut potterin' over queer-looking wheels and whirligigs in his garret yonder. [I've peeped in sometimes. You never saw such a sight o' wheels, and bands, and rollers, and crinkum-crankums, i' wood, and iron, and brass; as if all the clocks in the world had been smashed to bits and put together again, wrong way upwards;] and he says he's making summut that will spin, without wheels or hands either. [The oud gommock!]

Arkw. So, so! I must have a look at his crinkum-crankums before I go.

Nancy. And while he's spendin' time and brass over them, there's Maggie spinning her fingers to the bone to pay for 'em [and can't neither, and that's how they're come to t' bailiffs]. (MAGGIE *appears at garret door.*) Hush! here she comes. Not a word to her of what I told thee. She's as proud as proud.

Arkw. Never fear!

[MAGGIE *slowly descends, sunk in deep thought.*

Nancy (*to* ARKWRIGHT). Shall I get her to show you her hair?

Arkw. Leave that to me. And I say, lass—two's company and three's none.

Nancy. Thou'rt right, lad.   [*Exit.*

Arkw. (*looks at her*) Aye, a rare head o' hair, sure enough; and a grand figure, and a bonny face, if it were not for the cloud on't.

Margt. (*comes towards where wheel ought to be*). The old wheel gone! Our bread-winner! (*Cries.*) Nay, what a fool I am! I know it's in good hands. But old friends are sad to miss.

[*Hides her face in apron, sobbing.*

Arkw. (*comes forward, touches her gently*) Nay, cheer up, lass. April skies may be bonny, but May's sunshine is bonnier still.

Margt. Who are you? Not one of the bailiffs?

Arkw. No, thank'ee. Dick Arkwright, o' Bolton, at your service.

Margt. I never heard the name. What brings you here?

Arkw. Business; buying hair for the trade. I've seen some good heads o' hair in Leigh market this morning, but none like thine. Two pound ten's been my top price to-day, and it's not business-like to offer more without handling, but I don't mind saying three guineas down for thine—eye-bargain.

[*Margt.* Thank you, I've no mind to part wi' my hair.

Arkw. Few lasses have at first; it's most women's glory; but I never saw a face that could spare it better than thine.

Margt. Nay, I'm in no mind to listen to fooling.

Arkw. Nor I to talk it. I always stick to business, and I mean business now. But yours is a bonny face: and if it's so bonny i' the shade, what should it be i' the sunshine? Let's see. Try and smile a bit.

Margt. It's light hearts breed smiles, and mine's heavy.

Arkw. There's nought to lighten hearts like loading purses. Let me put three guineas into thine.]

Margt. I'd sell clothes sooner than hair, if it was come to that!

Arkw. Unluckily, I'm not in the old clothes' line, or I'd mak' you a bid, if it were only for good will. (*Pause.*) But I see your hair is not what it looks.

Margt. (*firing up*) Not what it looks?

Arkw. For quantity, I mean. You Leigh lasses ape your betters—wearing those new-fashioned pads that make hair go twice as far. Nay, I'm up to the trick; don't I make 'em?

Margt. (*angrily*) There's no more padding about my head than thine own!—I don't say aught in praise of my hair.

Arkw. Nay, you may leave that to the men.

Margt. But such as 'tis, 'tis my own, every bit on't.

Arkw. I don't believe it.

Margt. Thou doesn't? Thou shalt see. (*Takes off cap and kerchief, lets down hair.*) There!

Arkw. Thank you; but I should like to feel the weight of it.

Margt. Feel away, mon! and welcome.

Arkw. (*takes hair in his hand*). Eh, but it's bonny, bonny; as smooth as satin, and as soft as velvet.

Margt. Nought false there, mon, is there?

Arkw. I never thought there was.

Margt. Then why did'st say so?

Arkw. To mak' thee let it down.

Margt. 'Twas a mighty saucy trick o' thee.

Arkw. Only a trick of the trade. They don't count. I don't mind if I give thee another guinea.

Margt. (*aside*) Four guineas! It's three months' spinning. And what's losing my hair to clearing scores here before we go? None ever lost by the Hayeses till now.

[*Cries.*

Arkw. Nay, never cry.

Margt. I think it's missing the old wheel.

Arkw. It will come back; and if it shouldn't, thou would be well rid o't. Those little fingers were made for better work than drawing slivers into yarns for the weavers. (*Takes her hand.*) Nay, why should any fingers do such work, when wheels and rollers can do it better for them?

Margt. Wheels and rollers? Nay, now he's talking like poor father.

Arkw. Shows his good sense. The inventor the lass spoke of. (*Aside.*) Can he be on the same tack? So father talks about wheels and rollers, does he?

Margt. Aye, till I'm sick o' them; so please, no more o' that. If thou must ha' my hair, the sooner the better. (*Puts white cloth over shoulders and sits.*) I'm ready; where's thy scissors?

Arkw. Nay, there's no hurry; and I'd like to look a bit first. I've never seen just this shade [and I'm hair-dyer as well as hair-dresser. I'll be bound thy father makes machines, as well as talk about them?

Margt. That's his business, not mine or thine; cut, I tell thee.

Arkw. Nay, let me catch the colour first.

Margt. Thou canst do that when it's thine.

Arkw. Dead hair's not like living, and I never saw such a brown. It changes and changes; gold i' the sun—chestnut i' the shade. I've cut and carried hundreds o' crops], but somehow I feel it would be cruel to rob thee o' thine.

Margt. Nay, it's I who am going to rob thee—of four golden guineas. Cut away, man, and no more talk o't.

Arkw. (*is about to cut; then lays scissors aside*) It's a sin to part such a face and such hair—to strip that bonny head o' its crown o' glory.

Peter (*appears at garret door with wheels*). Marget, lass—canst find me a bit o' rope to tie these wheels together?

Margt. Hush, father! I'll look.

Peter. A stranger—a spy, perhaps! (*Sees her hair down—comes downstairs.*) Why, whatever art thou at, lass?

Margt. Having my hair cut, if this man would only begin.

Arkw. I can't—and won't.

Peter. Having thy hair cut? Is the lass crazy?

Arkw. Your servant, Mr. Hayes. It's my doing. I'm a dealer in hair—I tempted your daughter wi' a good price.

Margt. Four golden guineas!

Peter. Four guineas! (*Aside.*) That would just finish my six-roller model.

Arkw. I happen to know you want the money.

Peter. Thou seems to know a deal o' other folks' business, lad.

Arkw. Happen I do; for I know what you want it for. (PETER *stares.*) I'm not like Leigh folks, Mr. Hayes—I honour ingenuity and invention.

Peter. The devil thou does!

Arkw. If you will let me have a sight of your models, I don't mind if I advance the money as a loan, and let your lass keep her hair.

Peter. Let thee see my models?

Arkw. Mere curiosity. I'm no mechanic, you know—only a Bolton barber!

Peter. But thou'rt open to reason, more than these fools here are—happen thou't understand. But if the bailiffs were to come on us?

Margt. Nay, father. Hilkiah said they'd not seize thy models.

Peter. Not seize my models? Hilkiah said so! And thou believed him? The one thing i' the place worth seizing. Thou fool! Dost not see their drift?—To keep me easy, lest I shift the things? And this fair-spoken chap! who knows but he may be in league with them? A valuer from Warrington, perhaps.

Arkw. Now, Mr. Hayes, if you'll lead the way.

Peter. Stand back! I'll none o' thy offers! I'll show thee nought!

Arkw. Nay!

Peter. Stand back, or it may be the worse for thee! I'm prepared for such visitors—I keep a loaded gun in there!

[*Exit into garret.*

Margt. You mustn't mind an old man's moods. As for this offer—I doubt not you meant it kindly. But anyhow, if you lend this money, let it be to me and not to father.

Arkw. Nay; you settle that between you. I only want to help you over a pinch.

Margt. But it was to me you offered first—and 'tis I must have it. Promise me you'll not give a shilling to father.

Arkw. Why, he's the head of the house, you know, and if he insists——

Margt. No matter. Tell him you have given me the money already. [Don't think I care for your guineas or grudge my father, but if he gets it 'twill but go as all has gone before, in work that brings no return (in models that cost heavy for making, only to be pulled to pieces when they are made. It seems a sin to wish aught ill that God gives us, but I feel in my heart as if I could pray there was no such thing as a machine in the world—nought but bare hands and plain tools, such as our fathers used before us.) My wheel has brought us honest bread; what have all his inventions brought us—but the bailiffs?

Arkw. And what is thy wheel but a machine? Perhaps he that invented that had a daughter that hated wheels, and sighed for distaff and spindle. Nay, what is this pretty hand o' thine but the most wonderful of all machines? It will never do to raise that against inventors.

Margt. I have seen the misery invention brings to them that toil at it in vain, and all who trust to them. I have seen mind and heart and feeling bent all to one thought, till they are made blind to the suffering and slow decay of those

x

they loved once, and that loved them still. I've seen a generous man grow selfish, and a wise man wild and wilful. I've seen a bright hearth grow cold, and a happy home emptied of all but sorrow—and then you tell me not to curse invention!

Arkw. Hush, lass, hush! You may come to a different way o' thinking one day. I think I could teach thee—and I'd fain have thee to teach. It's not all inventors that are as fierce and feckless as thy father—nor as unlucky. There's them among them who can make a home, and keep a home too.]

Enter HILKIAH, *hurriedly.*

Hilk. Oud Crookmouth—I was just in time wi' t' wheel. Lord! if he'd caught me !

Enter Bailiff.

Bailiff. I'm sorry for this, Marget! Where's thy father? (MARGARET *points to garret.*) Here, Peter! Peter Hayes, you're wanted! Gang up, Hilkiah! Won't show, won't he? Door locked, eh? Put thy shoulder to t' jamb—we mun sarve. [HILKIAH *breaks open door.* PETER *appears.*

Peter. T' bailiff—too late !

Bailiff. I'm sorry for this, Peter, but Learoyd would wait no longer.

Peter. I looked for better things from Will; but what must be must. (*Comes down. Bailiff puts writ in his hand.*) Nay, I'm sarved—right enough. Here's the things; you see all you have to look to. (*Points round.*)

Bailiff. Nay, I must know what's in the upper room.

Peter. Nobbut a ruckle of old iron, and bits o' clockwork—no use to Will, or anybody but me.

Bailiff. We must book 'em.

Peter. Nay, you've the value of th' rent here. You've no right to seize beyond th' rent. (*Getting between him and stairs.*)

Bailiff. Nay. I tell thee I must.

Peter (*snatches up gun*). If thou values thy life, mun!

Bailiff. A rescue! Nay, Hilkiah, we must do our duty.

Margt. Father! father!

Arkw. (*coming forward*) You'll find the law too strong for you, Mr. Hayes.

Peter. Aye, it always is too strong for honest folk. Here,

Crookie, let Will take all that's here—table and chairs—meal ark, and eight-day clock—she's a real good 'un, with a new escapement o' my own—the beds from under us—Marget's wheel; only leave me my gimcracks yonder—an oud man's playthings! Thou knows oud men are bairns over again.

Bailiff. It's no use talking, Peter.

Peter. They're worth nought i' t' market but for oud iron —and, oh! they're worth so much to me! [*Exit into garret.*

Arkw. (*calling to Bailiff*) What's the amount of the writ?

Bailiff. There's t' figures. (*Giving paper.*) You mak' out the list here, Hilkiah. I'll go and look round wi' Peter up yonder. [*Exit.*

Margt. Aye, let all go—the cradle his dead bairns were rocked in—the bed they and mother died on—the wheel that's been bread to us—and all to save the bits o' brass and iron that have been his ruin!

Arkw, Look here, Marget. Excuse me calling you Marget; but sorrow makes speedy friends. I've offered once—I offer again—let me pay out t' bailiffs. I've the money handy, and you can owe it me.

Margt. Pay out the bailiffs? But who's to pay out you?

Arkw. What need to pay me out at all? I'll stay as man in possession, if you'll let me. Let me offer a home to you and your father—a home, and a husband to you.

Margt. A husband! why, man, I never set eyes on thee before to-day!

Arkw. Nought like love at first sight. Besides, I'll wait a month for thee before we're asked in church. Leave this house that's full of sorrowful memories, and come wi' me to Bowton.

Margt. You fairly take my breath away.

Arkw. Then you can't say no. Here you, Bailiff! what's his name?

Hilk. Oud Crookmouth when he's on t' job. His friends at the King's Yead calls him Bummie.

Arkw. Here, Bummie! (*Bailiff appears.*) Here's thy money. You may cancel the writ.

[PETER *and Bailiff come down, followed by* HAYES.
Hilk. Hurrah! [*Exit.*
Peter. The money—and they won't seize my mo— —, my playthings?

Arkw. Not a wheel. I've settled wi' your daughter here. You're to come wi' me to Bowton. You're to have a garret to yourself—playthings and all. (*Pays money.*)

Peter. Is't a dream? No, I hear t' money jingling. Does he want a finger i' my pie? He'll find that none's so easy. Bowton, eh! Dost hear, Marget? That's a big place—spins nigh on its half million pounds o' cotton wi' its own hands—hundreds o' looms—thousands o' money; sharp yeads at Bowton, happen they'll see farther than the fools do here. I wash my hands o' Leigh. Let's be off, lass; the sooner the better.

Margt. It's hard to leave the place you were born in, however it may have used you. I'm fair dazed. (*To* ARKWRIGHT). I suppose I may put up my hair now?

Enter NANCY *and* HILKIAH *in triumph with wheel.*

Nancy. Hilkiah's told me. Here's t' wheel back again!
Hilkiah (*singing*). 'See the conquering hero comes!'
Nancy. I'm so glad to see t' oud bread-winner again.
Arkw. Thou may'st say good-bye to it yonder.
Nancy. Yonder? (*To* MARGARET.) Why, wherever's thou goin', lass?
Margt. To Bowton, he tells me.
Nancy. And he's not bought thy hair?
Margt. Ay! It seems he's bought me, lass, hair and hand and all!
Arkw. And heart, too, Margaret?
Margt. Nay! I'll tell thee that when the month's out.

ACT-DROP.

ACT II.

SCENE.—*Preston.* Room *in* RICHARD AREWRIGHT'S *house, comfortably furnished. Panelled walls. Large door,* C. *Fireplace,* L. *Armchair beside it, in which* PETER *is seated, smoking. Street-door,* 1ST E. L. *Window* 1ST E. R. *and up* R. C.

Margt. (*looking in teapot by the chest of drawers*) Four guineas yesterday, and only three to-day! Dick would never have taken it without telling me. Can father have gotten to his weary machinery again and found out my hiding-place? I thought he was cured of that since we came hither. I must watch him—oh, dear!—oh, dear! I hoped that was all at an end. (*Shouts without.*) What's that, father, dear?

Peter. Some o' t' electioneerers—General Burgoyne's mob, I'll be bound. The less brains the more blether.

Margt. (*looking out of window*) Nay, they're not the General's colours. I pinned the rosette on Dick's coat before he went out to vote this morning. (*Shouts without.*) Hark!

Peter. Drunk!

Margt. Savage drunk—not happy.

Peter (*rising and looking out*). I see. It's the Jennyers from Blackburn.

Margt. The Jennyers!

Peter. The chaps that are going about smashing all the Hargreaves frames wi' more than sixteen spindles. Well for poor Hargreaves they don't smash him as well as his frames.

Margt. Poor Hargreaves! The people he's thrown out o' work have another name for him.

Peter. Nay, nought's bad enough for him. Hasn't he invented a machine to save men's muscles and double their gains?

Margt. Ah, what thou wert so set on once, father, before thou cam'st here to be happy with me and Dick. But that's all over now, isn't it? Thou canst take thy ease in the chimney-corner, and smoke thy pipe and chat to me, instead o' wasting thy life in thy garret among those weary wheels we brought from Leigh.

Peter. Aye, aye—I am wiser now. No more work o' that sort for Peter Hayes.

Margt. For all Dick gave thee yon room (*pointing to door*, R.) to store them in, just like the one he keeps for himself (*points to door*, C.) here——

Peter. And keeps locked—eh, Maggie? Some twelve months' wives wouldn't much fancy a husband having a lock-up place of his own.

Margt. Some wives have husbands that can't be trusted.

Peter. But that's not thy Dick?

Margt. No, father, that's not my Dick!

Peter. And thou'st been his wife all this while, and never peeped!——

Margt. Never, and don't mean to, till he gives me leave.

Peter. Nor asked what he locks up the room for?

Margt. Nay, what need to ask? Isn't it the passage to the old schoolhouse? Besides, hasn't he the secrets of his craft—the dyes he sells for the wig-makers? It's such a growing business. You know he hardly cuts, or shaves, or dresses hair at all now.

Peter. And I'll be bound it's hair-dyes that's taken him out o' late, hours and hours at a time?

Margt. A man must keep up his connexion. Hasn't he to meet and drink with his customers—from all the towns for miles and miles about?

Peter. Men-customers, think'st thou?

Margt. What should women-customers want with him?

Peter. Or he with them either. Nay, how should I know? Hair-dyeing, hair-buying—it seems but womanish kind of work altogether. But if only thou'rt satisfied, let him have half the lasses' heads i' Preston through his hands and welcome, for me.   [*Comes down.*

Margt. Nay, father. I'll hear no more such talk. I've my marketing to look after. Nothing like brisk wife's work to drive away silly wench's fancy! Make thyself easy about me and Dick; we'll none fight over a locked door while there's an open heart between us.   [*Exit door* L.

Peter. She's a chip o' the old block. It's hard to move her, but I'll manage it yet—open heart, locked door—quotha? The one's true enough, whatever the other is. (*Goes and tries lock of door,* c.) Locked, always locked! He takes good care I never get a peep; but I can see through more than a half-inch planking. Yes, I'd swear it —by the odds and ends of his talk, while he's tried to pick my brains—the way he's followed leads I've given him—a thousand things I can read if nobody else can—as sure as two and two makes four, Richard Arkwright's head's running on roller-spinning. He's in my grooves! [If he has kept me out of his shop, I'm well-nigh sure he's had one look too many into mine.] That room he gave me so kindly—to house my models—that key he put into my hands so handsomely! Like an old fool, I never thought to change the lock, till he had had time to steal my notions [and master my machine. I see now why he was so mighty ready to give my models house room]. But I'll be even with him yet, long-headed as he is. I've sown some seed already that grows apace. (*Chuckling.*) They don't like machine-inventors in Preston any more than they did i' Leigh, and the lads here are brisker than there, and think less o' smashin' man or model. (*During the speech he has lighted his pipe at fire.*) (*A knock.*) Come in, whoever you are.

Enter HILKIAH *and* NANCY.

Nancy. Eh! if it isn't Mr. Hayes!
Peter. Humph! Hilkiah Lawson and Nancy Hyde.
Nancy. Lawson, if you please, Mr. Hayes—this twelve-month gone. (*Sighs.*)
Peter. Another pair o' fools, eh?
Nancy. Not a pair, I hope. I don't complain, if Hilkiah's satisfied.
Hilkiah. For better, for worse—till death do us part.
Peter. But what brings you to Preston?
Nancy. Hilkiah's got a writing clerkship at Lawyer Ainsworth's, and now we are a bit settled, as he was coming here on business I thought I'd call and see Maggie. What a nice snug place she's got! (*Looks about.*)
Hilkiah. While Nancy talks over old times with you I can make my note for th' bill o' sale.
Peter. A bill o' sale here?
Hilkiah. [They're considered office secrets.] But I don't feel to like Mr. Arkwright so much—Nancy's hair an't scarce grown again yet—that you shouldn't know he's raising the wind on his furniture and effects.
Peter. Oh, he is, is he? Do you know what for, Hilkiah?—his wife's father has a right to ask.
Hilkiah. I don't know rightly, but master did let out something about his being on the fool's errand that turns so many heads hereabouts just now.
Peter. What's that?
Hilkiah. Machining—(*checking himself*)—I ask pardon.
Peter. Nay, never mind; happen I've grown wiser now. But if thou could'st find out for me what Arkwright's after, mayhap I could turn him from this wild-goose chase back to his [lawful] business.
Hilkiah (*aside*). A nice dog you'd be to lead a blind man! (*To* PETER.) I'll tell you aught I can learn and welcome. But Arkwright's mighty close, and so's Mr. Ainsworth. But I must get about my job. (*Makes a list of articles.*)
Nancy. Eh, but Maggie should be a happy woman, with all so well up and so comfortable about her—and here's the

old wheel, I declare! I thought she'd never part wi' that! I'll be bound her husband's one o' t' right sort.

Peter. Handsome is that handsome does.

Nancy. To take you in, as if you'd been his own flesh and blood!

Peter. Aye; there's few who would have cumbered their house-place with a queer, cranky, oud hunks like Peter Hayes. Is that what thou means?

Nancy. Nay, but a father-in-law's a father-in-law! And here you are wi' your pipe and your place in the chimney-corner, and a comfortable cushion to your back.

Peter. Aye, aye; Dick takes the best o' care o' me—a wonderful son-in-law is Dick Arkwright.

Nancy. Ah, they may well say, 'Neighbours' tongues for nagging.' Since we came to Preston we've heard things we didn't just like about Arkwright, haven't we, Hilkiah?

Peter. Things against son-in-law Dick? Whatten sort o' things, lad—whatten sort?

Hilkiah. That he was the sort o' chap to make his butter out o' other folks' churns.

Peter. Who doesn't, lad—who doesn't?

Hilkiah. And not likely to be over-particular, if aught fell in his way, who's earmark it carried.

Peter. Ah, they said that, did they? (*Aside.*) My seed's sprouted!

Nancy. Hout! folks will talk; but if only Maggie's happy——

Peter. She'll be here to answer for herself—(*aside*)—It's time for my gill o' ale. Nought like the tap for sowing prate-seed.

Hilkiah. I've a writ to serve a few doors down. If you'll allow me I'll go along with you, and so combine business with pleasure.

Peter. Which dost call pleasure, lad—my company or writ-sarvin'? [*Exit.*

Nancy (*examining furniture*). Right down honest oak, every bit on't, and not an inch on't but I could see to curl my hair in! She must be a happy woman.

Enter MARGARET.

Margt. Nancy!

Nancy. Maggie! (*Embracing.*)

Margt. I met Hilkiah. He's told me the news. And so we're to be neighbours.

Nancy. Aye, lass—who'd a-thought it?

Margt. An old friend was all I wanted! Why, to have thee here will be like bringing dear old Leigh to Preston. And how bonny thou art looking. Sit, lass, sit.

Nancy. I vow thy cheeks are rounder and thine eye brighter than the last time I saw thee.

Margt. To think we were both wenches then?

Nancy. Aye, lass. Lord! what a twelvemonth can do!

Margt. It can make a great deal of happiness.

Nancy. Aye, can it! if only a woman gets the right side of her husband.

Margt. Which side is that?

Nancy. The blind side, to be sure.

Margt. The blind side? Nay, I should always like to live full and fair in my husband's sight, and he in mine.

Nancy. Ah, but how would he like it, lass? Depend on't, we must all have our secrets, married or single. There's little thoughts and little corners a woman likes to keep to herself, or a man either.

Margt. Yes, I know. (*Sighs and puts off her things.*)

Nancy. And now thou must show me all over thy place. I've seen this room. (*Up to* c. *door*). What's in here?

Margt. That's locked.—it's Dick's room.

Nancy. Locked—oh, ho! What? Dick has his little corners, has he?

Margt. Yes.

Nancy. But thou keeps the key o't?

Margt. No.

Nancy. I never allowed Hilkiah a key, but I've another.

Margt. Dick never offered me one.

Nancy. Anyhow, thou'st been inside the door?

Margt. Never. (*Proudly.*) Dost think I'd ask?

Nancy. The more reason he should offer. Maggie, lass, I don't so much like this. And now I look at thee, I fear me there's more between thee and thy husband than this locked door.

Margt. (*bursting out*) There is, Nancy, there is! Oh, I'm so glad I've thee to tell all to at last! I've let on to no one—not even to father. I've held my heart in so hard! I thought it would burst sometimes! He's good, lass—he's loving—none better—none kinder: but he doesn't trust me as a wife should be trusted. He's never told me why that door is always locked; why, day after day, and almost every day of late, he leaves me for times and times, and when he's at home he'll often sit silent the hour together. I can see his thought is far away, but he never asks *me* to share it; and when I ask him, he puts me off with a kiss and a kind word, as if a hungry heart could be staid wi' *them*. And, worst of all—come closer, lass—only last week I had a terrible dream that he was taken from me. I sobbed myself awake, and his place i' the bed beside me was empty and cold. I got up, all i' the dark; I listened, I held my breath, I don't know how long, till at last I heard the key turn in the house-door lock. It was my husband come back as secretly as he had gone.

Nancy. And thou wert not out at him like a blast o' lightning?

Margt. I pretended to sleep, and swallowed down my sorrow.

Nancy. Thou shouldst have had it out with him there and then! Nought like catching a man i' the act. Hast thou told thy father?

Margt. He guesses something. He has said as much. I wish he hadn't—he has put thoughts into my head—of other women.

Nancy. Then tak' my word for 't: have it out with thy husband before thou'rt a day older. A jealous thought's like leaven—(*comes up to her*)—a thumb-nail breadth o't is enough to sour two lives. Tak' my advice, lass.

Margt. I'll try; but it seems so hard to own one's distrust; I wish it were harder to feel it!

Nancy. Where is thy husband now?

Margt. How should I know? (*Crosses to* R.) Away to vote, he said, but I know that's not all. Oh, its rarely he tells me the secret of his comin's and goin's.

Nancy (C.). Then when he comes home, lass, do thou tackle him—tackle him wi' thy woman's tongue; and if he stands that, try thy woman's tears. (*Kisses her.*) I never knew the man's heart yet that didn't wash soft. And now I must be looking after our Hilkiah. This Preston seems a desperate dangerous place for young married chaps. [*Exit.*

Margt. I will follow her counsel. I'll no longer bear this wall between me and my husband. But if I force his secret, only to come on knowledge that's worse to bear! That money I've missed of late; I don't think father can have taken it; and what should Dick want it for that his wife should not know? Ah, my husband!

Enter ARKWRIGHT, *wearing rosette (buff and blue).*

Arkw. Well, Maggie, lass. [*Kisses her; puts off rosette.*

Margt. I'm right glad to see thee back, Dick. Hast voted?

Arkw. Aye; and had a shake from the General's own hand, and a compliment to boot. To be sure, they come cheap enough at election-time.

Margt. Cheap as they are, I should like to hear it.
[*Sits on stool beside him.*

Arkw. Says the General, 'They tell me, Master Arkwright——'

Margt. He knew thy name?

Arkw. Happen one o' the committee whispered it. 'They tell me you've a rare secret for dyeing hair. I'm glad to see you don't turn it to dyeing ribbons,' and he pointed to my rosette. 'No,' says I; 'as long as 'tis the Burgoyne buff and blue, I'll never say die.' So with that they all laughed.

Margt. It was smartly said, and like my Dick. (*Reproachfully.*) But you let them keep you to drink!

Arkw. Only one glass to the General's luck, and then I came away.

Margt. Thou'st been a long time coming from the Granby.

Arkw. I came round about, not to cross the Blackburn mob. They've wrecked a good thousand pounds' worth at John Holt's mill, and now they are bound for the Burnleys—after the new frames they set up there last week. The fools—fighting their own best friends!

Margt. Dost thou mean the Burnleys?

Arkw. No; the machines, lass. When will our lads be sharp enough to see a man's place is on the box, not in the shafts; that it's easier to drive the coach than to draw it?

Margt. Thou hast learned that o' father.

Arkw. Thy father's head's longer than most.
[*Seeks in his pockets for light to his pipe; finds letter; reads it.* MARGARET *watches him, then draws near. Pause.*

Margt. What's that thou art studying so hard?

Arkw. I was seeking for a light to my pipe, when I fell on this?

Margt. A letter?

Arkw. Nobbut an order for a dozen bottles of assorted dyes, from an Ormskirk firm.

Margt. Let me see it.

Arkw. He writes a terrible bad fist; thou'dst never be able to mak' it out. [*Puts it in his pocket.*

Margt. I wish thou would'st let me be more help to thee in thy business.

Arkw. Help to me? Why, how could'st thou better help me than thou dost in thine own wife's place—the home place? Stick to that, Maggie; it's wide enough and to spare for most women.

Margt. Aye, that's always you men's cry. It's with your wives as with your horses—you swear we go best in bearing-reins and blinkers. If you would only give us a little more of our heads sometimes, and let us see a little more daylight——

Arkw. Take my word for it, Maggie, it's best as it is. Leave men the harvest work, and the mill; let the women knead the flour and bake the bread quietly at home.

Margt. Hadn't you better marry one o' the machines you and father talk of—made up of arms to labour for you, and wheels to be wound up at your will, but with no tongue to complain or heart to fret?

Arkw. Why, my lass, what's this?

[*Puts pipe down and rises.*

Margt. Nay, is it not rather for me to ask, 'What's this?' These absences I know no cause for; this work I have no part in; these letters I must not read; yon door I must not open; that money I must not seek account of?

Arkw. Maggie!

[*Margt.* Nay, I can count the guineas go, though I know not on what they are spent; I miss my husband, though I must not seek to stay him; I can see his thoughts are far away, though I must not try to follow them; I can feel there's something or somebody he cares for more than his wife, though I must shut the feeling in my heart till it will be shut there no longer; till it will speak out, as I, thy twelve months' wife, am speaking now!

Arkw. Thou hast thy father's mettle in thee; but the Arkwrights have wills o' their own too. It ill becomes wife to question husband in that style.]

Margt. Between true wife and husband there should be no need of question—only fulness of faith and love that casts out fear.

Arkw. I had thought to choose my own time for speaking. But suppose I took thee at thy word—made a clean breast to thee here, and now?

Margt. Thou canst? Thou will'st?

Arkw. I can, and I will,—though how thou'lt take it! Aye, Maggie, it's too true. There *is* another I care for.

Margt. No, no!

Arkw. That I cared for afore I knew thee; that I never ceased to care for all the while I have known thee; one that's fought wi' thee for the mastery o' my sleeping and waking thoughts.

Margt. And my own husband dares own this to me!

Arkw. It's a clean breast I'm making.

Margt. Who is she?

Arkw. Her name must 'bide a secret a while longer.

Margt. Where is she?

Arkw. Here!

Margt. Here, in Preston?

Arkw. Here, in this house!

Margt. Dick! Richard Arkwright! Husband!

Arkw. Here—I'll show her to thee.

Margt. He dares not!

[*He opens door, brings out machine. While doing so* PETER *enters and seeing what* ARKWRIGHT *is about conceals himself, while he watches intently.*

Arkw. There she stands, Maggie; thy rival!

[*Removing cover from machine.*

Margt. A spinning jenny!

Arkw. [Nay, poor Hargreaves has been beforehand wi' thee i' that christening. She has no name yet; my Maggie shall find her one.

Margt. A model, for all the world like one o' poor father's!

Arkw. But with a difference or two. A machine to do by the help of a few spindles and rollers what no wheels and no hands ever did or could do—spin cotton into yarn, long and fine, and strong enough for weft as well as warp.

Margt. But that was just what father used to speak of doing, and spent so much o' his time and money trying to do.

Arkw. Not thy father only, but scores o' keen heads in these Northern parts. Thy father was nearer than most.

Margt. Thou hast seen his models? I thought he never would show them thee?

Arkw. I never asked his leave to look (PETER *can scarce restrain himself*), poor old chap! He had the right notion o' the distance between the rollers, but he never could get them to work with equal pressure. See, here's th' weight that keeps the rollers together; and see the rollers themselves, the smooth leather sheathing above, and the fluted face below, to turn the loose sliver into an even yarn.] There, Maggie! there's the only rival thou hast had or art ever like to have; and she'll do for thee what never rival did—make thy husband about the biggest man, and thee the grandest lady, in all Lancashire, afore we die.

Margt. Father's dream over again! If I could only believe him!

Arkw. And that's not all [nor the best thou'lt do, my brave spinner. It would be poor work, if for one thou mak'st rich thou bring'st not bread and blessing to a thousand. Aye, Maggie,] not more surely were all the world's great oaks hid in the first little acorn, than mighty industries, such as Lancashire does not dream of, lie hid in this poor working model!

Margt. Father's dream; nay, all but father's words! If it should be but to end as his dream ended! [Husband, forgive me if my heart cannot be glad with thine.

Arkw. Not glad, Maggie? Not glad that thy husband's thought has prospered and come to this good end? Not glad to find a rival in wood and iron, instead of flesh and blood?

Margt. Nay; methinks I'd sooner have found a woman within yon door, than this cruel thing that minds me of the misery in my childhood; the suffering and sorrow of the life that thou cam'st to take us from; the blighting of a father's hopes; the ruin of a happy home.]

Arwk. But this is no dream; no half-grasped notion; no half-completed thought. [This is a solid thing, fixed in hard wood and hammered metal; a thing that goes, and works, and spins. It was because I knew thy past, thy father's blighted hopes and baffled seekings, that] I kept the secret so long, till the work was done, by stealth, all in the old school-house yonder. There have been times, whiles, when I was hard put to 't to find either spirit or money to carry on. Why, I've pawned my clothes, my watch, without telling thee. I've raised money on our furniture; nay, I've even gone to thy little store in the teapot yonder, without thy leave, and more than once, in the desperate stress of my need. But I've brought her through, and there she stands, thy only rival, ready to pay thee back all she cost thee of doubt and fear, by winning thy husband fame and fortune—that he may share them with thee! And yet thou dost not look glad!

Margt. How can I look what I do not feel? Oh, Dick, for mercy's sake do not set thy life on this terrible task! Turn from this doubtful, dreadful game of invention to hard, honest, humble work.

[*Arkw.* As well ask a man who has seen the sun to put up with a rushlight for the rest of his days.

Margt. There it is! Even so it was with father. I've seen him just as confident; just as angry with me not rejoicing with him. I've known his hopes raised just as high, and have felt the ruin when they fell. Man's heart and brain cannot stand the shock—not even thine, strong and springy as they are. This is but a model, and has yet to grow to a machine—to a multitude of machines—ere it does all thou hop'st from it; and where art thou to find the money to set them going? And if thou dost, what's to come of all the wheels and looms and spinners whose work thy machines will tak' away? Must they sit idle and clem?

Arkw. Why, thou dear little blind buzzard, this will make work for thousands, where there's work for tens now!

Margt. But while the work is making?]

Arkw. I'll hear no more croaking. (*Puts machine in room.*) Look, I can trust thee henceforth? No more locked doors; or if we must lock them against silly spies and prating meddlers, the key shall be in thy keeping. (*Gives her key.*) There, I make *thee* her gaoler—with that key and this kiss. [*Kisses her.*

Enter HILKIAH.

Hilkiah. Ah, here he is at last. Eh, Mrs. Arkwright, it's lucky I've found thy husband. Here's a mighty pressing note from our Mr. Ainsworth. (*Gives note to* ARKWRIGHT, *who reads.*) Hark ye, Maggie, what flea hast thou been setting in our Nancy's ear?

Margt. Nay, none that I know of.

Hilkiah. She was down on me like a fire-flaught, tucked me under her arm, and walked me down to the office, as if I'd been a cut-purse in charge of a constable!

Arkw. Now, lad, I'll come with thee at once. My laced hat, Maggie, and rosette. It's to meet some Nottingham gentlemen at the Granby. I may have good news for thee anon. Good day [little woman], and good hope.

[*Exit* ARKWRIGHT *and* HILKIAH. PETER HAYES *comes forward, pale, hands clenched, trembling in every limb.*

Margt. Father! you here?

Peter. Aye, I'm here!

Margt. What's the matter?

Peter. The matter! I've been here, all the while thy husband was showing thee that—that thing—in there. That's the matter! Give me that key!

Margt. Nay, father, Dick trusted it to me; I can only give it with his leave——

Peter. His leave? Did he wait for *mine* to use *my* key? The sly, smooth, behind-backs rogue!

Margt. Whom dost thou mean, father?

Peter. This Richard Arkwright! this villain! this thief!

Margt. I must not hear such words used of my husband.

Peter. Not strong enough, aren't they? Find me stronger and I'll use them! The key, lass, that I may find out all he has robbed me of!

Margt. Father, are you mad?

Peter. Not now; I *was*, when I let him pay out the bailiffs; when I laid him on the scent o' my invention; when I brought my models hither, that he might pick and plunder at his will.

Margt. I will not hear my husband ill said; least of all by thee, father, to whom he has been so kind.

Peter. Kind! the black-hearted robber! The key! I tell thee, the key!

Margt. I will not.

Peter. Tak' care! (*Threateningly.*)

Margt. I'm your own bairn, I've your own blood in my veins. You may tear the key from my dead hand, but while I've life to keep it, keep it I will!

Peter. Nay, then, I will bring those to thee that shall need no key. The Blackburn Jennyers are in the town! Think of what they did for Kay and Hargreaves! They have sworn the next time they turn out they will not stop with *machines!* Have a care for thy precious Dick, lass; if they fall in with him, see if thy love can save him then.

[*Exit* PETER HAYES.

Margt. Bring the Blackburn mob upon us! What had I best do? Oh, Lord guide me! This is terrible. I wished ill to his invention, but that it should come so sudden! Shall I warn Dick to shift his model? But where to find him? Is there time? Will father be as bad as his threat, angry as he is? Will they be my husband's best friends that stand between his model and the mob? I should feel proud of his work, but how can I, who have so often seen the blank end of hopes as fair? It is a will-o'-the-wisp he is following, that must end him in slough and sorrow. What if those desperate men come but to make him a short, sharp deliverance from what I know will be *his* ruin, as it was father's? (*A knock.*) Who's there?

Hilk. (*without*) Me, Mrs. Arkwright, Hilkiah Lawson.

Margt. (*opens*) Hilkiah!

Hilk. (*enters*) Where's thy master?

Margt. I've not seen him since he left with thee.

Hilk. Let's hope he's 'scaped them.

Margt. 'Scaped? Whom?

Hilk. The Jennyers! If they catch him, Lord ha' mercy on his limbs! And if they come here, Lord ha' mercy on the furniture!

Margt. But thou'lt stand by me?

Hilk. Aren't we both from Leigh, and isn't thou a woman? But I can't carry all this solid oak on my back, as I could thy wheel.

Margt. Never mind the furniture.

Hilk. I'm bound to; we've got a bill o' sale on't at our office.   [*Distant roar of mob.*

Margt. Hark!

Hilk. Those Blackburn devils! Better try and find your husband, and warn him.

Margt. I might set the mob on his track.

Hilk. Better they should have it out with him in the street, where there'll be nought there to smash except himself.   [*Cries of mob, nearer.*

Mob. No machines! Down with the jennies! Break and burn!

Margt. (*at window*) They passed the house before to-day; perhaps they'll pass again. Father never can have told them.   [*Yells repeated outside.*

Jack o' Dicks (*outside,* c.). Open t' door.

Bob o' Chowbent. Or we'll open it for ye.

Y

Hilk. Hast ere a weapon handy?

Margt. Father's old gun. [*The yells are repeated.*

Hilk. 'Twould be more danger to us than them.

Dick. Now, you inside there!

Margt. Here's none but a helpless, harmless woman.

Hilk. That's right, sink *me*, for I daren't shoot.

Bob. We'll none harm a woman; open t' door.

Nancy (outside). Do nou't o' t' sort, Maggie.

Hilk. There's our Nance among them, contradictin' as usual.

Bob Haud thou thy blether, or I'll mak' thee!

Hilk. You'd best try!

Dick. Open t' door, lass!

Peter. Open, Margaret, to thy father.

Margt. I will not. This is my master's house; I'll hold it against all.

Nancy. That's right; give it 'em hot, lass!

Margt. Ruffians and robbers as you are!

Nancy. Robbers is too good for them!

Dick. Throttle t' wench, and forward wi' sledges! Now wi' a will, lads!—once, twice, thrice! (*Sledges are used against the door.*) Now tak' breath!

Hilk. I can't do any good. It'll only vex 'em to talk law. I'd better get in somewhere (*tries cupboard*), or under summat. (*Gets under table.*) But if they offer thee any harm I'll be out on them! [*Withdraws.*

Dick. Now lads, another rouser! once, twice, thrice!

[*Door is burst open. Enter* BOB *and* DICK, *heading a mob of desperadoes armed with clubs, sledges, and pieces of machinery; followed by* PETER HAYES *and* NANCY, *held by two men.*

Margt. Are you men? Are you Englishmen? (*Confronts them.*) Here I stand—one woman to a mob of cowards. What do you want here?

Dick. This new jenny o' thy man's mak'—another gimcrack thrust between honest folks and their bread.

Peter. It's in that room (*points*); she's got the key.

Nancy. For shame o' thyself, Peter Hayes.

Dick. Come, missus, hand over.

Bob. Thou will not? Nay, then, out wi' master key!

[BOB *and another go up, smash* C. *door open, and fetch out machine.* BOB *raises hammer, about to smash it.*

Margt. (*rushes forward*) Stop! There stands my husband's work; you are here to destroy it.

Dick. Aye, are we, as we have smashed such devil's gins all t' country round. We'll none of such whirligigs, to do man's work and throw out man's labour.

Margt. And what am I but a labourer like yourselves —one o' the hand-spinners those cranks and rollers will undo? There stands my wheel. (*Points to it.*) No lass in Leigh or Preston has worked harder or earned more at hand-spinning than I have. No lass in Leigh or Preston either better knows the curse invention brings to the inventor and his home. Have I not prayed my master but now, as I have prayed my father for years, to turn from these things—to leave Lancashire to the warp and weft that was good enough for our fathers, and to the old wheel and shuttle on which our hands were most at home?

Mob (*murmurs*). She's reet.

Bob. Curse me, but thou talkest like a book.

Dick. Or like a man; that's more to the purpose.

Margt. But none the more will I see this wondrous work of my master's brain and hand—the thing he has made and loved—that's been to him as a bairn—that may well be more to him than a wife—smashed by those that wish as little good to him as to his work. I will not see the home-placed wrecked, where he has wrought at his trade, where we have been so happy, where he had made a home for this old man (*points*) who hounded you on. Shame on him, though he were ten times my father!

Mob (*groans and murmurs*).

Bob. Enough said; now for smashin'! (*Raises his hammer to smash the machine.*)

Margt. Hold! Better, if his work must be destroyed, it should be by my hands! Give me the hammer! (*Wrests hammer from* Bob.) Oh, husband! this will be a heavy blow for thee! but it was the one that loved thee best that struck it! (*Smashes machine.*)

Nancy. Hold thy hand, lass! he'll never forgive thee!

[*Mob shout exultingly.*

Margt. (*throwing down hammer*) Oh, what have I done? What have I done?

Dick. Our work, lass. Let's spare the place for her sake.

Bob. Thou'st saved thy man's gear, and done a good deed for Lancashire. But let Dick Arkwright set up one of his devil's frames again, and we'll limb him as well as his work!

Dick. Now, lads! down to Bremley Clough! Armstrong's gettin' six new twenty-spindle frames that want our sledges to set 'em goin'.

[*Mob exit shouting and yelling.* HILKIAH *emerges from under table.*

Nancy (*seeing him*). Hilkiah, thou wast here all the time, and never wagged hand or tongue?

Hilk. I thought that wasn't wanted, wi' thee here.

Nancy. This 'll be a sorry sight for Richard Arkwright.

Hilk. Lucky it warn't included in bill o' sale.

Nancy. Maggie, lass, I fear me thou hast done a bad day's work!

Margt. Oh, Nance, Nance! 'Twas in my heat of blood! Father, it was thou that brought them hither. How ever shall I face my husband? Is this the end of all his labours—all his hopes?

Peter. His labours! his hopes! And what o' mine, lass—what o' mine?

Arkw. (*outside*) It's all right—it's all right! (*Enters.*) Maggie, thank God thou'rt safe! Nought wrecked here! I'm all of a tremble. I saw the Blackburn lads turn out o' the street as I came in. I feared they had got sight o' my bonny bairn in yonder, and just as I had settled to set her to work for the Nottingham gentleman. Lord forgive me! I hardly know if I thought of thee or her first, Maggie. (NANCY, HILKIAH, *and* MARGARET *have been standing in front of the wreck. On moving* NANCY *aside discovers the destruction.*) Almighty God! dost thou see this? My life's work a wreck! (*Falls prostrate beside it.*) Villains! oh, curse——

Peter. Nay, best know whom thou'rt cursing, that thou may'st curse home. This was none of the Blackburn boys' doing.

Arkw. Whose, then?

Peter. Mine and hers. Thou hast robbed me, and I have but done with my own after my own fashion. But with her help though, if that mak's it any better to bear.

Arkw. My wife's?

Peter. Even so.

Arkw. Maggie! Speak, lass! But it's not true. The old man's crazed with fright or dazed with drink. Speak, lass, and give him the lie, father as he is. Dost thou hear? he says it is thou who hast done this!

Margt. He says true.

Arkw. True? Margaret Arkwright, dost thou know what thou'rt saying?

Margt. He says true. It was my hand that wrecked thy work. But, oh, husband! 'twas in love I did it, to take the deed out of less loving hands. I think I thought—if I thought at all—but it all comes back to me like a dream—the shock of this might stay thee, might turn thy mind from thy invention back to quiet life and common life's work; but, oh, husband! there was love in it all—there was love in it all!

Arkw. Woman!—for I can call thee wife no longer—

Margt. No, no! Richard! Husband! Master! do not look at me with those cold, cruel eyes!

Arkw. Henceforth our ways in life must lie apart! (*Throws her off.*) Old man! this is no home henceforth for thee or her!

TABLEAU.

CURTAIN.

ACT III.

SCENE.—*Birkacre Clough. A picturesque ravine. New mill,* R. *Cottage in the distance. Practical bridge,* R. C. *Charity school children, country lasses, workmen, and village lads with flags discovered. Ale-cask,* R. *Bank set at foot of bridge; another ditto,* R. 1 E. NANCY *marshalling the children, &c.* HILKIAH *studying programme of proceedings; all cheering; lively music as curtain rises.*

HILKIAH. There—there, lads! It's all very gratifying, but there's a saying in law, never leap until you come to the stile; keep your breath and your beer for the right moment, or when it comes you may find you've nought left i' craw or cask. Now, Nancy—I mean Mrs. Lawson—hast thou got those loppets o' school bairns to know right hand from left?

Nancy. Bless the man! I've stuck every one a cake i' one fist and a flower i' t' other, and they can all read cake-hand and flower-hand.

Hilkiah. That's practical. Now, Joe Higgins, you tak' t' flagmen and band down to th' last turn o' Bolton Road, and don't let 'em show till you see Sir Richard's carriage.

Nancy. And mind, Joe, you don't start too soon wi' your blastin' and blarin', for Sir Richard 'll be drivin' his own four the last stage, and they be spirited cattle.

Hilkiah. Jim o' Lankey's, thou see the ale-cask trundled down to the triumphal arch; it's there I want most enthusiasm, and naturally you'll want most beer. Come, Nancy, get school bairns started. (*Ale-cask taken off.*)

Nancy. Now, honies! 'Tention!—o' cake-hand—march. (*Exeunt children.*) Now, you lasses wi' posies—now, you lads wi' flags. (*School girls, country lasses, men, &c. march off in rough order*). They're off at last! (*She fans herself.*) I'm all in a muck o' sweat!

Hilkiah. In an advanced state of perspiration, you mean, my dear; sweat's all very well for mill hands, but nothing short of perspiration for the lady of Hilkiah Lawson, Esquire, attorney-at-law, Under-Sheriff for the Southern Division of the county of Lancashire. [*Takes snuff.*

Nancy. Wi' Sir Richard Arkwright, Knight, High Sheriff o' the county! And eighteen years ago thou wert sweepin' out lawyer Ainsworth's office, and he was scrapin' chins for a penny the shave! It's enough to mak' a body sweat.

[*Fanning herself.*

Hilkiah. That's your weak point, my dear—I mean one of your weak points—if you have one; you don't meet the chances and changes of this mortal life coolly enough. Depend on't, my rule is the right one. Take all good luck as if you expected it, or folks will never think you've earned it. And if ever there was a man that's earned every stroke of luck that's come to him, from the first day he scraped a chin till this day that he comes back from London, it is Sir Richard Arkwright, knighted by the King's own hand, pricked for High Sheriff, partner in a dozen mills in the three counties, and the first master spinner in Lancashire—which is about all one as to say i' the world, I reckon.

Nancy. Ah! If it wasn't for the thought of poor Maggie! He was too hard to her, Hilkiah. Don't you tell me—if he was here now I'd say so to his face, for all he's gone up like a lad's kite, and we after him like t' tail.

Hilkiah. It's a comfort to know that tails are useful to kites. In fact, they can't fly without them. [But here come Justices.]

Enter SIR RICHARD CLAYTON, MR. OMEROD, HAWORTH, CHADWICK, *saluting* MR. *and* MRS. LAWSON. (U. E. L.)

Sir Rich. Mrs. Lawson, your most humble servant; as blooming as ever. [*Crosses to* R.

Nancy. Get out wi' your nonsense, Sir Richard.

Sir Rich. Well, Mr. Lawson, this is a great day for Birkacre. (*The others cross to* NANCY *and converse with her.*) Quite a concatenation of excitements. The starting of the new weaving-shed (*pointing to mill*), with all Arkwright's latest improvements, and the welcome home of the new Knight.

Chad. For my part, I don't much fancy another Sir Richard on our Bench.

Sir Rich. Nay, I protest, Arkwright has quite as good, if not quite as old, a title to the handle as I have.

Chad. More's the pity.

Sir Rich. We must all have a start. Methinks the Claytons were no more than the Chadwicks once; and if the King likes to knight a cotton-spinner, why, the King can do no wrong, you know. That's good Tory doctrine.

Hilkiah. And Mr. Chadwick has the comfort of feeling he has tried his best to prevent it.

Chad. I don't quite understand you, Mr. Lawson?

Hilkiah. By trying, with Mr. Haworth here and the rest of the Master Cotton-Spinners' Association, to break down his patents, and eat up his profits in law!

Chad. And didn't Mr. Justice Bullar declare he'd not a leg to stand on?

Hilkiah. He's gone on uncommon well without one.

Chad. And as to his right to profits—wasn't it clearly proved that his inventions, as he called them, were all pickings out of other people's brains—poor old Hayes's, for instance?

Nancy (*aside*). Ah, poor Maggie!

Chad. If all had their rights——

Hilkiah (*interrupting*). There'd be many big folks who'd look uncommon small before Richard Arkwright.

Chad. Humph! birds of a feather! Others have risen besides the Bolton barber.

Nancy. Meaning our Hilkiah? Aye, Mr. Chadwick, while there's such a deal o' fools to fling away their brass at law, it's well there's a wise man here and there to pick 't up.

Hilkiah (aside). One for his nob from our Nance !
[*Distant shouts.*

Sir Rich. Where's the address, Lawson? (HILKIAH *looks for it.*) Gentlemen, we shall do ourselves most credit by receiving our High Sheriff handsomely. May I have the the honour, Mrs. Lawson——
[*Offering his arm to* NANCY.

Nancy. Nay the honour's o' my side, Sir Richard. But I'll bide beside Hilkiah. If he wanted a word, there's nobody could gie 't him as well as me.

Sir Rich. (*bowing*) A model wife! (*To* CHADWICK.) Come, Chadwick; best forget all about Justice Bullar's judgment and the Bolton shaving-shop.

[*Exeunt over bridge* CLAYTON, CHADWICK, OMEROD, *and* HAWORTH.

Hilkiah (*takes out MS. of his address and studies it*). I shall have five minutes to spare for a squint.
[*Cheering renewed.*

Nancy. They're they go! He's at turn o' t' road now. (*Reflectingly.*) Eh, if poor Maggie had but been here to see this day, Hilkiah! I wonder how she's living?

Hilkiah. With her old father, na doubt. It's under cover to him I've always paid her over the very handsome allowance Sir Richard makes her.

Nancy. Handsome! and I'll be bound best part o' t' goes to that mad swallow-hole o' a father. What dost think last news I heard o' him?—that he'd gotten started a sort of a show—o' sun, moon, and stars.

Hilkiah. An orrery, I daresay——

Nancy. Happen 'twas some such rubbish! and that he was trampin' country side wi' 't, and draggin' poor Maggie after him, I'll be bound. She'd never leave him, I know; she was hard whiles, but as true as steel—she'd *that* o' the Hayeses. (*Cheering repeated* R.) Hark! Come, Hilkiah, they've gotten to triumphal arch. [*Loud cheering,* R. H.

Hilk. Yes, that's the beer! I must take my place wi' the gentlemen o' the Bench, to read their address—my own composition.

Nancy. Nobbut tak' care o' thy stops; and mind, thy wife's listenin' to thee! [*Exeunt* R. I E.

MUSIC.

Enter over bridge PETER HAYES *and* MARGARET, *followed by a boy with box over his shoulder. They look weary and travel-stained.*

Peter. Now, lass! we've had a het trudge from Chorley. Rest thee a bit here under t' birken shaw i' the cool o' the beck; and thou, lad, carry t' orrery into village (MARGARET *sits on stone at foot of bridge, dreamily*), to King's Arms, and hire us two rooms for th' neet, and put one o' my show-bills up i' th' tap, and say, Peter Hayes is comin' after, wi' his wonderful machinery o' the heavenly bodies that goes by clockwork. [*Exit boy over bridge.*

Margt. What's the name of the place, feyther?

Peter. Birkacre.

Margt. It's a winsome spot, with the bright beck wimplin' down the clough, and the pretty slender birch-trees swingin' their fair green branches over the dark pools, like bonny lasses, that love to see in the looking-glass how they look wi' their loosened hair.] Dost know this place, father?

Peter. What foot o' Lancashire, Derbyshire, and Nottinghamshire but the sole o' Peter Hayes' clogs has ta'en a measure o't?

Margt. Ah, you were tramping them all those weary years I staid at home i' Leigh. It was sadder there, sitting by myself, with my hands in my lap, always thinking and thinking, and waiting for what never came [than out here wi' thee, under the open sky, footing the wild roads that wind on and on across moor and marsh, through clough and over edge, as if they'd never come to an end. It was end—end—nothing but end yonder i' Leigh.] But still I've thee to look after. A woman must have something she loves to spend her care upon.

Peter. Aye, thou's been a good daughter to me—better than afore yon——

[MARGARET *rises from stone, goes to* PETER, *and lays her hand on his shoulder.*

Margt. Don't, father! It's sore looking back for both of us!

[*Peter.* Sore, is it? I like nought so well. The Hayeses have long memories. There's debts I like to keep fresh i' mind, and scores I mun' go on reckonin', over and over, till the time comes to wipe 'em out.

Margt. I know—I know. [I've heard so much of that kind of talk, and I'm so weary of it.] But thou'st not told me the name o' this place?
Peter. Birkacre—[I told thee afore.]
[*Margt.* I had forgotten.]
Peter. There's that about it for *thee* to know it by, above all. See'st thou yon grand house o't hill-side yonder (*points off* R.) and this big bright bran-new mill that looks down on t' clough and village, as much as to say, 'Come, thou bonny beck, and turn my wheels [and wash the dirt out o' my yarns], And *you*, men and women and bairns, bring your fresh springs o' life, the strong thews and sinews o' your prime, and the aches and pains o' your old age, that I may spin them into water-twist, and turn all alike into money for my master!' [*Crosses* R.
Margt. Nay, father! Methinks I hear another song and a sweeter. I hear the mill-wheel whisper to the beck, 'Why should thy bright waters run to waste? Let me find cranks and beams for them to turn, as they spin and weave the white yarn, and set busy hands to work [far, far away, on Indian isles and American savannahs!] Methinks I hear *my* mill-bell, not harsh and hateful like thine, sounding its call to prayer—for is not labour prayer?—and rousing the village to a hard but honest day's work for a fair day's wage. Yes, father [I've not looked on all these years for nought; I've watched how things were going about us —even as he said they would]. I've learned to find a sweetness in the mill-bell now that I could not find in earlier days.
Peter. I think it would scarce sound so sweet if thou knew'st whose house yon is—who owns these mills!
Margt. Who?
Peter. Richard Arkwright.
Margt. (*starting up*) My husband!
Peter. Aye, lass! thy husband, who leaves thee and thy father to tramp for bread while he battens on the inventions he stole from *me!*
Margt. These mills my husband's? But we've come on others you told me were his, already.
Peter. Aye, lass. He's too knowin' a chap to risk all his eggs i' one basket: he plants his frame-sheds here and there, as he finds water-power handy, roads convenient, labour in his reach, and capital at command: and there's no lack o'

partners, for Dick has the reet knack that makes money breed money. He ever had, from the day he paid the bailiffs out o' our house at Leigh, that he might repay himself a thousand and a thousand times out o' my foolish brains, that I left him free to unlock wi' his own key—and be d—— to him!

Margt. Again, father! (*Starts up angrily, but checks herself.*) The old fancy, that I am weary of gainsaying! Oh, if thou could'st but give thy enemy his due!

Peter. I do give him his due—don't I hate him? And as thou'st thy father's bairn, I hoped, ere this, thou'd'st ha' come to hate him too. The one pleasant thought I brought away from Preston was o' thee smashin' his model! Ha! ha! ha! that was rare fun!

Margt. Oh, father! do not turn my thought to that wretched day and wicked deed. [Thou see'st there was a higher power at his back; he was working for good—the good of Lancashire—of England—of the world—and he saw it afar off, though I could not]. In my madness I destroyed his work, and yet see what it and he have grown to, and to what thou and I have fallen. [*Distant shouts and cheering.*

Peter. [Working for good, was he?] Wait a bit! Thou could'st not kill the seed, 'tis true : let's see if I cannot destroy the harvest. Poor old Peter Hayes may be man enow to pull down lusty Dick Arkwright yet—and the higher the fall the heavier.

Margt. What do you mean, father? [*Cheering renewed.*

Peter. I'll tell thee as we go along. (*Enter over bridge one or two women and a boy, forerunners of crowd shouting.*) This way : best give the slip to yon noisy crowd. (*To boy.*) Say, lad, what's yon fules shoutin' for?

Boy. Why, wherever's thou come from, thou old gommock, not to know? It's master come home—Master Arkwright.

Woman (*cuffing boy soundly*). Say Sir Richard! thou lazy young loppet!

Margt. Sir Richard?

Woman. King George has given him t' title, and he ought to get it from man, woman, and child here i' Birkacre, that he and his water-frames ha' made out o' nout!

Margt. Do you hear, father?

Peter. Aye, I hear.

Margt. And lay to heart?

Peter. [Aye, lass, and lay to heart!] Come thy ways, I tell thee. [*Exit* PETER, 2 E. L.

MUSIC, &c., BELLS.

Enter over bridge NANCY, HILKIAH, *school-children, country lasses, mill-hands, lads, and men carrying flags, cheering, while the band plays* 'See the Conquering Hero,' *followed by* SIR RICHARD CLAYTON, HAWORTH, CHADWICK, SIR RICHARD ARKWRIGHT, OMEROD, &c., &c.

Arkw. Thank ye, friends—thank you all, kindly. And you, working folks, that I have known longest—come o' the same stock—taught i' the same school—and not one but has the same road before him, if he nobbut keeps clear the hard Lancashire head on his shoulders to guide the strong Lancashire hands! (*Cheers.*) And as for you, gentlemen——

Sir R. Clay. (*shaking hands*) And brother Justices, Sir Richard.

Arkw. You're mighty kind to own me among you worshipful gentlemen of His Majesty's Commission and old county blood. I fear I'll scarce feel as much at home o' the Bench for a while yet, as lookin' after my bonny bit throstles, i' their nests yonder. (*Pointing to mill.*)

Chad. And some of us not only brother magistrates, Arkwright, but brother manufacturers, you know.

Arkw. Aye, Mr. Chadwick. Elder brothers, that have done me elder brothers' service—taught me to look to my own labour for my own living, and to trust my own hands to guard my own head. But let by-gones be by-gones; our bonny North Country is broad enough for all. There's elbow-room for working or fighting either, so the work's above board and the fighting fair.

Chad. Nay, nothing like a clear stage and no favour!

Arkw. That I'm sure of. Now, lads and lasses! there's a free tap and fiddlers at the 'King's Arms,' and the merrier you are, the more I shall like it.

Hilkiah. One cheer more for Sir Richard Arkwright!

[*The crowd troop off huzzahing.*

Arkw. Now, gentlemen, if you'll do me the honour to look over the new shed—you'll find some improved carding machinery, Mr. Chadwick—for all my patents haven't a leg to stand on—and a lot o' new things i' roving gear, Mr.

Haworth. There's the foreman ready to lead the way. (*Enter from mill the Foreman, and holds gates open.*) And after that there'll be a bit o' dinner at t' Hall, if you'll do me the honour.

Sir Richard. Egad! we must christen the new title! And, luckily, Sir Richard's port is older than his knighthood. Come, gentlemen!

[*Exit into mill* CLAYTON, CHADWICK, HAWORTH, OMEROD, &c., &c.

Hilkiah. Let's off, Nancy. I'm too much excited for eating and drinking. [*They are about to go.*

Arkw. Nay, I can't spare *you*, old friends. Besides, on such a day I shall want a lady to do the honours at the Hall. (*With a sigh.*)

Nancy (*half-aside*). More's the pity!

Arkw. Thou's right there, lass. Nay, I've quick ears! Aye (*bitterly*), believe it or not, Nancy Lawson—busy and prosperous as I am, wi' more mills than I can manage, more machines buzzin' i' my head than I shall ever gi' shape to, more money than I want, and more honour than sits easy upon me, I sometimes feel I should be thankful to change lots wi' the worst-paid spinner that sits i' the poorest o' yon chimney-corners, wi' wife and bairns about him.

Nancy. Aye, home's home!

Arkw. And what home can there be without a wife? (*sighing.*) Thou knows—if only she'd been here to-day!

Enter lad running with a note from L. 1 E.

Boy (*to Arkwright*). 'Tis for thee.

Arkw. For me, lad? (*Takes and reads.*) 'Oud shaver.' Free and easy at any rate. 'Look out for sky-scrapers. Them that blazed Rawmarsh mills have a lowe left for Birkacre. There's red-coats at Chorley Barracks. This is a hint from thy friend. Anominous.' Ominous indeed! Who gave it thee, lad?

Boy. A travellin' mak' o' chap I never see here before—chuck'd it ower t' churchyard dyke to me, and a groat, to tak' it to thee straight.

Arkw. Good lad! There's another for doin' thy errand. (*Exit lad, joyfully.*) A hint, eh? I never tak' hints.

Hilkiah. But hadn't you better make inquiry?

Arkw. (*tearing up paper*) Nay; if I heeded such trumpery I'd never know a night's sleep. [Besides, think how Chadwick and Haworth would chuckle if they came to know. No; I must do the honours of the new shed yonder. So I'll e'en leave you. You'll not mind that, I know.

Nancy. Nay, we'll stroll up to the Hall. It's a fine even', and the young birks smell so sweet—it's as good as a posy.

Arkw. And, I say,] Nancy, just thou cast an eye into t' kitchen, and over t' table and things, there's a bonny woman. I've none to do for me, thou knows, nobbut t' housekeeper. (*Mastering his feelings.*) There, what's use i' frettin'? I don't often; but somehow the thought of *her will* keep coming back to-day. [*Exit into mill.*

Nancy. Ah! there goes a sad heart—for all the laced waistcoat.

Hilkiah. There's a skeleton i' every cupboard, as the saying is; though we hav'n't set up one yet—and don't mean to (*aside*), I hope.

Enter MARGARET, *running*, L. 1 E.

Margt. Who are these? Bettermost folks! They must be friends o' his—all here are. Perhaps they'd help me. I beg your pardon, sir. [*They turn; mutual recognition.*

Nancy. Why—nay—Lor' a mercy! Hilkiah! It's niver——

Margt. Nancy! Oh, lass! that I should ha' come on you two!

Nancy (*embracing her*). Maggie! Eh, but I knew thee, for all thou'st so changed! Thou here, i' this poor plight!

Margt. Never fash wi' me! I've no time now. (*To* HILKIAH.) Thou'st thy home here? (*He nods.*)

Hilkiah. House and office, with appurtenances.

Margt. Hast e'er a trusty man (*he nods*) and a swift horse that'll carry him into Chorley afore nightfall?

Hilkiah. My grey gelding has covered the three miles within the eighteen minutes.

Margt. Then send him off, for the Lord's sake, to bring the dragoons from Chorley Barracks here, as fast as they can ride!

Hilkiah. Dragoons? But what the dickens——

Margt. (*with eagerness*) No questions; but do as I tell thee! There's life and death hangs o' the doing!

Hilkiah. The dragoons! They'll none move without a regular magistrate's order.

Margt. Get one at once! or tell me where to find them that can.

Hilkiah. Nay, if the thing's to be got, I am the man to get it (*tears page from his pocket-book and writes rapidly*). Here lad (*beckons off—lad approaches*), ask Sir Richard—he's in the new shed—to give me his signature on this paper. Say, Mr. Lawson wants it particularly.

[*Exit lad into mill.*

Margt. Run! lad, run!

Nancy. Is she gone crazed, I wonder?

Hilkiah. What does all this mean?

Margt. It means that but for such swift help as that may bring, before this night is two hours older, Birkacre Mill may be a heap of ashes!

Hilkiah. The new mill burnt!

Nancy. Mercy on us!

Margt. And not Birkacre Mill only! Its blaze is watched for on the hills for ten miles round. 'Twill be the signal for firing every other mill in the three counties that Richard Arkwright has money or machines in!

Hilkiah. Lord defend us! (*Lad enters from mill; takes paper from him, and writes.*) Tell John Allen to ride wi' this to Chorley Barracks as fast as thy grey gelding can lay legs to ground. (*Exit* L. U. E.) And who's at the bottom of this hellish plot?

Margt. Oh, don't ask me that.

Hilkiah. I must know.

Margt. Oh, must I tell?

Hilkiah. Yes, if I'm to trust.

Margt. Woe's me that I should say it!—my father! 'Tis for this that he has guided our journey hither, so that the blow may fall to-day, the birthday of the new mill, [and the new honour. 'Tis a long-planned purpose, though I never knew. He has been a wanderer for years, and still in his wanderings he has laid his train of dark designs and desperate men, chosen secretly, to meet and rise with fire and gunpowder, for the ruin of Richard Arkwright and his inventions. The work is to begin to-night.] Pray Heaven it may be prevented. [Not Richard Arkwright's property only—his life is in danger!]

Hilkiah. Yonder goes John Allen, full gallop.

Margt. The Lord speed him!

Nancy. Thou'lt 'bide with us, Maggie? We've a bed for thee.

Margt. No rest for me to-night. They'd best be on their guard at the mill.

Nancy. Be off, Hilkiah, and warn them. I'll go bring thee thy blunderbuss from the office.

[*Hilkiah* (*aside*). A most unprofessional weapon, but these rascals will mind lead more than law. (*Going.*) But if they ask who gave me warning?

Margt. (*struggling with her feelings*). Say a poor woman, a poor travelling woman, who wished well to Richard Arkwright, because she thought he had done good to the country.]

Nancy (*to* MARGT.). Thou 'bide till I come back. I'll bring the blunderbuss to thee by the short cut through the garden. [*Exit* NANCY *over bridge;* HILKIAH *into mill.*

Enter PETER HAYES, L. 1 E., *jubilant.*

Peter. Where's gotten to, lass? It's none wise thou and me should be seen glommerin' about t' mill, wi' what's comin'. (*In a half-whisper.*) The lads are hard at hand, wi' [Black Bob o' Chowbent and Dick o' Rawmarsh, to show 'em t' way. They're nobbut fettlin' up a bit, takin' a drink and a pipe just ower t' 'edge. I've seen Bob; he says the lads are mad for mischief.] We've nobbut to let spring click? [*Going.*

Margt. Father, if you can loose these desperate men, you can stay them—you must stay them now!

Peter. [Stay them?] Nay. Oud Nick's easier loosened than laid!

Margt. Tell them [Nay, what good to tell *them* the devilry they're upon—not destroying the means of one man, but the bread of thousands—but tell them] they are rushing to their undoing!

Peter. Pshaw! Who's to harm them? [They know nought i' t' mill, master nor overlookers. Birkacre folk are a poor lot, but they'll none turn out for mill or master;] and if they do, our chaps has gotten guns, and Bob's melted all his oud aunt's pewter into bullets, and she left him a rare dresser-full.

Margt. Armed! Then, do what I may, there will be blood spilled yet!

Peter. Never fear; [t' pensioners 'll be flayed and t' constables will none fight, for all that oud Clayton. There's Chadwick, and Haworth, and a deal o' that mak', will look on wi' a laugh i' their sleeves, justices though they be.]

There's nobbut t' red-coats could hinder, and they're safe at Chorley, three miles away!

Margt. Do not trust that. They may have had warning.

Peter. Nay, nay, niver.

Margt. [Father, they have had warning.

Peter. T' red-coats? And who's warned them? Bob and Dick ha' kept their chaps i' t' dark. Save them and me, there was none knew t' day and t' deed.

Margt. You told me]—*I* have warned the soldiers.

Peter. Thou? Marget Hayes! My own flesh and blood! [Have a care, lass! I love thee, as thou knowest; what I should do without thee I cannot think, but if thou hast done this, thou'rt no more child o' mine!

Margr. My father casts me off, as my master did eighteen years ago. But 'tis even justice wipes out the score against me. 'Tis for right done now, as it was for wrong done then!]

Peter. But, come, lass, come! Thou says this nobbut to scare me and t' lads? Thou'st none split, Maggie?

Margt. Father or no father—I tell you again, I have sent a swift rider to Chorley Barracks.

Peter (*fiercely, then checking himself*). Thou hast? Dost know if I let on to yon lads o' this, they'd limb thee as soon as look at thee?

Margt. Tell them, father; let them do their worst. Better wreak their mad wrath on me than on the mills.

[R. *Loud murmurs off.*

Peter. It's too late, lass. They're here, and red coats isn't. Fire is a swift servant. Happen t' soldiers may come to find white ash and black brands where Birkacre Mill stands now. (R. *Murmurs.*) Hark to yon! (*Murmur.*) Dick's loosed his lads! Let's away, and leave them to their work. Come——

Margt. Nay, then, father. If you will not lift hand to stay them I will!

Peter. Thou!

Margt. Have I not stood before this between his work and a misguided mob? But then I was mad—the blind tool o' their madness and thy hate. I am wiser now.

Mob enter, headed by Bob *and* Dick, *armed with sledges, &c., and carrying a beam slung,* L. 2 E.

Dick. Now, lads, there's t' mill, and here are we! and

z

one on us is bound to go down ! Beams and sledges to t' front. (*Shouts.*) Firemen, ready wi' your tows and your quickmatch. When's gate's smashed, then bleeze her up. (*Yell.*)

Margt. (*interposing between them and mill-gates*) You know me—Maggie, Peter Hayes' daughter !

Peter. Never heed her ! She's mad, I tell you. 'Tis Peter Hayes's self that says so. [*Movement of men to front.*

Margt. No, no—'tis he—'tis you are mad—not I ! Think o' what you are doing. Look at all those homes— like your own—lying so quiet yonder ; and here, the mill— that finds bread for all those bread-winners. What ha' yon poor wives and bairns done, that you should burn them out o' their bread like this—and there's many a blaze I know to be kindled at this one, and every fire will be the wasting of a hundred homes. [*Murmurs,* 'She's reet !'

Dick. Stop her gab.

Margt. 'Tis not mills and machines you would be burning, but bread and meat, the clothing and comfort of hundreds on hundreds o' happy firesides. 'Tis not the masters you are undoing, but your fathers and brothers, your sisters and your wives, your own bonny bairns—(*Murmur.*)

Dick. Haud' thy gab, I tell thee—or—— (*Threatening her with pistol.*)

Margt. (*strikes up pistol*) Who cares for thy pistol ? I will not hold. (*Mob shout,* 'Down with the machines!')

Margt. Down wi' the machines ! oh, wise cry ! Down wi' the horses, and let us draw t' coach ourselves ! Down wi' the brains, and let men be like the brutes [that toil but with their thews and sinews and dead weight of flesh !] Down with all that spares strength, saves waste, and cheapens cost !

Dick. Nought's working-men's friend that maks one man's work worth ten——

Margt. And so sets free the wasted strength of nine for work that's wanted.

Dick. That's masters' talk—not men's.

Margt. Men's or masters', it is truth ! And woe to them that will not hear it. (*Crowd are becoming impatient; a shout.*)

Dick. Poise her over !

Peter (*interposing*). Leave her to me.

Margt. If you care not for the poor folk yonder, mayhap you will have some pity for me—I am Richard's Arkwright's wife.

Peter. And see how he has sarved her.

[*Mob,* 'Shame, shame!

Margt. But as I deserved. He put me from his heart and his home. He had a right. I was false wife to him then—I will be true wife to him now!

Dick. Enow o' t' crazy wench's talk—down wi' gates, lads! [*Tremendous shout, and the mob rush on.*

Margt. If nought else will stay you, think of the danger to yourselves—you are giving your lives to the dragoons, who have been sent for from Chorley—who will be here anon.

Peter. Never heed her!

Dick. Dragoons! Who sent for them?

Margt. What matters—suppose I did?

Peter. 'Tis a lie, I say; but, lie or truth, there's time to burn the mill before they come.

Dick. To the gates! You beams and sledges there!

[*Mob cheer, and make a movement forward.*

Margt. I tell you again—'tis your own ruin you are working—not Richard Arkwright's.

ARKWRIGHT *appears at the gate with gun, followed by* CHADWICK *and gentlemen.*

Ark. That's a true word, whoever spoke it. I am armed, and so are my friends here.

Enter HILKIAH *quickly from gate with blunderbuss.*

Hilkiah. And so am I.

Ark. I've done you lads nought but good, and I'm not disposed to put up with ruin in return, be it from Jack or gentleman.

Hilkiah. You see, lads, we were warned—you'd best be.

Bob. Gang in at 'em, lads!

Arkw. The first that raises his hand against this gate will never raise another.

Hilkiah. The dragoons have been sent for from Chorley.

Bob. And 'twas your lass that's split on us! (*To* PETER.) —Chuck her into mill-lead, lads.

[*They seize* MARGARET *and drag her towards mill-stream.*

Nancy (*entering quickly over bridge*). Save her, Richard Arkwright—'tis thy wife! (*Officer appears.*) You are under the fire of the dragoons, my lads!

Clayton. Drop your weapons!

[*Mob shrink back cowed.*

Arkw. (*rushes up, strikes down* BOB, *and saves* MARGARET) Let mine be the first voice she hears—mine the first face she sees. Margaret, speak, lass—'tis Dick, thy husband; speak, my long-suffering, ill-used wife!

Margt. She that was thy wife once—when she was not worthy thee.

Arkw. She that was my wife when I was a poorer, and oft a happier man—she that shall be my wife now, if she'll only forget and forgive.

Margt. Forgive, but not forget!

Arkw. Peter Hayes, I was hard upon thee, too; wilt take this hand—a clean hand—from Richard Arkwright?

Margt. Oh, come with us, father, and let our love make happy the evening of thy days!

Nancy. Take it, Mr. Hayes, take it—they have to mak' a grandfather of thee yet.

Peter (*taking his hand*). There's my hand, Dick; but remember, I was first with th' rolling machine.

Arkw. Aye, so thou wert, and thou shalt have a royalty out of mine.

Margt. And be mine the woman's royalty—the ruling of a well-ordered home! Oh, I dreamed not of such happiness! Friends, do not call me back to a waking less happy than my dream!

CURTAIN.

NOTE.—This play was suggested to me by a story, 'Joan Merryweather,' one of a collection of tales by Miss Katherine Saunders, in which her father had a share. As Miss Saunders wished her father's name to appear in the play-bills rather than her own, the name of John Saunders stands on the bills as joint author, in accordance with the very proper French practice of so recording the name of the author of a story which has served as the groundwork of a play.

ANNE BOLEYN

An Original Historical Play

IN FIVE ACTS

This play was produced at the Haymarket Theatre, in March, 1875.

DRAMATIS PERSONÆ.

KING HENRY VIII.
EARL OF SURREY (*afterwards Duke of Norfolk*).
EARL OF NORTHUMBERLAND.
SIR THOMAS BOLEYN (*afterwards Earl of Wiltshire*).
LORD HENRY PERCY (*Earl of Northumberland*).
EUSTACE CHAPUIS (*Envoy from the Emperor Charles V.*).

THOMAS WYATT.　⎫
HENRY NORRIS.　⎬ *Gentlemen of the King's chamber.*
FRANCIS WESTON.　⎪
WILLIAM BRERETON.⎭

GEORGE BOLEYN (*afterwards Viscount Rochefort*).
THOMAS CRANMER (*Archbishop of Canterbury*).
SIR WILLIAM KINGSTON (*Lieutenant of the Tower*).
MARK SMEATON (*a Musician of the King's chamber*).
CONSTANTINE (*a Gospeller*).

ANNE BOLEYN (*Maid of Honour to Queen Katherine, afterwards Queen*).

MARGARET WYATT　⎫
(*afterwards Lady Lee*).　⎪
JANE PARKER (*afterwards Lady Rochefort*).　⎬ *Maids of Honour to Queen Katherine.*
ELIZABETH CAREW.　⎪
MADGE SHELTON.　⎪
MARY CHEYNEY.　⎭

JANE SEYMOUR.　⎫ *Queen Anne's Ladies.*
ANN GAISFORD.　⎭

LADY KINGSTON.
MARIA DE ROJAS, LADY WILLOUGHBY (*Mistress of the Robes to Queen Katherine*).

ANNE BOLEYN.

ACT I.

Time: Towards the End of 1523.

Scene.—*Chamber of the Queen's Ladies at Hertford Castle. A room, panelled, below, and with richly decorated stucco arches above the panelling. The room is set obliquely, a wide door communicating with the corridor, 1 and 2 entrances, R. A window in a deep square recess, with raised floor, occupies the 2nd and 3rd entrances, L. In the centre, a doorway communicating with the Queen's apartments, with tapestry before it. Small door, 1 E. L.*

Margaret Wyatt, Jane Parker, Elizabeth Carew, Madge Shelton, Mary Cheyney *discovered at their embroidery frames, seated on the raised floor of the window recess.*

Jane P. Who yawned there?
Madge. Rather ask, who did not yawn?
Did Heaven make girls with light hearts and light heels
To peak o'er 'broidery frames?
  Mary.   And at such 'broidery!
  Madge. Treason! 'Tis of her Majesty's ordering—
A set of cushions for our sour duenna,
The Lady Willoughby.
  Margt. That Spanish clock-case in a farthingale,
Whom even an English lord has not unstarched!
  Mary. Such subjects!
  Madge.   Parables and Christian virtues!
  Mary. When she has all of them.
  Jane P.   And we none to spare.
  Mary. Wer't scarf or sleeve to grace a tilting helm!
  Madge. Ill fall these wars! 'Twas never merry time
Since all our lustiest gallants left the court
For hard fare and hard knocks round Guisnes and Calais.

Mary. Nay, we've some men left still. There's Harry Norris,
Frank Weston, and Will Brereton.
    Margt. (*to* JANE P., *significantly*) And George Boleyn.
    Jane P. (*to* MARGARET, *in same tone*) Anthony Lee.
    Mary.   Thy brother, Margaret.
    Madge. Pshaw! He's a married man. I count not him.
    Margt. No more do I thy friends of the King's chamber.
Holiday gallants—carpet knights.
    Jane P.   Nay, Meg,
Give French kings minions, English kings need men;
And most a king like this, a man of men;
Foremost in battle, as in tilt and tourney;
Best hand on horse, best cheerer of a hawk;
Holds knaves at quarter-staff, as knights at barrier;
As light i' the dance as if his shoulders bore
No weight of manhood; book-learn'd as he is,
They say, to hold priests tightly to their Latin,
Master of lute and viol, as he'd made
Such minstrelsy his life's work; debonair
In hall, as he is terrible when crossed
In sport or earnest. Is not here a king
For men to fear and love?
    Margt. Hush! Walls have ears, and palace walls, they say,
The longest. Let's talk what will make no echoes.
And so, with Madge, I say, beshrew these wars,
That thrust between the Court and the French fashions.
    Madge. A year, and nothing new in hoods or gowns!
    Jane P. You forget one good we owe the French wars.
    Margt. What's that?
    Jane P. They've brought Anne Boleyn back to Court.
    Madge. To set our caps, and show how hanging-sleeves
Ought to be worn.
    Jane P. (*bitterly*) To hide ill-shapen hands.
    Mary. Or how a pearl rope makes a fair neck fairer——
    Jane P. And masks a mole at need!
    Margt.   Out, slanderer!
Tell me of marks and moles; me, that have known her
From baby days at Allington and Hever!
My brother made her lady of his song;
I made her—what she is—friend of my heart!

[SCENE I.] *ANNE BOLEYN.*

Jane P. Marry and amen! What the French Court
  made her
We all know, since we called her one of us.
A cunning gipsy, with her velvet eyes,
And nut-brown cheeks that pale or flush at will;
Her knack of tongues, trick of new-fangled dresses,
Dances, devices! Tell me of Anne Boleyn——

Enter ANNE BOLEYN, C. D.

Anne B. Nay, that were needless, with Anne Boleyn here
To tell you of herself. Largesse! Largesse!
So heralds cry for bounty when they bring
Good tidings; and for the brave news I bring
I will but ask more and more of your loves!
For Christmastide the Court goes back to Greenwich.
There'll be a Twelfth Night pageant. Such a pageant!
A castle kept by ladies—*Beauty*, *Honour*,
Kindness, and *Constancy*, and *Perseverance*,
Bounty, and *Pity*—all in Milan gowns
And French cauls of white satin broched with gold.
And in a base-court underneath the castle
Danger, *Disdain*, and *Jealousy; Strangeness, Scorn*,
Unkindness, and *Malbouche*—that's evil-speaking.
Then to those ladies shall come in eight lords—
Chief of their company his Grace the King,
Ardent Desire, in crimson full of flames—
And they to assail the castle, while the ladies
Shoot at them shot of comfits and rose-water.
At last the lords to take the ladies prisoners,
And all to dance together.
  All.   Brave! oh, brave!
  Jane P.   And what part
Do you play?

The Gentlemen (NORRIS, WYATT, LEE, WESTON, BRERETON, *and* GEORGE BOLEYN) *of the King's chamber appear in the corridor listening.*

  Anne B. Norris tells me I may choose.
  Jane. P. 'Twixt *Beauty, Honour, Kindness, Constancy?*
  Anne B. As you 'twixt *Scorn, Disdain*, and *Evil-
    speaking!*
That choice will keep. Meantime, to choose the dance.
What say you to the new French round I showed you—
The last I learned at Blois?

Margt.   Show us again.
Jane P. and all. Oh, rare! A hall! a hall!
Anne B. Where's partners?

Enter NORRIS, WYATT, LEE, WESTON, BRERETON, *and*
         GEORGE BOLEYN, *&c.*

Norris.   Here!
Wyatt.   And here!
Boleyn. And we have brought Mark Smeaton with his
   music.

Enter MARK SMEATON *and Musicians.*

     Anne B. In good time! That new French round,
     Master Smeaton?
I gave it you at Eltham once.
     Smeaton.   So please you,
'Tis in my book. (*Aside.*) And where I treasure all,—
Each word, smile, look, vouchsafed me,—in my heart.
     Norris.   Fair ladies!
        [*The Gentlemen take partners*—LEE *and* MARGARET
         WYATT; BOLEYN *and* JANE PARKER; NORRIS *and*
         MARY CHEYNEY; WESTON *and* MADGE SHELTON;
         BRERETON *and* ELIZABETH CAREW.
Wyatt (*coming forward to* ANNE B.). Grant me to touch
   the hand whose touch awakes
The music that my heart breathes to my pen.
     Anne B. My poet still!
     Wyatt.   While he has voice to sing,
Cœur Loyale is my name—my service yours.
     Anne B. See, the dance waits!
        [*They all join in a round. In the midst of the dance*
         MARIA DE ROJAS, LADY WILLOUGHBY, *a severe*
         dame of middle age, in stiff Spanish garb of black
         brocade, with ruff, farthingale, and mantilla, sud-
         denly draws the curtains of the doorway to the Queen's
         chamber, c. *Dismay. The music gradually dwindles*
         down. Those who see the lady stop. A couple who
         have had their backs to her continuing to dance come
         suddenly face to face with her and stop short.
     Lady W. How now? What Shrovetide skippings have
     we here?
My masters! Ladies! (*To the girls.*) You had work to do—
To 'broider—not enact—the Foolish Virgins.

Meantime, the Queen bids you attend upon her
To chapel. For you, sirs, I marvel much
At your slack service. Even now is come
A post from my Lord Cardinal. I saw him
Out of my closet window. Must he wait?
 Norris. Nay, good your ladyship, had we been praying
Instead of dancing, he must wait. The King
Is yet abroad. He went to try a cast
Of young hawks; they have led him far afield.
 Lady W. Hawks and men have their lures. Methinks
  'twere well
You, gentlemen, that are of the King's chamber,
Bore in mind this room is for the Queen's ladies.
 Norris (aside). We bear the fact in mind and act on
  it.
 Lady W. Bachelors will be bachelors, but I marvel
At Master Wyatt——
 Wyatt. Madam, I am here
To keep these boys in rein.
 Anne B. (playfully) And on his warrant,
Being an ancient, sad, and married man,
I thought no harm to lead our company
A dance.
 Lady W. You are too fond of leading dances,
Young mistress. Meanwhile, lead your dance to chapel.
Cover and range these frames. You, Mistress Anne,
You made this coil; 'twere well you set it straight.
     [*Points the way off to the Maids of Honour.*
 Wyatt (to ANNE B., *who is going to arrange the frames*).
Who think you's come from my Lord Cardinal?
 Anne B. Who?
 Wyatt. My Lord Percy.

   Enter attendant, who whispers NORRIS

 Lady W. Pray you, gentlemen,
Avoid the chamber.
 Norris (to LADY W.) Madam, by your leave,
Here is the Earl of Surrey come for audience;
And your good father, from o'er sea.
 Anne B.   Oh, joy!
 Norris. Come, gentlemen.
 Anne B. (to WYATT, *aside*) My poet, if you love me!
 Wyatt. I will tell him

That you are here alone.
> [*By this time* LADY W. *has guarded off the Maids,
> while the gentlemen have retired by the* R. E.

Anne B. 'Tis all for *me* he lackeys this proud priest!
He is love's post, not my Lord Cardinal's.
Let me hold him the higher in my heart,
The lowlier he makes himself to win it.
> [*Enter* PERCY.

My Percy!

 Percy. Sweet heart!

 Anne B.   Thou hast ridden fast.

 Percy. Did I not ride to thee? But 'tis not haste
Alone disorders me. I've stood this morning
Under the storm of my Lord Cardinal's wrath—
Been rated like a page.

 Anne B.   Would I could bear
Some of thy smart!

 Percy.   I scarce had tamed my tongue,
But for the thought a better life than mine
Might hang on favour of this butcher's son.
The hand that plucked down Buckingham can reach
Buckingham's brother-in-law, Northumberland.

 Anne B. Had I the opening of King Henry's eyes!

 Percy. His anger 'gainst me was that I had dared
To tangle and ensnare myself (his words)
With a fair foolish girl (his words again),
Anne Boleyn. Then spoke large and loud, and threatened
The King's displeasure—worse, his own disfavour—
If I broke not with thee.

 Anne B.   And thou wert silent?
Priest or no, I'd have given him cuff for cuff.

 Percy. I swallowed down my anger—answered him.
I was of years to choose; though you were only
Knight's daughter, that the best blood of two kingdoms
Met in your veins—that your rare gifts and graces
Raised you above your blood, made you a jewel
A king might set within his crown, and feel
The crown less honoured it than it the crown.

 Anne B. Brave words and true—all but their praise of
  me.
Methinks we should love closer, were't but crossing
Of this high-stomached priest, who dares to thrust
His crosier 'twixt our hearts. There's danger now

In loving thee. Something for *me* to dare
And do, to prove me worthy a man's choice.
Hold *thou* firm, *I* will hold, come what come may!

Enter WYATT.

Wyatt. Break off! Your father would have speech of you.
(*To* PERCY.) And you are called for on the bowling-green.
   Percy. I come. Keep a brave heart.
   Anne B.   Fear not for that.
   Percy. I'll see thee ere I ride.
   Anne B.   'Tis hours till then!
                  [PERCY *embraces her and exit*, R.
   Wyatt. Quick! to thy 'broidery—I to my lute.
Poets were ever feigners. Let me feign
I sing to speed thy needle. Woe the while
When 'tis to mask thy love game. Hapless poet!
   [ANNE B. *sits at her frame.* WYATT *takes a lute which
      is in the window-seat and plays.*

Enter SIR THOMAS BOLEYN, R.

   Sir T. My Anne!
   Anne B.   My lord and father, on my knee
I crave your blessing. (*Kneels.*)
   Sir T. (*Raising her and folding her to his heart*) Take
   it, in my arms!
Tom Wyatt, here, will give us neighbours' freedom.
   [*Holds out his hand to* WYATT, *who takes it and bows
      reverently over it.*
   Wyatt. Let me but share her blessing, sir, I'm gone.
   Sir T. God bless thee too, lad. Still at the old trade?
(*Points to lute.*)
   Wyatt. Alas! 'tis in grain!
   Sir T.   How does thy good father?
My oldest friend and best!
   Wyatt.   Well, and will be
Right glad to see you back again in Kent.
   Sir T. I'll wager him a hobby, not more glad
To see me back in Kent than I to see
Green Kent again, after these frowsy Flemings
And their sea-sodden polders. (*Exit* WYATT.) Bless thee,
   girl!
I have not seen so sweet a face since last
I looked on thine. Our English air hath browned thee!

Stay—while I think on't, here are letters for thee,
From the Archduchess. Sure she loves thee, Anne.
If ears e'er tingled at good words unheard,
Thine should have glowed, so well she spoke of thee.

  Anne B. 'Tis a kind lady! But her praise will wait—
Give me the latest news of pleasant Hever
And all I love there.

  Sir T.   Nay, I scarce drew rein
From Dover hither—passed almost in sight
Of my own chimneys. But home news will keep
For home. My time's the king's, as all I have
And am——

  Anne B. (*playfully*) And but the leavings for thy daughter?

  Sir T. What if she too be part of the King's business?
Thou knowest the coil I've had, this many a year,
Touching that red-headed, red-handed rogue,
Piers Butler's usurpation of the title
And lands of Ormond—mine by blood and law.

  Anne B. I know; his son, my cousin James—sweet cousin!
Is here, at school of Court and Cardinal;
And he needs schooling—an unmannered lout!

  Sir T. I warrant me we'll tame this eyas hawk
Under thy falconry.

  Anne B.   Let him fly wild,
Down wind, for me—he's no bird for my hand.

  Sir T. That older heads must judge. Sir Richard Pole,
The French King's puppet, would plant the white rose
I' the Irish bogs. False Desmond is his friend.
To check the Desmonds the King needs the Butlers—
The Butlers' following obey Red Piers.
Now, if his toward son and my fair daughter
Made English right and Irish might shake hands,
Our feud might sleep, the daughter's son succeeding
In peace to what his grandfathers must fight for.

  Anne B. Father, is this a jest; or do I dream?
Marry me with James Butler; Heaven forefend!
That Irish wolf-hound whelp! Was it for this
You sent me, still a child, to the French Court,
To learn its manners, breathe its perfumed air,
Glass me in its most gracious womanhood—
Take my mind's impress from its poets, painters,
Scholars, and sages?

Sir T. Think to whom you speak!
Or I shall think you bring from the French Court
The worst point of its manners—to forget
The duty that a daughter owes her father.
  Anne B. I own a father's duty. All I am
Is yours, as yours the King's; but there's one thing
Lies beyond pale of duty, will, or force—
That's love—that comes of nature. Such a love
I cannot give James Butler.
  Sir T. Love! a toy
For girls, a lure for men—no barrier
To raise between a father's will, with reason
To guide it; and a girl's like or misliking——
Here comes your uncle. Let him find in you
A better mind.

Enter the EARL OF SURREY, R.

  Surrey (*kissing* ANNE). Fair day, fair niece! Well, has your father told you
What we propose?
  Anne B. (*in a low voice*) He has.
  Surrey. And, knowing you
A buxom daughter, fair and uncontracted,
He has—what he but asks as 'twere for form—
Consent from you?
  Sir T. (*to* ANNE B.) You hear—what say you?
  Surrey. Silence
Is woman's best consent.
  Anne B. Then I must speak.
I cannot marry him whom you would have me.
  Surrey. Can or can not, you must, and there's an end——
  Anne B. Of me, ere of this marriage.
  Surrey (*after a pause of astonishment*). Brother Boleyn,
I thought that you had trained this sparrow-hawk,
As hawks and women should be trained, to soar
And stoop upon the call?
  Sir T. I thought so too.
  Anne B. (*imploringly*) Father! My lord!
  Surrey. Then the Court gossip's true
I heard i' the bowling-green—Norris and Bryan
And these plumed popinjays of the King's chamber
Breaking their poor jest-points on my Lord Percy!

This was the Mistress Anne whose name they bandied
So light among them.
　　Anne B.　　　　　　And Lord Percy brooked it?
　　Surrey. Nay, even then a summons called him thence
To attend the Earl, his father (*to* Sir T.), whom the King
And my Lord Cardinal are ill-content with,
For his refusal of the Wardenship
Of the North Marches—laying it on my shoulders!
Let him look to his earldom and his head.
　　Anne B. His father here!
　　Sir T. (*to* Anne B.)　　　Ha! you turn red and pale!
　　Surrey (*roughly*). Is this the man?
　　Anne B. (*throwing herself in her father's arms*). Father,
　　　I'll tell you all.
But my lord's questioning's not of the fashion
That I can stomach, or that I will answer.
　　Surrey. The Howard blood spoke in her there. Well,
　　　wait.
The King's will goes with ours in this. Let's see
If that old fox Northumberland will run
Athwart it, and for stuff of boy and girl.
　　Sir T. Here comes his Grace.
　　Surrey.　　　　　　　In good time.
　　Sir T.　　　　　　　　　His son with him.
　　Surrey. My life upon it, he has ridden post-haste
To break betwixt this pair of turtle-doves.
Let him work; if he fail, 'tis time for us.
Come, cousin; and you, mistress, be advised——
　　Anne B. Oh, not so stern, dear father! (*Seizing his hand.*)
　　　Bless me still! (*Kneels.*)
　　Sir T. Heaven bless thee, Anne, and teach thee to obey.

　　　　　　　　　　　　[*Exeunt* Surrey *and* Boleyn, R.

　　Anne B. In all but this; where to obey is treason
To more than daughter's duty—to my faith
Given him, whose strength must stay me in this pass.
Percy! be thou true, and I hold them all—
Father and uncle, King and Cardinal—
At vantage of a woman's heart and will.
I'll know the best or worst, by warranty
Of mine own ears!

　　　　　　[*Passes behind the arras that overhangs the entrance
　　　　　　　to the Queen's apartments.*

Enter the EARL OF NORTHUMBERLAND *and* HENRY PERCY.

 Percy. The lady is not here. I told you, sir.
As for confronting me and Mistress Anne——
 North. Perchance 'twere best thou first confront thy
  father.
Know, then, that I and my Lord Shrewsbury
Have come to good conclusion for a marriage
Betwixt his daughter, Lady Mary Talbot,
And thee.
 Percy. My lord, I hardly know the lady.
 North. You will have time to know her after marriage.
Enough, *I* know her, and she likes me well
For my son's wife.
 Percy.   I grieve, sir——
 North.   Grieve, son Percy?
 Percy.   Your conclusion
Left me out. Where conclusions end in marriage ——
 North. They are for father's shaping. What of that?
 Percy. Marriage so made proves often marriage marred.
 North. And what of marriage without father's warrant?
Headstrong pre-contracts closed in heat of blood!
Such flimsy nets, as my Lord Cardinal
Warns me that thou hast tangled thy fool's head in
With this Anne Boleyn. Say, boy, is it true?
What has passed 'twixt you? Answer.
 Percy.   No pre-contract
Of formal troth-plight, but such interchange
Of rings and vows as binds a gentleman
More than mere form. In brief, I'm hers—she's mine.
 North. She is her father's, sirrah, as thou thine.
Are children's hands and hearts for their own giving?
And great ones too!
 Percy. But see her, know her, sir, for what she is—
So bright, fair, brave; so rich in all good graces,
Arts, and accomplishments—whose choice of me
Brings me, methinks, more honour than the blood
I draw from you.
 North.   That blood upon a block
Shows but like baser puddle. I've no mind
To mix mine with my brother Buckingham's.
 Percy. But, good my lord——
 North. Was't it for such toys I sent thee

To my Lord Cardinal? He hath forbid
This dalliance betwixt thee and Anne Boleyn.
She is not for thy market. Dost thou hear?
  Percy. I do, worse hap!
  North.   And wilt obey?
  Percy.   My lord,
Bethink you, you were young once——
  North.   When I was
I did my father's bidding.
  Percy.   How should I
Discharge my conscience, were I base enough
To yield her up for fear of consequence?
  North. I have more boys than thee to make my heirs
Of lands—if not of lordship. Go thy ways!
Forbear this folly and amend thy manners,
And take with thanks the wife that I have chosen;
Or 'twill be worse for thee.
  Percy.   An evil strait;
Betwixt a father's wrath——
  North.   A father's life
It may be.
  Percy. And the strong voice of my love!
Let me have time to think—to speak with her.
  North. Shall I speak with her rather?

    Enter ANNE B. *from behind arras,* C.

  Anne B.   She spares both!
You, my Lord Percy,—who, so brave but now,
Swore to defy all obstacles that stood
Between our hearts and hands, and now turn pale
For fear of King, and Cardinal, and father—
The pain of telling me you dare not stand
To your stout words! And you, my lord, his father,
The shame to own to me you have a son
In whose regard safety is more than honour!
'Tis I cast off Lord Percy—not he *me!*
I'll no half-hearted love; nor have I fallen
So low to cry and crave your nobleness
To let me keep the man who more repents
Of having won me than of having lost!
(*To* PERCY.) It was not thus I thought that we should part;
But, as it is, briefest farewell is best.
May you be happy in the fitter marriage
My lord hath made for you!

Percy.   Oh, Anne, forbear
To trample on my heart! Could you but read it——
   Anne B. I would read two words only in the heart
Of him that I call husband, Truth and Manhood—
No more. (*She retires up.*)
   Percy. Lost love!
   North.   Lost lands, lost lordship, and lost life
Were heavier losses. This loss is their gain.
Bear we the news to my Lord Cardinal.
Fare you well, mistress; I'll report you fairly.
                        [*Exeunt* NORTH. *and* PERCY, C.
   Anne B. So snaps my cable—twisted from the sand
Of a slight heart. Better no love than one
Parted in pale with fear! What help is left me?
Father and uncle joined to force my hand
Into James Butler's; thought of *him* to root
Out of my heart, though heart-strings come with it!
Stay here for sacrifice, or mock—or worse—
For pity! No. If they deny me leave
To hide my wound apart, I will take leave. (*She looks out.*)
What stir without? The King—my father with him!
My uncle too! What if I cast myself
On his imperial strength, to help my weakness?
Butler and Boleyn, Surrey, Northumberland,
Cardinal's self, are straws before his breath.
There's life in't! Hold, my heart, and lend my voice
Persuasion to breed pity. They are here!
I'll bide my time. (*She retires behind arras.*)

Enter the KING, *with Falconers*, NORRIS, WESTON, BRERE-
   TON, *and* WYATT. NED MOODY, *a yeoman Falconer*.

   King. The falcon's well enough; but for the tercel
She's wild and wayward, and needs manning yet.
(*To Falconers.*) Have her put to the lure ere next I fly her.
   Norris. I fear she's haggard.
   King.   I'll lay thee a wager,
My Spanish roan against thy ten rose-nobles,
She holds that hulking Holderness bird of thine—
How call you him?——
   Norris.   Tis Hubert your Grace means.
   King. That's he—the best of three flights at the river.
Kite, crane, or hernshaw, mallard, rook, or partridge.
   Norris. I take your Grace.

  King. A wager! (*To Falconers.*) See the tercel
Enseamed against the trial. Be't on Thursday.
  Wyatt. Your grace has had good sport?
  King. Good, man? Right royal!
You slug-a-beds have lost the rarest chance—
A six-mile flight—the stoutest kite on wing
Falcon e'er footed—o'er a break-neck course,
Plashet and brook and marish! Where's Ned Moody?
  Ned Moody (*coming forward*). At hand, an 't please
   your Grace.
  King.   Ever at hand,
And nearest when most need. Look, gentlemen.
Know this good fellow, to whose brawny arms
You owe that I'm not bedded in three feet
Of Essex mud. How do you call the brook?
  Ned Moody. The Gravely brook, your Grace.
  King.   Marry, well named!
T'was all but dealing gravely with thy King.
The kite had soared, the falcon made his tower—
Two black specks in the blue. Grey Javelin swooped;
As I leapt at the brook. Down came the birds,
And down came I. Beshrew the false ash-pole
That snapped like a court-promise! Hark you, Norris;
Have me the rascal trounced who finds us staves.
Four feet of water and three feet of mud
Is drowning for a six-foot king or churl,
Without a difference. But Ned Moody here—
The rest were miles behind—leaped in and bore
My head clear of the water, till the rout
Came up and fished us forth, like two soaked apples
Out of a wassail-bowl.
  Wyatt.   But filled with liquor
Less pleasant than spiced ale.
  Norris.   Your Grace had best
See Doctor Butts.
  King. What! for a half-hour's wetting?
I shifted me at Hitchen. (*Takes a medal from his bonnet.
To* Moody.) Here, good fellow,
Wear't in thy cap; and, Norris, see him rated
As Master Falconer, at a hundred marks
A year.
  Ned Moody. God save your Grace! I care not, I,
How oft your pole breaks, so that no worse comes on't.

King. Amen. My bath has edged my appetite.
See dinner hastened. But, before we eat,
I, Norris, Weston here, will hold you three
The best of three bouts at the tennis-court.
See all prepared! [*Exeunt* WESTON *and Falconers.*
I'll come when I have seen
The Queen—lest rumour should have brought her news
Of my mishap, and drowned instead of ducked me.
[*Exeunt Gentlemen*, R.
Have me announced. Which of her ladies waits?

ANNE B. *appears from behind the arras.*

Anne B. So please your Grace, 'tis I.
King. Mistress Anne Boleyn,
I give you joy of your good father's coming
With such safe speed from Flanders. We have missed him;
Methought sometimes he never would come back,
For all he left such hostages in you
And my good George.
Anne B. But, now he *is* come back,
One of those hostages would fain be free
To leave the Court.
King. Ha! which?
Anne B. So please you, I.
I pray permission to lay down my service
For——
King. Shall I guess? The Castle of Kilkenny—
Or is it at Ross-crea the Butlers keep
Their honeymoons?
Anne B. I pray, your Grace, forbear—
That they would force me to this Irish marriage
Is true; but not more true than that I'd rather
Be cloistered than so wedded. To this end,
I ask your leave to go where I am wished for;
To the Archduchess Marguerite, at Mechlin,
To 'scape more urging, and not grieve my father,
Reminding him that once I crossed his will.
King. Nor his will only—my Lord Cardinal,
The Earl of Surrey, hold one mind in this;
They see in this match quiet days for Ireland.
Your soft hand is to sleek Butlers and Desmonds,
Macmurroughs, and Mackeoghs, O"Tooles, O'Donnells—
I know not what wild tribes of O's and Macs—

To lie down with each other like tame wolf-hounds,
Instead of tearing throats like wolves.   I grant
'Tis rude work for a woman, but the rougher
The horse, the lighter hand upon the rein.
We cannot spare you.
  Anne B.   Say you *will* not spare.
  King. Young Butler's wild, but he will tame, and all
Report in him the makings of a man.
  Anne B. Let him find one who'll set hand to such making;
So will not I.
  King. *Will* is no woman's word.
  Anne. It is a woman's weapon.
  King.   All the sharper
When, without phrase, 'tis out and at your throat.
      [*Approaching her and more softly.*
But why ask this, knowing I must deny you,
And all it costs me to say nay?   The Court—
The Queen—what if I dared to say the King?—
Cannot consent to lose you.   'Tis our wish
That you stay here.   I might have said, our *will;*
But kings should rather plead their wish than will
In such a dainty ear.   Say, shall my wish
Weigh no more than Sir Thomas's command?
  Anne B. In all but this I am your Grace's creature.
In this I would be mistress of *my* will—
None may command that—neither Queen nor King—
But only I alone.
  King. Ha! I bethink me
Of my Lord Cardinal's warning.   Is it hate
Of Butler pricks you, or love of Lord Percy?
  Anne. King as you are, sir, to such questioning
It is no treason to deny your right.
Yet, lest it touch Lord Percy's favour with you
Or any near him, I will answer you.
Betwixt us—be what has been—there is, now,
Nothing to bind him, or to bias me.
  King. I'm glad of that.   The Cardinal and Surrey
Will be still gladder.   Then 'tis fixed we keep you?
The Queen will thank me.   Will you thank me too?
(*More tenderly.*) And let me take my thanks upon your lip?
  Anne B. Bethink you, sir, we stand upon the threshold
Of my most gracious mistress, your good Queen.

I am here to lead you to her.   That's *my* service.
                          [*Retires towards* c.
   King (*aside*). Her coldness warms more than most
women's fire.
Kisses are not a tax I claim King's right in ;
They're like the Cardinal's war subsidies—
Free gifts ; yet sometimes it goes hard with those
That do deny them.   Sweetest Mistress Anne,
I speak in counsel, not threat, grace forfend !
Your grace as well as heaven's.   Now show me in.
       [ANNE B. *ushers the* KING *through doorway and follows.*

Enter WYATT.

   Wyatt. Not here ! 'Twere well I saw her ; she'll be sorry
To miss this messenger.   [*Re-enter* ANNE B.
You are flushed ?
   Anne B.   'Tis blood
That resolution calls up from the heart.
Wyatt, you love me.   Nay, I know the answer—
I mean no Beatrice or Laura fancies—
But as a sister ?
   Wyatt.   You know well I do.
   Anne B. Then help me hence. This is no place for me.
I'll tell you why hereafter.   Stay not now
To question.   Answer, will you help me hence ?
   Wyatt. What mean you ?
   Anne B.   The Archduchess bids me welcome
To Mechlin.
   Wyatt.   In good time.   The King sends letters
To her to-day.   Your father bade me warn you,
If you would write——
   Anne B.   What post goes with the letters ?
   Wyatt. Nicholas Broughton.
   Anne B.   Ah, the Kentish squire,
Our neighbour ?
   Wyatt.   Even so.
   Anne B.   He meets my need.
Quick ! take me where he is at once !
   Wyatt.   You'd put
Your letters in his hand ?
   Anne B.   I'd put *myself*—
Another day must see me over sea.

ACT-DROP.

ACT II.

Scene.—*In the pleasaunce at Hever. On the cloth the Castle. The stage represents the pleasaunce, with part of the bowling-green. Seats under the trees. A pleached walk of yew, with entrances cut in it.*

Servants, with baggage, cross the stage, the Earl of Wiltshire (*Sir Thomas Boleyn*) *directing them.*

Wilt. Now, stir, lads, stir! This gear not ready yet?
Ere this the horses should have been at Tunbridge.
    [*Enter* Lady Rochefort *from another part of the pleasaunce.*
Ha, Joan—I cry you mercy, faith—my lady! (*Kisses her.*)
Thou find'st me busy here on George's matters.
Those whom King Henry favours he finds work for.
    Lady R. Witness yourself, so long plain Knight, now Earl
Of Wiltshire and of Ormond both.
    Wilt.   The King
Far outpays my deserts; yet 'tis no boast,
I've spent my best of strength and skill for him;
But all's too little.
    Lady R.   Self—and son—and daughter!
    Wilt. For self, 'twas willing service; for my son,
His honour's yours——
    Lady R.   I prize it——
    Wilt.   For my daughter,
Her honour is her own!
    Lady R.   What better guard
Could she find for it—even against the King?
What woman, before *her*, e'er held King Henry
A four years' leaguer, quenching his hot fire
With her white shield of maiden-modesty?
    Wilt. If the King woo—'tis that he's free to woo——
    Lady R. And wed?
    Wilt.   Aye, wed—my lady nimble-wit—
By warrant of his conscience, of our Church,
Canonists, colleges——
    Lady R.   Deans, doctors, bishops,
Actual or expectant. Here comes George.

Enter GEORGE BOLEYN (*Viscount Rochefort*).

Roch. Father, good wife.
Wilt. Come, boy, the day wears on:
And they that ride upon King Henry's errands
Should wake the sun, and watch him into bed.
  Roch. I but staid to wish Anne good-bye. She's weak
Still from her sickness, and it went hard with her
To let me go, though left with so much love.
  Wilt. To horse, my boy! Heaven send thee a safe journey
To France! Thou hast my counsel and my blessing.
  Roch. Father, farewell! Come, my Joan, one last kiss.
Be kind to my sweet Anne!
  Lady R. Trust me for that.
  Roch. Even as myself.
  Wilt. I'll ride a mile with thee.
    [*Exeunt* WILTSHIRE *and* ROCHEFORT.
  Lady R. He trusts me, my kind George! I trust
    myself.
This marriage is not made yet. Why should she
Be Queen? If wives can be thrust off—why, so
May husbands be. And with a crown for winning!
He's jealous as he's amorous; yet one
For whom, without his crown, a woman well
Might risk her soul. How now? What bustle yonder?
Master Chapuis, the Emperor's Envoy, lighting
At the great gate! He told me he would come.
Is this Heaven's hand or Hell's? His keen eye notes me—
He moves this way.
  Chap. (*without*) Till my lord comes, I'll breathe
The sweet pure air awhile here in the pleasaunce.

Enter CHAPUIS. *He salutes* LADY R. *ceremoniously.*

  Chap. An angry man had stormed to miss Lord Wilt-
    shire,
And stood rebuked, meeting my Lady Rochefort.
  Lady R. My father-in-law has ridden with my husband.
  Chap. Doubtless for a last word of his ripe wisdom.
Were youth as keen to take as age to offer!
I come for conference on Lord Wiltshire's mission.
I would send letters with him.
  Lady R. (*uneasily*) Letters?

Chap. (*softly, but watching her closely*) Letters—
To my imperial master.
    Lady R.   Make your post
Of King's Envoy?
    Chap.   I said with, not by.
I have a good friend in his suite, of whom
I may, without presuming, ask so much.
It needs not that my lord should ever know
That I have dared to make posts of his servants.
    Lady R. He might chafe——
    Chap.   Yes, he might—*I* never chafe.
Two packets to my friend were no more load
Than one. You may remember certain letters
We spoke of late at Durham House together,
Between the King's Grace and your bright-eyed sister——
    Lady R. In law!
    Chap.   And love—sisterly, and the rest——
    Lady R. Say I had means and will to put these letters
Into your hand, what should they serve?
    Chap.   Yourself?
England? Spain? France? the Church? Your question
    stretches
So wide, the answer must stretch wide to meet it.
First, for yourself—self's a safe point to start from:
Gift of these letters makes Chapuis your friend,
And his friends are his master's. Then, for England:
It sets another bar 'twixt her and heresy.
It serves the Church, and Spain—mislikes not France.
For your fair sister-in-law—it may, let's hope,
Help to save her from the dark destinies
That dog all earthly crowns. And for King Henry—
Do you think Hercules loved Omphale
The better after he was caught a-spinning,
At *her* feet, in *her* gown, she lording it over him,
His club for sceptre, lion-skin for robe?
    Lady R. Yes, they must needs breed mischief.
    Chap.   Doubt not that!
Or think you I would take this pains to get them?
    Lady R. But ere you have the letters, what compact?
    Chap. The best—a common interest. We work both
At one mine, though our ends and tools may differ.
You hate Lady Anne Boleyn—I hate no one;
But can I love my master's aunt's worst foe?

And if the King must change his Queen for a younger,
Though he might not travel beyond the Boleyns,
It need not be for one of Boleyn blood.
I see you take me.
  Lady R. (*turning away in some confusion*) Nay.
 Chap. (*aside*) And I take you.

   Enter MARGARET WYATT (*Lady Lee*).

  Margt. Master Chapuis, Lady Anne Boleyn bids me
Greet you from her.
  Chap. (*respectfully*) My best thanks. A sweet lady!
But now we praised her—I and Lady Rochefort.
  Lady R. (*to* MARGT., *going*) Is Anne still in her chamber?
  Margt.   You will find her
In the west gallery.
  Lady R. (*aside*) Her chamber empty!
I have a key—of old——
  Margt.   Nor are *you*, sir,
The only one that waits Lord Wiltshire's coming.
Here stays the Duke of Norfolk, though he takes
Delay less patiently.
  Chap.   Send him to *me*.
Say that this sweet air's sovereign for impatience.
  Lady R. I leave you to the Duke.
  Chap.   I grieve to lose you,
But hope to see you yet, ere I ride hence.
  Lady R. I promise you. [*Exit* LADY R.
  Chap.   I know she'll keep her word—
For 'tis to serve her hate. Women would make
Our best Court-tools, were it not for their flaws
Of love and hate, that less mar the man's metal.
Ah, patience, patience! what a boon art thou!
A placid temper, that sleeps on the pillow
Of an elastic conscience! [*Enter* DUKE OF NORFOLK.
(CHAPUIS *bows low*.) My Lord Duke!
He wins that waits, when he gains speech of you.
  Duke. Beshrew the winning that is got by waiting!
It frets me. My way is a word and blow.
  Chap. 'Tis my own rule. Strike while the iron's hot!
That's why I love you English—frank and free.
No two ways round with you.
  Duke.   No—we go straight

At our leaps, to our ends, against our foes. (*Sits.*)
You come for speech of my good brother-in-law?
    Chap. (*demurely*) Before he starts for Italy.
    Duke.   Cock's blood!
Then you know?
    Chap.   Of his mission to my master?
Why, I have his instructions in my pocket.
    Duke. He knows not of it yet.
    Chap.   We are before him.
    Duke. How knew you?
    Chap. (*smiling*) Nay, if you knew how I knew,
How long should *I* know? May I know more yet?—
That you would not Lord Wiltshire had this mission?
    Duke. I think he holds his head too high already—
He and his.
    Chap. 'Tis, indeed, a marvellous rise!
Still he is Howard, by alliance.
    Duke (*impatiently*).   Zounds!
If Boleyn throw not Howard into shade,
As seems like. Father, son, trusted with missions!
Keepers of the King's secrets! and the daughter,
Keeper of the King's fancy!—soon to be
Made Marchioness of Pembroke; so the King
Told me but yesterday. Zounds! Who are *they*
To brave it thus? Nay, bid their house's head
Off-cap before their mushroom mightiness!
    Chap. As small men may indulge forecasts of great ones,
I have dared such a forecast of your Grace—
Or your house, rather. Pardon, my Lord Duke,
If I forecast too boldly. Thus it ran,
This dream of mine:—The good Queen was restored
To a wife's honour by the Pope's decree,
Backed by your help and that of all your following.
I saw your noble son, the Earl of Surrey,
That paragon of poets, star of knights,
Married to Lady Mary; and your daughter
Had honoured with her hand the Duke of Richmond,
The King's son, though it *be* wrong side the blanket.
So, let the lady's star or Duke's prevail,
There stood the House of Howard, sole in power,
On either side the throne.
    Duke.   Where were the Boleyns?
    Chap. In their fit place, below their house's head.

Duke. And where was Lady Anne?
Chap. I did not see her;
But I saw something covered with a pall—
It might have been a body, or a block.
Duke. Blocks are ill things to dream of. Hush! your
    fancy
Soars beyond mine.
Chap. A dream—an idle dream!
    [LADY ROCHEFORT *appears at one of the openings in
    the yew hedge, and shows* CHAPUIS *the packet for
    an instant, which he acknowledges by a slight move-
    ment.*
But dreams have often wrought their own fulfilment
With some nice guiding. (*Points off.*) Ha! my lord come
    back.
Duke. More of your dreams anon!
We'll go together.
Chap. Nay—I know my place—
After my Lord Duke!
    [*He bows; the Duke passes on. As* CHAPUIS, *fol-
    lowing, passes the yew hedge* LADY ROCHEFORT
    *puts the packet in his hand without a word. As he
    conceals it the Duke looks round for him, pausing.
    He repeats, with a deferential bow—*
After my Lord Duke. [*Exeunt.*
Lady R. (*coming forward*) None saw me—all's safe!
    Spite of haste and peril,
I could not hold from reading here and there.
If love e'er poured its molten soul in words,
Its hot breath smote my heart out of those letters.
At least she'll no more have the joy to read them!
In Chapuis' hands these burning lines may serve
For red-hot bars betwixt her and the Crown. (*Looks off.*)
So—she can face the air—with her fond poet
And saucy cousin! Good cause these, were't needed,
To rouse the lion's jealous mood. I'll watch,
And bide my time; I owe Chapuis that lesson.
                                        [*She retires*

Enter ANNE B., *leaning on* WYATT, *and accompanied by*
    WESTON *and* MARGARET. *She shows at first something
    of the langour of recent illness.*

Anne B. "Tis worth being sick to feel health come again,

Like a cool stream back to the pale, parched bed
That summer's fevered heats had left a-dust.
My trees and flowers smile welcome.
  Wyatt.   Shall I find them
A voice?
  Weston. Or let me speak for them, sweet cousin.
Two red lips can put more love in a breath
Than all the garden's green leaves in a lifetime.
  Anne B. (*playfully*) Nay, coz and poet, lute and lips
   are well,
But green leaves and fair flowers are better still!
  Wyatt. You'd have us leave you to them; that were hard.
  Weston. And after I have done a long month's penance,
Fasted from mirth and mocking, masque and may-game,
Not for my own sins, but to ease your sickness.
  Wyatt. And Master Smeaton, who had set my song,
And ridden, with his fellows, from the Court,
In hope to sing it to you at your levée.
Look, where he waits!—his soul strung like his viol.
  Anne B. And rode so far that I might hear his music!
He loves me well, I know. I would not grieve him.
  Wyatt. Then call him to your feet, and tell him so.
A gentle word from you is cordial to him.
He's high poetical, and, I believe,
Worships your shadow.
  Weston.   Let him worship *that*,
So he but leave the substance for his betters.
You spoil the knave.
  Anne B.   Knave! thou unmannered boy!
Because he's lowly born? The more behoves
That we do honour to Heaven's gift in him—
Music, that lifts the master of its magic
High, out of measure above state of kings.
(*To* WYATT.) I've beckoned him.
  Weston.   I can make music too,
As well as he. I'll show you. Ho! a lute there!
           [*Exit* WESTON.

    Enter SMEATON. *He kneels.*

  Anne B. Your hand, good Master Smeaton, not your
   knee.
Our friendship is too old for ceremony.
Now I'm abroad again, I hope that soon

We shall exchange instructions, you and I.
                            (*Re-enter* WESTON.)
I have a book of dances here which you
Must note. And we will try them—(*to* MARGARET)—shall
    we, Meg?—
In the great gallery.
    Weston.   I'll make one at *that!*
In legs I fear no rival.
    Smeaton.   'Tis my pride
To wait your pleasure.
    Anne B.   Now, your song.
        [WYATT *sings his own song,* '*Forget not yet,*' SMEATON,
            WESTON, *and Musicians accompanying with their
            lutes.*
Sweet words, and sweeter music. Thanks for both.
'Forget not *yet*'—nay, 'tis '.Forget not ever.'
    Smeaton. Would I had something more than my poor lute
To offer.
    Anne B. Nay, what could you give me better?
            [*She offers him her hand, which he kisses.*
    Smeaton (*as he retires, aside*). Only my life—and that's
too mean a gift.
Let me be humble, as my fortunes are.
    Anne B. (*to* WYATT) Be kind to him, my poet.
                    [*Exit* WYATT *after* SMEATON.
    Weston.   Meantime, *you*
Be kind to me. After six hours' riding
In muddy roads, with Norfolk's muddier wits
For entertainment—and he rating me
The whole way for my follies, as his wisdom
Is pleased to call them—I deserve some kindness.
Let me sing to you—laugh with you—unpack
My budget of Court scandal.
    Anne B.   Nay, I'll none on't.
Take him hence, Meg, and shut him with my uncle
For two good hours' more rating!
    Weston.   Mercy, cousin!
    Anne B. Go, Frank; in faith, I'm weary. When thou
        art wiser
I'll add my schooling to my Lord of Norfolk's.
    Weston. More penance. Wait till I get absolution!
                        (*She motions to 'him.*)
        Nay, an' I must, I must! I'll find Mark Smeaton,
And practise sarabands with my own shadow.   [*Exit.*

Re-enter WYATT.

Wyatt. I have made Smeaton happy.
Anne B. Thanks, my poet.
Wyatt. I'm not your poet now, but your nurse tender.
Anne B. The tenderest.
Wyatt. I bear the King's strict charge
To write him each day's red and white—meals, mendings—
How, yesterday, lady Anne picked a chicken—
To-day is dainty—turns up her fine nose
At aught more solid than a syllabub—
To-morrow—oh, joy!—looks forward to small ale.
But you've a duty presses—this first day
That sees you hail the sight of health's fair heaven—
That is, to pay your debts.
Ann B. My debts? Alas!
Methought I was near paying that great debt
Which wipes out all.
Wyatt. That payment is deferred,
Thank heaven! I mean your small debts—first, to me—
You owe me, sure, some set-off for the time
I've spent in sorrow, fears, and prayers for you.
A parlous inroad on a poet's sunshine!
My wife swears I'm an older man by years
Since you fell sick.
Anne B. What shall I give you? You've my love already.
Wyatt. The cinders the King's fire hath left of it.
Give me your tablets there, on whose fair leaves
As you write not my name, I may write yours;
Whose living virtue shall embalm my verse,
More than my verse it. Nay, I'll have the tablets!
Anne B. (*resisting*). You shall not! Nay, I tell thee they're a gift!
Wyatt. Gift to be given——
Anne B. Yes, but not taken thus.
Nay, I'll be angry! Wyatt, give them back.
Wyatt. The chain, too—fit wear for your slave.
[WYATT *detaches from* ANNE'S *girdle the tablets and chain which fastens them, kisses them, and places them in his bosom.*
Never! I'll consecrate the gift by penning
A sonnet in the first leaf. By *your* leaves! [*Exit* WYATT.

Anne B. I'm all too weak to struggle !
Margt. 'Twas in sport.
He'll give them back again.
Anne B. Nay, but he must—
They were my Henry's earliest gift. (*Lies back wearily.*)
  How far away
Seems all the past, across this blank of fever !
'Twas under this same tree, four years ago,
I met the King, after my flight to Mechlin.
He came and came—I learned to like his coming—
Look for it—live for it. Oh ! Margaret,
What woman had not laid her heart i' the dust
Before that princely presence ? And when passion
Bore his wild blood and lordly will beyond
Tide-mark of reverence, and I shrunk, and showed him
Passion with me must keep the pale of honour,
And all his lion-mood was tamed before me,
Who was I, not to love ? Though tongues cried shame—
Margt. Shame to the shamers ! (*Rises.*)
Anne B. Nay, why blame their hate ?
'Tis English pity for a hapless woman !
A wife unwived, a Queen discrowned, a heart
With all its treasures rifled ; at whose fire
The guest for whom 'twas lighted sits no more ;
Yet the fire's warm as ever—there's the sorrow.
Margaret, dost remember—'twas at Greenwich—
How one day, when I played at gleek with her,
Luck brought me still a king to take her queen ?
She sighed, and said to me, with her grave smile,
  [LADY ROCHEFORT *appears, listening.*
' 'Tis still your hap to stay upon a king—
Unlike the rest, you are for all or none.'
I glanced at Joan, who stood beside her chair——
Margt. And what said Joan ?
Anne B. She flushed and turned away.
Lady R. (*coming forward*) That she might leave the
  field for Lady Anne.
Anne B. Listening ?
Lady R. Your talk of those old Greenwich times
Tempted me. (*She kneels in mock penitence at* ANNE'S *feet.*)
  There—*confiteor* ! Shrive me, saint,
And set me penance.
Anne B. Hear first my confession.

Though love has been so long at end between them,
And their lives sundered—though the Church in England,
And both its Universities, have judged
The King's Grace free to woo and wed again—
Spite of the love my royal master shows me,—
Spite of my heart that love has overborne
And made his advocate—spite of ambition,
Which, you know, is my sin, or they speak false
That hate me and revile—throughout my sickness
A strong hand drew me back, a still small voice
Warned me, ' Forbear ! '
    Lady R.   And then came health again.
Hands filled with roses, and swept clear away
Those conscience-cobwebs, that are ever spun
In fever-troubled brains.
    Anne B.   My webs hang still !
Spite of this delicate air that breathes like balm,
This gold and blue, that pile their ceilèd pomp
Above my head,—were I a Queen indeed,
Could I have state like this ?—I feel a shiver
As if some chill, damp fear clung close about me.
    Margt. (*pointing off*) Here's shrift and solace both !
Look !
    Anne B. (*looking off, joyously*) Doctor Cranmer !

    Enter DOCTOR CRANMER.

    Anne B. (*rising and stretching out her hands towards him*)
Oh, joy ! And doubled that it comes unlooked for ! '
    Cran. (*drawing her to him tenderly and kissing her brow*)
My gentle pupil !
    Anne B.   Friends, your leaves awhile,
Till I lay bare my heart to *him* whose counsel
Still brought me cure and comfort.
    [MARGARET *and* LADY ROCHEFORT *retire.*
(*With passionate earnestness.*) Oh, kind tutor,
Tell me again—your strong mind nothing wavers
In its assurance—what has passed for marriage
Betwixt the King and Queen is null and void.
    Cran. Void from the first. Pope's Bull nor dispensation
(Had Popes the power they claim) can override
Heaven's will, revealed in word of Holy Writ—
' No brother's wife must share a brother's bed.'

Anne B. Oh, think how much hangs on your holy
    sanction!
For four years I have beat back the King's passion,
Holding my heart as a close-guarded fort,
With honour for its captain, nothing heeding
The traitor tenderness that whispered 'Yield.'
Then your ripe wisdom came, with terms of peace,
To which besieger and besieged might set
Their hands, with truth for witness, heaven for warrant.
    Cran. That warrant I avouch.   [*A bugle winded.*
    Anne B.   His bugle blast!
Shrill harbinger that rides the wind before him
To bid my heart prepare for its great guest!
    (*She stretches out her hand towards the sound.*)
My lord! my love! my King! my man of men!
    Cran. Bless thee, my child! I leave thee to thy joy.
                                        [*Exit* CRANMER.
    Anne B. (*looking off*) His horse's hoof makes music!
    How he hurls
Adown the hill and flashes through the stream,
Swift as a sunbeam, glorious as a god!
He flings him from the saddle. Look! he sees me!
He waves his greeting. Come! long wished-for, come!
Come to me—kiss me—clasp me in thine arms,
That they may buckler me from doubts and fears!

Enter HENRY *impetuously.* ANNE B. *goes eagerly to meet him, and half-sinks, half-throws herself into his arms. He caresses her ardently and fondly.*

    King. My poor pale darling! Yet the lovelier—
My damask rose transformed to a white lily!
Look up, and laugh into mine eyes with thine
As thou wert wont to do.
    Anne B. (*upon his breast*) No, let me lean
A little thus. I'm weak, and long for rest.
    King (*fondly gazing in her face*). This cruel sickness has
    been heavy on thee.
Oh, how I longed to lift its burthen off
And shift it to this big broad back of mine!
There's room, besides the public load it carries,
To bear my sweet Anne's suffering—and the will
To make it welcome too—e'en if a plague,

'Twere something of my sweetheart's. But all's now
O' the mending hand? (*Cheerfully.*)
    Anne B. (*faintly*)   Yes, all's well now—so well!
    King. But for Tom Wyatt thou had'st long since seen me
Lover and leech and nurse—in one great Harry!
    Anne B. Nay, thou hadst been too boisterous for a nurse—
Good Doctor Butts had bid thee from my chamber.
    King. I'd have shown him a short cut through the casement,
And taxed his surgery for his own bones.
But now I have thee back from death's dark door
I will not let thee go again.
    Anne B.   So held,
It seems as if no ill could come to me!
    King. These weary weeks of suffering for thee
Have been yet wearier for me.
    Anne B.   My own!
    King. 'Twixt hope deferred, love thwarted, joy delayed,
Life lopped in twain by severance of hands
That should have followed hearts, these years ago——
    Anne B. We must be patient.
    King.   Patient! By the mass!
(*Fondling her hand in his.*) Had man or angel told me this small hand
Had held me at the barriers six long years,
Angel or man, he would have had the lie
Deep in his throat. But patience hath its term.
This last month's fear of losing thee hath shown me
I cannot live without thee. My sweet Anne!
Mock not me nor thyself with more delays.
    Anne B. Thou art not free in law, though free in conscience.
    King. Show me the law that dares to cross my will!
    Anne B. The Queen lives!
    King.   Is to me as one that lives not.
Betwixt us is a gulf of sin and sorrow,
A barrier of graves. I have no Queen,
Until thou share with me my bed and throne.
    Anne B. But tarry sentence!
    King.   Though not yet awarded,
The Courts have judgment ready of 'no marriage.'
    Anne B. The Papal Courts of Rome?

King. Who spoke of Rome?
We've had enough of Papal japes and jugglings,—
'Tis English Courts should pass on English cases.
Cranmer has taught me that. His forthright counsel
Hath rid me of much cumber, packed and piled
By Rome's friends—thy foes—'twixt thee and the crown——
    Anne B. Ah, me! the crown! (*Presses her hands to her eyes.*)
    King. Let not that frighten thee,
With me at hand to lean on.
    Anne B. From afar
It beamed so bright and dazzling! But seen near——
I shudder at the thought; shall I not sink
Under the very thing?
    King. With me to stay thee?
    Anne B. Alas, poor Queen!
    King. 'Twere best not think of her.
    Anne B. Aye, best—if so it might be. Then the people
Cry out upon me.
    King. Let's see if a halter
Stop not the foul knaves' throats.
    Anne B. Nay, we'll no halters,
Scaffolds, or pillories, or gibbets darkening
The up-hill road I climb, that seems more steep
Each step I take. It is not yet too late
For pausing. Think, my lord, if you repent,
There's no harm done—'tis but to cast me from you,
To look back on a four years' golden dream—
So better than to fling me off hereafter
In hate, the bitterer that it once was love.
    King. Sweetheart, no more of that; thou'dst angered me,
Could I be angry with thee. Not a word!
The love thy coyness has held pent so long
Comes sweeping in, breaking all bars and bounds,
Flooding my soul deep with its soundless sea.
Mine as thou art by choice, thou shalt be mine
By Church and Courts! I'm King, and I command them;
Or I will know the reason. 'Tis for law
To follow love; love waits not upon law—
And, least, a royal love, like thine and mine.
    Anne B. Oh, clasp me not so closely!
    King (*seizing her hand*). Give me up
This ring, that binds thee to me for my wife.

Nay, I will have it. (*Wrests the ring from her hand.*)
    Anne B.   I am all too weak—
Somewhat your strength—more, my own love—o'erbears me.
Take me, my lord—do with me as you will ;
But love me ever, as you love me now !

ACT-DROP.

ACT III.

(TIME : 1533.)

SCENE.—*Room in Greenwich Palace. Painted roof, with arched timbers. State chair at the back. Doors* R. *and* L. *with tapestry pictures, showing rooms beyond. Two windows* R. *A fireplace opposite doors* R. *and* L. 1 E.'S. *Table under the windows. Chairs, cabinets, etc.* MADGE SHELTON *and* JANE SEYMOUR *near the fireplace, embroidering a pennon.*

  Madge. Three letters yet, and the jousts fixed to-morrow.
His Grace hates waiting—we must ply our needles.
  Jane S. How runs the legend ?
  Madge.   French—*Oncques ne désarde.*
  Jane S. In English, please. I'm a poor Wiltshire wench,
And know no French.
  Madge.   ' I never cease from burning.'
  Jane S. Poor King !
  Madge.   Rich King, with so much to burn in him !
  Jane S. What's the device on't ?
  Madge.   An asbestos lamp.
  Jane S. (*simply*) As——
  Madge.   Bestos.
  Jane S. (*in the same tone*). Lo, you now ! What is asbestos?
  Madge. A stone that's always burning and ne'er burnt—
Like my poor heart.
  Jane S.   Is that a stone ?
  Madge.   The men
Have done their best to harden it to one.
  Jane S. Let's hope 'twill soften now Sir Henry Norris
Has set light to it.
  Madge.   Hold thy saucy tongue !
  Jane S. Or is't her Grace's cousin, Francis Weston,
The new Knight of the Bath ?

Madge.   Fair Mistress Seymour,
Your service is of too short date to warrant
Such freedom; you, too, so prim and precise
Still sitting mumchance—you must pry into
The secrets of your elders—I mean, betters.
   Jane S. I cry you mercy; but indeed I knew not
It was a secret, so plain as you showed it.
In Wiltshire we keep hid what we want hidden.
   Madge. In Wiltshire, if they chid what they want chidden,
You would have been well whipped for sauciness.
   Jane S. Ah, none can whip me now I'm Maid of Honour.
My father bade me bear myself discreetly.
   Madge. Well said: discretion is a virtue always,
And worth the more at Court, it is so rare.
Methinks you'll rise.
   Jane S.   Why not? Queen Anne has risen
From just such place as mine.
   Madge.   Aye, so she has;
But 'twas not by discretion.
   Jane S.   How was't, then?
   Madge. Ask her, Discretion, and see what she answers.
   Jane S. But you, who know the Court and served
      Queen Katherine,
Think you Queen Anne is queen indeed?
   Madge.   In deed?
   Jane S. The Grey Friars here still preach that 'tis no
      marriage.
   Madge. They are traitorous rogues!
   Jane S.   But I heard Father Peto
Prove it from his own pulpit.
   Madge.   Did you so?
If you lend treason ear, 'twere more discreet
To keep it to yourself.
   Jane S.   Thanks for the counsel.
I will do so.
   Madge. And therein will do well.
You're a shrewd wench.
   Jane S.   You mean a simple one.
   Madge. Still waters run the deepest.
   Jane S.   That's a saw
In Wiltshire too.
   Madge.   More than a saw—a truth
That thou wilt one day put to proof, or much

I do misread that deep dark eye of thine—
Like a still pool, that may hide in its depths
More than folk wot of.
  Jane S.   Now you are mocking me,
Because I'm country born and new to Court.
But if the King laugh with the Maids of Honour,
What should they do?
  Madge.   That's left to their discretion.
Thus far the King laughs only with the Queen—
An eight months' honeymoon, and not tired yet!
Hush! here's grave company.

    Enter NORFOLK *and* CHAPUIS.

  Norf.   Your servants both!
  Chap. Sweet ladies, may we ask your entertainment,
Until their Graces be returned?
  Madge.   I heard
The mort awhile ago—a sign the hunters
Will not be long. Please you to wait the while.
      [MADGE *and* JANE S. *retire up.*
  Chap. (*coming forward with* NORFOLK) She might have
    been content with her Hart Royal.
She'll scarce find fatter haunch; and, as for horns—
Were scandal truth, they'd be ten-tined already.
  Norf. Tush! idle talk. Your Boleyns are too wary
To give hate handle.
  Chap.   That's the worst of her.
Ere this I had hoped to have caught her tripping—
But still she disappoints me.
  Norf.   A sly baggage!
Ah, Master Envoy, we were foully out
At Hever, when you dreamed—'tis two years now.
  Chap. Dreams may come truer for their slow fulfilment.
But grant your niece such queen as law can make her——
  Norf. Law! a fig's end! as love can make her, man!
And she's a dainty piece of womanhood,
As saucy as she is. That was a crowning!
I've seen some shows in my time—but her progress
From Greenwich by the river, and, next day,
Through the throng'd City's length, from Tower to Abbey—
One pageant—and my niece the sun of all!
I know few love her, but I heard, that day,

Curses pass into blessings, as she rode
Proud as a queen, yet gracious as an angel.
 Chap. My Lord of Norfolk, too, among her slaves!
 Norf. My Lord of Norfolk is no woman's slave,
Nor man's, but he knows beauty when he sees it,
As he does manhood. The King doats on her.
 Chap. And let him doat. 'Tis fires of straw blaze
  fiercest,
And burn out fastest. What to-day is doating
May be disgust to-morrow. Then the lady
Is of too free speech, and too skipping spirit,
For the nice steering that these troubled times
Ask to clear shoal and sand.
 Norf.   You politicians,
You look so far and wide!
 Chap.   What need to look
Farther than Greenwich? A young, bright, proud lady,
Lifted beyond her breeding, and so dizzy,
Whose very innocencies may be snares.
Her lord a King who knows no will but one,
And whose will must have way; of jealous mood,
And quick to change in love, as hot to burn—
If here be not matter enough for mischief,
I never made it—I mean, saw it made.
 Norf. Well, grant her reign a short one.
 Chap.   Make it so.
You keep your house and following well in hand,
Leave me to lodge the deer and lay the hounds
Upon her slot. Here comes one of my prickers!

Enter LADY ROCHEFORT. *Speaks to* MADGE *and* JANE S.,
  who retire.

 Lady R. (*seeing* LORD N. *and* CHAPUIS) My lord,
  Messire Chapuis. (*Saluting.*)
 Chap.   We wait their Graces.
 Lady R. Their hunting should be over.
 Norf.   I'll go meet
The hunters in the park. Good day, fair lady. [*Exit.*
 Chap. A blunt, bluff, brave, beef-witted lord as e'er
Ran his head at a wall or in a springe
Set by his betters in the way of wit.
No, give me ladies for the pretty game
Of policy. (*Bowing to* LADY R.)

Lady R. Do you not sometimes fear
They may tire of the game, deeming the stakes
Scarce worth the time and tricks it takes to win them?
    Chap. With ladies I do sometimes fear such folly,
And so set my she-players' stakes so high
They dare not quit the game, lest they should leave
Their heads behind them.
    Lady R. Sir, is this a threat?
    Chap. Only a warning. Well, how goes our game?
    Lady R. Ours?
    Chap. Ours. Are we not partners, you and I?
Nay, you and my great master, Charles the Wise?
    Lady R. I'm sick of looking on their happiness.
    Chap. The more need you should do your best to mar it.
Have you no likely root of treason yet?
Or even scandal? Fie! in this gay Court,
They should sprout thick as nettles in a graveyard.
Whom is she private with? Who comes about her,
In her sad moods or gay? How does she spend
Her leisure?

    Enter MARK SMEATON.

    Lady R. What's your pleasure, Master Smeaton?
    Smeaton. Her Grace bade me attend her in her chamber.
    Lady R. For what?
    Smeaton. Her lesson on the virginals.
    Lady R. You come too soon; the Queen is still afield.
    Smeaton (aside). 'Tis my heart's hunger that forestalls the hour.
    Chap. (aside) Bid to her chamber! He's a proper man.
(*To* SMEATON.) You have long taught her Grace?
    Smeaton. With intermission,
Since first she came to Court.
    Chap. So—her old master?
If that word fit the master of a pupil
So near in age. Her Grace is an apt pupil?
    Smeaton. She is in that, as all, a mistress born;
Whom to show is to teach, so quick she takes
All knowledge in.
    Chap. Her teacher should be happy
In such a scholar.
    Smeaton. Yes, he should be happy;
But there is happiness, as there is honour,

Too high for those whose low estate it mocks;
As the sun's smile but makes more mean the hovel,
Whose thatch it kindles into gold.
  Chap.   A trope!
Poet as well as lutist. Does her Grace
Take lessons of you in the *gaie science*,
As well as on the virginals?
  Smeaton.   Your pardon.
Sir Thomas Wyatt is her Grace's poet;
I am but her musician (*aside, and going up*), all whose
  music
Is in her voice! Her bondslave, not her master.
(*To* LADY R.) When her Grace comes say I attend her
  pleasure.   [*Exit.*
  Chap. (*to* LADY R.) One root of scandal there, and of
    rare promise!
I recommend it to your careful nursing. [*A fanfare.*
Here come their Graces—King Jove and Queen Dian!
Whose crescent waxes still—until it wanes!

Enter KING, QUEEN, NORFOLK, NORRIS, WESTON, BRERE-
 TON, *and* MARGARET (*Lady Lee*), *as from hunting:*
 MADGE SHELTON *and* JANE SEYMOUR *in attendance.*

  King. A lusty hart! an inch fat on the brisket.
And how he stood, till my Maid Marian here
Yerked him between the ribs!
  Norris.   I never saw
A fairer shot.
  King. When Harry Norris praises
Hawk's flight or bow's shot it is praise indeed!
So prize it, sweetheart.
(*To* MADGE *and* JANE S.) How now, merry maidens?
Why hunt not you with us? (*To* JANE S.) Here's a
  demoiselle
Has drawn a bow before, or I mistake
The breeding Sir John Seymour gives his daughters
Down at Wolf Hall. How say you, Mistress Jane?
  Jane S. So please you, my good father had me taught
To shoot; but I'm so fearful.
  King.   We must teach thee.
'Tis but to pattern by your mistress here—
Aim as she aims, and loose shaft as she looses.
  Anne B. I'll make a joy to teach her all I know.

Jane S. I thank your Grace. I'll do my best to learn.
  King. But, sweetheart, how shall we bestow the
    haunches?
She that brought down the deer should part the venison.
  Anne B. One to my good Archbishop, and the other,
If he'll accept it of his duteous niece,
For my kind uncle Norfolk here.
  King. Who owes thee
A greater gift. Nay, tell it him thyself.
  Anne B. My gracious lord is pleased, of his high favour,
To seal the contract of the Duke of Richmond
To your fair daughter, Mary.
  Norf. My best thanks
To his Grace and to you are all too poor.
(*Aside.*) Howards have wedded royal blood ere this.
    [*While he is speaking the* KING *pays a compliment
      aside to* JANE SEYMOUR, *who laughs.*
  Chap. (*aside to* NORFOLK) What of my dream?
  King. Messire Chapuis,
I'm glad to see you, and yet to say 'glad'——
  Chap. Is to take my word in your royal mouth.
'Tis my part to be glad when your Grace deigns
To see his humble servant.
  King. We'd be private.
    (*All are retiring; he stops the* QUEEN.)
Nay, go not thou, Anne; all our counsel lies
In thy wise ear.
  Anne B. If love gave counsel wisdom,
Your Highness should need none but mine. Alas!
That my wit equals not my will to serve you!
  King. Enough of humbleness. Look you, Messire,
You are close and crafty, like the prince you serve;
But think not all your closeness and your craft
Can mask the foul game you and he are playing
Here in our realm. You steel to stubbornness
The Princess Dowager, and the Lady Mary,
Styling *her* Queen from whom our Parliament
Hath stripped the title; hearten our proud Bishops
And saucy friars in their insolence
To this our most dear Queen and wedded wife.
You stomach-up the Pope until he dares
Threaten with excommunication us,
Our Queen and realm! Let him look to himself,

Or he may find the thin rope cut that still
Holds 'twixt St. Peter's bark and the Great Harry.
You spur on Scotland to invade our Marches;
Find arms and brains for Irish rebeldom;
And link our peevish nobles, North and South,
With her they dare call Queen. I give you warning
Out of your fine-spun cobweb threads of treason
I'll yet weave rope of strength enough to halter
Your friends—who knows?—yourself, perhaps.
  Chap.   An Envoy!
  King. When Envoys turn to traitors let them look,
For traitor's shrift. Ha! sweetheart, said I well?
  Anne B. Most well, my lord—like a right English King!
Messire Chapuis, wise as he is, can scarce
Read English weather-signs with English eyes.
But I am English born, and this I tell him:
Let but the Pope take one step more along
The road his Emperor points, and England's Church
Owns no more of allegiance to the Pope,
Than England's realm doth to the King of Spain.
'Tis but a woman's word, but 'tis the truth!
  Chap. Your Graces find me dumb for mere amazement!
I plot! I risk my master's name in treasons,
Or my own neck! Nay, then, let me take hence
My poor self from a Court where honesty
Is misread knavery, and simple faith
Judged for deceit. So I crave leave to leave you.
           [*Exit, bowing low.*
  King. A murrain go with him! A smooth-faced knave!
  Anne B. A rogue in grain, or I know nought of men.
  King. And who should know them better? Having witched
So many, and me first?
  Anne B.   And last, my lord!
  King. But he shall find us two more than a match
For lawyers' tricks and Savoy suppleness.
To-morrow I send Wyatt to his master.
He knows my mind—is charged to speak it soundly.
He comes for last instructions.
  Anne B.   So I leave you.
I'm glad my poet should serve for your Envoy.
  King. More than thy poet, sweetheart, or report
Wrongs him.

Anne B. Whose?

King. Suffolk's and a certain lady's.

Anne B. My Lord of Suffolk loves not me, nor Wyatt.

King. True, but the lady speaks from Hever days,
When you were sick, and Wyatt your nurse-tender.

Anne B. That he might pass between you and your Anne.
We both should love him better that he links
Our lives in memory of that happy time.
And so I leave you to transform my poet
Into a politician—a vile change!
True, poetry is feigning, and so's policy,
But of a baser sort. Look, here he comes. [*Exit* ANNE B.

King. Her poet! Humph! (*Looking off.*) She stays to toy with him!
Smiles! Hands exchanged! She rates his sonneting
Higher than mine. What need she tell me that?

Enter WYATT.

Ha, Wyatt!
I have instructions for thee.

Wyatt. Let your Grace
Dictate, and I will write. (*Taking out* ANNE'S *tablets.*)

King. What hast thou there?

Wyatt. My tablets.

King (*aside*). Ha! the tablets that I gave her
At Hever, ere her sickness.

Wyatt. I am ready
To write when it shall please you give me words.

King. You have a dainty case of tablets there,
And a fair chain.

Wyatt. Poets are curious
In such toys.

King. Show me. (*Takes the tablets.*) If I asked them of thee?
Perchance they'll bring some inspiration with them—
Blossom in verse as good as thine, or make
My lady think it so. Thou'lt give me them?

Wyatt. Good your Grace, pardon me. They are a token,
And clasp more memories than I care to part with.

King. A lady's gage? Ha! If you may not give,
You may, without *lèse tendresse,* lend them me.

I have something in my mind that I would write
Rather than dictate. So—let me consider.
          (*Waives back* WYATT, *who retires respectfully.*)
(*Aside.*) The token I gave her she hath given him!
Now, by St. George! this asks to be explained.
(*To* WYATT.) No more now; I will see thee after dinner.
I would con further what I have to tell thee.
                    [*Exit* KING, *moodily*.
  Wyatt. The King is in his moods. He's dangerous
When his lip whitens. What has moved him thus?
A light! Those tablets! Fool that I have been!
Is old love growing cold love that it calls
On jealousy to heat it hot again,
Or burn it into ashes? So the storm
Break all on me and spare her innocence!

       Enter SIR WILLIAM KINGSTON.

  Kingston. How now, Tom? I must clap thee on the shoulder.
  Wyatt. Arrested! The blow's sudden. To the Tower?
  Kingston. But to thy chamber. Tush! the wind will change—
This is some autumn humour in the King.
We'll have Butts let him blood. Meanwhile, thy sword.
  Wyatt (*aside*). Could I but warn the Queen! Ah, Lady Rochefort!   [*Enter* LADY ROCHEFORT.
(*To* KINGSTON.) One word alone with her—no treason.
  Kingston. Nay, I'm deaf.
  Wyatt (*rapidly, to* LADY R.) The King has ta'en my tablets—it mislikes him:
See that the Queen's advised of my arrest.
  Lady R. (*aside*) The match is fired—I laid the powder ready.
Mislikes him, doth it? It mislikes not me.
          [*Exeunt severally* LADY R. *and* WYATT, *attended by* KINGSTON.

Enter, by D. *in* F., MADGE SHELTON, *pursued by* WESTON, *who is trying to kiss her, she coquettishly resisting.*

  Madge. Hands off!
  Weston.   Nay, not till lips are on!
  Madge.   I'll scream!

'Twas Lady Rochefort! Had her lynx-eye seen you,
Here were old scandal.
    Weston.   Tut; she's jealous of thee.
    Madge. I tell thee, Frank—nay, cry you mercy, Sir—
Fresh from your Bath—Sir Francis Weston, Knight—
I'll none of your light suit.
    Weston.   I'd make it heavier.
    Madge. I've good as promised Norris. He's your friend!
    Weston. And when did friend's suit stand a bar to
        friend?
The loves of friends are interchangeable,
As are their purses, horses——
    Madge.   The poor loves
Are worse used of the three. You spend the purses,
But they can be replaced; you lame the horses:
The farrier mends them; but, for the poor hearts.
You take and break them. Hearts can't be put back
Like purse in pouch, or patched, like horses' knees.
Besides, you are contract to Mary Cheyney.——
    Weston. Hang contracts! They are mortal foes to love.
If ever man loved thee, until contracted,
I was that man. I swear it by this kiss. (*A struggle.*)

    Enter ANNE B., *attended by* LADY ROCHEFORT.

    Anne B. What madcaps have we here! How now,
        good cousins?
This is too warm for cousinhood! Fie, Madge!
With a good man's heart—a man to be proud of,
Like Harry Norris—waiting on thy word!
Kissing in corners like a light-o'-love!
And you, Frank Weston! Kinsfolk as we are,
I'll no such rake-hell doings where I come.
    Weston. Nay, but, fair cousin——
    Anne B.   Spare your cousining.
Was it for this I named you of the knights
Dubbed at my coronation? A true knight
Owes, before all, pure faith to plighted word,
And yours is Mary Cheyney's. Keep your lips
For her that claims your love. Ill fall the one
That plays false to the other!
    Weston.   Nay, but, cousin——
    Anne B. Cousin again! Best know your place and
        mine!

Weston. Were't love that drew me, there's one in your
 house
Whom I love more than Madge or Mary either.
 Anne B. Who may that be?
 Weston. Even your gracious self.
 Anne B. Boy as you are! this passes insolence!
Men's heads have fallen for less. This once I spare thee.
But such another word, and Kingston serves thee
As usher to the Tower. What have I done
That thou should'st so forget my place and honour,
The bond of blood, the favour I have shown thee,
To fling words in my face that make my cheek
Flame as a blow had stung it? But that kinship
And pity hold, thou'dst twined thy rope to-day!
Hence! nor dare show thyself here in our presence,
Till thou art summoned.
(*He makes a gesture of deprecation.*) Hence! [*Exit* WESTON.
 And, Madge, be wiser.
Good cousin, seest thou not how thick my path
Is set with pitfalls? Add not thou to them.
I'd not be harsh on young light hearts, Heaven knows.
Mine own is not so old nor yet so heavy
But it loves harmless mirth. Go. For this folly
I'm sorry more than angry. Think of Norris,
And think of me that have so much to think on.
 Madge. Forgive me, gracious Queen and loving cousin!
 [*She throws herself at* ANNE'S *feet, who kisses and
 raises her. Exit* MADGE.
 Lady R. (*aside, while this is going on*) The nettles grow
 apace that Chapuis spoke of—
I see them springing as I watch for them.
 Anne B. I must see Norris urged to speedy close
Of his contract with Madge, or there'll be quarrel
'Twixt him and Weston.
Mine eyes the loadstar of these popinjays!
They have enough to do to guide my lord—
So in these eyes he seek his loadstar still.

 Enter KING.

 King (*to* LADY R.). How now? Your leave, good mistress, for awhile.
Who was't went hence by the great gallery?
 Anne B. Sir Francis Weston.

King. He's not of thy chamber,
If he's of mine.
　　Anne B. Where there are maids in waiting
Gentlemen of the Chamber still will buzz.
　　King. Nor for maids' lips alone—their mistress's
Sometimes.
　　Anne B. My lord?
　　King. What of my lord, my lady?
Know you these tablets? (*Takes them out.*)
　　Anne B. (*joyously*). Now, a blessing on them!
And you that gave them first, and bring them now!
Know I those tablets? Why, they are the same
You gave me—almost your first gift—at Hever.
Wyatt in sport once snatched them from my girdle.
I struggled—I was still weak from my sickness—
He took them, kept them, would not give them back
For all my prayers and wrath—for I was wroth,
And chid him roundly. Then came the glad time
When he that gave me these gave me himself,
And the great gift drove out the memory
Of the lost lesser gift. But now I have them
Again, where is the man shall take them from me?
　　King (*aside*) Could aught but truth speak so in voice
　　　and eyes?
　　Anne B. But say, how came you by them?
　　King. From the thief,
As he wrote in them.
　　Anne B. And you challenged them?
　　King. Yes.
　　Anne B. And he owned the theft?
　　King. Not quite the theft.
He said they were a token——
　　Anne B. Of his sauciness
And strength—naught other.
　　King. I believe it, sweetheart! (*Kisses her.*)
(*Aside.*) I am a jealous fool!
Farewell, my own good wife. And when I doubt thee,
Why, then I'll doubt myself and that I love thee! [*Exit.*
　　Anne B. Doubt me! Alas! where doubt comes farewell
　　　love! [*Re-enter* LADY ROCHEFORT.
Joan, did'st observe my lord's look as he entered?
　　Lady R. 'Twas lowering, as I've seen it oft of late.
　　Anne B. Methinks 'tis these Church troubles that disturb
　　　him. [*Cries without,* 'Follow!' 'Seize him!'

Anne B. Go, see what means this stir i' the outer ward.
[*As* LADY R. *approaches the door a shot is heard.* CONSTANTINE *rushes in, disordered, and throws himself at the* QUEEN's *feet, followed by Apparitor and Guards in pursuit.*
Constan. Save me, your Grace!
Anne B. Back, you unmannered knaves!
(*To* CONSTANTINE.) What's this? Who art thou? Have no fear, man—speak!
Appar. Your Grace, I am the officer——
Anne B.   Peace, sirrah!
I bade him speak.
Constan.   My name is Constantine—
Once of Queen's College, Oxford: there a hearer
Of blessed Father Bilney—then a fleer
From fire and fagot—settled, late, in Antwerp——
Anne B. One of the fellowship of Master Tyndal?
Constan. Even so, madam. Sent by him to spread
His books in England—struggling on the edge
'Twixt light and darkness.
Appar.   Your Grace hears—he owns
His cursed heresy.
Anne B. Whose knave art thou?
Appar. A sworn apparitor of my Lord Bishop——
Anne B. Of London? I know Stokesley's heavy hand
On all who spread the light of Tyndal's torch.
Appar. We took this rogue in the act of sowing heresy—
I've here his pack of books prohibited. (*Producing a pack of books.*)
Anne B. Give me. (*Apparitor gives her book.*)
(*Reads title.*) 'The Books of Moses, Englished.'
Appar. Horrible! (*Gives another.*)
Anne B. (*looking at it*) 'The New Testament in English.'
Appar. Most horrible! Your Grace, they stand condemned
In my Lord Bishop's Court Diocesan,
And all that read and all that sell or spread them
Doomed—books and men alike—to fire and fagot.
Anne B. Thou art a bold-faced rogue. 'Like man,' they say,
'Like master.' Pity of poor souls that fall

Into thy Bishop's claws, till they are clipped.
'Tis time we saw to that—I and good Cranmer.
    Appar. Your Grace, how may I answer to my lord?
    Anne B. Send him to me, and I will answer for thee.
                      [*Exeunt Apparitor and Guards.*
(*To* CONSTANTINE.) For thee, my friend, stay here—I will
    protect thee.
    Constan. May Heaven still grant you life to guard the
    truth!
    Anne B. And is there so much light in this poor land
The Church should make it less? Or they that love
That which the Church is set to guard—the truth?
So help me Heaven! if I live long enough,
No house, wide England through, from hall to hovel,
But shall have God's Word in our English tongue—
The best book in the scholar's library—
The one book, if but one, i' the peasant's cottage.
    Lady R. (*announcing*) My Lord Archbishop!

              Enter CRANMER.

    Anne B. My good Cranmer, welcome!
I have not seen thee since thy putting on
The dignity thou fought'st hard to avoid
As most to reach. This visit—was't for me?
    Cranmer. For the King and your Grace. But first, for
    you.
'Twere well your Grace should know how on all sides
Those of the royal blood—Brandons and Poles,
Salisburys and Exeters—are bound and banded
For your undoing. How your uncle Norfolk,
Who works for his own house, would undermine you—
How the close Emperor and his puppet Pope
Point the black battery of their preaching friars,
The fears of your own Bishops, for your ruin—
How scarce a pulpit but rings 'Out on you'
For heretic and—worse—— (*He pauses.*)
    Anne B.   Nay, speak it plain.
    Cran. As the King's concubine!
    Anne B. (*after a struggle to master her feelings*) I thank
    thee, Cranmer,
For showing me their worst. Now let me show thee

What shall confront this worst, and wrestle with it,
And overthrow it, if there's force in faith
And time and truth.   That I'm no concubine
I have the warranty of thine assurance,
And mine own conscience.   That I am Queen
I'll show by a Queen's mettle.   They shall prove it
That dare assail my place upon the throne,
Or in my husband's heart—that still is mine !
Save that, and thee, I stand at guard—alone.
Father and brother both across the sea—
Knowing mine enemies, but not my friends.
I would have given them love for love.   Let's see
If I play not their game of hate for hate,
And then try which is sharpest, theirs or mine.
Now to the King.

ACT-DROP.

ACT IV.

ON MAYDAY.

SCENE.—*The Park at Greenwich on Mayday, with the hawthorns in blossom and the chestnuts in flower.   Trees and thickets, practicable.* JANE SEYMOUR *and* MADGE SHELTON *discovered gathering may.*

Madge.   This Maying's but dull sport without a gallant.
Jane S.   Look ! where one walks this way.
Madge.   I see him—Norris !
Let's make as if we saw him not.   He comes
To urge his suit on me.
      Jane S.   Since the Queen caught thee
At corner-kissing with her cousin Weston
She would have Master Norris make an end
Of all delays, by bond of Church and ring.
      Madge.   E'en so.   She wants me wed, the more the pity !
      Jane S.   Yes, better have two lovers than one husband.
Wooed, you rule both, laugh at both, set both tasks ;
Wed, one of them does all the three with you.
She should know love and marriage.
      Madge.   Yes, poor lady !
What they are like in, and wherein they differ.

Jane S. They say she would but couple thee and Norris
To keep him nearer to herself.
 Madge.   *They say?*
Who say? The foul mouths of still fouler scandals.
Heed'st thou such filth?
 Jane S.   A girl can't shut her ears;
And if the King himself repeat these tales?
 Madge. To whom? To thee?
 Jane S. (*laughing low*) A girl *can* shut her mouth.
 Madge. The time may come tongues will be hard on thee,
For thine own sake, wench, if not for the Queen's.
Be not too private with the King, still less
Too public.
 Jane S. Leave my wits to keep my honour.
 Madge. There's talk of thee already with his Highness.
 Jane S. Heed'st thou such trash?
 Madge.   They say he laughs with thee.
 Jane S. Who say? The foul mouths of still fouler scandals.
Poor King! with one wife dead, the other sick.—
I call her wife; the new Act makes it treason
To call her otherwise. Is't wonderful
If he should seek for smiles on fresher lips?
Trust me to keep myself this side the wall
Of maiden modesty and safe discretion.
 Madge. Trust thee? See Norris has plucked up a heart.
He comes this way.
 Jane S.   Let not me spoil your sport,
Though you are all so eager to mar mine!
         (*Runs behind a tree.*)

     Enter NORRIS.

 Norris. Fair Mistress Madge, may a blunt suitor seek
Plain answer to plain question? Will you have me?
 Madge. For partner in to-morrow's cinq-a-pace?
 Norris. Partner for life!
 Madge.   So bold! Frank Weston told me
You were the challenger in the lists to-morrow.
That should be enough daring for one bout.
 Norris. Be grave for once. My favour with the King

Forbids my deeming this my quest o'er-bold,
Even if your priceless graces be its goal !
'Tis true I am a widower.
    Madge.   Lo you there !
See you not how unfair that makes our tilt?
You have unhorsed one woman's will already:
I've still to learn how to bear down a husband.
    Norris. I have the Queen's voice for my suit.
    Madge.   Poor Queen !
Has her own married venture been so happy,
She would send others the same doubtful voyage?
    Norris. Let me but call thee wife, sweet Madge, we'll make
An argument for marriage to outweigh
All ill-starred couples—Kings or Lords or Commoners !
Come, there's the sweetest honeysuckle bank
Beyond that brake.   (*Drawing her off.*)
    Madge.   Defend me, woman's wit !
Woman's will grows so weak this soft spring weather.
                                          [*Exeunt* R.
    Jane S. (*peeping out*) They're safe. (*Distant chime. She comes forward.*)
The half-hour's chime from the Greyfriars.
He knows this is my breathing-time of day,
And this the chestnut walk I most delight in.
If the King love it too this fresh May morning
What wonder? And what harm? Let Mistress Madge
Say what she will, now Lady Anne grows peevish,
And poor Queen Katherine rests at Peterboro',
The King must seek some solace in his sorrow.
The Lady Mary says as much herself.
How kind her letters are ! She loves me well.
The King ! I need not see him—he sees me.

                Enter KING.

    King. Ha, pretty mistress, you are late a-maying ;
May-blossoms should be plucked with the dew on them,
Fresh as your lips, and fragrant as their breathing.
    Jane S. Your Grace is pleased to jest.
    King.   You ne'er said truer.
My grace is pleased to jest. But little jesting
He has now, what with mad nuns, stiff-necked priests,
Pope's threats, and Parliaments, and White Rose plots !

Jane S. I grieve at all that grieves you.
King. Joy forbid!
Or grief would leave thy red lips robbed of smiles;
And 'tis for smiles I come to thee. For poutings,
Pale cheeks, and heavy looks, and sick-room qualms,
These the Queen gives me, and to spare.
Jane S. Poor lady!
She is so good, pity she's not more merry.
King. 'Blessed the poor in spirit,' say her chaplains.
I hear enough of her good works, Heaven knows!
Her shirt and smock-making, help to poor scholars
And craftsmen, ancient folks, widows and orphans.
What a plague! If poor spirits must be poor
In buxomness and health and lustihood,
Give me my wealth of these, and leave poor spirits
To cut out smocks and rock girl babies' cradles.
Jane S. What pity the Princess was a princess!
King (*impatiently*) Come, shall we see my hawks?
Or shall we try
A flight-shot at the butts? Thou know'st I promised
To make thee a Maid Marian, as befits
Mayday, and Maypole revels, and May garlands,
Wherein there blooms no flower fresh as thy cheeks,
No bud so tempting as those cherry lips.
Jane S. Nay, these are flowers to look at, not to gather.
King. Then you should hide them in a velvet vizor.
But once seen, 'tis too late—not if you sconced
Your winsome face in steel instead of sammet.
Come, let me go a-maying in this garden
Of spring delights. (*Kissing her.*)
Jane S. Fie, you unset my hood,
And chafe my poor cheek with your great rough beard.
Why wear it you so long?
King. Since those curst Friars,
Haughton and his mad monk o' the Charter House,
Went to the scaffold, I've a vow to wear it.
Jane S. A penance?
King. Maybe. But enough of that.
I'm but a rough-faced fellow at the best.
Jane S. Nay, I hate smooth-chinned men—that is, I think
That I should hate—but what can a girl know
Who, were't not for her father and her brothers,
Has all to learn of lips?

King.   I'm here to teach thee.
Lips are Love's bows, and I'm thy bow-master.
  Jane S. You'll find me a dull pupil.
  King.   I shall find thee
The archest archer of King Cupid's guard,
Whose arrows, tipped with smiles, fledged with sweet breath,.
Go pointblank to the red—here in my heart.
Thou bear'st the bell from all the lady-archers
I e'er stood up for target to. See, here (*taking out a jewel
    with his miniature*)
For parlour-practice here's my face in little
To shoot at, when the target is not by.
  Jane S. The jewel's fair, but there is something fairer—
  King. What's that?
  Jane S. (*in a low voice*) The face set in its gems and
    gold. (*Putting the chain round her neck.*)
  King. Nay, wear't not so.
  Jane S.   How should I wear it?
  King.   Thus!
The lips on thy white neck. (*Kisses her and turns
    the miniature.*)
  Jane S.   Hark! some one comes!
                       [*Exit* JANE *hastily*.
  King. Plague on these madcap mayers! Dainty
    darling!
How she bounds o'er the fern and through the trees!
Light as a deer, and with as rare a grace.
The path turns at yon clump. I'll catch her there!
Hind, 'ware the hunter!   [*Exit in pursuit of* JANE S.
    (EARL OF WILTSHIRE *without*, R.)
  Wilts. Here, sirrah! Hold our horses. Through the
    pleasaunce,
Will be our nearest way to the Queen's lodging.

Enter EARL OF WILTSHIRE *and* LORD ROCHEFORT, *as from
    riding.*

  Roch. Who would ride roads upon an English Mayday
When he could tread on turf? Are you not glad, sir,
To be again in England?
  Wilts.   Am I glad!
If blue sky, sweet air, lush grass, and green trees,
The fragrance of May-blossoms, and the stir
Of May's pulse in the heart, sufficed for gladness,

I should be glad. But, since Anne bore her babe,
Her letters that should brim with mother's joy
Have a sad note in them that soundeth rather
Of coffin than of cradle.
  Roch.   You have read them
By light of rumour, that still spends the venom
Of all its hundred mouths on our sweet Anne.
  Wilts. May it so prove! Come, let us learn the worst.
  Roch. Or best—there *is* a best even at Court!
Heaven hold me all! Faith, father, you have drawn
May's mirth out of the air with your ill-bodings.
    [*Exeunt* WILTSHIRE *and* ROCHEFORT, U. E. L.

  Enter, from the other side, CHAPUIS *and* NORFOLK, R.

  Chap. Was not that my Lord Wiltshire and my Lord
   Rochefort
That went before us?
  Norf.   It might be. I know not
The Boleyns by their backs; I only know
They hold them stiffer than befits their duty
Before their house's head. They come to find
Her tether shortened.
  Chap.   I give her two months
To weary out the King.
  Norf. (*impatiently*) So your curst Pope——
  Chap. (*gravely*) Curst Pope, my lord?
  Norf.   Plague on't—I would say 'blest'—
Mar not our plans for Anne's defeat by lighting
His Church-petards and blowing us in air
Instead of her.
  Chap. Oh, we've the Pope in leash,
To slip or check as my imperial master
Lifts his hand.
  Norf. Then I would he kept him shorter
Upon the chain. See you not for each blow
The Pope deals out the King returns a buffet?
Pope seals a Bull 'gainst King's divorce and marriage:
King makes it treason to appeal to Rome!
Pope talks of banning: King stops Rome's Church pickings.
Pope bastards Anne's brat: King names her successor.
Pope growls with thunders of anathema;
King dubs himself 'Supreme Head of the Church.'
Pope burns a batch of spleeny Lutherans:

King strings me up a fellowship of monks,
Till the death-dance is led up to Tower Hill
With Fisher's good grey hairs and More's ripe wisdom.
    Chap. And see you not how, at each stroke King fetches
The Pope, some of the force that weights the blow
Oozes away? How Rome's cause in the North
Spreads and still spreads, till England beyond Trent
Is leagued to raise up the true Church again,
And set the Pope, its head, above the King?
That is what comes of buffets with St. Peter.
But leave the Church to hold its own—our business
Is first to make short work of Lady Anne
And Cranmer, arch-contrivers of all ill
That the King wishes Rome or works against her.
    Norf. Since Anne has been a mother I've a scruple
To strike at her across her baby's cradle.
    Chap. Yet that blow must be struck, much as it grieves
Your kindly heart and mine.
The Royal palate longs for change of diet,
So seeks it in Anne Boleyn's opposite—
That sly piece of mock-maidenhood—Jane Seymour.
I've watched her at her angling. Beautiful!
Dangling the bait before her Royal fish;
Then—twitch!—it flutters high beyond his reach!
Anon 'tis dropped back—close to the great jaws.
All fishing's sport for a philosopher;
But where's such fishing as a cool close maiden's,
Who knows her craft and has a fish worth catching?
    Norf. You love the sport; I seek what comes of it.
    Chap. The pear will soon be ripe. But go we now
To ask, as duty bids, how fares the Queen,
And offer welcome to her noble father
And gentle brother.
    Norf.   Hang that devil's grin!
Canst thou not frown upon an enemy
As I do?
    Chap. Nay, you do that so much better!
To me a smile comes far more natural.
This way the hawthorn blossom smells the sweetest—
Your English Mays are gleams of Paradise.   [*Exeunt.*

Enter SMEATON.

    Smeaton. May flower on bush, May music in the brake!

And merry bells of May from tower and tower!
What have *I* with these glad sights and glad sounds?
I thought to tune my lute to Mayday mirth
This morning in her gallery, that on waking,
A thought of me might blend with the sweet spring.
But ever more my music died in sighs.
'Twas my heart spoke in them—its hopelessness,
Its bitter sense that I am naught to her,
Who must be all to me.   Hark! 'tis her voice,
And tuned again to joy, as fits the season.
Who come with her?   Her father and her brother!
They make her mirth.   I may but look and listen.
[*He hides.*

Enter ANNE B., ROCHEFORT, WILTSHIRE, LADY ROCHEFORT,
and MARGARET.

  Anne B. (*with forced gaiety*) *I* sick?   *I* sorry?   You
   believed this gossip?
Nay, father, and you, George, I thought you both
Knew more of courts than to give ear to news
That comes with ill-will.
  Wilts.   I'm glad 'tis other
Than we had heard.
  Roch. (*aside to* LADY R.) If it indeed be other?
  Anne B. 'Tis the best jest.   They come to find me laid
In a close-darkened chamber, and they meet me
Here in May's green pavilion, hawthorn-hung,
Set about with the chesnut's silver sconces—
I, and my ladies, and my pretty babe—
My little first-born—my Elizabeth!
Look, yonder wait your horses.   I am glad
I met you coming.   His Grace would be vexed
You sought me first.   Ride you round to the Palace
To lay your duty at his royal feet,
And then find me out.   I'll but draw a breath
Of this soft air.
  Lady R. I'll see you to your horses.
I've much to hear and tell.
  Wilts. (*kissing* ANNE B.) Beshrew my bodings!
Thou look'st as bright and blythe as e'er I saw thee.
[*Exeunt* WILTSHIRE, ROCHEFORT, *and* LADY R.
  Anne B. Thank heaven they've gone, and still believe
   me happy!

What's cheating them that cannot cheat myself?
The unloved mother of an unloved babe!
    Margt. Neither unloved. The King is but impatient,
As having set his heart upon a boy——
    Anne B. (*fiercely and bitterly*) As having set his heart
        on a fresh face!
'Tis the man's nature—as he is most a man
He shows that nature most—what he liked best,
When it has once palled, is thrust farthest from him.
If he but loved my babe I could content me
To stand aside, and know my treasure hers.

       Re-enter LADY ROCHEFORT, *behind.*

But to be rivalled where I reigned alone,
To see my dues laid at usurping feet!
Humble me as I will, and pray my best
For resignation and the strength to suffer.
Still it is bitter, bitterer than gall
Offered to parching lips upon the rack.
It makes me mad.
    Margt.   But is there such a rival?
    Anne B. 'Is there?' Had'st thou been here these last
        three months,
Thou'dst not asked 'Is there?' Yes, Meg, yes, there is.
    (LADY ROCHEFORT *lays one hand on* ANNE'S *arm and
    points off with the other.* ANNE *looks in the same
    direction.*)
And see, where she walks yonder!
    Margt.   Mistress Seymour!
    Anne B. Mistress Jane Seymour—that coy Wiltshire
        wench,
Who dared not lift her dropped lids in the presence,
Practised no arts, knew no accomplishments—
She it is that has thrust me from the heart
Of my brave Harry! Me, upon whose smiles
He waited years and years, for whom he braved
Pope, Parliament, and people, and bore down,
As he bears down opposers in the lists,
All that withstood his will or barred his way.
    Margt. She takes this turn.
    Anne B.   Let's couch—nay, I've a right
To watch her. Think how oft she has watched me!
                    (*They conceal themselves.*)

Enter JANE S., *with a bow, arrows, and bracer* (*an arm-piece to guard the wrist from the chafe of the bowstring*) *in her hand.*

   Jane S. A fair bow and a richly broidered bracer!
His Highness told me they had been the Queen's.
She offered once to teach me how to shoot—
I've learned without her teaching, on her chase too.
              (*Puts down bow and arrows on the seat.*)
       (ANNE B. *shows herself, in spite of* MARGARET'S *attempt
          to restrain her.* ANNE B. *grasps* MARGARET'S *arm
          convulsively.*)
This jewel the King gave me ere I fled
And he came after, and caught and clasped me close,
And I was angry; and to purchase pardon
He took me to the mews and gave me these.
                     (*Points to bow and arrows.*)
I like being hunted; shall I like as well
To hunt, I wonder? with his kingly face
To smile on me for drawing a good bow,
       (ANNE B. *is about to rush on her, but restrains herself,
          and draws nearer and nearer to* JANE S.)
And when I shoot foul to cry 'Ha!' and frown,
'Till I chase off his frowning with a look
Of pretty penitence?
       (ANNE B. *grasps her arm.* JANE S. *stands aghast.*)
The Queen! Your Highness! Oh! Let go my wrist!
You hurt me!
   Anne B.   The King's picture—he gave it thee!
Nay, lie not—thou canst lie!
I heard thee talk to it: I saw thee smile
As it had been his face. If that smiled on thee,
This picture never shall. Let it go, woman!
                 (*She wrenches it from her hand.*)
As he that gave thee this has set his heel
On my heart, so I set my heel on this,
And stamp it into powder—(*stamping on it*)—as, please
       Heaven,
I will stamp thee, that hast crept like a thief
Into my treasure-house, to steal my jewel—
Jewel it was to me—my husband's love.
What is betwixt you?

Jane S. No worse, please your Highness,
Than jests and laughs and idle compliments.
 Anne B. And gifts like that. (*Pointing to miniature.*)
(*Looking at bow and bracer.*) And these, that once were mine!
Whisperings in window-seats, and secret meetings—
Paddling of ready hands—claspings of waists,
And clinging kisses. Out, thou harlotry!
Nay, thou should'st brazen it better! Cower not thus,
But set a face of flint against thy Queen,
And dare her, and defy her in the strength
Of what he is to thee and was to me!
 Jane S. Your words are fierce and bitter—you have called me
A foul name.
 Anne B. You have done me a foul wrong!
 Jane S. None worse than words——
 Anne B.   And thoughts!
 Jane S.   Nay, thoughts are free,
Queen as you are, till you can fathom mine
You have no right to tax them. If his Grace
Have deigned to seek in my poor company
Disport he finds no more where he once found it,
Is the blame mine?
 Anne B.   She bandies words with me!
 Jane S. Not till you flung at me a name to rouse
A serving-wench to speech—much more a lady
In whose veins runs the royal blood of England.
Aye, madam, humble as you hold Jane Seymour,
My mother was a Wentworth, and the Wentworths
Draw line from Hotspur. I've a touch of him
In me—best not awake it!
 Anne B.   She defies me!
Come, this is better.
 Jane S.   Had yourself been by
And heard and seen——
 Lady R. (*who has been looking on*). Look, madam—from the mews
The King comes hasty hitherwards. Were't well
He found you here, with her?
 Anne B.   And were it well
He found her without me? I will confront him,
As I've confronted her—set them together—
Speak all my wrong, and try which is more easy—

To make her cheek blush or his hard heart pity.
    Margt. 'Twere madness.
    Lady R. (*aside*). And must make the worst still worse—
If there's a worse. In faith I'm sorry for her,
For all my hate.
    Anne B.   Tell me not—I will watch.
(*Seizing* JANE S.) Ah, would you fly? (*Seizing the bow.*)
Look! this bow was once mine—
You've seen how I can use it. These sharp arrows
Are mortal to a woman as a deer.
Thou swear'st there's no worse 'twixt thee and my husband
Than words, jests, toys—I'd see what is betwixt you,
Unseen myself. But, if thou stirrest step
For flight, breath'st word of warning to the King,
Winkest or wavest, or e'en willest signal—
There's listeners in the brake and lookers on—
That grey swan's feather is red with the blood
Of thy false heart. (*Imperiously to* LADY R. *and* JANE S.)
Come you, I am still Queen!
(*Relenting.*) Yet I would spare my husband. Leave me to
him.
Who bears the sorrow should have all the shame.
    [*Exit* MARGARET, *beckoning* LADY R. *to follow.*
    Lady R. (*aside*) I claim my share in't. Yet I hate the rival
Worse than the wife,—my rival—as she's hers.
    [*Exit* LADY R. *after* MARGARET.
    Jane S. (*in an agony of terror*) For mercy's sake, your Highness——
    Anne B.   Stir not, speak not,
If thou set'st store by life! (*Disappears behind tree.*)

    Enter the KING, *impetuously.*

    King.   Ha, pretty one!
If Harry dared to chase thee, he must make
Huntress of hunted. Where's the bow and bracer
I gave thee? But what's this? How pale thou'rt grown!
Those ripe red roses, my lips revelled in
But now, turned to pale traitors? Nay, beshrew them.
I'll no white roses in my lady's cheeks.
Was it the falcon fluttered the soft dove?
Nay, let me make atonement—let me show thee
How gentle I can be, how woman-tender

To her I love. (*Impetuously.*) Nay, shrink not. Time for shrinking
Is past for thee and me. (*Seizes her in his arms and draws her on to his knee.*)

  ANNE B. *comes forward, unseen by the* KING.

Jane S. (*seeing her*). Forbear! The Queen!
King. You here? In hiding! This was queenly done!
Anne B. (*pointing to the group of* HENRY *and* JANE S.)
As this was kingly. Oh, my lord, my husband!
Should this have been while yet our baby's face
Smiled up, incarnate innocence, between us?
When those soft fingers should have drawn our bonds
Of wedded love more close. You take my crown
And set it on her head——
 King.   What crown?
 Anne B.   Thy love—
My husband's love!
 King.   Perchance, had I that crown
To give again, ay, or the Crown of England,
I'd bestow neither as I once bestowed them.
 Anne B. What need to tell me that in naked words,
Which slights and scorns and coldnesses more cruel
Have told already?
 Jane S.   Please your Grace, forbear
To grieve her Highness. Who am I, to make
Such sore division? Let me leave the Court,
Wherein I breed but ill-will for myself,
And grief for you.
 King.   No, mistress, here you stay,
Depart who will.
 Anne B.   Methinks you might have hid
This fancy, that dishonours her it falls on
Even more than it wounds me.
 King. You do well to rate me. If there be blame,
I take the blame upon my own strong shoulders.
 Anne B. Strong as they are, they'll scarcely bear the load
Of shame and scorn this day should pile upon them.
Think not I'll sit down patient with my griefs,
To peak and pine and dwindle to my grave.
No, I'll proclaim my wrongs, and challenge pity
Of England!
 King (*fiercely*). Hold there! Speak'st thou of thy wrongs?

Then I must loose a tongue I would have bridled,
Had'st thou been wise enough to wink——
    Anne B.   Meet wisdom
For a wronged wife!
    King.   Aye, when the wronged has taught
His lesson to the wronger.
    Anne B.   Taught? What mean you?
    King. Thinkest thou thy light words and lighter acts
Have had no eyes to witness, tongues to carry?
I know a load of guilt to bear thee down
Wert thou three times my wife—ten times my Queen!
    Jane S. (*frightened*) Oh, my lord!
    King (*to* ANNE B.). Say you nothing?
    Anne B.   Not a word.
    King. 'Tis well you blench at sight of what you are.
    Anne B. I do not blench, false husband! cruel King!—
Save for amazement such vile witnessing
Could find your ear—even if your weariness
Had grown to loath the woman you once loved!
Had I no sins but sins against your bed,
I were an angel, ready winged for Heaven!
    King. That let them test that try thee. For to trial
This innocence thou boastest shall be brought.
(*To* JANE S.) Take thy farewell of her whom never more
Thou shalt obey as mistress or as Queen!
                              [*Exeunt* HENRY *and* JANE S.
    Anne B. (*stretching her arms towards him*) King! husband! Henry! (*Enter* MARGARET.)
                                  Ah! his words were death!
What need of block or axe? (*Throwing herself into* MARGARET'S *arms.*)
                              Oh, Margaret!
He could not be so cruel! Yet, not so—
Who knows how cruel man can be to woman
When he is wearied of her? Now it comes,
The thought of that poor Queen whose place I took,
As she takes mine.
    Margt.   Not so—you had full warrant.
There was no marriage bond between them.
    Anne B.   True;
And yet thought of her misery should have stayed me.
No, no; 'twas too much love, and some ambition,
Drew me on to the doom that, gathering long,

Has fallen at last. Oh, if my sin was great,
Great is my punishment! (*She sobs on* MARGARET's *shoulder.*)

Enter SMEATON. *He throws himself at* ANNE's *feet.*

Smeaton. Oh, most unhappy lady! Crownéd Queen
Not so much of this England as my heart!
Anne B. How now, Mark Smeaton?
    [*As the* QUEEN *stands in silent amazement* LADY
      ROCHEFORT *appears from her concealment.*
Lady R. (*aside.*)   So falls the last blow!
My witness to those words seals both their fates!
                        [*Exit* LADY R.
Anne B. What make you here?
Smeaton.   Oh, pardon, if thy servant
Have dared to listen. He was strong enough
To hold the hand and sword that fain had leapt
To wreak your wrong on your traducer's head,
Though 'twas a crowned one.
Margt.   Smeaton, art thou mad?
Smeaton, Aye, lady, mad for wrath of her great wrongs—
Mad that my wrath must vent itself in words—
Mad that the reverent love I dared to cherish
When she was high in state and happiness
Should now find voice, but to lay idle offers
Of duty and devotion at her feet.

Enter behind HENRY *and* JANE SEYMOUR, *led by* LADY
    ROCHEFORT.

Lady R. Hark! 'At her feet!'
King.   The action to the word!
Anne B. I thought thee my true friend. He's no true
    friend
Who at this moment speaks of love to me,
Though 'twere as pure as loves of angels are.
    King (*coming forward*; SMEATON *rises in confusion.*) Ha!
Jane S. Many said it—I scarce thought to see.
Now, madam, take your foul name back again!
    [SMEATON *attempts to draw his sword, but pauses,
      checked by a look from* ANNE B.
Anne B. Lost!
King. 'Loves of angels,' quotha! Even now
You were an angel ready winged for Heaven!
Kind will to kind! Here's the companion angel—

Whose wings need caging, till his flight to Heaven
Can be helped with a halter. Cry you mercy,
If I have followed the example set me
Of breaking on your May-game unannounced !
If wives are free to play it, why not husbands ?
Only for Queens, in whom law calls it treason,
The hazard of the game is—heads for hearts !

    Anne B. My lord, I knew not——
    King.   Nor had I known either
But for this lady here.
    Anne B.   Betrayed !
    King.   Unmasked !
Ho, Kingston !
    Anne B.   Standing even on the brink
Of death—nay, worse—of shame, I raise no voice
To plead for pardon—pardon is for guilt—
But to proclaim my clearness of all wrong,
And his of worse wrong than a hopeless love—
That ne'er found tongue till now—when I for wonder
Scarce found a tongue to strike his dumb again.
    King. Plead not for him—you'll have enough anon
Of pleading for yourself.   (*Enter* KINGSTON.)
                         Arrest the Queen !
    Anne B. Arrest me—'tis your right—but hear me still,
By our old love.
    King.   'Tis dead !
    Anne B.   By our sweet babe !
I am your true wife; guiltless of all fault,
But listening to what amazed me more
Than it should anger you.
How gladly would I kneel before the block,
Could my last words but move thee to believe
My woman's innocence and wife's true faith !
    King (*impatiently*). No more !
    Anne B. But hear me ! Husband ! Henry ! King !
    King. No more. Thy prayers knock at a heart of stone.
                (*She clings to him ; he shakes her off.*)
Away ! (*To* KINGSTON.) Hence with her—and him (*pointing to* SMEATON)—to the Tower !

                      ACT-DROP.

ACT V.

Time: 1536.

Scene.—Presence Chamber in the Tower. A large and handsome room, of Norman architecture, hung with tapestry between the arches, as it was for the Queen's lodging before her coronation. A state, C., stools, chairs; window recess, R.

Enter Kingston, *meeting* Ann Gaysford.

Kingst. Where's her Grace?
Ann G. In her closet at confession
With Doctor Latimer.
Kingst. Have you told her Highness
The Presence Chamber here is free to her
From nine?
Ann G. She had your message—thanked its kindness,
Then smiled, and said 'twas strange in three short years
To leave the same room for a throne and scaffold.
But why not free till nine?
Kingst. That is the hour
Fixed for her friends to die. Their nearest road
To Tower Hill lies through this room. You may see
The scaffold from your window. Tell her Grace
After confession, my Lord Wiltshire waits
To take farewell.
Ann G. Poor father! A sore parting.
Kingst. 'Tis well she's stout of heart as she is gentle.
Ann G. Oh, Master Kingston! what a saint men's hate
Has blackened to a devil! I could talk
Such treason——
Kingst. Better keep it to yourself.
I must report, above, whatever passes
About her Grace.
Ann G. Sweet lady! Never servants
Had such a mistress. [*Exit* Ann G.
Enter Stokes.

Kingst. How now?
Stokes. Here's the Spanish Envoy with Master Secretary's order
To see the gentlemen ordered for execution.

Kingst. They'll pass this way. Admit him. Hark ye: is all in readiness upon the Hill?

Stokes. All ready, so please you. And a fair new block and a new black kersey for the scaffold. Half a mark the ell.

Kingst. Thou seest, Stokes, this is no common occasion. A lord and three of the King's gentlemen in one batch, and for light dealing with the Queen. I would have all things handsome.

Stokes. Never fear, your worship. They say, your honour, these gentlemen are like to die hard. Master Reynolds tells me they are all in a tale. All clear the Queen.

Kingst. All the gentlemen. Only the musician, Mark, confesses to naughtiness with her.

Stokes. And that was after a week of Little-ease—a day of the Scavenger's Daughter and six turns of the rack. And they say after he was unbound, as soon as he fetched breath, he unsaid his confession, and cursed his faint heart that made it.

Kingst. Many do that.

Stokes. So many, your honour, that I don't count much myself on what men say under persuasion of winch-rope and pulley.

Kingst. 'Tis not our business to weigh confessions.

Stokes. No, your worship, no. We've enough to do with keeping bodies safe first, and chopping heads off handsomely after; and a rousing trade we've driven, to be sure, since the King came to years of discretion. Bless him for a pleasant prince! He likes all the world to live—even the headsman—one that has not so many friends as another.

Kingst. Touching that, is this Frenchman yet arrived? The excutioner—thou know'st—from Calais?

Stokes. Ah, the mounseer, whose new-fangled sword is to give our honest old axe a lesson. Will your worship hear me? I've had forty years of the Tower, man and boy, and I've never seen any harm of the axe. A man may miss his cut sometimes, but it comes right in the end. I see no need to fetch any over-sea jackanapes to teach honest Ned Grimes.

Kingst. Nay, Stokes, 'twas none of my wish. 'Twas the King himself gave order for the fetching this Calais headsman.

Stokes. Ah! had a fancy, as 'twere, to try the new weapon on the young Queen.

Kingst. How, sirrah! Crack'st thou thy scurril jokes on royal heads?

Stokes. Nay, Sir William, I crack no jokes on heads—royal or rascal. I know better what belongs to a Tower warder than to jest on matter of business; but, methinks, English heads are best cut off English fashion; and so they'd tell you, if they could speak after proof on't

[*Exit* STOKES.

Kingst. Hither come some of the lords from the Council. I must bid the gentlemen make ready. But his Donship is waiting. Faith, what with Frenchmen to do our heading, and Jack Spaniards to look on, an honest English gentleman will soon feel strange upon a scaffold.

[*Exit* KINGSTON.

Enter NORFOLK, L., *with Lords, who pass on. Enter* CHAPUIS, R.

Norf. You come to see a sorry sight.
Chap. An Envoy
Must not know natural sorrow.
Norf. Like a king.
They say he hunts to-day—the day they die!
Chap. Our hunt is at an end—our hart pulled down.
Norf. I've not forgot your figure, trust me, sir.
I'm used to cheer the hounds, and love the chase;
But 'tis of a stout stag—with horns for harm,
And speed for safety. But this poor young hind,
Still weakly from her fawn, without defence
From nature but her tenderness and beauty——
Chap. And not bad weapons.
Norf. Think of the foul odds—
When she stood there at bay, her large sad eyes—
Larger for sorrow—wandering, wistful, round
To find a friend.
Chap. Nor likely to find many
In that Tower Court, selected with such judgment.
Norf. And then, after that first look round the Court,
So calm and firm of cheer, not speaking much,
But each word to the point, and still denying
All but things done or said, as she averred
In innocence—vouched herself loyal subject

And wife unstained. Said she knew how to die,
And cared not to live longer—but it were
For her babe's sake—and grieved much for the others,
As innocents, she said, who needs must suffer
Along with her. But trusted as she went
To death with them, so with them she should rise
To life eternal.
    Chap.   Tut, tut, my Lord Duke;
You think too much of this. Think of the Crown
That her death brings within your children's reach.
    Norf. Would they had not named her father of the Court!
All Boleyn as he is, proud as he once was,
I'd give much to forget that poor old man,
Struck in one week from green age to grey dotage.
    Chap. See you not how it stops mouths out of doors,
Her father's voice, among those that condemned
His daughter and his son?
    Norf.   Will Kingston tells me
The first day she was brought into the Tower
She said she only prayed she would have justice;
    Chap. And she that knew the King too! 'Justice,'
    quotha!
You English are a marvellous strange people.
Give you but husks of form to stay your stomachs,—
Your Parliaments and Courts, judges and juries,—
And you yield purse, land, liberty, or life
To the one will, be't King's or Cardinal's,
That rules the roast. Where my great master reigns
We look the one will naked in the face,
And bow to it, or break, and there an end.
Here comes Sir Thomas Wyatt. Who is that with him?
His father?
    Norf.   He's in Kent.
    Chap. (*recognising him*) The Earl of Wiltshire. Poor old
    man!

Enter WYATT, *supporting on his arm the* EARL OF WILT-
SHIRE, *who walks feebly with the aid of a staff.* WYATT
bows gravely and is passing on. The EARL *stops and
accosts them with senile politeness.*

    Wilts. (*making an effort to recollect Chapuis*) As I think—
    Wyatt (*explaining*). Sieur Chapuis, the Spanish Envoy.
    Wilts. I knew him well—a shrewd and supple man.

Wyatt. Nay, this is he, sir.
Wilts.   Pardon, sir; my eyesight
Has failed of late. I bear not such a brain
As I was wont to do. But this, I think,
Is my good brother-in-law, the Duke of Norfolk.
We met in a court lately, you presided
Here in the Tower, to judge my—the Queen's matter,
But the King's business before all. And yet
A father, sirs, and my poor boy—my George!
'Tis hard to stand alone, sirs, at my years.
   Wyatt. Your barge is waiting, sir, to take you home.
   Wilts. Home, Tom? Home, said you? Would I were at home!
   Wyatt (*aside*). Under the grey stone in the Boleyn vault.
Poor stricken, solitary, childless father!   [*Exeunt.*

Enter Mayor, Aldermen, and Members of the Council, R.
ROCHEFORT, NORRIS, WESTON, BRERETON, *guarded*, L.

   Chap. Here come the gentlemen.
   Norris (*to* ROCHEFORT).   Speak, George, for all.
   Roch. Sirs, we are not come here to preach to you.
The law has found us guilty. To the law
We all submit ourselves, not fearing death,
Or what may follow death for guilty men.
You, lords, are high and mighty; many a year
You have known my friends and me as you are now.
Your turn may come. If it lead to Tower Hill
May you kneel at the block with as clear souls
As we to-day. Said I well, gentlemen?
   Norris. Right well, my lord. As I am innocent,
The Queen is innocent. I'd rather die
A thousand deaths than soil her with a lie
From dying lips.
   Norf.   Confession yet might save you.
   Norris. Shame us, you mean, my lord. I know I speak
For my friends as myself.
   Weston.   God save the Queen,
And make her innocence as clear on earth
As it shines now in heaven.
   Brereton.   Amen, quoth Brereton!
I am a man of sword, not speech, but evil
Did I, nor knew I, never of the Queen.

Norris. Set on, good Kingston.
Roch. Farewell, summer sun!
Our next sun will be brighter.
Kingst. Forward, yeomen!
[*Exeunt all.*

Enter ANNE BOLEYN *from her closet, with* ANN GAISFORD *and* MARGARET WYATT.

Anne B. Here's space to breathe. It needs, after the wrench,
Of such a parting! Fare thee well, dear father.
'Tis not for long. (*Goes to window.*)
    Ann G. Nay, not that window, madam.
    Anne B. 'Tis well I learn to look on what to-morrow
I must take part in.
(ANNE BOLEYN *looking from the window.* MARGARET LEE *in attendance.*)
    Anne B. How the crowd presses! 'Twill press more anon.
My brother! my sweet George! That soul of honour,
Sent by his wicked wife, a sacrifice
On that black altar. And my gallant Norris!
Poor Madge! 'Twas well they wed not, as I wished them.
Frank Weston, with his brown hair and fair face,
And step as light as for a Mayday revel;
And Brereton, with the sun and swarth of warfare
Upon his cheek, that blenches not to meet
Death, his old battle comrade, at the block.
Margaret! Thank heaven thy brother is not with them!
'Tis strange they should spare him. One tongue to speak
My innocence to England yet unborn.
Thou'lt tell my child, when she is grown to woman,
What her poor mother was when she lay smiling
A baby in her arms.
    Margt. Think not of her,
Dear Anne! The thought must needs unfix thy heart
    Anne B. Nay, next to having her is thinking of her.
But I forget, in joy of her young life,
Those that, for me, end yonder all too soon. (*Bell and muffled drum.*)
    Margt. (*who has been at the window, suddenly turns away in horror*) Oh, heaven!
(ANNE B. *turns to the window.* MARGARET *stops her.*)

No madam! No! You must not look.
 Anne B. Now Heaven have mercy on their faithful souls!
  (*She falls on her knees at the table, burying her face in
  prayer, as does* MARGARET. *Enter* KINGSTON.
  MARGARET, *hearing his step, signals him not to
  disturb* ANNE B. KINGSTON *holds up a paper to*
  MARGARET, *who rises to go to him. They whisper.*)
Their pain is ended—mine is yet to come.
To-morrow upon daybreak, was it not?
  (*Looking round for* MARGARET, *she sees* KINGSTON.)
 Kingst. Your pardon if I interrupt grave matters,
But 'tis for graver. I had warned your Highness
For twelve to-morrow, but, lo! here an order
To hasten execution.
 Anne B.   What! so soon!
 Kingst. (*to* ANNE B.) I must entreat you to prepare for
  death.   [*Exit* KINGSTON.
 Anne B. (*to her women*) Farewell, true friends; and
  speak me after death
As in my life you found me. (*Taking out paper.*) Let the
  King
Have what I have writ here—if Master Cromwell
Perchance should keep it from his hand; that prince
Had never wife more loyal in all duty
And true affection than he in Anne Boleyn—
With which name I could have been well content,
Heaven and his Grace so pleasing—that I never
In my receivèd Queenship so forgot me,
But I looked for such chance of alteration
As I have found—the ground of my preferring
Being, not my own merit, but his fancy,
Which now I know another's. For my death
I pray God pardon his great sin therein,
And all my enemies, its instruments.
And tell the King, too, he hath still been constant
In heaping honours on this head of mine—
From simple maid he made me Marchioness;
From state of Marchioness raised me to Queen;
And now he hath no higher earthly crown
He crowns my innocence with martrydom!
(*To* MARGARET.) Farewell, dear friend! Be mother to my
  babe.
Tell her I blessed her with my dying breath.

I have not much to give, but I've had ordered
Some little books of high and holy thoughts
For thee and Madge and Ann here and the rest.
See that they have them. I ask Heaven's forgiveness
For all unkindly deeds or words or thoughts
Done, said, or thought by me to anyone.
Chief I pray pardon of the Lady Mary ·
For aught she may have suffered at my hands,
Or for my cause. (*Rising.*) And, that done, there is
    nothing
But thanks and still thanks for your loving-kindness,
In this my sore strait and my doleful prison.
                              (*Looking round.*)
'Twas hence I set forth for my coronation;
All is as it was then—only a Queen
Who goes to take a higher crown than England's.

Re-enter SIR W. KINGSTON, *Guards appearing behind him in the entrance, but outside.*

CURTAIN.

PLOT AND PASSION

An Original Drama

IN THREE ACTS

*First Performed at the Royal Olympic Theatre, on Monday,
October 17, 1853.*

ORIGINAL CAST OF THE CHARACTERS.

FOUCHÉ (*Duke of Otranto, Minister of Police*)	MR. EMERY.
M. DESMARETS (*Head of the Secret Department of Police*)	MR. ROBSON.
The MARQUIS DE CEVENNES (*a Legitimist*)	MR. LESLIE.
BERTHIER (*Prince of Neufchatel, Grand Chamberlain*)	MR. WHITE.
DE NEUVILLE (*Secretary to De Cevennes*)	MR. A. WIGAN.
JABOT (*House Steward to Madame de Fontanges*)	MR. LINDON.
GRISBOULLE (*a subordinate of Desmarets*)	MR. H. COOPER.
MADAME DE FONTANGES	MRS. STIRLING
CECILE (*her Maid*)	MISS TURNER.

TIME: THE BEGINNING OF 1810.
SCENES—ACTS I. AND III. IN PARIS. ACT II. NEAR PRAGUE.

COSTUMES OF THE PERIOD.

Fouché.—First Costume—The long black soutane of an Abbé, with black skull-cap, covering the tonsure; black bands, with narrow white edging and narrow black cloak at the back; silk stockings; shoes and buckles; white wig. Second Costume—Blue velvet court coat, embroidered with gold, in the fashion of the Empire; white satin waistcoat and breeches; sword; silk stockings and shoes; iron-grey hair, cut straight on forehead, long at sides and back.

Desmarets.—Black suit, breeches, and buckles. In Second Act—Long boots; iron-grey hair, cut close in front, long behind.

De Cevennes and De Neuville.—Maroon and chocolate coats, with high collars and lapels, satin waistcoats, and breeches. *De C.*, in Act II.—Leather breeches and long-topped boots. *De N.*, in Act II.—Blue stockings, rich pantaloons, and high boots.

Berthier.—Crimson velvet court suit, white satin waistcoat and breeches, and sword.

Jabot.—Livery.

Grisboulle.—German peasant's dress.

Madame de Fontanges.—Elegant evening dress. Act II.—White dress, broad-leafed straw hat, blue sash, cloak. Act III., as in Act II.

Cecile.—Madras on the head, long hose mittens.

NOTE.—The subject of Fouché and his employment of women of fashion and ruined character as what was called his 'cohorte Cythérienne' to keep him informed of the political gossip in places of play and public resort, and, on occasion, to lure compromised persons within his reach, was suggested to me by Mr. John Lang. His name was on that ground originally associated with the authorship of the play.

PLOT AND PASSION.

ACT I.

SCENE.—*An apartment in the house of Madame de Fontanges. The room is spacious and handsomely furnished in the semi-classical style of the Empire, with large folding doors communicating (in flat) with an adjoining room. A secret door in the wall (R.) concealed by a picture, and another side-door communicating with the staircase. Windows practicable (L.) A writing-table, with writing materials. (L. C.) Caraffe of water and glasses. Fauteuils disposed about the stage. Fireplace between the windows, with bronze pendule and candelabra, and a glass over it.*

CECILE *at the fire place.* JABOT *arranging the inkstand and a breviary on the table.*

Cecile. Seven o'clock, and Madame not returned! Astonishing!

Jabot. Cecile, how often must I repeat to you that servants in a good family ought never to be astonished? Madame is young, charming, a widow, and may choose her own hours.

Cecile. For her visitors—yes; but you forget this is her night for receiving her Confessor; she never would dare to keep the Abbé Lenoir waiting?

Jabot. Pooh! she must leave a few of her sins to stand over till next week—there's a running account between them. When the Abbé arrives show him in here, and take care he is not disturbed in his pious exercises.

Cecile. Hark! there's a fiacre in the court. (*She looks out.*) The Abbé! (*She arranges her cap and hair at the glass. A ring is heard.*)

Jabot. What! even for an Abbé!

Cecile. Why not? One must show some respect for the Church, Monsieur Jabot. [*Exit* CECILE, C.

Jabot. Oh, woman! woman! As if that walking monument of mortification had eyes for a waiting-maid!

Re-enter CECILE *showing in* FOUCHÉ, *in the dress of an Abbé. He walks with an air of pious abstraction, his hands folded, and his eyes cast down.*

Jabot (R., *wheeling an arm-chair forward*). Madame, unfortunately, has not yet returned—but she expected your reverence's visit.

Cecile (L.). And directed that we should show every attention to your reverence's wishes.

Fou. Thank you, my children—I wish to be alone—see that no one enters this room, except your mistress, or my other penitent, M. de Cevennes, should he arrive.

JABOT *bows,* CECILE *curtsies and exeunt,* L. FOUCHÉ, *rising, takes a rapid survey of the room, then closes the window curtains, places the lights on the mantelpiece, and bolts the door by which they have gone, and also the folding doors.*

Fou. Never trust an order while there's a bolt. Now for my ferret—to all but me, M. le Bon, the respectable proprietor of the house next door—to me, Maximilian Desmarets, the most unmitigated rascal and most invaluable head of a secret department in Europe. It was a good idea of mine to establish him next door to Madame de Fontanges. We meet here unobserved. (*He touches a spring in the frame of the picture,* R. *It moves, and discovers a secret door.*) Hist! Desmarets!

Enter from the secret door DESMARETS, *with a despatch-box and papers. He takes a chair at the table, opens his box, unfolds his papers* (R.), *and sits looking at* FOUCHÉ.

Fou. At least I am sure to find you at your post. (DESMARETS *chuckles and rubs his hands.*) These women think only of pleasure.

Des. So do I—my pleasure's here. (*Pointing to papers.*)

Fou. I pay Madame de Fontanges enough to ensure diligence, too.

Des. Madame receives exactly double what I do. Suppose you reversed the proportions?

Fou. You would serve me no better, and she would not

serve me at all. Besides, she has the enormous recommendation of an unblemished character.

Des. She!—so much for the world's judgment of a confirmed gambler!

Fou. That is her only vice—a secret confined to us and her mask. It was a good thought to allow of masks at the public tables.

Des. Do they hide many blushes?

Fou. They save many reputations. No, my excellent Desmarets, I have not spent twenty years in gauging the price of consciences without arriving at a tolerably fair estimation of the money value of my species, from kings downwards.

Des. And you think my fidelity is worth just four thousand francs a month?

Fou. With your character I think no one would pay half as much for your treachery.

Des. You think so?

Fou. If anybody should make the offer let me know, and we can enter into a fresh arrangement.

Des. Ah! you know my heart is devoted to you.

Fou. I know your *head* is, and, as times go, that is perhaps a better security. But to work. First, your despatches from England.

Des. Two. (*Takes papers.*) One from Mons. Ouvrard, announcing that he has opened a negotiation for peace in *your* name with the Foreign Secretary, but that he fears your other agent, Mons. Fagan, is not to be trusted.

Fou. Ordered—that M. Ouvrard keep a strict watch over M. Fagan. (DESMARETS *makes a note on the despatch.*) And the other?

Des. From M. Fagan, stating that your overtures for peace have been most favourably received by the English Prime Minister, but that he has reason to believe M. Ouvrard is in the pay of the Emperor.

Fou. Ordered—that M. Fagan establish a close espionnage on M. Ouvrard. (DESMARETS *makes a note on another despatch as before.*) I have long found the advantage of running my agents in couples. Two rogues so employed are as good as one honest man.

Des. And so much easier found.

Fou. The Envoy of the Emperor has not yet arrived in London?

Des. (*referring to another paper*) No; he reached Amsterdam on the 3rd, but he will not sail for three weeks. I have made the necessary arrangements.

Fou. Good; by that time I shall have concluded my negotiations, and the Emperor may have found himself once more anticipated by his Minister of Police. We must teach these people that they cannot do without us.

Des. It is a dangerous lesson sometimes, with such pupils as the Emperor.

Fou. H'm!—he has trusted me too far, Desmarets. Those letters, from his own hand, extending over the last ten years, are my security. While I have those, I stake his credit against my portfolio.

Des. And those letters, thanks to my skill in iron-work, are safe in their secret deposit yonder. (*Pointing off to secret door.*) How lucky the Revolution made a locksmith of me, when it made a Member of the National Convention of you!

Fou. Yes, we have both been able to serve the State and ourselves. Go on.

Des. (*takes up a pamphlet*) From our London correspondent for printed papers—another of those pamphlets signed 'Timon,' which have been already found so disagreeable in high quarters.

Fou. Another? Is the Emperor never to be released from these attacks? Has this one reached France?

Des. Thirty thousand copies have been distributed, but I am sorry to say I have not yet discovered by what channel, which is the more annoying, as this one is not directed against the Emperor.

Fou. Indeed! against whom, then?

Des. Against yourself!

Fou. Ah! (*Starts up.*)

Des. It gives a very minute and apparently accurate account of your career.

Fou. No matter. (*Uneasily.*)

Des. From the date of your Professorship at Nantes all is recorded—your strong measures in the Convention—your speeches in the Jacobin Club——

Fou. Enough, enough!

Des. What he calls your peculations in the Nièvre—your vote for the death of the King—your establishment of the Goddess of Reason in the Nivernais——

Fou. Pshaw! A truce to those youthful indiscretions.

Des. Your massacres at Lyons—your——

Fou. (*striking sharply on the table*) Desmarets, the mind of France must not be poisoned in this way!

Des. Unfortunately the facts are supported by regular official documents.

Fou. They are forgeries—I destroyed all those papers when I became Minister.

Des. They may have been preserved, or copied.

Fou. Impossible. You alone had access to them besides myself. Desmarets, how comes it this man is not discovered before this?

Des. Ha! ha! ha! What do you say to this? (*Rising and showing a written paper much frayed.*) If we have not the man we have his handwriting.

Fou. Give it me. How did you get this?

Des. Through one of *my* agents—a compositor of the London printer, who puts into type these detestable calumnies.

Fou. Your register of handwritings—quick! (DESMARETS *gives* FOUCHÉ *a book from the box.*) Peltier, Fontaine, De Coigny, Talon. None of the known hands. Yet it is clearly not a feigned character. It is flowing, bold, natural.

Des. Like that of a man who believes what he writes, and glories in writing it. The wretch! (*Rubs his hands.*)

Fou. I must have this scribbler, Desmarets. (*Stopping.*) Do you hear? I must have him; the author of these miserable calumnies must be found—must disappear—a cell in Vincennes first, and then a file of grenadiers. Find him for me, and I will not say what I will not do for you, Desmarets. (*He walks up and down, rapidly turning over the pamphlet.*)

Des. (*aside*) Ha! ha! ha!—I think I know—ha!—it stings, it stings! (*He chuckles and rubs his hands.*)

Fou. Abominable! (*To himself.*)

Des. (*aside*) Excellent! (*Aloud.*) Oh! atrocious!

Fou. Infamous!

Des. (*aside*) Beautiful! (*Aloud.*) Horrible!

Fou. (*stopping short and flinging down the pamphlet*) Mons. Desmarets, I can dispense with a chorus. You have ordered De Cevennes to attend me here?

Des. Yes—at half-past seven. 'Tis close on the time.

Fou. And have you prepared his false despatches?

Des. They are here, expressing your great anxiety to conclude the Emperor's marriage with the Arch-Duchess Marie Louise.

Fou. And the real ones, communicating my negotiations in favour of the match with Russia?

Des. Here, as you directed, in the inside of the bonbons in this box. (*Noise of carriage.*) Hark! a carriage! (*Goes cautiously to window and looks out.*) It is De Cevennes.

Fou. Good!—another lesson for you, Desmarets. Fools make the best agents, provided they are skilfully hoodwinked.

Des. (*aside*) I'll make a note of that for future use. Shall I retire?

Fou. Yes.

[FOUCHÉ *goes up, and unfastens door.* DESMARETS *retires by secret passage, with box and papers.* FOUCHÉ *unlocks the door,* C.

Enter the MARQUIS DE CEVENNES, *ushered in by* JABOT.

Jabot. Monsieur le Marquis De Cevennes! (FOUCHÉ, *who has taken up his breviary, and appears absorbed in it, lifts his head, rises, and bows.*)

Fou. Leave us, my son. (*Exit* JABOT, R.) (FOUCHÉ *watches him out and locks the door.*) You were summoned here in the name of the Police. I am Fouché.

De C. (*stammering*) Monseigneur, I am charmed to have the honour of making such an acquaintance.

Fou. Monsieur De Cevennes, you are a man of the world—(DE CEVENNES *bows*)—so am I. You wish to know why you are summoned here? I will tell you. Your intrigues with the exiled family are discovered.

De C. (*confused*) Your Excellency!

Fou. Do not interrupt me. A word from me would consign you to Vincennes for life.

De C. Pardon me, your Excellency, and I will confess all.

Fou. Let me see first what there is to confess. (*He reads from a paper very rapidly.*) On the 6th you obtained a passport for Ostend on pretence of sea-bathing—you travelled by post in a green caléche without arms—dined at Amiens, and complained of the amount of your bill—you then purchased a woodcock pie—for refreshment in the carriage, I presume—slept at Montreuil, and swore at the damp sheets—arrived at Ostend on the 9th—had an interview with Mons. Delbecq, agent for facilitating the passage of the Bourbonists to England—were landed by his men on the beach near Dover at 8 p.m., after suffering much from sea-sickness—proceeded next morning to Hartwell—had an interview with the exiled Louis XVIII., at which you presented a statement of services, professed devotion, and asked for a dukedom.

De C. Good gracious! All known! But I was alone with the King.

Fou. Mons. de Blacas was in the room. When two persons are together I generally know what passes—when three, invariably.

De C. Is it possible?

Fou. You subsequently assured Mons. de Blacas that Napoleon Buonaparte was the man most detested by all classes in France——

De C. Oh, no! your Excellency?——

Fou. Except the wretch Fouché! Thank you, Mons. De Cevennes.

De C. But I assure your Excellency——

Fou. One moment—where was I? 'Except the wretch Fouché!' Shall I go on, or can your confession add anything to this tolerably complete detail?

De C. Oh, Monseigneur! as you are omniscient, be merciful. If the devotion of a life——

Fou. That is a kind of a devotion I have not, hitherto, found very available.

De C. If my gratitude——

Fou. In my experience fear is a more efficacious stimulus. Listen. I have need at the Austrian Court of a trusty envoy—(DE CEVENNES *bows*)—a man of high rank—(DE CEVENNES *bows again*)—and of polished manners. (DE CEVENNES *bows still lower.*) I offer you the mission.

De C. I fly, your Excellency——

Fou. You had better receive your instructions first. You are among Madame de Fontanges' guests to-night. (DE CEVENNES *bows.*) In an hour a carriage will be waiting in that courtyard, furnished with money, passports, and all that is necessary for a rapid and uninterrupted journey to Prague. You will stop at the Kaiser Karl Hotel, and ask for Madame Schoenbrunn. You will be shown to a lady masked. You will deliver to her these despatches (*giving them*), and return at once, without pushing curiosity or gallantry further.

De C. I will be as mute as a fish and as cold-blooded.

Fou. And—yes, I think I may trust you so far—you will also present to that lady a *bonbonnière* from Mons. Lenoir. Remember the name.

De C. Mons. Lenoir. It is engraved, monsieur, here (*touching his forehead*), as your clemency and confidence are here (*touching his heart*).

Fou. And this is the suspicious and double-dealing Fouché! Confess, your friends of the Faubourg St. Germain do us injustice, Marquis.

De C. I will undeceive them. Oh! your Excellency, I have been so ill-requited for my services to the Royal Family! Here is my statement of them. I presented it six times without any effect to the King—I mean the exile. If you think it would serve me with the Emperor—— (*Shows a paper;* FOUCHÉ *catches sight of it.*)

Fou. Let me see your memorial.

De C. (*gives it*) Modestly but firmly expressed—is it not?

Fou. (*aside*) The same hand. Perfect alike in style and calligraphy. (*To him.*) Your own composition?

De C. (*simpering*) Yes.

Fou. And your own handwriting?

De C. No—copied by my secretary, a young man, a native of Guadaloupe, where his father was Governor, under Louis XV.

Fou. What is his name?

De C. (*aside*) He charged me to keep his name and arrival a secret. (*Aloud.*) His name?

Fou. Yes, I wish to make a note of it for employment in my bureau. Such a writer ought to be at once laid hold of.

De C. (*aside*) What a chance for him! (*Aloud.*) His name is Henry de Neuville.

Fou. So!—De Neuville!—Guadaloupe! (*He reflects a moment.*) Like yourself, an adherent of the Bourbons, I presume?

De C. A rash young man; but one, I have no doubt, whose eyes may be soon opened to the error of his ways.

Fou. As yours have been. I should like to see him. Bring him with you to-night; but remember that, in this house, I am not Fouché, the Duke of Otranto, but the Abbé Lenoir.

De C. I pledge you the honour of a De Cevennes; and

when did a De Cevennes succumb to either fear or temptation?

Fou. (who has unlocked the door, goes up stage) Enough, enough—I know what precisely what one De Cevennes is worth, and by him I estimate the whole of the family. *(Bows.)*

De C. I will be punctual to a minute. *(Aside.)* Decidedly one of the most agreeable persons I ever met.

[*Exit* DE CEVENNES, C.

Fou. (eagerly comparing the paper given him by DE CEVENNES *with the paper given him by* DESMARETS) Line for line and letter for letter the same!

DESMARETS *enters noiselessly by secret door and watches*, R.

Fou. I have this bravo of the pen—this stabber of reputations. To-night he shall sleep in Vincennes. *(Turns and sees* DESMARETS.) I did not call.

Des. (R. C.) But I heard the door close, and I knew I was wanted. I have not yet got through my despatches.

Fou. They will keep, Desmarets — they will keep! *(Exultingly.)* You look astonished.

Des. I am not accustomed to see you indulge in the vulgar emotions of joy or sorrow.

Fou. You are right. A Minister of Police, under the Emperor, cannot afford the luxury. Look here, my old friend—here! *(Holds up the two writings.)* There, Desmarets, what say you to that?

Des. Eh! I do not perceive. *(With some confusion.)*

Fou. Where are your eyes? The characters are identical to the turn of a hair-stroke—and more, I know the writer—and more than that, he will be here in half-an hour.

Des. (agitated) Indeed!

Fou. You do not seem to relish this discovery. *(Suspiciously.)* Ah! I see—you can't bear that I should have made it, instead of yourself; but enough; I feel I hold him fast. Order a coach here at nine—a gendarme in disguise on the box. Plant a double file of mounted gendarmes in the stable, who will take their posts on either side when the prisoner is in the carriage; and resist to the death any attempt at escape between this and Vincennes. Let that coach take its place to the right of the courtyard; the carriage to convey De Cevennes to Prague, to the left. I will write a letter to the governor of the fortress, from your

cabinet. You will wait here to receive Madame de Fontanges. Why, Desmarets, you look confounded!
Des. Your excitement stupefies me!
Fou. It is unworthy of me—I admit it; but the Minister is but a man; he must be allowed his moments of weakness.
[*Exit* FOUCHÉ *by secret door.*
Des. De Neuville discovered—arrested! Will he have mettle to resist and keep the secret? Should he turn coward and purchase pardon by discovering that it is from one of Fouché's confidential agents he received the information contained in the pamphlet—should he have preserved the letter which sent it—should Fouché discover that letter came from me! He must not be arrested, or my life is not worth an old pen-stump. But how to baffle Fouché? Let me see— let me see—I am as much excited as he was—I can't think coolly. (*Sits down and pours out glass after glass of water, which he drinks rapidly, then presses his head with his hand.*) Eh! yes; I have it! (*Flings himself back in his chair and gives a long low chuckle.*) Ha, ha, ha! betray his secrets— rifle his papers—release his prisoner! Ho, ho, ho! he can dispose of my place, but I can dispose of his head! Ha, ha, ha! the great Fouché at two millions a year, and the little Desmarets at four thousand francs a month! Ho, ho, ho! there is some compensation in the world, after all! (*A hurried knocking at the door,* L.) Come in! (*Opens door,* L.)

Enter MADAME DE FONTANGES (*taking off a mask as she enters, agitated and parched,* L.)

Mad. de Fon. The Duke?
Des. He is busy in my cabinet; can I not supply his place?
Mad. de Fon. What money have you about you?
Des. Money?
Mad. de Fon. Yes, you ought to understand the word —money.
Des. My last month's salary was paid to-day; it is here —four thousand francs. (*Shows pocket-book.*)
Mad. de Fon. Give it me—quick!
Des. Eh! give it you?
Mad. de Fon. Your master—our master, Fouché, will repay it on my order. (*Writes hurriedly.*) Here! now the four thousand francs!

Des. Madam, I have an infinite respect for you, and the most implicit confidence in your note of hand, but you will forgive my hesitating, at least, till I know——

Mad. de Fon. Till you know what I want this money for so urgently? 'Tis the old story, then, if you will have it. I have played again to-night; I have lost all, down to my bracelets—see! (*Holds out her arms.*) I want my revenge. (*Hoarsely.*) I shall win all back—I feel I shall. Quick, the money!

Des. Madame—Madame de Fontanges, I would give you anything—everything I possess in the world—but this money I will not give you.

Mad. de Fon. Insolent! you dare to refuse me?

Des. I will not supply you with the means of ruining your beauty—your health—your happiness—your peace of mind—at the gaming-table.

Mad. de Fon. Youth—beauty—peace of mind! Ha! ha! ha! (*Bitterly.*) You forget to whom you are speaking.

Des. To Marie de Fontanges—the daughter of a noble father, the widow of a brave gentlemen, the ornament of the Faubourg St. Germain.

Mad. de Fon. No, no!—that is the world's Madame de Fontanges. You speak to Marie de Fontanges, the gambler, the spy, the creature of Joseph Fouché, and, lower still—if there be a lower—of Maximilian Desmarets! No more words; but the money, man, the money!

Des. You use a strange way to charm it out of my pocket.

Mad. de Fon. Pshaw! Do you want me to cringe for it—to wheedle and cajole? I am low enough even for that. But do not force me.

Des. Why will you repay with scorn my respectful interest?

Mad de Fon. Interest! You forget to whom you are speaking.

Des. You have reminded me—to the gambler, the spy, the creature of Joseph Fouché.

Mad. de Fon. True, true—why will you awaken in me a pride I ought to forget?

Des. Because I love you.

Mad. de Fon. You?

Des. Why not? By your own showing we are equal. But it is not that I would level you with me; I wish you to be a thing that I may look up to—that may teach me to be better myself, and to think better of others.

Mad. de Fon. No more of this, Desmarets. Desperate necessities, and an absorbing passion, may have driven me to Fouché's service; the chances of the table, and some love of secret power, may keep me there. I seldom look into myself; but you almost awaken me to reason, when you show me how near I am fallen to the level of a creature like you.

Des. I am low—I know it; but love works such wonders! It will save me. It is the one spark of good left here—(*touching his heart*)—do not trample it out—do not! (*He kneels.*)

Mad. de Fon. Miscreant! dog! slave of a slave!—stand up, or I will tread you under my feet!

Des. Take care—I might hurt your heel. Marie, listen to me.

Mad. de Fon. Silence! Oh, I hear foul words enough about the green table, and try to shut my ears to them; but I would like to remember them all, that I might pour them on your sordid head. Serpent! let go my hand. (*She tears her hand away from his.*)

Des. (*rising, and maliciously*) Ha, ha, ha!—my hand pollutes you, but you will touch my money. Here it is—bought with lies, and treachery, and blood—buy with it misery, and madness, and despair. Here, here, here! (*Forcing it on her.*)

Mad de Fon. How dare you? Keep your money—I will not take it. (*To* R.) Yet, no—give it me, quick—black came up eight times running—the colour must change—I will try a martingale on red—double or quits every throw—the luck must turn—it must—or there is laudanum at the worst. [*Exit furiously,* L.

Des. So, Marie de Fontanges! 'Serpent,' she said. Well, serpents are grovelling things, no doubt, and proud folks tread on them, but they sting, and so does Maximilian Desmarets.

Enter FOUCHÉ *at secret door*, R.

Fou. Has Mademoiselle de Fontanges not yet returned?

Des. Yes; from the gambling-table—plucked to the last feather, as usual.

Fou. Why don't she cheat?

Des. She has still some scruples left; another twelve-month under your tuition may remove them. Not finding you, she has gone back for another cast of the dice.

Fou. Her passion for play will be that woman's ruin.

Enter JABOT, C.

Jab. M. de Cevennes—M. de Neuville.

Enter DE CEVENNES *and* DE NEUVILLE, C.

De C. Abbé, let me present to you my secretary, M. De Neuville; M. de Neuville, the Abbé Lenoir. (*They bow.*)

Fou. The unworthy confessor of Madame de Fontanges.

De N. Pardi, Abbé! your task should be a light one, for Madame de Fontanges, the Marquis assures me, is perfect.

Fou. Perfection is not given to erring humanity; but Madame is unusually near it. A model for her own sex and a goddess for ours. (*Sighs and folds his hands.*)

De N. She seems to want one virtue, however—punctuality—for here we are in the temple, but where is the divinity?

Fou. Your language is profane.

De N. I beg your pardon. (DESMARETS *goes to window.*)

Fou. Nay, I know the warmth of a tropical temperament, and can excuse it.

De N. I will try not to sin again; but our Creole tongues, Abbé, have a terrible trick of running away with their masters.

Fou. You will find the need of a curb in Paris, my young friend.

De N. I will put the unruly member under your training. Luckily, here, in the Faubourg St. Germain, we are safe.

Fou. Alas! how little you know Paris! You may, even now, be surrounded by spies. May he not, M. de Cevennes?

De C. Eh! so they say; but I don't believe it! (*Aside.*) Incredible self-command!

De N. Well, I will promise to be rash only in the Marquis's hearing and in yours, Abbé, and then, at least, I shall be secure.

Fou. Let us hope so; but Madame de Fontanges does not appear. I suppose I must give up my game at picquet.

De N. If you will allow the Marquis or myself to replace

the lady for once, and then you can lecture me while we play—(*he approaches a table;* JANOT *places card-table*)—you will find me the most patient of penitents.

Fou. With all my heart, my son. But you will find me a bad schoolmaster; I have too much sympathy with the openness and ardour of youth.

Des. (*who has been at the window, aside to* FOUCHÉ) De Cevennes' carriage for Prague has arrived, and the coach for Vincennes.

Fou. Good. (*Aside.*) Now for our game.

Des. If you'll allow me, I will look on.

De N. (*aside to* FOUCHÉ) You can rely on him?

Fou. As on a second self: he is one of us. Come! (FOUCHÉ *and* DE NEUVILLE *sit at the table;* DESMARETS *and* DE CEVENNES *look on.*)

Fou. I conclude from your high spirits, my son, that you have not been long in Paris?

De N. Only a fortnight; and, to tell you the truth, I am disenchanted already. I had imagined it the home of pleasure, gaiety, and wit; the theatre of noble arts, the arena of great deeds——

Fou. And you have found it——

De N. The haunt of intrigue, servility, and treachery; a big prison, where every one is the gaoler of his own thoughts; a huge masquerade, but without the mirth, the music, and the champagne. I sigh for my native Guadaloupe! Oh, Abbé! if you but knew our island—its blue, unclouded skies, its palms, and summer seas, where, though slavery surrounds us, we whites at least are free to move and speak and think like men.

Des. You are primitive in your tastes, sir.

De N. Very. I hate laughter without joyousness, lovemaking without passion, society without confidence, and sanctimoniousness without piety. I fear I am very old-fashioned.

De C. Oh, savage! perfectly savage!

'*Tityre, tu patulæ recubans sub tegmine fagi!*'

Fou. Yes, Paris is sadly changed; but we must pay the price of imperial glory.

De N. The glory of one man bought by the misery of millions! There is no true glory so purchased, Abbé. Frenchman as I am, I feel dishonoured in this man's great-

ness. Blood tarnishes the gold of his crown; blood stains the purple of his imperial robe. His acquisitions are a robber's booty; his triumphs the brutal mastery of wrong.
De C. Hush, De Neuville! (*Behind table*, L. C.)
Fou. Let him talk—he refreshes me.
Des. It is most refreshing! Your card, M. de Neuville.
De N. And is it to this, Abbé, that the horrors of the Revolution are to conduct us? Must the high hopes of enthusiast and philosopher end in the heavy waking of the prison-house or the bloody delirium of the battle-field? No, this cannot be the end. This is a purgatory we are passing through—the glory is beyond.
Fou. (*aside*) The very style! (*Aloud.*) Ah! could we but find pens to write these truths!
De N. Why not, if there are swords to maintain them? But the swords will come, for when were such thoughts spoken but they found echoes in a thousand breasts?
Fou. Yes, thank the spirit of old French chivalry, we have still some who dare utter all we feel. The author of those recent pamphlets, for example, signed 'Timon,' those masterpieces of indignant eloquence——
De N. What—you have read them?
Fou. I know them by heart.
De N. (*grasping his hand*) If you knew the good these words do me!
Des. I have read them too—that last, for example, against the monster Fouché.
Fou. Ah! how the wretch must have writhed!
De N. I thought he was invulnerable to shame, as he is inaccessible to pity. Depend upon it, Fouché is one of that lowest class of rogues who imagine shamelessness, heroism, and consistent rascality, statesmanship. Oh, I know him well, Abbé.
Fou. I have heard him called inscrutable.
De N. Only because few are base enough even to conceive the acts which he practises habitually. No, that pamphlet traces his career, step by step, through every doubling, from disguise to disguise, from treachery to treachery, and only leaves him, at his present post, on the right of the imperial throne, the tricky head to guide the desperate hand. Does that pamphlet contain one word beyond the truth?
Des. Not one.

De N. Every document cited was authentic, for I had information——

Des. (*breaking in hastily*) Monsieur, you've lost a fish— two fish—four. You'll be ruined if you don't attend to your cards.

De N. Thank you for your warning, but the subject of these pamphlets has a peculiar interest for me.

Fou. A nearer one, young man, than it would be safe to avow here. Nay, do not start—our friend De Cevennes has hinted.

De C. (*deprecatingly*) Oh, sir!

De N. What, De Cevennes, you cannot have been so imprudent?

Fou. Oh! he knew his man. Do not blush. Great writer, scourge of tyranny, barer of the face of fraud, let me embrace you. (*Embraces him, then speaks aside over* DE NEU- VILLE'S *shoulder to* DESMARETS.) Now!

Des. M. de Cevennes, have you brought with you that list of your services which you promised us?

De C. Unluckily I have forgotten it.

Des. Careless man that you are! It is most unfortunate, as the Abbé wanted to forward it.

De N. I will go for it with pleasure. I know the paper— I copied it only yesterday. (*Rises.* DESMARETS *writes on a card unseen.*)

Fou. Nay, I cannot allow you to take this trouble.

De N. Yes, yes. If only to hide my confusion at your praises.

Fou. Stop; my coach is below; suppose you take it? The night is damp.

De N. A thousand thanks.

Des. I will show it you from the window, if the fog will permit. (*Takes him to window.*) There, the fiacre on the right of the entrance. (*Quickly, and aside.*) Take the car- riage on the left—not a word! Read (*giving card*) before you get in—it's life or death!

[*Exit* DE NEUVILLE (C.). DESMARETS *returns to* FOUCHÉ *and* DE CEVENNES.

Des. (*aside to* FOUCHÉ) It's done!

Fou. (*aside to* DESMARETS) Excellently managed!

Enter MADAME DE FONTANGES (L.). *Her manner is entirely changed—she is radiant with joyous excitement.*

Fou. At last, daughter!

Mad. de Fon. A thousand pardons, Abbé! Marquis, what penance should he impose? (*Aside.*) M. Desmarets, your money, doubled! (*He takes it, and goes up* L. H.)

De C. (*crosses* L. *to* MADAME) Ah, Madame! always charming—always radiant! How lovely you are to-night!

Mad. de Fon. Hush, hush, or the Abbé will scold you! I have to confess to him, and your delicate compliments will oblige me to add another to my list of sins. Item—to one indulgence in feminine vanity. No, not a word will I hear. (*Crosses to* R. H. *to* FOUCHÉ.)

De C. Ah! cruel! (*Goes up* L. H. *to* DESMARETS.)

Fou. (*talking to* MAD. DE FONTANGES, *forward.*) What is the meaning of this? Desmarets tells me you have been playing again.

Mad. de Fon. Yes, increasing your revenue, M. Fouché. Nay, don't frown at me. What would become of your secret service money without the contributions of the gaming-houses? And what would become of their contributions. without me, and those like me? You see I am logical for a woman.

Fou. Woman never yet wanted logic to guide her to ruin.

Mad. de Fon. Ruin! (*With a bitter laugh.*) Who first lured me to the table?

Fou. My agents; but that was to drive you into my nets —now you are there, I wish you to avoid those places.

Mad. de Fon. And our compact—do I not keep it? Do I not play your spy at those places?

Fou. No, you get so excited by your cards that you lose your faculties of observation. Once for all, you must and shall give up play. Do you hear me?

Mad. de Fon. And you tell me this—*you*, and to-night, when I have broken the bank at Petiot's! See. (*Thrusts her hand into her bosom and brings it out filled with bank-notes.*) Why, man, I am independent of you for a week. (*She goes up* L. C.)

Fou. (*aside*) It is hopeless to speak to her now. I must get her away from Paris.

De C. (L. C., *looking at the pendule*) It is nine o'clock, the hour fixed for my departure. (*To* FOUCHÉ.) M. le Duc, my time is come.

Fou. You are punctual—a good sign. Your despatches are in the carriage.

De C. And the *bonbonnière?*

Fou. Ah, I had forgotten that, in weightier matters. (*Takes it from his pocket.*) There.

Des. (*taking him to the window*) The carriage on the right of the entrance.

De C. Thank you. I am infinitely obliged.

Des. Oh, do not mention it. [*Exit* DE CEVENNES.

Mad. de Fon. (*throws herself into a chair,* L. H.) Thank Heaven that coxcomb is gone at last; I could not have borne his chatter a minute longer. I feel faint. Some of that water, Duke.

Fou. (*giving it to her*) Fool! you see what this excitement leads to.

Mad. de Fon. Do not scold me now—I cannot bear it. Leave me to myself a little. I have a calculation to make. (*She takes a pack of cards on the table and begins to combine them, marking their colours with a pin on a card, as they turn up.*)

Fou. I will stay; and stay you, Desmarets. (*A noise heard without.*) What is that? (*Two shots fired.*) The prisoner!

Des. He leaps from the carriage. He runs this way.

Mad. de Fon. I thought my house safe—at least from this. (DE CEVENNES *rushes in, followed by an officer and two gendarmes,* C.)

Fou. De Cevennes!

De C. Save me—M. le Duc—Abbé, I mean—say it is a mistake—say I'm not the man. DESMARETS *speaks aside to the officer, who orders the gendarmes. They fall back respectfully.* DESMARETS *goes off after them,* C.)

De C. There—I said I was not the man! But they would fire; though, thanks to the fog, they missed me.

Fou. (R. C.) Now, sir, what is the meaning of this?

De C. R.) That is what I was about most respectfully to ask you.

Re-enter DESMARETS. *He and* FOUCHÉ *come forward.*
DE CEVENNES *talks to* MADAME DE F.

Des. (R.) A mistake of the carriages, owing, no doubt, to the fog. De Neuville is, by this time, beyond the barrier, on his way to Prague, in the carriage intended for M. De Cevennes.

Fou. Quick, the telegraph!

Des. I thought of that, but unfortunately the fog is too thick for the telegraph to work.

Fou. Baffled! Confusion! Desmarets, this is your bungling.

Des. (*shrugging his shoulders*) I really cannot undertake to control the fog.

Fou. By to-morrow morning pursuit will be in vain—nothing can stop him!

Des. What a pity it is I had made such perfect arrangements that the Marquis's journey should be uninterrupted!

Fou. Marquis De Cevennes, this will cause a day's delay in our plan; but be ready to start to-morrow. (*He reflects.*)

De C. Certainly, M. le Duc; but I do hope you will give the gensdarmes orders to be a little more particular about firing. Madame, I have the honour.

[*Exit* DE CEVENNES, C.
[MADAME DE FONTANGES *has returned to her occupation with the cards.*

Fou. Your plan, Desmarets?

Des. He will be on friendly territory at Prague—it won't do to carry him off by force.

Fou. I know an infinity of schemes that won't do—tell me one that will.

Des. Suppose you sent her (*pointing to* MAD. DE FON.) to draw him back to Paris? She is a stranger to him, and she has attractions, till you know her. (*Aside.*) Ho, ho, ho! my proud lady won't like that task, I think.

Fou. A good thought! (*He touches her on the shoulder.*) Madame, your health is evidently impaired by the excitement of Paris—you require change of air. A young gentleman has just succeeded in escaping from Paris whom it is essential I should have brought back again.

Mad. de Fon. Well, sir, what is that to me?

Fou. You must follow him to Prague, where he has taken refuge, and employ those charms which are so irresistible, when you like to exert them, to attract him again to Paris.

Mad. de Fon. No! I have been your spy, but I will not be your decoy. (*Rises and crosses* R.)

Fou. As a request is insufficient, I regret to change it into an order.

Mad. de Fon. And I must meet that order by a refusal. Oh, I know you can imprison me—torture me—murder me, perhaps—I shall not be the first. I have not forgotten Pichegru and Cadoudal.

Fou. They were state criminals. But, my dear madam, when did you ever know me rude to a lady? No, you are free to refuse—do so, and to-morrow I have you proclaimed in every drawing-room in Paris as the paid agent of the police—the salaried spy of Fouché.

Mad. de Fon. You will not; you cannot have the heart to put this choice upon me. You know me for what I am, but still I have a high place and fair fame in the world. I will be your slave—your unquestioning tool in all besides this—but do not set me between such business and such dishonour.

Fou. Choose!

Mad. de Fon. I know you cannot feel respect for me, but there may be some woman in the world you reverence and love—a mother, a sister, or a wife. If there be, think of her, and spare me. Do—do—only in this! only in this!

Fou. Choose!

Mad. de Fon. He is pitiless!

Fou. I give you five minutes. (*Takes out his watch. A pause.*)

Mad. de Fon. Better face my own conscience than the world. I will go. (*She faints.*)

Fou. I thought she would.

Des. (*aside*) I hoped she would not. (*Moves towards the bell.*)

Fou. Do not alarm the servants. A glass of water!

[DESMARETS *brings one.* FOUCHÉ *leisurely sprinkles her brow.*

END OF ACT I.

ACT II.

SCENE.—*A prettily furnished room in a cottage, overlooking the Elbe and the City of Prague; large French windows opening on a spacious terrace, with a balustrade and vases of flowers; a light verandah, covered with creepers, shades it from the sun.* R., *a door leading to* MADAME DE FONTANGES' *dressing-room; door* L., *leading to the entrance to the cottage from without. Rustic but elegant furniture, books, flowers, &c., an embroidery frame.* CECILE, *in a great chair, with work in her hand, stretching and yawning.*

Cecile. Oh, dear! oh, dear! what a length these German

days are, to be sure! I suppose it's because one measures time by laughs in Paris, and by yawns in Prague. Two months have we been here—two months with nothing to look at but those stupid trees, and flowers, and clouds, and that great long, lazy river, run, run—running—shine—shine—(*yawning*) shining in the sun all the day long! Whatever could bring Madame to a place like this? Prague! as if anybody in their senses ever went to Prague! (*Takes a long stretch.*) And she pretends to enjoy it too! To be sure, she has M. de Neuville to make love to her, and very nicely he makes it. And I've nobody but that stupid Karl, who makes nothing but hay. Madame could not bring a valet from Paris, so we took Karl with the cottage. He's dreadful
[*Enter* GRISBOULLE, D. L.
—doesn't even talk, only snorts; and he's always at your elbow when you're not thinking of him.

Gris. (L.) Note! (*Holds out letters.*)

Cecile (R.) Oh, Lord! (*starts*) there he is! Good morning, Karl.

Gris. Note!

Cecile. Oh! for Madame, from M. de Neuville! I wondered we had been a whole day without seeing him. He hasn't spent much time in his own little cottage since he made Madame's acquaintance. I never saw a poor young man more in love; but Madame doesn't treat him as I should treat such a lover. (GRISBOULLE *retires and busies himself with the flower-vases on the terrace.*) She is wearing his life out. They've had a tiff, and this note's to make it up again. Coquette that she is! never satisfied but when she's flirting with somebody. I wish I'd anything to flirt with—Karl does not know how—and he won't learn. Karl— (*tenderly*)—Karl.

Gris. (*gruffly*) Eh?

Cecile. What are you about, Karl? Will you make me a bouquet. (*Insinuatingly.*)

Gris. Can't.

Cecile. There! was there ever! (*Shrugs her shoulders.*) Shall I teach you, Karl?

Gris. No.   [*Exit*, D. L.

Cecile. Dear, dear! one might as well try to amuse one's self with a German primer. 'Ach,' 'Och,' 'Ich!' all in grunts of one syllable. But here comes Madame.

[*Enter* MADAME DE FONTANGES *from the terrace.*
A note, madame, from M. de Neuville.

Mad. de Fon. So: you may go, Cecile. (*Gives her hat to* CECILE, *who puts it on couch, and exit,* L.) He has been playing truant for the last twenty-four hours, and this explains his absence, I suppose. Poor fellow! I fear my dart has pierced rather deeper in that bare bosom than into the well-padded chests of my Parisian adorers. The vehemence of his passion startles me sometimes. It is his tropical temperament, I suppose. The sun, which has bronzed his cheek, may have enriched his blood and quickened his susceptibilities, but can it make nature truer, or affection more constant? No; he may be as changing and hollow as the rest. If one could but believe in man, what a glorious thing love would be! The few tranquil weeks I have spent here, since by a simple artifice I made his acquaintance, I really think have been the happiest in my life. I have not once missed the excitement of the cards! Strange! in playing with his heart there have been moments when his earnestness has shot a sudden thrill through me which I never felt before. If it were the first stir of love! Pshaw! let me remember what I am, and what I have to do. I wish Fouché had found another instrument. But his note. (*She opens it and reads.*) ' Madame '— Madame! we are distant this morning, Monsieur—'if I listened to the promptings of my heart I would not begin thus coldly '— listen to them, Monsieur! happy you if you hear anything—'but I dare not, and yet I cannot stifle them. I love you madly '—poor fellow!—' with a passion violent like my nature, but reverential as my worship of that saint whose sweet name you bear.' Pretty! 'My love is so real, so ungovernable—you must have seen it.' What were eyes given us for? 'And yet you will not deal with me as a true-hearted woman should.' Alas! if truth and heart both be wanting! 'I would live for you—die for you—and you but trifle with me. Either tell me I am indifferent to you, and then I will go and wrestle with my grief alone, or show, by a tenderness like my own, that you are worthy of as true a devotion as ever man felt for woman.' (*She pauses.*) 'I have struggled with myself the whole night through before writing this—I am almost mad. If I am too bold, forgive me—for I cannot live out of your sight. May I come for your answer?—Henri de Neuville.' (*She *sits and lets the letter fall on her lap.*) If it should be true that his heart is of a different mould from those that till now have found their best use as my playthings, what a terrible task is this I am about? I will go no further with it. But Fouché's orders are irrevocable ; and, alone as I am here, so far away from Paris, I feel as if his cold relentless eye was on me at every turn. Who knows? this man may after all be only a more consummate actor than the rest. This show of rough sincerity may be art. No, no; I feel in my inmost self that he is true and noble. To win such a heart might make any woman proud ; but to win it on a cold, passionless calculation—to win it that I may place it under the point of Fouché's stiletto ! Oh ! foul, foul ! The more noble it is, the more hideous is my treachery. What is to be done?

Enter HENRI DE NEUVILLE *by terrace,* L. H.

De N. Your pardon, madame, if I have come without a summons. You have read my letter ?

Mad. de Fon. Yes, M. de Neuville ; and shall I tell you the truth ?

De N. Tell me nothing but the truth always.

Mad. de Fon. The tone of it is new to me.

De N. It may be, for it is the voice of a real, a devoted love—the love of a man who has never felt before what it was to hang with all his being upon the breath of another. Till now I have shared the hopes and fears and projects of my party—of those who looked to the restoration of our rightful King. But now ambition, projects, plots, hopes, fears, all are dead within me—my life, my soul are yours !

Mad. de Fon. (*restraining herself*) I believe you feel all this now, but who can answer for himself a week hence? Love ! Who that knows the changefulness of the weather and the fashions can believe in the eternity of anything, much less of love, which we change oftener than an April day or a spring bonnet ?

De N. I cannot believe her frivolous who awakens in me what I feel.

Mad. de Fon. At least do not conclude too soon. I shall soon return to Paris, and absence will test your devotion.

De N. Absence ! You do not think I can leave you ?

Mad. de Fon. Nay, it is impossible you can return to Paris, where Fouché threatens your liberty—indeed, your life!

De N. Ha! so danger is to deter me! Go, go! that you may see if I will follow—aye, though Fouché's spies were ranged at every barrier, and I must run the gauntlet of them all! But why return to Paris? You are free. Our positions are equal. I offer you my hand, for the hundredth time. Oh, make me happy with yours, and we will live here in an exile that we shall bless, because in it we shall be all in all to each other.

Mad. de Fon. (*aside*) This is real. And shall I be his destroyer? Forgive me, M. de Neuville, if I have appeared sometimes to trifle with you, but there are obstacles which even with love on both sides cannot be surmounted.

De N. Obstacles! Name them, that I may prove to you they are none.

Mad. de Fon. Suppose I were to say I will never marry—that I find the liberty of widowhood too agreeable?

De N. I would not believe you. Give me a better reason.

Mad. de Fon. You have grave duties to our party—duties which love distracts you from. Till your King is restored to France you have no right to chain your destiny to a woman.

De N. The King was first in my heart till I knew you—now he is second. A better reason still. Do you love another? De Cevennes has boasted——

Mad. de Fon. He! Oh, no; my heart is free. But why force me to say there are motives—I regard you too much to tell you them. Do not ask me, if you would still love me as you say you do.

De N. Oh, why will you not lay bare your heart to me, as I do mine to you?

Mad. de Fon. How do you know that I have one?

De N. By the colour that mounts to your cheek when I speak to you of love; by the langour that veils your eyes when we sit together and watch the sunset in a silence too passionate for speech; by the trembling of your voice when we bid each other farewell; by the thrill that shoots from my being to yours, from yours to mine, when our hands meet or a tress of your hair brushes my cheek. By these signs, and the thousand subtler that a lover's eye can see but no tongue can describe, so delicate are they—you have a heart, Marie de Fontanges, and that heart is mine! (*He seizes her hand.*)

Mad. de Fon. (*overcome*) Henri, my own! (*Starts back from his embrace.*) Sir, you forget yourself. You have no right to put my nervous susceptibility to the proof of such excellent acting.

De N. Acting!

Mad. de Fon. Yes; do not talk to me, after that tirade of your inexperience. Talma might take a lesson from you. I remember uttering just such a scream after his grand burst in 'Orestes.'

De N. Oh, you will drive me mad! (*Starting up.*)

Mad. de Fon No, no; but seriously (*sits*), are you wise in yielding to this passion for one you scarcely know? Why, I may be an adventuress—who knows?—an emissary of Fouché's, perhaps.

De N. No; the instincts of such a love as mine are infallible;—it would shrink up at the contact of baseness as the sensitive plant at a touch. I know you as if I had watched your actions from a child—I know you as your own conscience knows you.

Mad. de Fon. Hush—hush, Henri!

De N. Oh! let me throw myself where the slave should be—at his tyrant's feet; where the worshipper should be —prostrate before his saint. (*He throws himself at her feet.*) Let me but lie thus, and look up into your eyes, and rest my brow upon your hands, and forget time, duty, danger, all in the delirious happiness of my love! (*He suits the action to the word.*)

Mad. de Fon. Oh, Henri! check this passion—you must; it is not that my heart is cold to it. If I durst listen to its promptings!

Enter CECILE, C., *comes down* R. HENRI *rises.*

Cecile. A gentleman, madame—oh, I beg pardon!—who gave his card. (*Aside.*) Very pretty!

Mad de Fon. M. Lebon. (*Aside.*) Desmarets! (*Rises and goes to* L.)

De N. My preserver! Oh, show him in here, Cecile, at once. (*Exit* CECILE, C. *and* L.) I long to see and thank him. He saved me, Marie, on that night I was to have been arrested from your house.

Mad. de Fon. (*aside*) Fouché distrusts me. The taskmaster is sent to overlook the slave. It is too late!

Enter CECILE, *showing in* DESMARETS, C., *from* L.

Cecile. M. Lebon. [*Exit* CECILE, R.
Des. Being on my way from Vienna, whither a little money affair took me, I ventured to pay my respects to Madame.
Mad. de Fon. (*bows*) You are at home in my house, sir, as you know.
Des. You are too kind.
De N. Failing Madame de Fontanges, you have a sacred right of asylum with me, M. Lebon. You remember me?
Des. Ah, M. de Neuville!
De N. Your timely warning saved me on the night Fouché was to have arrested me. I have bewildered myself in endeavouring to discover a clue to the treachery which betrayed me. Can you explain it?
Des. We live in wretched times, my young friend. The son is not safe from the father, the husband from the wife, the lover from his beloved. (*Looks at* MADAME DE FONTANGES.) Fouché buys up all affections and all dignities.
De N. Say, rather, all treacheries and all basenesses. But here I can defy him. Spies cannot breathe the air of purity and peace that bathes these blue hills and scarce ripples that placid river. I only think of him as of an adder, whose spring I have escaped, and whose hisses I laugh at. But how came you to be warned of my danger?
Des. Oh, one of his creatures, the wretched Desmarets, had a scruple of conscience, or rather some fear of his own safety, which led him to reveal the plot to me, that I might warn you.
De N. So!
Des. By the bye, what interesting documents that last pamphlet of yours brings to light! How did you procure them?
De N. From an unknown correspondent, one evidently having access to the archives of the Police.
Des. You have, of course, preserved the letters transmitting them?
De N. No; fearing they might some day endanger my

unknown informant, I burnt every scrap I ever received from him.

Des. (*aside*) I am safe! (*Aloud.*) Ah, that's a pity; you might, in case of danger, have purchased safety by denouncing him.

De N. M. Lebon, that is a counsel no gentleman would take. I am surprised any gentleman should give it.

Des. Ah! you have the chivalry of youth, I the caution of riper years. But this conversation is not interesting to Madame.

Mad. de Fon. Pardon me, all that concerns Fouché has a strange fascination for me.

Des. Oh, I could tell you stories of him that would horrify you! Conceive his employing a troop of wretched degraded women, whom he calls his 'Cohorte Cythérienne,' to attract his victims within his reach—and they do too.

De N. Can there be women so base?

Mad. de Fon. (*aside*) Viper! (*Aloud.*) Before we condemn we should know the arts by which he has enslaved them. Once enslaved, it may be they are powerless.

De N. But surely death would be preferable to such baseness?

Mad. de Fon. Death?—yes! But he can disgrace these women; reveal their shame to the world—nay, worse—to those they love and who love them! What death is so sharp as that?

Des. Poor creatures—poor creatures! They are much to be pitied. I pity them, especially when I think there may be haughty beauties among them, who have been used to despise others.

Mad. de Fon. (*aside*) He chafes me to distraction! (*Aloud to* DE NEUVILLE.) M. Lebon is a stranger to our valley, M. de Neuville; will you show him the lovely prospect from these hills?

De N. With pleasure, if M. Lebon will accept me for a guide; but I warn you it is rough climbing.

Des. Never fear; I've a strong sense of the picturesque.

De N. But have you a strong pair of legs? You have, eh? Then come along; I'll show you every sight worth seeing within a league round—(*aside, to* MAD. DE F.)—and dream of you, dearest, at each point where we have sat together.

Des. Au revoir, madame!

[*Exeunt* DESMARETS *and* DE NEUVILLE *by the terrace.*
Mad. de Fon. Yes, the mask is off at last! I see my hideous self. And he thinks me pure! The sincerity of his own nature reflects itself in mine! What an awakening, should he learn the truth! And Desmarets, malignant as he is, will soon find out I love him. What is to be done? Fouché alone can relieve me from this task, which, base always, is now a sacrilege; for I love him—love him as he is worthy to be loved—love him with my whole soul! Yes, I will write to Fouché. (*Enter* DESMARETS *by the terrace.*) I feel a power within me that will work even upon *him*. I will write at once. (*As she turns for writing materials her eye falls on* DESMARETS—*she stands staring at him, then sinks into a seat.*) You here again!

Des. I have despatched M. de Neuville into Prague for my calèche. Let me congratulate you, madame, on the restorative effects of the Austrian air. You look so much better—that is—you did until you saw *me*. You were going to write to Fouché—pray write—unless you think I can save you the trouble.

Mad. de Fon. He has sent you down here?

Des. Yes; he was naturally anxious about your health, and he sent me to enquire—merely to enquire. He was also anxious to know how our little ruse was succeeding—when we might expect to see the Siren wing her flight back to Paris, with her captive in her clutch.

Mad. de Fon. M. Desmarets, I have lived a new life since that promise was made. I cannot keep it.

Des. Ah! M. Fouché will be sorry to hear it. He is so particular about promises, so very particular!

Mad. de Fon. Sir, you have professed an interest in me. If you retain a spark of that interest still, release me from the degrading task to which M. Fouché has condemned me.

Des. Listen to me, Marie de Fontanges. I am not young, not pleasant to look at; I have no graces of speech; I am what the world calls a spy, an informer—what you will that is more ignoble and treacherous; but I have a will like iron, and a head which, under any other chances, might have made a different man of me. Till I knew you all my species were alike to me—counters to be pushed about as suited my game; but at sight of you I felt that you were my fate—my good angel, if you chose to be so.

Mad. de Fon. Oh! no, no; we are our own good and evil angels.

Des. Let me finish. You spurned me once in a fashion that few men of a less determined spirit would provoke or endure twice. Yet I provoke it again, for, proud as you are, I love you still!

Mad. de Fon, Oh! no, no!

Des. I love you still. There is but one way to save you from Fouché—it is by sacrificing him. Give me but hopes that time will change your scorn of me to endurance—leave me to change endurance into pity, and pity into love. From the day which gives me that hope, Joseph Fouché's fall and your rescue are both begun!

Mad. de Fon. This from you! I thought you were devoted to him?

Des. Oh, so I am—so I am!—ha, ha, ha!—but my devotion never stands in the way of my will—never.

Mad. de Fon. But surely it is madness in you to dream of striking at one placed so high and seated so securely?

Des. Ho, ho, ho! (*Chuckles.*) A small worm may sink a big ship. Listen!——

De Cevennes (*without*). At least you can announce me, my taciturn friend. The Marquis de Cevennes—de Cevennes!

Des. That fool! Will you see him?

Mad. de Fon. No, no; not now.

Des. He is here. We will resume this conversation when he is gone.

Mad. de Fon. (*going to her room*) Oh, sir, have pity on me!
[*Exit into her room,* R.

Enter DE CEVENNES, C., *from* L., *shown in by* GRISBOULLE.

De C. He is certainly the man of the fewest words I ever —— Ah! madame not here, eh? The excellent M. Lebon (DE CEVENNES *carries in his hand a common stout walking-stick with a silver head*), one of our party on that eventful night when I was so highly honoured and so nearly shot. You have not forgotten me?

Des. Few that meet the Marquis de Cevennes can forget him.

De C. Ah, monsieur, you are very polite. Yes, it was a delightful soirée—that is, all but the little mistake which concluded it. Would you believe it, sir? I've been three times to Prague and back since that eventful evening! But it's very odd—many as are the despatches I carry, I never bring back any answer—'*vestigia nulla retrorsum!*' Not that I return empty handed, either—the ladies of the Court employ me about their little commissions—give me things to carry—the oddest things, sometimes. Now, on this occasion, what do you think the Duchess von Kaiserleben gave me to take to the Duke of Otranto? Only guess?

Des. Oh, I give it up.

De C. A stick—this stick—(*holding it up*)—neither more nor less. Odd present from a Duchess to a Duke, is it not?

Des. (*takes it and sways it in his hand*) Very; dukes have given such things to duchesses now and then.

De C. You can examine it at your leisure while I wait for madame.

Des. Shall I order you some refreshment?

De C. Eh! well, really—if you can take the liberty—but shall I not see her first?

Des. I am afraid not—she was denied to me—she is not well.

De C. Poor creature! excitable always! Well, if I cannot see her, I think a cutlet and a bottle of Geisenheimer—

Des. Karl! (GRISBOULLE *appears on the terrace and comes down.*) Karl, luncheon for the Marquis. (*Aside to him.*) Not here.

Gris. Good. (GRISBOULLE *goes off*, L.)

De C. A thousand apologies for the trouble. By the way, I have been so constantly on the move since the eventful evening, I have never been able to recover any trace of my secretary, M. de Neuville. You may remember the young man the Duke took such a fancy to who disappeared so mysteriously on the same eventful evening? What can have become of him?

Des. Ah! from discretion I've never enquired.

Gris. (*appearing at door*, L.) Lunch!

De C. Ah! my friend of the limited vocabulary! Have you observed how very sparing he is of words?

Des. Dis—cretion.

De C. Yes; I have remarked the Germans are discreet.

Gris. Lunch! (DESMARETS *makes him a signal.*)

De C. I'm coming, my abrupt friend, I'm coming. (*As he goes off looking at him.*) A most repulsive physiognomy!

[*Exit* DE CEVENNES, L.

Des. The chattering ape has left behind him the only thing worth a thought—this stick. Ah! he little knew I turned it! (*He screws off the head of the stick, which is hollow, and draws out a roll of paper.*) The answer to Fouché's last despatch, which went, by the way, in a paté of snipe. (*Opens paper.*) Why will Joseph not trust his old friend? Why will he force him to this sort of thing? (*Looks at paper.*) So, Joseph: more counterplotting the Emperor, and in his marriage too! He wants an Austrian wife, and you insist on giving him a Russian one. Have a care, Joseph, have a care. It's a game of heads, Joseph, and thine totters, Joseph—totters! totters! Karl!

Enter GRISBOULLE, L.

Gris. What?
Des. A fac-simile of this paper immediately.
Gris. Good! [*Exit*, L.
Des. A very valuable man, Grisboulle. He can assume any disguise, copy any handwriting, drink any quantity of wine, and never goes beyond monosyllables.

Enter MADAME DE FONTANGES, D. R.

Mad. de Fon. Has the Marquis gone?
Des. No; but he is at table, where, as I don't hear him chattering, I conclude his teeth are employed. Let me resume the conversation he interrupted.
Mad. de Fon. You ventured to threaten Fouché!
Des. I never bark when I cannot bite. Papers of his are in my hands that would condemn him were he ten times Fouché!
Mad. de Fon. And he knows this?
Des. A man must trust somebody! He has trusted me! Ho, ho, ho! And I will trust you. I contrived the place of deposit for these very papers. You know the picture on the left of your drawing-room?
Mad. de Fon. Yes.
Des. Press the third ornament on the right side of the frame—the picture moves and discovers a passage. It leads from my house to yours.
Mad. de Fon. Ha!
Des. Touch the rosette of the third panel in that passage—it slides away. In the recess stands in the box containing Fouché's treasonable correspondence with Bernadotte,

with Murat, with all who have an interest in the Emperor's death, or hopes of sharing the spoil of his downfall. There, too, are the Emperor's private letters and instructions, the security to which Fouché trusts when all else fails him. Madame de Fontanges, I have given you my secret. I have put into your hands the master-key to my life and fortunes—you know my secret!

Mad. de Fon. (*reflects*) Your secret is safe with me.

GRISBOULLE *enters silently*, C., *and, unseen by* MADAME DE FONTANGES, *lays paper on table and exit, with look at* DESMARETS, *noiselessly.*

Des. I have surrounded Fouché himself with the meshes of my police. He is inquisitor over France. I am inquisitor over him. (*Takes papers* GRISBOULLE *has left.*) See here: this is a secret despatch which that ass, De Cevennes, is bearer of without knowing it. That was never intended to come to my knowledge; yet here is a fac-simile of it, which goes to Fouché, while I retain the original. (*He places fac-simile in stick.*) You see I show you my cards.

Mad. de Fon. And having overthrown Fouché, you would aspire to his post?

Des. If alone, yes; if with you, no. I will go where you bid me—be what you will—if you will not refuse the endurance, which is all I ask, in return for restoring you to honour and happiness.

Mad. de Fon. (R. C.) Give me some time for reflection.

Des. Oh, certainly, certainly. Weigh my offer well. I will wait for your answer before I return to Paris. Work with me if you will—betray me if you dare!

[*Exit by terrace,* L.

Mad. de Fon. He dare attack Fouché to serve his ambition! Shall I fear him to save my love? These secrets! Without betraying him I might use them to extricate myself and to save Henri. Desmarets does not know I love Henri; he must not see us together. I must fly to Paris without leaving any trace of my route. There I will see Fouché, and, failing prayers, this secret must serve me against him. But how to leave this place undiscovered?

De C. (*without*) My carriage at once!

Mad de Fon. Ha! his carriage!

Enter DE CEVENNES, D. L.

De C. Ah! madame, this is indeed happiness. I was

going away a heart-broken pilgrim without a sight of the fair saint of my pilgrimage.

Mad. de Fon. A truce to compliments, Marquis. It is important I should return to Paris speedily and secretly. Will you give me a seat in your calêche?

De C. Ah, madame, the felicity will be overpowering. (*Aside.*) Dis-cretion!

Mad. de Fon. I will meet you at the turn of the road. Not a word to anyone!

De C. Not even to that dear M. Lebon?

Mad. de Fon. To him least of all.

De C. I fly, a happier man in every respect. (*Aside.*) A perpetual tête-à-tête with a lovely creature all the way to Paris! [*Exit* DE CEVENNES, C. *and* L.

Mad. de Fon. Yes, I will go. But Henri, what will he think of this departure? Oh! I cannot leave him. And yet, with Desmarets here, I dare not risk a parting, or our love will be known, and with it my infamy. Yes, I must go for his sake; and, once at Paris, I may save him, and free myself from the sword which is always hanging over my head. Yes, though my heart break, I must leave you, Henri! And yet to go without one word! No—no—I cannot. (*She writes a note hastily and leaves it on the table.*) And now, dear home where I have first known peace and love, good-bye—good-bye—good-bye! (*She throws herself down and buries her face in a chair, then rising, looks passionately about her. Then, after tying on her hat, she takes a flower from one of the vases and exits hurriedly along terrace and* R.)

Enter DESMARETS, C.

Des. Ah! not here!

[*Enter* CECILE, *door* R.

Where is your mistress?

Cecile. Out, I suppose, sir.

Des. She has not passed out by the terrace.

Cecile. All I know is, she's not in her room.

Des. Where can she be? I'm in a cold sweat till she
[*Enter* GRISBOULLE, C.
pronounces her decision. Ah! here's one who will know something. Where is Madame?

Gris. Gone!

Cecile. Gone?

Des. Gone? with no word for me?

Gris. (*seeing note on table*) Note! (*Gives it,* R.)
Des. (*looking at address*) For me?
Gris. No.
Des. (*reads address*) M. de Neuville! (*Reads.*) 'Farewell! I leave this place—perhaps for ever. Ask not why or whither. I love you passionately. But I must leave you.—Marie.' Gone! By what means?
Gris. (*at terrace*) Look! (DESMARETS *turns up and looks out.*) [*Exit* GRISBOULLE.
Des. De Cevennes' carriage stops at the turn of the road—a woman gets in—it is she! The carriage starts again at full gallop!
Cecile. Gone! (*She runs off,* D. R.)
Des. Oh! fool that I was to leave my calêche at Prague! She carries my secret with her! My fortune—my life may depend on my outstripping them to Paris. But this note to De Neuville!—'I love you passionately!' Can she really love him? Then her listening to me was a trick to worm my secret out of me, and then use it for herself. I see it all, all now! Oh! gull, idiot that I am! She loves him, and so flies to escape the revelation of her infamy face to face. What hinders me from revealing it to him still? Or shall I keep the secret and let him follow her to Paris? Were he brought there, Fouché's end would be gained. He has burnt my letters. I have nothing to fear from his arrest now. Yes, it shall be done—he shall follow her to Paris. She has gone with De Cevennes—ah! jealousy—jealousy!—I will detroy him, reveal her shame, and break two hearts—all at one blow. Ho! ho! ho! 'Tis a revenge might satisfy Bëelzebub, or Fouché himself.

Enter DE NEUVILLE, C. *from* L., *in joyous excitement, speaking as he enters.*

De N. M. Lebon, your calêche will be here in ten minutes; I saw it brought out, and the horses harnessed. I am sorry you leave us so soon, and so will Madame De Fontanges be, I am sure; but at least you must not go without a stirrup-cup. Here, Karl!—wine! Cecile, tell Madame M. Lebon is going.
Des. Madame is gone herself!
De N. What do you mean? Gone! Where?
Des. Nobody knows.
De N. Surely she has left some word—some letter——

Des. Nothing!

De N. But when—how did she go?

Des. Just now—in the carriage with the Marquis de Cevennes.

De N. The Marquis de Cevennes! (*He stands aghast.*) Gone with De Cevennes! What can this mean? With De Cevennes, my friend?

Des. 'Tis the privilege of friends at Paris.

De N. This accounts for her caprice—her hesitation—her trifling with my passion. She was only playing with me, to pass away time, while that frivolous coxcomb was in her heart all the while! Gone! (*Crosses,* R.)

Des. Forget her.

De N. Forget her! Old man, she has grown part of me. To tear out her image I must tear out my heart-strings with it! Oh! to know what road they have taken!

Des. We have no chance of overtaking them.

De N. We have! What speed can outstrip revenge?

Des. Revenge!

De N. Do you think that when one of my blood is so wronged he that wrongs him is allowed to live? (*Crosses to* L. *He is going.*)

Des. My carriage will be here immediately. It is at your service. We will go together.

Enter GRISBOULLE, C.

De N. Thanks, my friend, thanks. But their route, their route? How to discover that? No matter, the instinct of revenge will guide me—come!

Grisb. I know. (*Stops,* C.)

De N. Ah! their road!—speak! speak!

Grisb. To Paris.

De N. To Paris! to Paris! Quick!

Des. Think of the danger. Arrested by Fouché on French soil, you are a dead man!

Re-enter CECILE, R. H.

De N. Death may be there, but revenge is by its side. give me that first: then let death come! To Paris, to Paris!

Des. He is mine! (*Following* DE NEUVILLE, L. U. E.)

CECILE, R.   GRISBOULLE, R. C.

END OF ACT II.

ACT III.

Scene as in Act I.—Night—stage dark—candles unlighted on table, R. C., *and mantelpiece.*

Enter MADAME DE FONTANGES *shown, in by* JABOT, C. D., *who is in dressing-gown and has a lantern in his hand.*

Jabot (R. C.) A thousand excuses, madame, for having kept you at the door.

Mad. de Fon. Enough, my good Jabot; I accept them. I was not expected.

Jabot. I had retired unusually early.

Mad. de Fon. No more apologies; light the candles and leave me.

Jabot. Madame—— (*Hesitating.*)

Mad. de Fon. Well, why do you not light them?

Jabot. A thousand pardons, madame, but——

Mad. de Fon. (*feeling for and finding them*) Here they are.

Jabot. Yes; but madame will understand—I am not in a fit state; I ask pardon—but my—my déshabille; I am not fit to appear——

Mad. de Fon. (*laughing*) Oh, my poor Jabot!—I understand—leave your lantern—I will light the candles.

Jabot. You are too good, madame; you have relieved my mind. You require nothing more, madame?

Mad. de Fon. Nothing, Jabot. Good night!

Jabot. I have the honour. (*Bows.*) In two minutes I will be prepared to appear before you as propriety requires.

Mad. de Fon. Do not come unless I ring.

[*Exit* JABOT, C.

[MADAME DE FONTANGES *lights the candles hastily.* Thanks to fortune, and the Marquis's liberality to the postilions we have reached Paris before Desmarets. While De Cevennes slept I have extracted the fac-simile of the secret despatch from the cane. It is another arm against Fouché. Now to secure the papers Desmarets described: with them I may conquer Fouché at his own weapons. He shall find I have not served in his school for nothing. (*Goes towards picture and feels for the spring.*) The spring should be in this ornament—(*she feels for it*)—yes, the picture yields! (*The picture moves away and discovers the entrance of the passage, with* FOUCHÉ *in it, a dark lantern in his hand.*) Fouché! (*The candle begins to tremble in her hand from the violence of her agitation.* FOUCHÉ *remains calm and unmoved.*)

Fou. The candlestick is too heavy for your hand, madame; allow me to relieve you of it. (*He takes the candlestick from her and puts it on the table.*) (*Aside.*) A minute sooner and she would have found me at the recess. (*To her.*) You are agitated; pray sit down and compose yourself. (*She sits mechanically* L. *of table.*) (*Aside.*) Can she know anything? (*Aloud.*) I was not aware you had the secret of that passage.

Mad. de Fon. I discovered it by an accident.

Fou. (*aside*) I told Desmarets it was unsafe. (*Aloud.*) I ought to apologise for making such a breach in your partywall without notice, but I have such an objection to being announced, and I hate front doors.

Mad. de Fon. You have reason.

Fou. (*sits* R.) You seem startled to see me.

Mad. de Fon. I did not know—— (*Pause.*)

Fou. Oh! my visit, then, is an unexpected pleasure! Not so yours. (*Aside.*) What can have brought her back?

Mad. de Fon. You knew I had left Prague?

Fou. How else should I have been prepared to receive you?

Mad. de Fon. No news could have reached you. I left suddenly, and we travelled as fast as four horses could carry us.

Fou. (*aside*) We? A companion! (*Aloud.*) Four leagues an hour is good travelling, but the telegraph beats it.

Mad. de Fon. Inscrutable man! Then you know all?

Fou. Not all, precisely, but most; your travelling companion, for example.

Mad. de Fon. De Cevennes has told you?

Fou. (*aside*) So, it was he! (*Aloud.*) My dear madame, if I gave up my sources of information I should not long hold my portfolio of the Police. Enough that I know of your leaving Prague in company with the Marquis.

Mad. de Fon. You had your spies even there! Perhaps you know my reasons for leaving?

Fou. The reason you gave the Marquis, of course. But

a lady's real reasons are beyond even my penetration. Perhaps you will favour me with them—I am all attention.

Mad. de Fon. You know how I struggled against the duty you imposed upon me. (*He bows.*) But your hold over me was too strong. (*He bows again.*) I yielded, and set about my work—reluctantly, at first, but by degrees the devil of womanly vanity got the upper hand, and I laid siege to De Neuville's heart with all the arts that my experience of Parisian society had taught me. Impassioned and inexperienced in woman's wiles, he was an easy conquest.

Fou. You see I chose my emissary well.

Mad. de Fon. You did not.

Fou. Ah!

Mad. de Fon. You thought the hot wind of play had dried up in me all that was good or akin to good. I thought so too. Neither of us knew how vital the roots of love are in a woman's nature. At contact with the fresh and springing life of his passion my dead affection wakened, till what we both thought a stone became a living, leaping, loving woman's heart. I found him ready to follow me to the jaws of death——

Fou. And you did not lead him to Paris? It was a blunder.

Mad. de Fon. I resolved to risk my life to save his. I knew all I exposed myself to in disobeying your orders. I knew that shame, imprisonment, perhaps death, lay in the path of duty. There they sit in you—and here (*rising*) stands love in me to meet and grapple with them!

Fou. (*rises*) You would have made a capital actress. But no heroics, pray—leave them to the theatre and Mademoiselle Georges. You have told me what brought you back; and now oblige me by explaining how you mean to conduct this struggle between 'shame, &c.,' or Joseph Fouché and ' love, &c.,' or Marie de Fontanges?

Mad. de Fon. I should not have said 'struggle.' How can an unfriended woman struggle with the potent Minister of Police?

Fou. Exactly the question I wished to ask, better expressed.

Mad. de Fon. I meant, after telling you the truth, to have appealed to the good I cannot believe utterly dead in you, now that it has revived in me. Ah, Fouché! think of all that virtuous love means in a woman like me—self-scorning, self-loathing, living only to be the prey of frantic excitement, or the tool of dark intrigue. It is the branch that sweetens the bitter waters of my life—the ray that breaks upon the labours of the prisoner, to tell him he has pierced the outer wall of his dungeon. Till I knew it, I had nothing to believe in—nothing to venerate—nothing to live for. Having it, a future of peace and purity opens before me. Do not darken this future! Spare him, that I may love him—far from Paris, far from plots, and intrigues and passions. Spare him, Fouché! spare him!— and spare me! (*She has risen while speaking, and now falls on her knees grasping* FOUCHÉ's *hand.*)

Fou. (*who has once or twice betrayed slight signs of emotion*) What eloquence earnestness gives! I never could feel in earnest, or I should have been eloquent. Rise, madame. We will talk of this again when you are less excited.

Mad. de Fon. No—now—here. I will not leave this spot till you have answered me.

Fou. I am sorry for it, as I must refuse.

Mad. de Fon. Refuse! Oh, you cannot!

Fou. (*shrugs his shoulders*) You cannot understand State reasons, or you would see I must. What would the world say of Fouché if they heard that, having the serpent under his heel, he forbore to crush it, out of consideration for a woman's unreasonable passion? My dear madame, I should have all the serpents hissing at once. No—once for all—it cannot be. I will listen to no more. (*Crossing,* c.)

Mad. de Fon. (*rising, her figure dilated.*) Beware! Joseph Fouché!

Fou. (*turning and smiling*) Eh! you spoke?

Mad. de Fon. You have laughed at my love—fear my hate!

Fou. Come, this is better; your grief pained me, your rage amuses me.

Mad. de Fon. Take care lest the time should come when you will sue to me.

Fou. Eh? Ha, ha! Excuse my laughing, but—when shall I sue to you? Ha! ha! ha!—though you are charming enough, especially when excited, to render it not improbable.

Mad. de Fon. Mocker! I tell you I have means of action against you you little dream of—I will use them—I warn you of it—ruthlessly—remorselessly—if by them alone I can save the man I love!

Fou. (*aside*) Can she know anything? Pshaw! a woman's bravado. (*He turns and bows.*) Madame, I have the honour——

Mad. de Fon. (*crosses* L.) Then we separate on my terms.

Fou. No—on mine. Return to Prague. Fulfil your contract, and all shall be forgotten that has occurred to-night. Refuse—and to-morrow your connection with the Police is the topic of conversation in every salon of Paris.

Mad. de Fon. Very well. Then it is war between us—war to the knife! Be it so. [*Exit*, L.

Fou. She has a man's courage, at all events. I rather like her. But these threats are childish. My papers are safe—I saw them a quarter of an hour ago. It is now ten o'clock. You are mistress of the situation to-night; to-morrow it will be too late. (*A ring heard.*) Ha! a late arrival! (*Looks out of window.*) The Marquis de Cevennes, come, no doubt, to enquire after the health of his travelling companion. He will be surprised to find me.

[*Exit by secret door*, R.

Enter JABOT (*dressed*), *showing in* DE CEVENNES, C.

Jab. I will announce M. le Marquis to Madame.

De C. Do. Say I merely wish to assure myself she has not suffered by our rapid journey, (*Exit* JABOT, C, *closing doors*) or been annoyed by my attentions on the road. A charming *tête-à-tête*. Unluckily I was so fatigued I slept most part of the way. (*Enter* FOUCHÉ *by the secret door unseen by* DE CEVENNES.) I will see madame first, and then for the dear Duke.

Fou. No; the dear Duke first, and then Madame.

De C. (*turning*) Ha, the Duke here! Why, how did you enter?

Fou. My movements, like my intelligence, are rather mysterious, Marquis. But here I am. I congratulate you on your quick return, and on your fair *compagnon de voyage*.

De C. Your Excellency has heard! It's incredible!

Fou. (R.) You delivered your despatches?

De C. Yes.

Fou. They required no answer. I think I may dismiss you at once to Madame.

De C. Ah! I had almost forgotten. The Duchess Von Kaiserleben—really, 'tis too odd, too ridiculous—particularly requested me—you'll excuse the absurdity—to present the Abbé Lenoir—now, don't be angry—with this walking-cane.

Fou. Give it me. (*Coolly taking the cane from the* MARQUIS.)

De C. You are not surprised?

Fou. Never! So—a pretty cane. The handle is a souvenir. (*Looking at the head.*) See! (*Shows it him.*)

De C. Why, I never observed before; 'tis a Death's head and cross-bones!

Fou. Yes; an appropriate present to me, in my spiritual capacity; very pretty and cheerful!

De C. Remarkably! (*Aside.*) How very lugubrious!

Fou. You are impatient to see your travelling companion? You will find her in that room. (*Pointing to folding doors,* L.) Return to me before you leave the house. I may have a fresh commission for you—a new mark of the imperial favour.

De C. Oh, Monseigneur! (*Aside.*) I wish, though, he'd give me a little time for repose between my journeys; I am worn to a skeleton. [*Exit* DE CEVENNES, L.

Fou. So—and now for Czernitcheff's despatch; it should announce the final stipulations for the Russian alliance. (*Begins to unscrew the head of the cane.*) The Emperor's heart is set on the Austrian Archduchess; but my head on the Russian. Head against heart is desperate odds always. (*He has unscrewed the head, and has found the hollow empty.*) How's this. Empty! Can Czernitcheff be retreating, or has this fool discovered and abstracted the paper? No, no; it is incredible! Or can some sharper sight have penetrated the secret? I must find out, for this is a matter of life and death to me. I have gone between the lion and his prey, and have no inclination to try the weight of his imperial paw.

Re-enter DE CEVENNES, L.

De C. So now for this new mark of imperial favour, Monsieur le Duc. Madame having retired, I am at your Grace's service.

Fou. (*angrily*) So! sir—this is the way you discharge your commissions! The Duchess's present has been tampered with.

De C. Tampered with! The stick is as when I received it—upon the honour of a De Cevennes.

Fou. The Duchess's letter, describing it, speaks of diamonds in the eyes of the skull. They have been abstracted.

De C. No—upon my honour!

Fou. The stick must have quitted your hands.

De C. Never. I kept tight hold of it all the way from Prague to Paris.

Fou. You slept in the carriage?

De C. Not a wink—on the honour of a De Cevennes.

Fou. Then you extracted the diamonds yourself.

De C. Oh! M. le Duc—what a slur on the honour of a De Cevennes!

Fou. That for the honour of the De Cevennes! (*Crosses L., snapping his fingers.*) I am dissatisfied with you, sir. I know your intrigues with the exiled family. You may need to take better care of your own head than you have of this cane's. Look to it, sir! And now sit at the table and write, briefly, the stages of your journey, your places of stoppage, the persons you met. (*Aside.*) I must at once despatch another messenger to inquire into this. In the meantime, lest there should be anything in Madame's threat, there can be no harm in setting a watch to see that she does not leave the house to-night. [*Exit by secret door.*

De C. (*writing at* L. *of table, and not aware the* DUKE *has left the room.*) You shall have every information, M. le Duc. (*Writes.*) 'Left Prague on the 16th, at ten. Lunched at Madame de Fontanges' cottage.' (*Aside.*) Shall I say I met M. Lebon? I had better tell the truth—as he knows everything. 'Started with madame'—he knows that too. What was the next stage? Eh! Oh! those dreadful German names! I haven't the least notion how to spell Skratzenellenbogen—I must appeal to the Duke. Monsieur, M. le Duc, how do you spell— (*looks round*)—eh! spell—— Why, I declare he's gone! (*Rising. The folding doors open.*) Here he comes! (*He runs to table and begins to write diligently.*)

Enter MADAME DE FONTANGES, L.

Mad. de Fon. The doors are guarded. The officer has orders not to allow me to quit the house! What is to be done to get this paper carried? Ha! Fouché not here, and De Cevennes alone! May I trust him? I must, Monsieur. (*She comes forward.*)

De C. Eh! not the Duke! Madame, you come to save me.

Mad. de Fon. How?

De C. Madame, for the love of mercy, how do you spell Skratzenellenbogen?

Mad. de Fon. Pshaw! You have seen the Duke?

De C. I have. (*Dolefully.*)

Mad. de Fon. And this new mark of imperial favour he promised you?

De C. There's a hitch somewhere. In fact, I'm a disgraced—a ruined man, and it will be entirely owing to the Duke's good nature if I'm not denounced to-morrow, for my secret correspondence with the King. He says there are diamonds missing from the head of that cane.

Mad. de Fon. Hush! there is missing from that cane what is more precious to Fouché than all the diamonds of Golconda. There needs but one quarter of an hour's resolution to enable you to save yourself and to ruin him.

De C. Only a quarter of an hour's resolution? Madame, I am prepared for any danger—speak!

Mad. de Fon. The cane concealed a secret dispatch.

De C. A secret dispatch!

Mad. de Fon. Which I abstracted in the carriage while you slept.

De C. Oh, madame! How could you?

Mad. de Fon. Many lives depended on it. That paper involves Fouché in the guilt of high treason. (*She produces despatch letter.*) It is here. Take it instantly to the Grand Chamberlain—yes, there is a ball at the Tuileries to-night—he will no doubt conduct you to the Emperor. Say you came from me——

De C. But this letter?

Mad. de Fon. Only stipulates for the safety of one who is very dear to me, as the price of this intelligence. Quick! Fouché may be back every moment—and soon, no doubt, egress from my house may be as impossible for you as it is for me. Quick! do not hesitate. For my sake!

De C. But the risk?

Mad. de Fon. For your own sake.

De C. I will go at once!

[*Exit* DE CEVENNES, C. *and* L.

Mad. de Fon. And now, Duke of Otranto, it is a race for life between you and me!

Enter JABOT, C.

Jab. A gentleman to see Madame instantly. Here is his card. (*Giving it.*)

Mad. de Fon. Desmarets! He here! I was just in time! And Henri—he will bring the news of Henri! Yes, admit him. (*Exit* JABOT, C.) Should he have betrayed to him what I am—with what intention I followed him to Prague! He is cruel enough! Oh, if I could read his face!

Enter JABOT; *shows in* DESMARETS, C., *and exit.* MADAME DE FONTANGES *stands eagerly and keenly looking at him.*

Des. Delighted to see you once more, madame; but you have given me a hard journey. (*He takes a light from the table, goes rapidly to secret passage, and exit by it.*)

Mad. de Fon. I cannot read through the mask!

Re-enter DESMARETS.

Des. So our deposit is safe! Your departure from Prague was so abrupt, I fancied you were in a hurry to transmit certain papers to the Emperor.

Mad. de Fon. You see I have respected your confidence.

Des. Hm! At least I see you have not had time to make use of it.

Mad. de Fon. M. Desmarets, pardon my sudden flight. I had motives.

Des. Oh, a lady is not supposed to have any, you know, nor to tell them if she has.

Mad de Fon. But tell me—what did M. de Neuville think, say of my disappearance?

Des. Oh, you don't expect me to repeat a lover's incoherencies—for I find he is a very warm lover. I congratulate you on the success of that part of your mission. But the best of it is, he is under the impression, poor innocent, that you love him!

Mad. de Fon. That I love him! Ah, he is so inexperienced—and these Creoles are so passionate! And then I played my part so well! It was my part to appear to love him. Love him! (*Forcing a laugh*) No! Ha, ha, ha! I was not there to love him! But what matter what he thinks? You know the truth.

Des. (R. C.) I do. Shall I tell it you?
Mad. de Fon. (L. C.) Me, Desmarets?
Des. Yes, you, Marie de Fontanges. You do love this man.
Mad. de Fon. Oh! no, no, no—you must not believe him.
Des. It is not from him I know it, but from you.
Mad. de Fon. Me! I tell you it is not so—I do not love him.
Des. Will you tell him so?
Mad. de Fon. Oh, if that will satisfy you, I will write as much to him at once. (*Aside.*) I need not send the letter.
Des. Why write, when he is here?
Mad. de Fon. Here! Here, in the very den of the wolf?
Des. In your house, madame!
Mad. de Fon. You have not told him what I am—with what intentions I came to Prague?
Des. Eh! (*Looks at her maliciously.*)
Mad. de Fon. Oh! for mercy's sake. You have not told him of my shame?
Des. What matter if I have or not?—you do not love him, you know. But it is time to undeceive him. I will send him to you, that you may tell him you do not love him. [*Exit* DESMARETS, C. *and* L.
Mad. de Fon. One moment will decide all.
[*Enter* HENRI DE NEUVILLE, C.
Oh, Henri, Henri! my love!
De N. Your love! that name was not meant for me. I am Henri de Neuville, madame!
Mad. de Fon. For you—for whom else but you? Do not look at me so! Speak to me—the worst, if it must be —anything rather than this silence!
De N. Better silence than the truth.
Mad. de Fon. The truth!
De N. Your pardon. I forgot myself. The man whose heart you made the plaything of your summer leisure, when he wakes to the truth, may suffer—it is a compliment to your fascination—but that he should complain—absurd! I do not come to complain, madame. (*Sternly.*)
Mad. de Fon. (*clasping her hands*) Henri! why are you here?

De N. (L. C.) To revenge!

Mad. de Fon. (R. C.) Has that man betrayed me?

De Ne. Oh, you use the wrong word—he has opened my eyes—I know all!

Mad. de Fon. All!

De N. The mode of your departure—it was admirably contrived—your companion—he was well chosen, for he was my friend!

Mad. de Fon. Ah! De Cevennes!

De N. I expected to find him here. It is from him, and not you, I come to ask an explanation.

Mad. de Fon. (*aside*) Ah! it is but jealousy, after all. (*Aloud.*) Oh, Henri! be more just to me, if not to yourself, than to imagine that coxcomb could hold a place in my heart.

De N. I did not imagine he held a place in your heart, madame, but in that which does duty for your heart—your vanity. Besides, he had prior claims. How often has he not proclaimed himself your adorer—long—long before I had the misfortune to know you?

Mad. de Fon. Henri de Neuville, look at me well. It was necessary, to save you, that I should leave Prague secretly and speedily. The Marquis De Cevennes' carriage offered me the only means. I took that means for you—and you doubt me.

De N. Marie! Is this the truth?

Mad. de Fon. Look into my eyes, as I swear to you this is the truth.

De N. There is conviction in your look, Marie—I do believe you. Forgive me.

Mad. de Fon. No! no! It is I who must ask for forgiveness. Oh! if you knew all!

De N. I know only this, that we are once more together, and that we will never part more. (*They embrace. Suddenly she starts from his arms.*)

Mad. de Fon. Hush, Henri! in my joy, I forget all!—to stay here is death.

De N. Nay, nay. Fouché is the only enemy I have to fear, and here I am secure from him.

Mad. de Fon. Oh! no, no—what place is safe from that man?

De N. Yes, this place is safe. (*Holding her in his arms and looking on her fondly.*) Falsehood never sat on that pure and open brow. Treason never lurked in the depth of that clear eye. Poison never seethed in the honey of these lips. (*He kisses her.*)

Mad. de Fon. His kisses scald like molten lead. Oh! Fly! fly! Henri! Every minute may be too late!

Enter DESMARETS, C. *from* L.

Des. (*at the window*) I begin to think it is too late already. (*Crosses to* R. C. *behind.*)

Mad. de Fon. Ah! (*Going to window.*) Gendarmes in the court!

De N. Has treason followed me so close? I will not die without a struggle.

Mad. de Fon. (*crosses in front to* R. *Aside to* DESMARETS.) Stay! (*Pointing,* R.) There is a passage here. (*She rushes to picture—tries the spring.*) It will not work!

Des. Oh! I forgot to explain to you the counter-spring.

Mad. de Fon. Lost! lost! Oh! no. (*Crosses to* L.) At least stay here, Henri. The gendarmes may retire; we do not know they come for you.

De N. Doubtless they do. I am betrayed. I may yet discover the traitor.

Des. (R.) You may, easily. Shall I reveal his name?

De N. (C.) You? Where is he?

Mad. de Fon. (L.) No, no—for mercy's sake!

De N. (C.) Where is he?

Des. (R., *smiling coldly and pointing to* MADAME DE FONTANGES) There!

Neuv. (*laughs scornfully*) M. Lebon, our rapid journey has disordered your wits. This is Madame De Fontanges! a pure and stainless woman, and my love! Her honour is mine.

Des. I am sorry for it. I tell you——

Mad. de Fon. Oh, mercy! mercy! Do not!

Des. There stands the woman who, when you escaped hence, followed you to Prague to win your affections and lure you back to Paris. Your affections are hers—you are in Paris—she has obeyed her orders—(*she sinks on her knees,* L. C., *hiding her face*)—as becomes the spy, the decoy of Fouché.

De N. Liar!

Des. (*shrugs his shoulders*) Look there! (*Points to her.*)

De N. Marie, you hear him? Tell him—as I have told him—he lies! lies like a coward! How's this? No word? You hide your eyes, when they should strike him dumb! Marie, speak to me, if not to him; say he lies! Oh! God! he lies! Marie, does he not lie?

Enter FOUCHÉ, C., *in Court dress.*

Fou. (C.) Let me answer that.

De N. The Abbé Lenoir—in this dress!—but you know her, Abbé?

Fou. First let me set you right about myself. I am Fouché, though, thanks to Madame's complaisance, I have been occasionally allowed to usurp the character of her confessor.

Des. She needs one no longer now; I have confessed for her.

Fou. Let her agony save her the pain of an avowal. Accept my assurance that what this gentleman has said is, oddly enough, the truth. (DE NEUVILLE *sinks into a chair,* R. C., *and hides his face on his folded arms.*)

Des. (*to* FONTANGES, *who has dragged herself up to a chair and sits on it, ghastly pale*) I told you the serpent could sting! (*Crosses to* L. C.)

Fou. The shock is naturally overpowering at first, but you will get over it—particularly with the advantages for cool reflection which you will have in Vincennes, to which safe and retired residence I have a particular pleasure in consigning the brilliant and sarcastic Timon! (*Goes up stage.*) Lest you should make any attempt to escape, I may inform you that the house is guarded at every exit. And now, Desmarets, perhaps we had better leave them together a little—they may need some mutual explanation. (*Looking at* MADAME DE FONTANGES.) Poor creature! she threatened me, Desmarets! (*Going off,* C. *and* L.)

Des. Ah!—and she spurned me—but I bear no malice.

[*Following* FOUCHÉ *by* C.

Mad. de Fon. (*struggles up and walks falteringly to where* DE NEUVILLE *sits. She stands before him with her head bent down*) Henri! M. de Neuville!

De N. Still here! I hoped I was alone. (*He turns from her, at first as if in scorn; then sobs bitterly. She approaches him and tries to take his hand; he looks up fiercely.*) Do not touch me! I wish I could have spared you the sight of this humiliation. It is not for myself I am so shaken, but that you—you, whom I had set so high in my heart, should have so fallen! A spy! worse—a decoy!

Mad. de Fon. It is true; but let me not hear it from your lips. Spare me! spare me! I cannot bear it.

De N. (*passionately*) Why cross my path? What wrong have I done to you that you should wreck my happiness thus? Why do you stay? Is it to look at the ruin you have made? Why are you not with them for the wages of your work? You have earned them too well—too well!

Mad. de Fon. No, no, no!—do not look at me so—speak so! I was not vile enough to finish what I had the vileness to begin. I loved you, Henri, at last—truly, fondly loved you—with the love before which life and death are indifferent. Only one thing I could not bear—your scorn! It was dread of this that kept me from avowing the shameful truth that sometimes made your softest words daggers. If you knew the weight of self-scorn I bore under my happiness in your love—my nights of bitter tears—my days of hidden shame—fallen as I am, you would pity me, Henri—indeed you would! (*Still kneeling.*)

De N. How am I to know this tone does not mask some new treachery?

Mad. de Fon. No; my shame is revealed now—and that —that was all I ever concealed from you.

De N. And your flight was not to draw me to my destruction?

Mad. de Fon. No!—as I live, no! It was to try one last appeal to Fouché for release from my infamy.

De N. But what could she have been who could first lend herself to such ignominy?

Mad de Fon. A gambler, Henri!—enticed to the table by Fouché's arts—beggared there by his agents—and then, when ruin and dishonour beset me, the tempter was ever at my elbow with gold. I listened—I fell—I became his spy. Once fallen to that, the man who tempted me ordered me to tempt you—and I did tempt you—wretched woman that I am—you, for whom if I had a thousand lives I would give them all!

De N. Poor, poor Marie! My suffering dates but a few hours back, and yours has been the misery of years!

Mad. de Fon. (*rises and advances*, c.) But is the agony I feel now no atonement for my past, Henri? I feel as if it might be. My suffering has been so bitter—so bittter! You will let me take your hand, Henri? (*She takes it; he does not resist.*) There are tears in your eyes—you look upon me as you did in those happy days when you thought me worthy of your love. I feel that I have destroyed you, Henri—forgive me, I did not mean to use that word!—may I still call you so?

De N. (*in a broken voice*) Yes, yes!

Mad. de Fon. Ah! I am forgiven! Speak!

De N. Yes! yes, my poor Marie! I forgive the past—such suffering and such repentance redeem all! (*She falls into his arms; he presses her to his heart.*) And so we will meet fate together! They did not look to find us thus—thy wet cheek on my loving heart! I can face imprisonment, death, now, if it must be, without a shudder! (*They embrace and remain in each other's arms.*)

Enter FOUCHÉ *and* DESMARETS, *with soldiers*, C.

Fou. (*speaking at entrance*) We will try that! Madame, I regret to disturb your *tête-à-tête*, but the carriage waits to conduct this gentleman to Vincennes.

Mad. de Fon. Kill me! kill me! How can I live with his blood upon my head? Henri! Henri! (*The soldiers advance.*) Where he goes, I go!—to prison with him—to death with him!

De N. (L. C.) One moment, gentlemen. Joseph Fouché, so sure as there is an eternal justice above us, so surely shall this wickedness be atoned for! Aye, smile, and tremble while you smile—for you feel that truth speaks out of him, who, on his way to the grave, pauses here to give you your true titles of knave and coward!

Fou. (C.) Do your duty!

Berthier (*speaking without*). Stay without, gentlemen; the carriage for Vincennes may wait.

Enter DE CEVENNES, *accompanied by* BERTHIER, *in a Court dress*, C.

Mad. de Fon. Ha! Berthier! Prince, my prayer?

Ber. (R. C.) Is granted.

Mad. de Fon. He is free! Henri, you are free! free! Do you hear? I said so; I knew they could not part us now!

You are safe—something here at my heart told me so—you are safe! God bless the mouth that tells me so!

Ber. M. le Duc, my errand is to you. (*Beckons* DE CEVENNES *and takes paper.*) A glance at this paper may spare painful avowals. (*Hands despatch.*) You will wait the further directions of the Emperor on your estate of Pont Carré.

Fou. (*looks at despatch, then to* MADAME) Admirably done, madame; worthy of yourself, upon my honour!

Ber. Your Grace will not wonder, after this discovery, that I am charged to demand your portfolio: you will give up your cabinet and papers to the Duke of Rovigo.

Fou. (R. C.) Savary—poor Savary! (*Takes snuff.*) Savary —after me!

Ber. (C.) Among the papers to be given up, the Emperor includes all his autograph letters and instructions.

Fou. (*to* BERTHIER) I regret extremely not to be able to oblige the Emperor; but, fearing so delicate a correspondence might fall into bad hands, I have burnt it.

[*Exit* DESMARETS *by secret passage.*

Ber. Burnt it! You will find it difficult to convince the Emperor of that.

Fou. I have always found him difficult to convince. But it is nevertheless true. His autographs are burnt. (DES- MARETS, *returning with box, crosses behind* FOUCHÉ *to* C.)

Des. Not all, I think, M. le Duc—not quite all.

Fou. You, too, Desmarets! Then I *am* down!

Des. Your Highness will find his Majesty's revered autographs in this box, besides much interesting correspondence with Marshal Bernadotte and the King of Naples. (*Aside.*) I should not like Joseph to fall without my having a hand in it. (*Crosses to* R.)

Fou. Prince, I am a victim to calumny. I resign my portfolio and myself, until his Majesty again requires my services. Desmarets—no—I leave you to my successor *ad interim.* I have only to hope he will find you as trustworthy as I have done.——

Des. (R.) Adieu!

Fou. (R. C., *looking at him fixedly*) No, *au revoir!* Madame, permit me to congratulate you on the skill of your play! M. de Neuville, you have acquired a jewel. Treasure it, but don't forget you took it out of the mire.

De N. (L. C.) I will remember it, Duke of Otranto.

H H

Think *you* how precious must be that jewel, which, for a moment soiled by contact with your hands, is yet worthy of being set here—in the heart of an honest man! (*He takes her to his arms—she falls on his neck.*)

    Mad. de Fon. If from the whirl of passion, plot, and play
      My storm-tossed bark seeks wedded life's calm bay,
      What tamed the gambler's passion in my heart?
      What 'gainst the plotter turned his own deep art?
      What made weak hands strong for a giant's fall?
      The master-passion, Love—' that still is lord of all.'

SOLDIERS.
DE CEVENNES.
FOUCHÉ.
DESMARETS.   MADAME DE FONTANGES.   DE NEUVILLE.
R.   R. C.   C.   L. C.   L.

CURTAIN.

www.ingramcontent.com/pod-product-compliance
Lightning Source LLC
Chambersburg PA
CBHW051857300426
44117CB00006B/438